Lecture Notes in Information Systems and Organisation

Volume 15

More information about this series at http://www.springer.com/series/11237

Francesca Ricciardi · Antoine Harfouche
Editors

Information and Communication Technologies in Organizations and Society

Past, Present and Future Issues

Springer

Editors
Francesca Ricciardi
Dipartimento di Economia Aziendale
University of Verona
Verona
Italy

Antoine Harfouche
Université Paris Ouest Nanterre La Défense
Paris
France

ISSN 2195-4968 ISSN 2195-4976 (electronic)
Lecture Notes in Information Systems and Organisation
ISBN 978-3-319-28906-9 ISBN 978-3-319-28907-6 (eBook)
DOI 10.1007/978-3-319-28907-6

Library of Congress Control Number: 2015960226

Printed on acid-free paper

This Springer imprint is published by SpringerNature
The registered company is Springer International Publishing AG Switzerland

Preface

The first ICTO conference (ICTO2015) took place in Paris on March 12 and 13, 2015. This conference focuses on the impact of information and communication technologies (ICTs) on organizations and society, and aims to shed light on how these technologies are understood, adopted, adapted, assimilated, and used within organizations and, more generally, within the society as a whole to solve complex social problems.

In its first edition, the ICTO conference called for contributions on a wide range of issues, such as new business models, competitive strategies, knowledge management, marketing, human resources management, project management, operation management, and innovation management, in both private and public sectors. ICTO2015 was especially interested in papers investigating the role of ICTs in the value creation processes through which organizations impact the society.

The conference attracted more than 70 submissions in all areas of ICTs and information systems. Several innovative and rigorously developed submissions raised interesting debates at the conference. The conference accepted papers from 13 countries: France, Italy, UK, Canada, USA, Austria, Singapore, Lebanon, Greece, Tunisia, Algeria, Slovakia, and Oman.

This book includes 22 papers. Among these, invited scholars (namely Paola Dameri, Sami Dakhlia, and Daniele Pederzoli, respectively) who participated in ICTO2015 as keynote speakers and/or roundtable chairs produced three articles. The remaining 19 papers included in this book have been selected through a double-blind review process as the best and most interesting ICTO2015 submissions.

The 22 contributions have been clustered around the following three headings: (1) ICT and the Pursuit of Public Good; (2) ICT, Innovation, and Organizational Change; and (3) Interacting in an ICT-Enabled Relational Landscape.

1. *ICT and the Pursuit of Public Good*. In this section, six papers explore the importance of technological innovation to address some key societal challenges, such as e-government, corporate social responsibility, healthcare quality and sustainability, smart cities, and quality of urban life.

- Walter Castelnovo, Maddalena Sorrentino, Rania Fakhoury, and Marco De Marco describe the long and complex process through which a radical ICT-enabled simplification of the interactions between the citizens and the public administration has been pursued in Italy in the last two decades. Then, their study draws some suggestions to guide the implementation of "one-stop government" in Lebanon, where the process is still in the beginning stages.
- The paper "Cloud Computing: Risks and Opportunities for Corporate Social Responsibility," by Norberto Patrignani, Marco De Marco, Rania Fakhoury, and Maurizio Cavallari, focuses on a relevant topic: the potential impact of cloud computing on ethically sensitive organizational issues, such as responsible governance, contractual obligations, or market openness.
- In her study "The Electronic Health Record: A Comparison of Some European Countries," Sabrina Bonomi conducts an interesting comparison across different countries (Italy, Great Britain, Norway, Finland, Denmark, and Sweden) highlighting the different solutions adopted to collect and leverage digital information in order to improve healthcare quality and sustainability.
- Danila Scarozza, Alessandro Hinna, Stefano Scravaglieri, and Marta Trotta concentrate on a recent, important reform of the Italian Public Administration that introduces stringent requirements for programming, evaluation, and transparency. Through document analysis, the authors explore the perceived and expected role of ICTs in enabling this important transformation.
- The paper by Roberta Pinna, Pier Paolo Carrus, and Fabiana Marras concentrates on the pharmaceutical logistic process. The authors investigate this issue through the analysis of a case: the introduction of an ICT-enabled integrated drug logistic system in the healthcare system of an Italian region. The results confirm the advantages of the ICT-enabled system, in terms of cost containment and the traceability of drugs.
- In her study, Renata Paola Dameri provides a synthetic overview on the smart city phenomenon and related literature. Then, she focuses on smart mobility initiatives as part of a larger smart city initiative portfolio, investigating the emerging role of ICT to address the challenges of today's transportation systems, which are crucial to improve public value and quality of life.

2. *ICT, Innovation, and Organizational Change*. This section includes eight papers that investigate emerging aspects in management issues such as the organizational implications of information technology (IT) innovation and assimilation, supply chain management, knowledge management, human resources management, and the acquisition of hi-tech start-ups.

- Nabil Badr presents a paper titled "A Framework of Mechanisms for Integrating Emerging Technology Innovations in IT Services Companies." His paper focuses on a systemic issue in IT organizations of companies in the sector of IT services. In order to innovate their business models, these companies often rely on emerging technologies, which affect the stability of IT services. Through in-depth case studies, field interviews, and focus group discussions, the study brings forth mechanisms that may serve as guidance to develop organizational capabilities for IT-based business model innovation projects.

- Moufida Sadok and Peter Bednar present the paper "Relating ICT to Organizational Change in Research and Practice." Their paper discusses key information system (IS) paradigms in some of the content of commonly adopted IS academic textbooks and research papers. The paper highlights original differences between two dominant IS paradigms and considers that the distinction between IS as a data processing system and IS as a human activity system provides a frame of reference to explain why the gaps in understanding the transformation process continue to be relevant issues to explore in IS research.
- Mary Ann El Rassi and Antoine Harfouche propose in their paper "e-Business Assimilation Levels in Lebanon" an investigation into the factors that explain the differences in e-business assimilation. Based on the perceived e-readiness model adapted to the Lebanese context, they develop a dynamic model, tested through the analysis of quantitative data collected from a sample of 171 executives from three different industries: banking, retailing, and tourism.
- In "Supply Chain Management and the Role of ICT: DART-SCM Perspective," Lucia Aiello, Iana Dulskaia, and Maria Menshikova analyze the main literature on service-dominant logic (SDL) and Dialogue-Access-Risk Benefits-Transparency (DART) framework in order to investigate how the academics and practitioners put this framework in action in the international scenario of supply chain management. Through a case study focused on e-procurement in a multinational enterprise that operates in the chemical–pharmaceutical sector, the paper aims to highlight the coherence of e-tools with a DART perspective.
- Alessandra Lazazzara and Stefano Za, in "How Subjective Age and Age Similarity Foster Organizational Knowledge Sharing: A Conceptual Framework," review the literature on knowledge sharing, examining the influence of subjective age and age similarity within the work context. They propose a conceptual framework that highlights how subjective age and age similarity may affect the extent to which the people in an organization are inclined to share and the knowledge-sharing route they prefer.
- In "Information Technologies and Quality Management. Towards a New Idea of Quality?" Teresina Torre examines the relationship between technology and quality. She investigates which of the many IT solutions used in enterprises affects more directly the quality levels and underlines the main effects they produce. The study considers the specific case of an Italian software house, where it is possible to clarify and understand the role of each specific IT solution.

- Roberta Fantasia presents a paper entitled "Acquihiring: A New Process for Innovation and Organizational Learning," which aims to give an academic contribution to comprehend the "acquihiring" strategy and its success for organizations in fostering innovation and consolidating a competitive position. Her work is based on a theoretical background and includes a field study on organizational learning and the dynamic capabilities focusing primarily on the post-acquisition phase conducted on an Italian firm.
- Claude Chammaa, in "The Optimization of the HRM at the 'LSCA' in an Economy with Delay in Modernization of Systems," reviews the literature of development and adaptation of information technology to human resources departments. The paper describes the implementation process of a new human resources information system in a Lebanese company.

3. *Interacting in an ICT-Enabled Relational Landscape*. This section presents eight papers that focus on how new technologies are shaping the emerging landscape of business interactions. The topics addressed in these papers include privacy, trust, branding, customer relationship management, and the nexus between technological and social networking.

- Imed Ben Nasr, Lisa Thomas, Jean François Trinquecoste, and Ibtissame Abaidi, in "The Brand Website as a Means of Reviving Memories and Imaginary," explore mental imagery in the consumer online Web site navigation experience. They examine qualitative and quantitative attributes of mental imagery as influencers of consumers' e-satisfaction and brand attitude.
- Wen Yong Chua, Klarissa Chang, and Maffee Peng-Hui Wan present a paper entitled "Location Privacy Apprehensions in Location-Based Services among Literate and Semi-Literate Users." Their empirical study draws upon theories of restrict access/limited control and familiarity to identify the antecedents of location privacy apprehensions related to personalized services provided by location-based services (LBSs) and user literacy. The proposed research model is tested in a laboratory experiment. The findings show that the different types of LBS affect the degree of location privacy apprehensions between the literate and semi-literate users.
- In "Towards an Ontology for Enterprise Interactions," Youcef Baghdadi presents a typology of enterprise interactions toward a lightweight ontology for interactions that can facilitate their engineering. His paper distinguishes different types of interactions by their nature, their issues, and their current realizations and conceptualizes them for the purpose of their modeling, design, realization, evaluation, and analysis.
- Eliane El Zoghbi and Karine Aoun, in "Employer Branding and Social Media Strategies," analyze the evolution of employer branding on social media platforms. They conduct a study to better understand the new facets of employer branding created by social media. Based on nine interviews with hotel managers in Paris, they describe the evolution of this concept and summarize the different facets of e-employer branding within social media.

- Christine Bauer, Natalia Kryvinska, and Christine Strauss, in "The Business with Digital Signage for Advertising," present a detailed analysis of the potential of digital signage. The authors emphasize challenges in performance measurement and implementation, operating and using a digital signage system, display blindness, and negative externalities. The article presents possible solutions as well as best practices.
- Sami Dakhlia, Andrés Davila, and Barry Cumbie, in "Trust, but Verify: The Role of ICTs in the Sharing Economy," propose a pedagogical note that offers a short primer on some of the underlying economic concepts related to peer-to-peer sharing platforms. They underline the main challenges of the feedback-driven reputation that can boost trust by reducing risk while keeping transaction costs small. To do so, they propose two complementary approaches: (1) developing ID verification solutions that link and aggregate a user's reputation profiles from various communities and (2) using connected monitoring devices.
- Francesco Bellini, Fabrizio D'Ascenzo and Valeria Traversi, in "Internet Service Providers: The Italian Scenario," present the characteristics of the Italian Internet providers' market. They analyze the Italian Internet market based on fundamental parameters such as demand, global turnover, and different methods of access to the network. They underline the technical, economic, and financial characteristics of the sector. They provide an analysis of the economic and financial structure exploring companies' efficiency through performance indicators.
- Daniele Pederzoli, in "ICT and Retail: State of the Art and Prospects," analyzes the diffusion of technologies in the retail sector. He categorizes four different fields for technologies impacting retail activities, and he analyzes some examples for each category that can illustrate these trends.

ICTO2015 was hosted by the ESCE International Business School (a member of Laureate International Universities) and co-organized by the CIRCEE research center (Centre Interdisciplinaire de Recherche sur le Commerce Extérieur et l'Économie) and PRIMAL (Paris Research In Norms Management and Law).

We would like to thank Dr. Pierre Pariente, President of the ESCE Group, Prof. Eric Pezet from Paris-Ouest Nanterre La Défense University—PRIMAL, and Prof. Alexandre Sokic, the Dean for Research of the ESCE, for their excellent organization of this conference. We also thank all the ESCE and PRIMAL members for making this event a success. We extend our gratitude to Prof. Cecilia Rossignoli and Prof. Frédéric Gautier, Conference Co-Chairs, and the ICTO2015 keynote speakers: Yohan Ruso, the founder of Praditus and Former Managing Director of eBay France, as well as Prof. Paola Dameri from Università di Genova and Prof. Alessio Maria Braccini from Università della Tuscia. A special thanks to Prof. Marco De Marco, who received the ICTO Golden Medal for his lifetime achievement during the ICTO2015 conference.

Last but not least, we want to thank the 103 reviewers who generously gave their time and knowledge, and especially Ibrahim Abunadi, Mokhtar Amami, Georges

Aoun, Jamil Arida, Nabil Badr, Youcef Baghdadi, Imed Ben Nasr, Sabrina
Bonomi, Papetti Catherine, Marco De Marco, Sami Dakhlia, Andrés Davila, Alain
Devalle, Eliane El Zoghbi, Soraya Ezzeddine, Roberta Fantasia, Nizar Ghamgui,
Kalinka Kaloyanova, Atif Khan, Nasri Messarra, Beba Molinari, Jessie Pallud,
Daniele Pederzoli, Eric Pezet, Elpida Prasopoulou, Daphne Raban, Moufida Sadok,
May Sayegh, Alexandre Sokic, Hirotoshi Takeda, Teresina Torre, Claudio
Torrigiani, Sara Trucco, Stefano Za, and Alessandro Zardini.

September/October 2015   Francesca Ricciardi
                                                               Antoine Harfouche

Contents

Part I
ICT and the Pursue of Public Good

One-Stop Government in Italy and the Lebanon: When the Law Alone Is no Silver Bullet

Walter Castelnovo, Maddalena Sorrentino, Rania Fakhoury and Marco De Marco

Abstract The paper investigates the implementation of One-stop government in Italy and the Lebanon. The Italian government's One-Stop Business Shop ('SUAP') programme is first analyzed to discover why it has taken 12 years of legislation to get Italy's municipalities fully on board, and whether it has returned the expected benefits by effectively lightening the administrative load that drags on the competitiveness of the country's business sector. The critical discussion of the "innovation by law" approach identifies the stumbling blocks that have deterred the Italian government from achieving its mission to set up the One-Stop Business Shops and to deliver e-government. From the analysis of the Italian case some lessons are drawn that can be useful to guide the implementation of One-Stop Business Shop in Lebanon where the process is still at the beginning also due to the effects of the instability that affected the region during the past years.

Keywords E-government · One-stop shop · E-services · Digital agenda

W. Castelnovo
University of Insubria, Varese, Italy
e-mail: walter.castelnovo@uninsubria.it

M. Sorrentino (✉)
University of Milan, Milan, Italy
e-mail: maddalena.sorrentino@unimi.it

R. Fakhoury
Grenoble Ecole de Management, Grenoble, France
e-mail: rania.fakhoury@grenoble-em.com

M. De Marco
Uninettuno, Roma, Italy
e-mail: marco.demarco@uninettunouniversity.net

© Springer International Publishing Switzerland 2016
F. Ricciardi and A. Harfouche (eds.), *Information and Communication Technologies in Organizations and Society*, Lecture Notes in Information Systems and Organisation 15, DOI 10.1007/978-3-319-28907-6_1

1 Introduction

Keen to harness the many benefits generated by One-Stop Government for citizens, business and the public sector itself, the past twenty years have seen governments the world over put it at the top of their policymaking agendas [1–3].

The rush to define 'one-stop government' was led by the supranational organizations [4–7] and the large consulting firms (e.g., [8–10]), while the e-government scholars see the one-stop solution as the hub and spokes of each e-government system [11–19].

One-stop government is a concept that translates into a variety of shapes and sizes but implementation usually comprises:

- the bundling and/or integration of public services [20] that can be accessed from a single point of contact, although they can be delivered by different public authorities that have competences on them [11, 21];
- the re-design of the services architecture and the service delivery so that users are able to access the services in a well-structured and well understandable manner, meeting their perspectives and needs [11, 22];
- the availability of a multiplicity of delivery channels, including the online channel that makes the services available 24 h a day [23, 24].

More recently, the topic has fallen under the scrutiny of the Information Systems scholars, who are especially interested in key conceptual aspects such as:

- public agency interoperability/integration to support the execution of inter-organizational workflows, as required by the single-point-of-contact idea itself [25–30];
- the study of inter-organizational transformation/innovation processes and reengineering process models from the perspective of inter-organizational cooperation between different public agencies [31–35];
- the study of business and service delivery models, particularly in terms of the single point of contact's delivery of online services [36–41].

The simplification of administrative procedures, single points of contact (SPC) and online services are the three distinct features that make one-stop government particularly conducive to not only smoothing business-government relations, but also easing the bureaucratic millstone that crushes business [28, 31]. Take the example of enterprises in countries like Italy and Lebanon, where highly fragmented government systems force them on a daunting race from one type of government agency to another in order to comply with the many, often idiosyncratic legal requirements for business start-up, change of activity and closure [42].

It is now recognized that leaner administrative procedures are the categorical imperative for new business development and economic growth. Indeed, administrative simplification remains a key priority for many countries in both the developed and the developing world [43] and is usually achieved by streamlining procedures and the setting up of One-Stop Shops, either physical or online (or a combination of both) [44].

This qualitative paper investigates the approaches taken by both a developed country, Italy, and a developing country, Lebanon, to implement the One-Stop Shop model. However, the two countries differ vastly not only in terms of government and economic systems, but also in terms of e-government development status (the 2014 UN E-Government Survey ranks Italy at 23 and Lebanon at 89).

The approach of Italy to the One-Stop Business Shop (in Italian, Sportello Unico per le Attività Produttive or 'SUAP') began with the enactment of Law 447 in 1998, better known as the SUAP law, the specific aim of which was to simplify the authorization process for the start-up, change of activity and closure of a business. Law 447 mandated that each municipality set up a SUAP to deal with the tasks therein defined and to put in place the relative technological and organizational innovation processes. However, the lacklustre response to Law 447, mainly due to many municipalities lack of resources and skills, meant the Italian government had to intervene several times to impose increasingly tougher rules in order to get them fully on board the SUAP programme. In fact, it took as much as 12 years of law-making, ending with Law 160/2010, to get the municipalities to deliver a full menu of online business services as typical e-Government services.

The Lebanese government embarked on its One-Stop Shop (OSS) programme in 2002 with a two-point agenda: (i) to assist investors in obtaining the permits required for industrial, tourism and real estate projects and to assist people in obtaining their residence and work permits, as well as to fulfil other similar formalities; and (ii) to inform and guide investors through the legal and administrative framework, the financing options and choice of location.

However, in 2005, the Lebanese citizens lost a certain degree of control when Lebanon was caught up in regional instability and political unrest, mainly as a result of the crisis that hit its Middle Eastern neighbours, the effect of which has stalled the approval and/or implementation of many policy programmes and the relative legislation, especially those related to administrative simplification and reform. This had consequences also on the implementation process of the Lebanese OSS that slowed down significantly.

The article maps the diverse challenges faced by both Italy and Lebanon in setting up their One-Stop Business Shops and offers a timely reflection on their current state of play. The Italian SUAP programme and the Lebanese OSS programme share the same goal, that of reducing the administrative burdens on enterprises by simplifying procedures and establishing a Single Point of Contact (SPC), i.e., one sole platform from which the enterprises can conduct all their government business. In Italy, the SUAP is now up and running as a typical e-government service, enabling enterprises to communicate with the authorities through exclusively the online channel. On the other hand, the Lebanese OSS is still struggling to hit target. Therefore, while the current divergence in the status of the SUAP and the OSS prevents us from making a full comparison of the two approaches, we believe the insights and weaknesses highlighted by the Italian case analysis can usefully guide the Lebanese OSS implementers through the rocky terrain that leads to the virtualization of the OSS.

Now that the SPCs are effectively on stream in Italy, the paper can attempt an ex-post assessment in order to understand whether the diverse SUAP interventions have succeeded, which, to the best of our knowledge, has not yet been done. Given the aim of the paper, the scope of the analysis will be delineated by the factors that can help us respond to three interrelated research questions:

1. Has the SUAP programme lightened the administrative millstone that crushes Italy's businesses, thus helping the country to reboot the economy and increase its competitive status?
2. Is the exclusively legislative approach a true driver of innovation?
3. What can be learned from the Italian case that could be useful for Lebanon?

The Introduction is followed by Sect. 2, which first sets out the approaches taken by the Italian and the Lebanese governments to implement the One-stop Shop model and then outlines a reference framework against which to gauge the development of both the Italian SUAP and the Lebanese OSS. Section 3 discusses the outcome of the now fully operational SUAP programme, using secondary data sources to assess whether it has reduced the administrative burdens on businesses and, if so, whether it has thus achieved its mission to reboot the growth and competitiveness of the Italian economy. This same section also discusses the SUAP programme's "innovation by law" approach, which we believe is the main reason for the lacklustre results. Section 4 presents the study's conclusions and discusses how the lessons learned from the Italian case can help to guide OSS implementation in Lebanon.

2 One-Stop Shops: Background

2.1 One-Stop Shop in Italy and Lebanon

In Italy the SUAP programme was launched in 1998 with Law 447/98 as part of the policy to spur the country-wide adoption of e-government and to simplify relations between government and business. The Law gave each municipality the option of setting up a SUAP either independently or jointly with other municipalities (through inter-municipal cooperation) provided that only one single organization was responsible for handling the relevant administrative procedures from start to finish.

Prior to Law 447/98, the Italian municipalities were free to apply the procedures, forms and tariffs of their choice. This legacy system meant that those business owners operating in complex and/or sensitive sectors had to plough through an obstacle course where the barriers were the different public offices and their idiosyncratic procedures, and which translated into yet more red tape and even higher costs. The SUAP thus was tasked with streamlining the entire business authorization/licensing/permit process by coordinating all the public agencies involved (e.g., local healthcare authorities, fire brigade, provincial and regional governments, regional environment authorities) and ensuring the entrepreneurs a single point of contact (SPC) from which to start the process of compliance and permits needed to start-up, change the activity or close a business.

Since 1998, the SUAP programme has undergone a continuous adjustment process, mainly determined by issuing new laws that mainly aimed at making the SUAP more technology driven and to transform it, ultimately, into a virtual service centre, i.e., a computerized and connected unit that delivers government information and services to business users via the new digital technologies, internet and new media.

From 1998 to 2012, the Lebanese Government has made several attempts to introduce a One-stop Shop programme as part of its Public Administration reform package. The municipal one-stop shop programme was initially adopted by the Minister of State for Administrative Reform (OMSAR) in September 2001 as part of the 'Strategy for the Reform and Development of Public Administration in Lebanon' with the goal of simplifying citizen administrative procedures [45]. The e-government strategy document was approved by the Ministerial ICT Committee in December 2002 but not by the Council of Ministers.

The first milestone the Lebanese one-stop shop programme wanted to achieve was to reduce bureaucracy and modernize service delivery, while the ultimate objective is to deliver more streamlined e-government services that both lighten the red tape for citizens and make the country more attractive to investors. The Lebanese government wanted to make the municipalities responsible for kicking off its digital agenda and facilitating relations with the citizenry. A full review of first the e-government strategy and then the Strategy for the Reform and Development of Public Administration in Lebanon was made in 2008 and 2011, respectively, but again it failed to receive the blessing of the Council of Ministers [46, 47]. In addition, as part of both those strategic review processes the OSS programme also was reassessed and its importance highlighted.

The Lebanese OSS programme was designed to create a standard model with standard procedures accessible from a single platform that enables the governmental agencies to deal with the requests of a large number of citizens. The main role of each ministry's OSS is to put their human resources to effective use to facilitate the processing of specific government transactions and thus reduce the overall timeframe and the waiting lists. Despite these good intentions, the several pitfalls (mostly administrative and technical) encountered by the various ministries mean that by 2012 only the Ministry of Tourism had managed to implement its OSS, mainly delivering services to exclusively business users but without having managed to simplify the procedures.

Overall, Lebanon is having trouble getting over its digital agenda teething problems, mainly due to the long delays in enacting the much-needed ICT [47]. Nonetheless, the lack of appropriate legislation has not stopped the OSS and similar projects from getting off the ground.

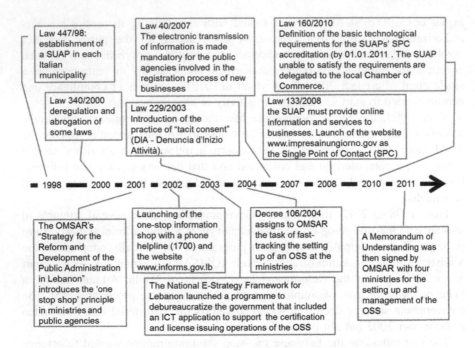

Fig. 1 The timeline of the Italian SUAP and the Lebanese OSS programmes

Figure 1 summarizes the main steps of the Italian legislative journey to the SUAP from 1998 to 2010, comparing it with the development along time of the Lebanese OSS programme.

2.2 A Reference Framework for One-Stop Shop Development

As explained above, the Italian SUAP and the Lebanese OSS are at quite different development a stage, which makes it hard to fully compare the two cases. However, if we use the One-Stop E-Government reference framework defined in [24], it is possible to gauge their progress according to the different stages identified by the model (Fig. 2).

The first major challenge addressed by the One-Stop Business Shops in both Italy and in Lebanon was to bundle the different services provided by the public agencies (Step 1 of Fig. 1). The programmes implemented by the governments of each country in the past few years then took the One-stop Shop to Step 2 of the development path, when it became a service center.

The top quadrants shown in Fig. 1, outline the two successive stages in which the public agencies proceed to "virtualize" their service delivery activities. In Italy,

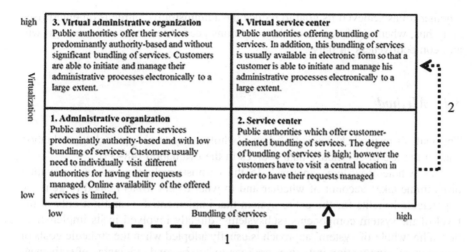

Fig. 2 One-stop e-government reference framework [24]

the issue of digital inter-agency communications and workflows was not addressed until the launch of the 2003–2008 Italian National Action Plan for E-Government, which provided the municipalities with the funding and support needed to transform the SUAPs into virtual portals. To transform the SUAP into a virtual service centre (Step 2 of Fig. 1), most of the funded projects had the objective of laying the technological foundations needed for electronic inter-agency communications and workflows, even when these did not explicitly include the implementation of business e-services. In fact, that particular goal was only achieved after Law 160/2010 made the electronic submission of all business authorization applications mandatory, signaling the end of the lengthy process of change that called for Italy's municipalities to set up a virtualized SUAP.

Unlike the Italian SUAP, the Lebanese OSS has remained at Step 1 (Quadrant 2) of Fig. 1, achieving that preliminary status only after surpassing many challenges. In fact, the inter-agency agreement between, principally, the Ministry of Tourism and the Municipality of Beirut has not yet been signed.

3 Assessing the Italian SUAP Programme

Given that more than four years have passed since the last SUAP law was enacted (Law 160/2010), it should be possible to assess whether the programme and the chosen implementation methods have effectively achieved the desired innovation benefits. Accordingly, this section investigates the impact of the SUAP programme on the Italian municipalities; above all, it analyzes whether they have been able to comply with all the requirements laid down by the various laws issued from 1998 to 2010. We then seek to respond to the paper's first research question by assessing whether it has achieved its goal to reduce the administrative burdens on enterprises and, thus, whether it has created the conditions needed to reboot economic growth and competitiveness in Italy.

3.1 Method

The analysis method chosen is based on a 'whole-of-system' approach to evaluation and on the use of secondary data sources in the evaluation [48–53].

The 'whole-of-system' approach to the ex-post evaluation of an innovation programme takes account of whether and to what extent it has helped to generate appreciable benefits for the entire system that implemented it, and not only at the level of the system components (subsystems) directly involved in its implementation. The 'whole-of-system' approach is usually adopted when the strategic goals of government's innovation initiatives are seen to "go beyond efficiency, effectiveness and economy, and include political and social objectives such as trust in government, social inclusion, community regeneration, community wellbeing and sustainability" [50, p. 134]. This approach calls for shifting the focus of the evaluation from inputs and outputs to outcomes and impacts that are not normally indicated as the direct objectives of an initiative, but rather as societal objectives to which a successful initiative should contribute, such as economic growth, jobs, democracy, inclusion, quality of life, etc. [54].

From that perspective a 'whole-of-system' evaluation can be likened to an assessment of impact, seeing that both approaches use 'information on the overall impact of a program, as opposed to specific case studies or anecdotes, which can give only partial information and may not be representative of overall program impacts' [55, p. 4].

System-level evaluation usually is resource and data-intensive, requiring time-series data that are not always available and that would cost too much to gather directly [56]. The use of secondary data sources for the ex-post evaluation of government's innovation initiatives can sensibly reduce the evaluation costs since it can use already available data. As well as reducing the costs for data collection, there are other advantages to using secondary data sources, such as ease of reproducibility, ability to generalize the results arising from larger datasets, reliability of the data deriving from their having been compiled by trustworthy organizations, taking into account suitable procedures for ensuring reliability and validity [51, 57].

3.2 Impact of the SUAP Programme on the Italian Municipalities

There is no question that the diverse laws enacted by the Italian Government in the 12 years from 1998 to 2010 have increased the number of municipal SUAPs, although Law 160/2010 was the key turning point, propelling approximately 94.5 % of Italian municipalities to implement a SUAP by June 2013, whether managed by the municipality itself, through inter-municipal cooperation agreements, or by the local Chamber of Commerce. In fact, Law 160 provided the vital catalyst by requiring the SUAP to obtain national SPC accreditation and legally forcing the municipality to transfer the management (but not the cost) of the SUAP to the local Chamber of Commerce if it failed to meet the 1 January 2011 deadline.

Indeed, the boost in performance was clearly thanks to this latter obligation, given that a good 2951 (75 % micro municipalities with 5000 residents or less) of Italy's 8092 municipalities had delegated SUAP management to the Chambers of Commerce by June 2013. On the other hand, 4698 municipalities gained SPC-accreditation for their SUAP, while 443 had still not set one up [58].

Paradoxically, however, although 5718 municipalities had set up a SUAP by October 2007, the number of SPC-accredited SUAPs at June 2013 was lower than before Law 160/2010 came into force, which means that about 18 % of the SUAPs set up prior to 2010 lacked the basic technological requisites needed for SPC accreditation. That and the fact that 443 municipalities (5.5 % of the total) had not yet managed to comply with the law and actually set up a SUAP is a clear sign of the hurdles faced by even the most willing councils. But it is the micro municipalities that face the biggest obstacles to implementing and running the SUAP, whether directly or through inter-municipal cooperation. Indeed, 44 % of Italy's 5693 micro municipalities have either failed to set up a SUAP or have had to delegate it to the local Chamber of Commerce [59].

So what is stopping the small municipalities from setting up self-managed SUAPs? Firstly, the smaller municipalities rarely have either the resources or the skills needed to set up and run this kind of services unit, an issue that was evident from the outset of the SUAP programme but which has worsened over the years with the major spending cuts decreed by the Italian government as part of its crisis recovery package. Secondly, the law has made the SUAP responsible for coordinating multiple governmental agencies over which it has no authority, hence, to comply with its legal obligations the SUAP has no choice but to rely solely on the good will and cooperation of these agencies. In the words of Lanzara [60, p. 34], legal procedures must be able to travel across administrative bodies and ICT infrastructures 'without raising exceptions of sorts or problems of recognition, legitimacy, accountability or validity'.

Further, the smaller municipalities do not have the negotiating power needed to implement third-party agreements for sharing the inter-organizational workflow, even though these are essential to its proper functioning [69]. This perceived difficulty, and the fact that the penalties for non-compliance were only introduced in 2010 with Law 160, has further discouraged the smaller municipalities from setting up a SUAP.

3.3 Impact on Businesses

The main objective of the SUAP programme was to reduce the administrative burdens on enterprises, thus creating the conditions to reboot economic growth and competitiveness in Italy [61]. After a journey lasting more than 13 years, it is now time to investigate whether the SUAP programme has achieved this objective. Figures 3 and 4, show Italy's ranking in two well-known international surveys in the period in which the SUAP programme was expected to start generating benefits:

- World Bank Ease of Doing Business Index—EDBI (www.doingbusiness.org/ rankings), which measures a country's capability to create a business-friendly environment with better, usually simpler, regulations for businesses;
- World Economic Forum Global Competitiveness Index—GCI (www.weforum. org/issues/global-competitiveness?), which ranks the institutions, policies, and factors that enable a country to sustain current and medium-term levels of economic prosperity.

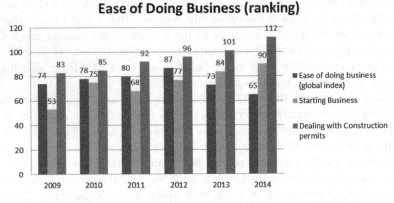

Fig. 3 The ranking of Italy in the EDBI

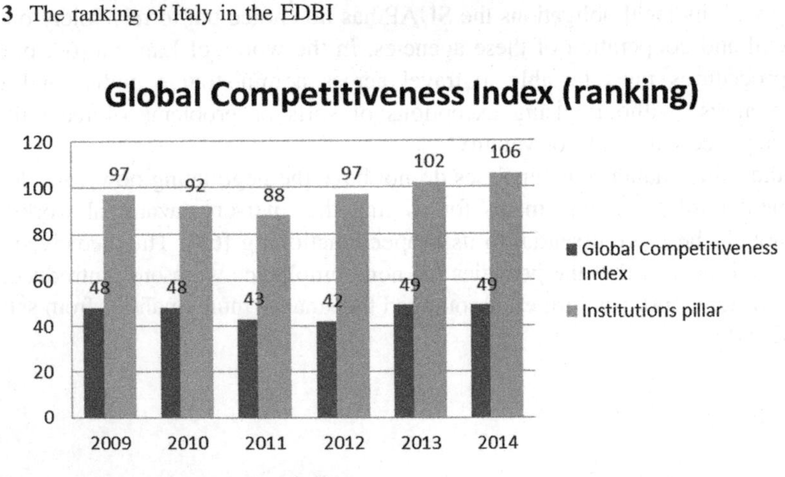

Fig. 4 The ranking of Italy in the GCI

The low rankings recorded by the two indices shown in Figs. 3 and 4, are a clear indication that the SUAP programme has not yet enabled Italy's local governments to provide more effective services to support competitiveness and economic growth. Indeed, the trend tracked by both indices suggests more of a decline as opposed to an improvement in the municipal indicators (i.e., the "institutions pillar" in GCI, and "starting a business" and "dealing with construction permits" in EDBI).

In fact, the SUAP programme alone has done nothing to help matters as far as Italy's competitive deficit is concerned, given that, as reported in [62] it has failed to both cut the cost of dealing with the public administration for businesses (especially SMMEs), which on average spent 23.9 man-days on bureaucratic requirements in 2007 rising to 30.2 in 2013, and raise the business users' level of overall satisfaction with the public administration (on a scale 1–10, 4.9 in 2007 vs. 4.0 in 2013).

Denting that performance even more, the Italian SMMEs continue to rate the weight of bureaucracy and administrative burdens a major risk factor to survival, ranking it 8.5 on a scale of 1–10 [62], suggesting that the SUAP programme has been a total flop in detangling the red tape process.

4 Lessons Learned from the Italian Case and How They Can Be Useful for Lebanon

As mentioned earlier, the implementation delays suffered by the Lebanese OSS programme mean that it is yet too early to make even a preliminary assessment of whether it has succeeded in delivering the expected benefits. It is therefore impossible to directly compare the outcomes and impacts of the respective administrative simplification programmes on the economic systems of Italy and Lebanon. Nevertheless, since the Lebanese OSS seems to be pursuing the same development path as the Italian SUAP, we believe the Lebanese implementers can use the insights and weaknesses highlighted by the Italian case analysis offered here to chart a smoother path to the virtualization of the OSS in Lebanon. To this end, in this section we draw some lessons from the Italian case that could be useful for Lebanon.

As observed by Rebora [63], any attempt by Italy to reform its Public Administration has erred heavily on the regulatory side, ignoring the most fundamental question of all: whether the public organizations are actually equipped with the capabilities and/or the funds needed to comply effectively with the new legislation and, if not, how to first address this aspect. In fact, because policy makers assume that the collective interest's chief concern is the decision-making process, they tend to dismiss the policy implementation process as a given, seeing it as a 'technical' phase and, thus, as neutral and devoid of discretionary power, which, of course, is not the case at all [64].

Instead of using legislation to create the conditions for innovation and, thus, as an enabler, the single-minded approach to reform taken by all the Italian governments for the past 20–25 years has been 'innovation by law'. This use of a specific legislative framework to impose change explains the snowball effect triggered by the failure of the first SUAP policy intervention. In fact, the belief that the law alone would generate the desired results and benefits was sorely tried when the government was forced to enact not one, all-encompassing law but several laws, which served only to further tighten the rules and, in the event of non-compliance, subjected the already financially pressed municipalities to higher and higher penalties. The SUAP programme also shows how the 'innovation by law' approach can spark the path dependency syndrome, given the cultural and institutional attitudes that dominate the Italian administrative landscape [65, 66].

As seen in Sects. 3.2 and 3.3, above, the SUAP programme has yet to produce the expected benefits. That translates into a negative response to our first research question, 'Has the SUAP programme lightened the administrative millstone that crushes Italy's businesses, thus helping the country to reboot the economy and increase its competitive status?' which leads us to ask why it has failed, and what is the lesson to be learned?

Implementation of the SUAP programme suffered all the start-up problems common to ICT-based innovation processes [67]. However, the aim here is not to analyze the critical success/fail factors of innovation processes, which are already well known and well covered in the literature, but to analyze two of the SUAP programme's most critical aspects, which we believe are the main culprits of the poor results achieved so far: (i) Italy's exclusively "innovation by law" approach to PA reform; and (ii) the risk of over-estimating the effectiveness of delivering the services online.

By making it mandatory for the municipalities to establish a One-Stop Business Shop, Law 447/1998 paved the way for its transition from Administrative Organization (AO) (Quadrant 1, Fig. 1) to Service Center (SC) (Quadrant 2, Fig. 1), while Laws 133/2008 and 160/2010 required the SUAP to advance to the Virtual Service Center (VSC) stage (Quadrant 4). However, only a user-centred approach can ensure the effective transition from AO to SC, a stage in which it is essential to closely integrate/coordinate the bundling of services at both the intra-organizational level, i.e., among all the offices involved in the delivery of a service, and at the inter-organizational level, i.e., among all the local agencies involved in the business authorization process. Nevertheless, although Law 447/1998 had already issued a clear set of requirements for intra- and inter-organizational integration/coordination, according to the SMME rankings, the functioning of the Italian PA never fully complied with even the basic organizational prerequisites of the SC model. Law 133/2008 and Law 160/2010 then called for the SUAP to advance from SC to VSC status, making it compulsory for the One-Stop Business Shop to provide its services online and for the relative public agencies to use ICT to manage information flows. Even so, these additional laws made little positive difference to the overall situation.

Italy then wrote European Directive 2006/123/EC into law as part of Law 160/2010, launching the national www.impresainungiorno.gov website and standardizing the SUAP front-office but failing to define how the back-office activities, including the inter-organizational workflows, should be organized or which technological solutions to use to manage the intra- and inter-organizational information flows. This has significantly undermined the efficiency and efficacy of the municipalities' effort to transform the SUAP into a fully connected digital business service provider.

The fatal flaw of taking an exclusively 'innovation by law' approach is that it glosses over the major organizational criticalities of setting up one-stop government, such as the fact that the smaller municipalities lack the resources needed, in primis, the skills to not only implement the model's standardized procedures, but also to manage relations with the relevant PA actors and stakeholders. By tightening the regulatory screw and expecting the practical side of implementation to sort itself out on its own, the various governments have charted a course that could only lead to an unhappy ending. Indeed, the findings of the Italian case study teach us that unless reform is tackled from the grass-roots perspective (addressing the problems of resources and competences from the bottom up to help the municipal organizations provide an effective response to business needs) it will never have the desired effect. Giving the municipalities the much-needed organizational support to set up their SUAP would have made all the difference. Instead, Italy continues to chase the elusive ghost of simplified administrative processes and, as a result, has made no headway in improving the Italian economy's competitive edge.

And so to our second research question, 'Is the exclusively legislative approach a true driver of innovation?' The belief that the law alone can drive innovation is disproved by the impact of the SUAP programme on the users. In fact, on a scale of 1–10, the 2013 PromoPa Italian SMME survey ranked the SUAP as a means of simplification at a lowly 4.3. Moreover, even though the various laws issued in 1998–2010 eventually pushed 94.5 % of Italian municipalities into setting up a fully operational SUAP by 2013, most of them did not even bother to inform the potential users either about the new service or the relative opportunities to simplify and ease the administrative burdens; in fact, only 37.6 % of the SMMEs said they knew about the latest SUAP requirements introduced in 2010. Hence, the municipalities seem to have set up their One-Stop Business Shops in name only, providing yet further evidence that more than regulatory compliance is needed to generate the desired benefits of innovation.

The second critical aspect revealed by the SUAP case study is the risk of over-estimating the effectiveness of delivering the services in online format. Despite the fact that Law 160/2010 called for the full virtualization of the One-Stop Business Shop, making the online channel mandatory for the delivery of its business services, the PromoPa 2013 survey shows that the SMMEs rank the online delivery of services as less important than debureaucratization, the synergic organization of the offices, the competence of staff [68], and even the opening hours of the public offices. That the SMMEs do not consider the virtualization of the One-Stop Business Shop a strategic priority is confirmed also by the efficacy rating of the latest SUAP interventions (especially those aimed at transition to full VSC) designed to simplify government-business relations. In fact, the high 2011 rating

(6.2 on a scale of 1–10) had already retreated to 5.5 in 2012 before sinking even further, to 4.3 in 2013. Hence, it appears that the hurdles encountered by the SUAP programme were at least in part created by getting the priorities wrong and misjudging the demand for online services.

Naturally, the potential of a virtualized SUAP to deliver more efficient and effective services should not be underestimated solely because the priorities of the SMMEs diverge from those identified by the SUAP programme (for the transition from SC to VSC). Rather, what the SUAP case underscores is the risk shared by many e-government programmes that the delivery of services online is expected to happen as if by magic, i.e., without doing the appropriate ground work, or at least making a simultaneous effort to deal with basic problems such as organizational structure. Indeed, the simple act of virtualization actually risks emphasizing instead of resolving this issue.

A final observation on the case of the Italian SUAP is that the policymakers' focus on the law has swept aside other primary considerations. For example, not only the implementation factor, but also the behaviour of the civil servants, the responses and reactions of the regulated subjects and interference from pressure groups. In addition, the Italian public system is an idiosyncratic organism that has a bad habit of neglecting other, interrelated aspects. In the SUAP case, the spate of regulations was not issued in a vacuum but loaded onto an already complex framework made up not only of other legislation, but also habits, behaviour models [68] and beliefs. Second, ICT itself yields regulatory effects; in consequence, the design and use of artefacts depends not only on considerations of technical feasibility and usability, but also on interpretation, power relationships and administrative procedures [60].

5 Conclusion

The paper has followed the empirical trail left by the e-government programme dynamics of Italy and Lebanon since 1998, drawing on the framework developed by Hogrebe et al. [24] to map the routes taken to implement their online One-stop Business Shops. Moreover, although the aim of the study was not, initially, to make an original contribution to the evaluation literature, it is hard to ignore the important implications that have emerged from our analysis of the SUAP case.

The macro-level assessment suggests a negative response to the first research question: 'Has the SUAP programme lightened the administrative millstone that crushes Italy's businesses, thus helping the country to reboot the economy and increase its competitive status?'

The current status of the SUAP programme indicates that the Italian government's strategic mission of simplification with its expected benefits continues to dance out of reach. As observed above, many institutional, organizational and technological problems have hindered the development of the virtual One-stop Business Shop in Italy. The need of providing appropriate solutions for these problems before evolving the One-stop Business Shop toward the virtualization stage is the main lesson for Lebanon that can be drawn from the Italian case.

In Italy, the local governments have had to deal with the major issue of how to incorporate the SUAP into the municipality's organizational boundaries, its degree of autonomy in the given context and how to find the resources needed to make it function. Another key aspect to consider is whether the businesses themselves have the technology needed to access the online services, given that the Italian business landscape is made up chiefly of small and very small firms not all of which are computerized.

The response deduced from the analysis to the second research question 'Is the exclusively legislative approach a true driver of innovation?' leaves no room for doubt that while administrative simplification by law is necessary, it is far from sufficient. In other words, the legislative intervention is only one of several inputs. Compared to the earlier measures, the latest SUAP law not only opens up new scenarios of discontinuity, but also introduces elements of uncertainty and complexity that weigh on the decisional processes, with the smaller municipalities penalized by contextual factors, not least the traditional attitudes of Italian administration.

Lebanon does not seem to suffer from the problems related to the 'innovation by law' approach that affected the SUAP programme in Italy. On the contrary, in the Lebanese case it is precisely the lack of legislation that is the stumbling block to OSS implementation. The four main pillars of Lebanon's Public Administration Reform (PAR) of 2002 were technical, service, capacity building and legal. However, the fact that the review and modernization of the country's laws and regulations is still a work in progress has hindered any advances in the first three areas. The PAR relies heavily on equipping the ministries and the public institutions with ICT infrastructure and applications in order to upgrade the public administration. However, any attempts at reform in Lebanon are blocked by the country's political situation and the government's lack of interest in the appropriate follow up. In addition, most ministerial decisions are taken by consensus so imposing a legal framework on the ministries or the institutions is already a lost cause. The challenge is to introduce an approved legal framework into the governance of the public administrations, making them an integral part of the public sector modernization effort. From that perspective, Lebanon might find the "innovation by law" approach more advantageous, on condition, however, that it learns from the Italian case to use legislation to enable instead of to coerce innovation. The Lebanese legislator has already created the conditions for the adoption of a user-centered approach, but both the legal and the technical frameworks need to become firmly embedded in the mainstream modernization policies and service design.

This shift to a technological and legal framework would seem the most workable path to reorganizing Lebanon's public administration but demands the coherent and strategic planning of PAR policies across all areas and levels. In this respect, the situations of Lebanon and Italy are very similar. In Italy, the failure to address the municipalities' basic organizational requirements led to the overestimation of the effectiveness of the online delivery of services. Therefore, the ensuing implication for the Lebanon case is the need to work on mainly transforming the organization, the structure and the processes of government (i.e., administrative reform) while encouraging the active participation of citizens.

The selective assessment exercise presented here is limited to the current status of Italy's SUAP and Lebanon's OSS and their respective contextual effects. A more in-depth assessment of the one-stop government programme that covers a broader platform of stakeholders (e.g., other public agencies, business intermediaries) would require further knowledge gains and an interdisciplinary analysis. Nevertheless, the authors firmly believe that the approach to increase our understanding of how the reform processes develop, as proposed by the paper, needs to go further than just analyzing the regulations and the policy tools in order to encompass the multiple contextual factors and their dynamics.

References

1. Wimmer, M.A., Tambouris, E: Online one-stop government—a working framework and requirements. In: Proceedings of the IFIP world computer congress, August 26–30. Montreal (2002)
2. Scott, M.: A click and bricks strategy for e-government. In: Proceedings of the 17th bled e-conference. Bled, Slovenia (2004)
3. Janssen, M., Joha, A.: Motives for establishing shared service centers in public administrations. Int. J. Inf. Manage **26**(2), 102–116 (2006)
4. UN: World public sector report 2003—E-government at the crossroads. United Nations, New York (2003)
5. OECD: Cutting red tape—national strategies for administrative simplification. Online: http://www.oecd.org/gov/regulatory-policy/cuttingredtapenationalstrategiesforadministrativesimplification.htm (2006)
6. OECD: Why is administrative simplification so complicated? Looking beyond 2010. Online: http://www.oecd.org/regreform/regulatory-policy/cuttingredtape-whyisadministrativesimplificationsocomplicated.htm (2010)
7. World Bank: how many stops in a one-stop shop? A Review of Recent Developments in Business Registration. The World Bank Group, Washington DC (2009)
8. Accenture: From e-Government to e-Governance—using new technologies to strengthen relationships with citizens. Online: http://nstore.accenture.com/egovernance/x/From%20e-Government%20to%20e-Governance.pdf (2009)
9. PwC: Transforming the citizen experience—one stop shop for public services. PricewaterhouseCoopers. Online: www.pwc.com.au/industry/government (2012)
10. Deloitte: The functioning and usability of the points of single contact under the services directive—state of play and way forward—final report. Report commissioned by the European commission, directorate-general internal market and services. European Union (2012)
11. Wimmer, M.: A European perspective towards online one-stop government, the eGOV project. Electron. Commer. Res. Appl. **1**, 92–103 (2002)
12. Wimmer, M.: Integrated service modelling for online one-stop government. Electron. Markets. **12**(3), 149–156 (2002)
13. Glassey, O.: Developing a one-stop government data model. Govern. Inf. Q. **21**(2), 156–169 (2004)
14. Bannister, F.: E-government and administrative power: the one-stop-shop meets the turf war. Electron. Govern. Int. J. **2**(2), 160–176 (2005)

15. Tambouris, E., Wimmer, M.: Online one-stop government: a single point of access to public services. In: Huang, W., Siau, K., Wei, K. (eds.) Electronic government strategies and implementation, pp. 115–144. Idea Group, Hershey, PA (2005)

16. Skaggs, B.L., Poe, J.W., Stevens, K.W.: One-stop shopping: a perspective on the evolution of electronic resources management. OCLC Syst. Serv. **22**(3), 192–206 (2006)

17. Gouscos, D., Kalikakis, M., Legal, M., Papadopoulou, S.: A general model of performance and quality for one-stop e-Government service offerings. Govern. Inf. Q. **24**(4), 860–885 (2007)

18. Verdegem, P., Hauttekeete, L.: The user at the centre of the development of one-stop government. Int. J. Electron. Govern. **1**(3), 258–274 (2008)

19. Howard, C.; Rethinking post-npm governance: the bureaucratic struggle to implement one-stop-shopping for government services in Alberta. Public organization review, pp. 1–18 (2014)

20. Kubicek, H., Hagen, M.: One-stop-government in Europe: an overview. In: Hegen, M. (ed.) One-stop-government in Europe: results from 11 national surveys, Universität Bremen, Germany (2000)

21. Ricciardi, F., Rossignoli, C., De Marco, M.: Participatory networks for place safety and livability: organisational success factors. Int. J. Network. Virtual Organ. **13**(1), 42–65 (2013)

22. Dulskaia, I., Menshikova, M.: New service development: best practice of the Itaian postal sector. In: MCIS 2014 proceedings, AIS electronic library (AISeL). Online: http://aisel.aisnet.org/cgi/viewcontent.cgi?article=1008&context=mcis2014 (2014)

23. Dias, G.P., Rafael, J.A.: A simple model and a distributed architecture for realizing one-stop e-government. Electron. Commer. Res. Appl. **6**, 81–90 (2007)

24. Hogrebe, F., Kruse, W., Nüttgens, M.: One stop egovernment for small and medium-sized enterprises (SME): a strategic approach and case study to implement the EU services directive. In: Bled 2008 proceedings. Paper 8 (2008)

25. Charih, M., Robert, J.: Government on-line in the federal government of Canada: the organizational issues. Int. Rev. Admin. Sci. **70**(2), 373–384 (2004)

26. West, D.M.: e-government and the transformation of service delivery and citizen attitudes. Public Adm. Rev. **64**(1), 15–27 (2004)

27. Guijarro, L.: Interoperability frameworks and enterprise architectures in e-government initiatives in Europe and the United States. Govern. Inf. Q. **24**, 89–101 (2006)

28. Colarullo, F., Di Mascio, R., Virili, F.: Meccanismi di coordinamento nei SUAP (Sportelli Unici per le Attività Produttive): il caso Enterprise. VII Workshop dei Docenti e dei Ricercatori di Organizzazione Aziendale, Salerno (2006)

29. Bekkers, V.: The governance of back-office integration. Pub. Manage. Rev. **9**(3), 377–400 (2007)

30. Vaast, E., Binz-Scharf, M.C.: Bringing change in government organizations: evolution towards post-bureaucracy with web-based IT projects. Paper presented at the ICIS 2008 Conference (2008)

31. Ongaro, E.: Process management in the public sector: the experience of one-stop shops in Italy. Int. J. Pub. Sect. Manage. **17**(1), 81–107 (2004)

32. Kraemer, K., King, J.L.: Information technology and administrative reform: will e-government be different? Int. J. Electron. Govern. Res. **2**(1), 1–20 (2006)

33. Mele, V.: Explaining programmes for change: electronic government policy in Italy (1993–2003). Pub. Manage. Rev. **10**(1), 21–49 (2008)

34. Leeuw, F.L., Leeuw, B.: Cyber society and digital policies: challenges to evaluation? Evaluation **18**(1), 111–127 (2012)

35. Hansson, F., Norn, M.T., Vad, T.B.: Modernize the public sector through innovation? A challenge for the role of applied social science and evaluation. Evaluation **20**(2), 244–260 (2014)

36. Janssen, M., Kuk, G., Wagenaar, R.W.: A survey of web-based business models for e-government in the Netherlands. Govern. Inf. Q. **25**(2), 202–220 (2008)

37. Schellong, A.: Citizen government interaction: the promise of the E-channel. In: Meijer, A., Boersma, K., Wagenaar, P. (eds.) ICTs, citizens and governance: after the hype!, pp. 13–20. IOS Press, Amsterdam (2009)
38. Kohlborn, T., Weiss, S., Poeppelbuss, J., Korthaus, A., Fielt, E.: Online service delivery models—an international comparison in the public sector. Paper presented at the ACIS 2010 Conference (2010)
39. Peters, C., Kohlborn, T., Korthaus, A., Fielt, E., Ramsden, A.: Service delivery in one-stop government portals—observations based on a market research study in Queensland. ACIS 2011 proceedings. Paper 66 (2011)
40. Casalino, N., Cavallari, M., De Marco, M., Gatti, M., Taranto, G.: Defining a model for effective e-government services and an inter-organizational cooperation in public sector ICEIS 2014. In: Proceedings of the 16th international conference on enterprise information systems, 2, pp. 400–408 (2014)
41. Singer, P., Ferri, M.A., Aiello, L., Cacia, C.: Internet as a "point of synergy" between communication and distribution: hypothesis of model applied to tourism. JDCTA 4(7), 23–37 (2010)
42. Mola, L., Carugati, A.: Escaping 'localisms' in IT sourcing: tracing changes in institutional logics in an Italian firm. Eur. J. Inf. Syst. 21(4), 388–403 (2012)
43. OECD: Overcoming barriers to administrative simplification strategies—guidance for policy makers. Online: http://www.oecd.org/regreform/42112628.pdf (2009a)
44. OECD: Better regulation to strengthen market dynamics—Italy 2009. Online: http://www.oecd-ilibrary.org/governance/oecd-reviews-of-regulatory-reform-italy-2009_9789264067264-en (2009b)
45. OMSAR.: Strategy for the Reform and Development of the Public Administration in Lebanon. Online: http://www.omsar.gov.lb/SiteCollectionDocuments/www.omsar.gov.lb/PDF%20Files/ICT%20Strategies%20and%20Master%20Plans/Strategy_Reform_and_Development_English.pdf (2001)
46. OMSAR.: E-government strategy. Online: http://www.omsar.gov.lb/Cultures/enUS/Publications/Strategies/Documents/a563d88a47764e59ae833410e0967ea1ExecutiveSummary.pdf (2008)
47. OMSAR.: Strategy for the reform and development of public administration in Lebanon. Online: http://www.omsar.gov.lb/SiteCollectionDocuments/www.omsar.gov.lb/PDF%20Files/ICT%20Strategies%20and%20Master%20Plans/Strategy_Reform_and_Development_English.pdf (2011)
48. Arnold, E.: Evaluating research and innovation policy: a systems world needs systems evaluations. Res. Eval. 13(1), 3–17 (2004)
49. Esteves, J., Rhoda, J.: Developing a framework for the assessment of egovernment initiatives. In: AMCIS 2006 proceedings. Paper 286. http://aisel.aisnet.org/amcis2006/286 (2006)
50. Grimsley, M., Meehan, A., Gupta, K.: Evaluative design of e-government projects: a public value perspective. In: Proceedings of AMCIS 2006 (2006)
51. Srivastava, S.C., Teo, T.S.H.: E-government payoffs: evidence from cross-country data. J. Global Inf. Manage. 15(4), 20–40 (2007)
52. Castelnovo, W.: A country level evaluation of the impact of e-government: the case of Italy. In: Gil-Garcia, R. (ed.) E-government success factors and measures: concepts, theories, experiences, and practical recommendations. IGI Global, Hershey, PA (2013)
53. Castelnovo, W., Riccio, E.L.: E-government evaluation using the whole-of-systems approach. In: Proceedings of the 10th international conference on information systems and technology management—CONTECSI. June, 12–14. São Paulo, Brazil (2013)
54. Verleye, G. (ed.) Measure paper 3: impact measurement, eGovernment monitor network, deliverable D 3.3 (2010)
55. Gertler, J.P., Martinez, S., Premand, P., Rawlings, B.L., Vermeersch, C.M.J.: Impact evaluation in practice, the World Bank. Online: http://siteresources.worldbank.org/EXTHDOFFICE/Resources/5485726-1295455628620/Impact_Evaluation_in_Practice.pdf (2011)

56. Gupta, P.: Challenges and issues in e-government project assessment. In: Proceedings of the 1st international conference on theory and practice of electronic governance (ICEGOV '07) (2007)
57. Srivastava, S.C., Teo, T.S.H.: E-government, E-business, and national economic performance. Commun. Assoc. Inf. Syst. 26(14) (2010)
58. MISE: Sportello Unico Attività Produttive - Iniziative di monitoraggio dell'attuazione della riforma. Ministero dello Sviluppo Economico, Roma (2013)
59. ANCI-IFEL: Atlante dei Piccoli Comuni 2013. Online: http://www.anci.it/Contenuti/Allegati/Atlante%20dei%20Piccoli%20Comuni%202013.pdf (2013)
60. Lanzara, G.F.: Building digital institutions: ICT and the rise of assemblages in government. In: Contini, F., Lanzara, G.F. (eds.) ICT and innovation in the public sector, pp. 9–48. Palgrave Macmillan, London (2009)
61. Dameri, R.P.: Defining an evaluation framework for digital cities implementation. In: Information society (i-Society), 2012 international conference on (pp. 466–470). IEEE (2012, June)
62. PromoPa: Imprese e Burocrazia – Come le Piccole e Micro imprese giudicano la Pubblica Amministrazione – VIII Rapporto Nazionale. Franco Angeli, Milano (2013)
63. Rebora, G.: Trasformare le Pubbliche Amministrazioni - Per un progetto di transizione nell'orizzonte 2020. Liuc Papers n. 260, Serie Economia e Istituzioni 29 (2012)
64. Sorrentino, M., Passerini, K.: Evaluating public programs implementation: an exploratory case study. Int. J. Electron. Govern. Res. 6(3), 1–13 (2010)
65. Sorrentino, M., De Marco, M.: Implementing e-government in hard times: when the past is wildly at variance with the future. Inf. Polity 18(4), 331–342 (2013)@@@
66. Zardini, A., Rossignoli, C., Mola, L., De Marco, M.: Developing municipal e-government in Italy: the city of Alfa Case. Exploring services science, pp. 124–137. Springer International Publishing, Berlin (2014)
67. Luna-Reyes, L.F., Melloulib, S., Bertot, J.C.: Key factors and processes for digital government success. Inf. Polity 18, 101–105 (2013)
68. Casalino, N., Buonocore, F., Rossignoli, C., Ricciardi, F.: Transparency, openness and knowledge sharing for rebuilding and strengthening government institutions. In: Klement, E. P., Borutzky, W., Fahringer, T., Hamza, M.H., Uskov, V. (eds.) Proceedings of web-based education—WBE 2013 conference, IASTED-ACTA Press Zurich, 11–13 February, Innsbruck, Austria (2013)

Cloud Computing: Risks and Opportunities for Corporate Social Responsibility

Norberto Patrignani, Marco De Marco, Rania Fakhoury
and Maurizio Cavallari

Abstract This paper studies the impact of the information and communication technologies (ICT) used by organizations in their Corporate Social Responsibility (CSR) strategy. In particular, it analyses the impact of the most recent technological development, Cloud Computing, on the corporate users that adopt this service. What key issues need to be addressed by companies that use Cloud Computing? What is the impact of these choices on their CSR strategy? What strategic approaches best marry the company's ICT decisions with its CSR reputation?

Keywords Cloud computing · Corporate social responsibility · IT services · Centralised architectures · Information security · Organization

1 Introduction

The subject of this article concerns the impact of choices relating to information technology on strategies for Corporate Social Responsibility (i.e. CSR).

The first part is devoted to the most recent revolution in the field of information technology—Cloud Computing—then follows a brief description of CSR.

N. Patrignani · M. Cavallari (✉)
Università Cattolica, Milan, Italy
e-mail: maurizio.cavallari@unicatt.it

N. Patrignani
e-mail: norberto.patrignani@unicatt.it

M. De Marco
Uninettuno, Roma, Italy
e mail. marco.demarco@uninettunouniversity.net

R. Fakhoury
Grenoble Ecole de Management, Beirut, Lebanon
e-mail: rania.fakhoury@grenoble-em.com

© Springer International Publishing Switzerland 2016   23
F. Ricciardi and A. Harfouche (eds.), *Information and Communication
Technologies in Organizations and Society*, Lecture Notes in Information
Systems and Organisation 15, DOI 10.1007/978-3-319-28907-6_2

The third part of this study examines the relationships that can link these two areas of primary importance for the life of businesses in the twenty-first century.

The context of the article is that businesses and organizations face complicated choices related to the migration of some or all of their information services and communications into the cloud [1]. This implies many technological and organizational changes, so it is necessary to assess their impact, especially for an organization with a solid strategy [2].

Information technology indeed offers many opportunities for businesses, but there are also multiple risks. This article aims not only to provide an overview of the most controversial aspects but also proposes some guidelines to face them.

2 Cloud Computing: An Overview

Cloud Computing is a classic example of a socio-technical system in which technology also includes organizational social values. For many businesses, it is advantageous to transfer the ICT capital expenditure (CAPEX) to operational expenditure (OPEX) and this is what cloud computing can offer [3].

Capital expenditure includes amortisation of investments in infrastructure, space for equipment, specialised personnel, etc. Operational expenditure enables consideration of the computer as a service on demand set against the basis of a payment based on consumption by eliminating the investment and depreciation thereof.

On the other hand, cloud computing is a step backwards towards a centralised structure where the only entities able to provide ICT services (both for processing and for data storage) are those with huge data centres.

The approach of more recent developments in the history of computing, known as Cloud Computing, is to make available a global infrastructure with the following characteristics [4]:

- Based on broadband networks available in many countries;
- Based on servers and pooled multi-tenant platforms;
- Can be easily scaled and flexible;
- Measurable (providing services based on consumption requires them to be quantified);
- Available on-demand and as self-service.

For many small businesses this concept represents a real opportunity. They can have access to all possible software and applications without having to install them on their computers [5]: the software becomes a service (SaaS, Software as a Service). They also have the ability to access any form of application development environment (PaaS, Platform as a Service) and virtualised ICT resources (IaaS, Infrastructure as a Service). All of these services allow them to reduce or eliminate space for ICT equipment, the acquisition and maintenance of server systems and staff for ICT operations which enables them to focus primarily on their business [6]. For this purpose, it is sufficient to have a broadband network and a series of access devices for users (PCs, smartphones, tablets), thereby using these devices as a simple interface to access the "cloud".

Regarding costs, the operation is advantageous because the ICT sector becomes a service paid according to consumption, moving from CAPEX to OPEX. For example, for a small business (such as a start-up in a university incubator), a Public Cloud offers the possibility to make computing power and storage space virtually unlimited, fast and on demand [7]. On the other hand, this system is a significant shift towards a highly centralised computer architecture. Dependence on large datacentres is becoming more and more evident. In the seventies, ICT abandoned the mainframe for the PC, yet today in the twenty-first century, it is doing the reverse by turning once more to highly centralised structures. Of the five core computer functions, only the input, output and communication via the Internet remain in the users' domain, while storage and processing are now in the cloud (see Fig. 1).

The new model is quite different from the peer-to-peer architecture of Internet history [8]. We are returning to a one-to-many architecture very close to centralised distribution (broadcasting). It happens more and more that users surf the net and use software in the cloud through a simple touch screen [2]. The centre of the cloud is even able to turn off machines and operational systems in the hands of users, using a

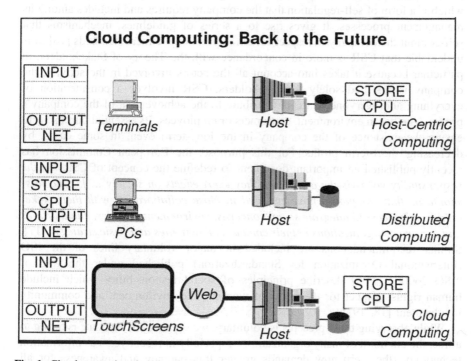

Fig. 1 Cloud computing: back to the future

device called a "kill switch" [9]. The risk of losing the status of digital citizenship to become a mere digital consumer is growing [10–12].

3 Corporate Social Responsibility: A Brief Overview

The realization of profits was for many years considered the sole purpose of businesses. Yet much research has been devoted to business ethics: "... the discipline of applied ethics that focuses on the moral aspects of the business" [13]. This form of applied ethics seeks to answer the question, "how, and in whose interests, ought the corporation to be governed?". For a long time and in many contexts, a single response was considered based on the Milton Friedman's Theory of Shareholders which says that the company's task is to maximize profits in the interests of shareholders [14]. However, more recently, other positions have emerged such as that held by Edward R. Freeman to whom we owe the Theory of Stakeholders that affirms that the company must be managed so as to take into account the interests of all stakeholders with whom it is in relationships [15].

The debate that ensued was not only academic in nature, but it has spread within the companies themselves. Often, this management model is assimilated to CSR which is a form of self-regulation that the company requires and includes among its management processes. It gives rise to a series of guidelines, mechanisms that self-commit the company to respect certain international ethical standards [16]. It is undeniable that CSR is more in concordance with the Theory of Stakeholders, in particular because it takes into account all the actors involved in the activity; the company is not tied solely to shareholders. CSR involves a consideration of everything and everyone that can contribute to the achievement of the company's profits, whether in environment, consumers or employees. Its essential purpose is to ensure the existence of the company in the long-term even, in some cases, by decreasing short-term profits. For this purpose, the European Commission has recently published an important document to redefine the concept of CSR "*as the responsibility vis-à-vis the companies they exert effects on society ... [To do this] should be that companies have engaged in close collaboration with their stakeholders, a process to integrate social concerns, environmental, ethics, human rights and consumer organizations in their commercial activities and basic strategy*" [17]. Similar recommendations are included in major voluntary lines of the ISO (International Organization for Standardization) published under the title of "ISO 26000". They describe principles of social responsibility which include human rights, respect for the rights of workers, the environment and community involvement [18, 19].

While observing these precepts is voluntary, we see that this mandate is trying to attract the attention of many organizations, especially in recent years as information technology (the web) now demands greater transparency and awareness for all business operations, and consumers are becoming increasingly sensitive.

4   Relationship Between Cloud Computing and Corporate Social Responsibility

The connections between the ICT tools used by organizations and their effectiveness with respect to customers and users has now been studied for some years to the point that cultural institutions such as museums have not escaped the analysis [20]. In the particular case of Cloud Computing, technology choices have far greater consequences at the organizational level in terms of customer service and corporate reputation.

This could also affect CSR strategies. In fact, organizations with a well-defined CSR strategy prefer to monitor closely the "borders" of the company and the behavior of their suppliers [21]. In general, they access ICT services that are outside their firewall only for some specific, non-mission critical applications.

As regards to cloud computing, the temptation to extend the acquisition of ICT services from outside is very strong. It can certainly be an opportunity for businesses, but it also raises several important issues which we examine here.

Governance. In IaaS and PaaS models, the company still has control of the final applications (IT levels on software application and services). It "rents" only basic computing resources (computing levels for servers, storage and network) from an outside vendor. With the SaaS model, the company entrusts the entire ICT protocol stack (applications, services, servers, storage and networks) [22, 23] to the cloud provider. For a socially responsible organization, governance of IT infrastructure is fundamental because nowadays they have become critical to any form of activity [24]. This outward movement of the control of ICT infrastructures related to the Cloud implies a radical revolution in organizational terms. Those responsible for ICT, as one of the main stakeholders of the company, may find their jobs in jeopardy. The problem of "shutdown" of the computer room and the loss of all the ICT skills of the people who work there, cannot be dismissed lightly by a company with a strong CSR.

The perimeter of the company. For many organizations the firewall, the security device that separates the corporate network (intranet) from the public network (Internet) is the main organization border. With the adoption of information technology services by the public cloud, this separation has decayed. The storage and processing of data takes place outside the corporate boundaries. The devices used by employees of the company are reduced to simple input and output interfaces. This puts socially responsible companies in a position to rethink their borders in line with those who are among the major stakeholders: customers [1].

Contractual obligations. If anyone can easily acquire computing resources in the cloud, then there will be organizations that buy resources simply to sell them. The risk for a socially responsible company is to entrust their data and processing to a simple "broker" and not to true computer professionals. The risk is to rely on a cloud provider who is not the real owner of the resources but merely an intermediary [25]. All research on the RSI confirms that the length of the chain of suppliers ("supply-chain") is one of the most critical aspects to be monitored [26].

System administrators. When there are too many people with system administrator privileges, there is the so-called "problem of many-hands" [27] in critical resources. For example, what if a cloud provider system administrator decides, for maintenance reasons, to stop a server? Will the related service just be interrupted? Will the company that has entrusted its ICT services to its cloud provider be warned? How will the cloud provider reconcile the need for maintenance with the need for continuity of service enterprise (cloud user) towards its customers?

Risk management. Although it is not admitted so explicitly in public, computer scientists know very well that software and complex systems are by definition unreliable (exhaustive testing is impossible, being subject to the so-called combinatorial "explosion" typical of finite state machines) and only the main functions are tested in the laboratory. What happens when you have a failure in the chain of user—network—cloud user—network—cloud provider? In fact, in a Cloud Computing scenario, responsibility of computer professionals in the design of complex systems becomes even more important [28, 29]. The reliability of systems and all matters related to software (from the limits of the reliability of the software to the responsibility of the software designers) are still present. They have simply moved from within the company to the "centre" of the cloud.

Legal issues. Many companies need to know, sometimes for legal reasons, the physical location of the data: the country and the relevant jurisdiction where the data is managed by the cloud provider. For example, it is essential for financial organizations or governments to know exactly where their data is located.

Open and free market. Often, companies must change providers for many different reasons (reliability, organizational change, business models, etc.) [30]. Will it be easier to change providers of ICT services in the cloud (cloud provider)? How can one avoid getting stuck with a provider ("lock-in") that has proven to be unreliable? Or with a supplier with a CSR strategy that is not consistent with the one that buys the services? In what formats are the data stored? Will they be open formats? These issues of standard formats of data and the risk of "lock-in" are the most critical issues associated with the adoption of Cloud Computing for an organization with a strong CSR strategy [1, 31]. In the ICT industry, Cloud Computing services are undergoing a process of consolidation that further worsens these aspects. The risk of having technologies that work with a supplier but that do not interface with any competitors is very high. The interoperability of open standards of the Web is seriously challenged by the titans of the network (for example, Microsoft, Apple, Google, Amazon, Facebook).

How to deal with the main issues. How can a company with a strong CSR approach equip itself to face the risks of Cloud Computing? Are the benefits of moving to ICT as a service, which does not require large investments, compatible with a policy of respect for all stakeholders of the company? For example, how will it change ICT governance? Is it realistic that there will be no more need for computer experts in a socially responsible business that adopts Cloud Computing? Is it realistic that the CIO (Chief Information Officer) is destined to disappear? It would not be the first time in the history of computing that organizations that manage technology have to undergo radical changes. Yet the trend towards the automation of many business processes and the growing importance of data ("Big Data") requires socially responsible organizations to design very carefully the process of migration to the cloud to maintain skills within them. One can turn off the computer room, but not the skills on the data, their security, their analysis and visualisation. Competent people able to "extract value" from the data will still be necessary for any business. The risk of lack of transparency in the supply chain (one of the most controversial aspects of CSR) can be faced by taking specific measures. For example, a company can ask the cloud provider to prove that they are actually the owner and controller of the infrastructure and not just a "broker". This is possible, for example, by including specific clauses in the contract. The same applies to the issue of too many hands on the systems; for some maintenance operations by the cloud provider, cloud users may require that directors from both sides agree ("four-hands authorisation").

An aspect not to be overlooked in the drafting of a Cloud Computing contract is the traceability of events. If a "computer crash" (data loss, software malfunction etc.) occurs, it must be possible to find out what happened ("cloud traceability"). It will be necessary to store the events log in a safe place, accessible only to the involved company (with the exact date of the events, all protected by "electronic signatures" and encryption). At the very least, the risk management plan of the company should be revised, taking into account the plan of the cloud provider. This will avoid the risk of having two plans either not in synch or even in conflict. It is not a coincidence that some have started to consider "cyber-insurance" to cover technology risks [32]. Many organizations require the cloud provider to provide explicitly the place of data storage or even demand that they be stored only in specific countries with adequate legal systems. The risk of "dependency" ("lock-in") still has much to mitigate in the world of cloud computing, and the spread of open standards is still a very difficult issue. Yet this aspect for CSR is fundamental. For example, many consumers are asking companies to be transparent about their environmental impact [33].

A company with a strong CSR may, for example, ask the cloud provider to explain the sources of energy used to power its huge datacentres. How many of these are sources of renewable energy? [34]. The company may have to change cloud providers if this does not fully meet its strategy of environmental sustainability, but changing providers without open standards may turn out to be very difficult, if not impossible.

5 Conclusions

The whole Theory of Stakeholders in the field of "business ethics" is based on balancing the interests of all the stakeholders. CSR translates this theory into practice. A company with a strong CSR strategy must be able to identify all the nodes in the network of stakeholders around it.

Cloud computing, on the one hand, simplifies the use of computer services (transition from CAPEX to OPEX), on the other hand, however, this simplification is done at the cost of greater complexity of the supply-chain in the ICT market. For a company, it becomes more difficult to design its network of stakeholders: not everything is under the strict control of corporate ICT and the ICT supply-chain becomes even more extended. A company may find itself managing a business providing products or services to its customers using a cloud computing infrastructure that is not consistent with the company's ethical principles, and this requires close attention in many aspects [35].

The Theory of Stakeholders (stakeholders) is not sufficient to prepare a solid CSR strategy; however, its definition helps to design precisely the stakeholders' networks around the company and this helps to make the right management of links between CSR and ICT. Cloud computing makes this task much more complex, but the most advanced companies in CSR and in ICT strategy are aware that the choices in these fields are becoming increasingly aligned. This article has analysed, from a company point of view, some of the most critical issues related to the adoption of cloud computing: the loss of control of the governance of IT, the loss of the very meaning of corporate boundaries, the assignment of services to simple "brokers" (which would lengthen further the supply-chain), the difficulty in ensuring continuity of services to its clients when the critical infrastructure is managed by an outside vendor, the further worsening of IT risks, the need for the company to revise its risk management plans to make them consistent with those of the cloud provider, the loss of control over data, the difficulty in changing supplier.

Cloud Computing exposes a company with a strong social responsibility to risks that must be addressed on time. This article aims to provide a contribution to companies that want to mitigate these risks, helping to define a strategy for migration to Cloud Computing consistent with their CSR strategy.

References

1. Aiello, L., Cacia, C.: Knowledge sharing and crowdsourcing as an enterprise opportunity. In: Khosrow-Pour, Mehdi (ed.) DBA (a cura di), Encyclopedia of information science and technology, 24th edn. IGI Global, International Publishing Company, International book USA (2014)
2. Tendulkar, V., Pletcher, J., Shashidharan, A., Snyder, R., Butler, K., Enck, W.: Abusing cloud-based browsers for fun and profit. In: Proceedings of 28th annual computer security applications conference—ACSAC12, 3–7 Dec 2012. Orlando, Florida, USA, pp. 219–228 (2012)
3. Marciniak, J.J., Reifer, D.J.: Software acquisition management: managing the acquisition of custom software systems. Wiley, New Jersey (1990)
4. NIST.: The NIST definition of cloud computing. National Institute of Standards and Technology, NIST special publication 800–145, p. 2 (2011)
5. Za, S., D'Atri, E., Resca, A.: Single sign-on in cloud computing scenarios: a research proposal. In: D'Atri, A., Ferrara, M., George, J.F., Spagnoletti, P. (eds.) Information technology and innovation trends in organizations, pp. 45–52. Physica-Verlag HD, Berlin (2011)

6. Ferrari, A., Rossignoli, C., Zardini, A.: Enabling factors for SaaS business intelligence adoption: a theoretical framework proposal. In: D'Atri, A., Ferrara, M., George, J.F., Spagnoletti, P. (eds.) Information technology and innovation trends in organizations, pp. 355–361. Springer, Berlin (2011)
7. Creeger, M.: CTO roundtable: cloud computing. Commun. ACM **53**(8), 50–56 (2009)
8. Hafner, K.: Where wizards stay up late: the origins of the internet, Simon & Schuster (1998)
9. Karim, A., Syed, A.S., Rosli S.: Mobile botnet attacks: a thematic taxonomy. In: New perspectives in information systems and technologies, Vol. 2, pp. 153–164. Springer International Publishing, Berlin (2014)
10. ACMA: The cloud—services, computing and digital data. Emerging issues in media and communications. Australian communications and media authority, Australian Government (2013)
11. Cavallari, M.: Information systems security and end-user consciousness—a strategic matter management of the interconnected world—ItAIS: The Italian Association for Information Systems, pp. 251–258 (2010)
12. Spagnoletti, P., Resca, A., Lee, G.: A design theory for digital platforms supporting online communities: a multiple case study. J Inf Technol **1**, 1–17 (2015)
13. Marcoux, A.: Business ethics. In: Zalta, E.N. (ed.) The Stanford encyclopedia of philosophy (Fall 2008 Edition). http://plato.stanford.edu/archives/fall2008/entries/ethics-business. 19 Sept 2014
14. Friedman, M.: The social responsibility of business is to increase its profits, The New York Times Magazine, 13 Sept 1970 (1970)
15. Freeman, E.R.: Strategic management: a stakeholder approach. Pitman Publishing, Boston (1984)
16. Wikipedia.: Corporate social responsibility. http://en.wikipedia.org/wiki/Corporate_social_responsibility. 19 Sept 2014 (2014)
17. European Commission.: A renewed EU strategy 2011–2014 for corporate social responsibility, (COM(2011) 681 final), http://eur-lex.europa.eu/LexUriServ/LexUriServ.do?uri=COM:2011:0681:FIN:EN:PDF, 19 September 2014 (2011)
18. Casalino, N., Cavallari, M., De Marco, M., Gatti, M., Taranto, G.: Defining a model for effective e-government services and an inter-organizational cooperation in public sector (2014) ICEIS 2014. In: Proceedings of the 16th international conference on enterprise information systems, vol. 2, pp. 400–408 (2014)
19. ISO.: ISO 26000—Social responsibility. http://www.iso.org. 19 Sept 2014
20. Pallud, J.: How web 2.0 tools impact the museum-visitor relationship. In: Geyer-Schulz A., Meyer-Waarden L. (eds.) Customer & service systems, pp. 91–102, Karlsruher Institut fuer Technologie (KIT) Scientific Publishing (2014)
21. Dameri, R.P., Sabroux, C.R., Saad, I.: Driving IS value creation by knowledge capturing: theoretical aspects and empirical evidences. In: Information Technology and Innovation Trends in Organizations, pp. 73–81. Physica-Verlag HD (2011)
22. Ferrari, A., Rossignoli C., Mola, L., (2012) "Organizational factors as determinants of SaaS adoption." *Information Systems: Crossroads for Organization, Management, Accounting and Engineering*. Physica-Verlag HD, 61–66
23. Mether, T., Kumaraswamy, S., Shaled, L.: Cloud security and privacy. An Enterprise Perspective on Risks and Compliance, p. 30. O'Reilly, Massachusetts (2009)
24. Ricciardi, F., De Marco, M.: The challenge of service oriented performances for chief information officers. In: Snene, M. (Ed.) Exploring service science. Third international conference, IESS 2012. Geneva, Switzerland, Feb 2012. Proceedings, pp. 258–270. LNBIP, vol. 103. Springer, Berlin (2012)
25. Schiering, I., Kretschmer, J.: The infrastructure level of cloud computing as a basis for privacy and security of software services. In Camenisch, J., Crispo, B., Fischer-Hübner, S., Leenes, R., Russello, G. (eds.) Privacy and identity management for life. Proceedings of the 7th IFIP WG 9.2, 9.6/11.7, 11.4, 11.6 international summer school, Series: IFIP Advances in Information

and Communication Technology. Trento, Italy, 5–9 Sept 2011, vol. 375, Springer, Berlin, pp 88–101 (2012)

26. Tate, W.L., Ellram, L.M., Kirchoff, J.F.: 2010. Corporate social responsibility reports: a thematic analysis related to supply chain management, journal of supply chain management **46** (1), 19–44 (2010)

27. Thompson, D.F.: Moral responsibility of public officials: the problem of many hands. APSR **74**, 905–916 (1980)

28. Gotterbarn, D.: Software engineering ethics. In: Encyclopedia of software engineering, Ed (1992)

29. Rogerson, S., Gotterbarn, D.: The ethics of software project management. In: Colleste, G. (ed.) Ethics and information technology. New Academic Publisher, Delhi (1998)

30. Cavallari, M.: A grand master and an exceptional mind. Eur. J. Inf. Syst. **14**(5), 463–464 (2005)

31. Cavallari, M., Adami, L., Tornieri, F.: Organisational aspects and anatomy of an attack on NFC/HCE mobile payment systems(2015) ICEIS 2015. In: Proceedings of the 17th international conference on enterprise information systems, vol. 2, pp. 685–700 (2015)

32. Pratt, M.K.: Cyber insurance offers IT peace of mind—or maybe not. Computerworld. 13 Jan 2013 (2013)

33. Menshikova, M.: Impact of corporate social responsibility and sustainability policies on consumer decision. Upravlenets No. 3/43/2013, pp. 46–51 (2013)

34. Greenpeace.: Cool IT Leaderboard, Version 6, avril 2013. www.greenpeace.org (2013)

35. Peng, G.C.A., Dutta, A., Choudhary, A.: Exploring critical risks associated with enterprise cloud computing. In: Cloud computing, pp. 132–141. Springer International Publishing, Berlin (2014)

The Electronic Health Record: A Comparison of Some European Countries

Sabrina Bonomi

Abstract The paper presents an overview of the Electronic Health Record (EHR) used in some European countries such as Italy, Great Britain (England, Scotland and Northern Ireland), Norway, Finland, Denmark and Sweden (called "Northern Europe"). An EHR is a patient's digital health data collection, to which physicians, nurses, health workers and the patients themselves add the patient's data progressively. It improves health care by using information and communication technology that can be different in various countries. The aim of the European Union is to establish a health system network with standardized guidelines. The paper describes the situation in the various European countries in order to compare dissimilar scenarios. It starts from the institutional and regulatory framework and its historic evolution and then describes the present situation and attempts to foresee future trends. It also tries to define the progress of the EHR process, by analysing the common characteristics, its advantages and limitations. It shows how historic paths, elements, procedures and future trends can highlight the strengths and weakness of national systems, as well as the similarities and differences among legislative, political and entrepreneurial activities. In the future it may be interesting to include other countries or carry out a longitudinal research on them.

Keywords Electronic health record · European countries · Standardized guidelines

1 Introduction

The Electronic Health record is a digital format for keeping an account of health information and consequently improves the quality of health care. Therefore, EHR can be defined as a set of electronic data and information concerning a patient's health, which is collected during his/her lifetime.

S. Bonomi (✉)
e-Campus University, Novedrate (CO), Italy
e-mail: sabrina.bonomi@uniecampus.it

© Springer International Publishing Switzerland 2016   33
F. Ricciardi and A. Harfouche (eds.), *Information and Communication Technologies in Organizations and Society*, Lecture Notes in Information Systems and Organisation 15, DOI 10.1007/978-3-319-28907-6_3

The information can be shared across the continuum of healthcare services and the patient's progress can be followed in the various care settings [1]. The EHR is continuously updated by the patients themselves and the various health professionals who treat National or Regional Health Service patients. This shared electronic medical record enables citizens to obtain information concerning their state of health and monitor their current and complete clinical record; they can add information regarding their state of health, or access the data entered by their healthcare workers.

An EHR must satisfy three principal requirements [2]:

- Data collection and processing; clinical, financial, administrative data are obtained from various information sources, i.e. hospitals, private hospitals, health care facilities, with the aim of facilitating the extraction of medical data in order to determine the disorder promptly and reduce waiting times;
- Support clinical procedures and decision making;
- Reduce administrative mistakes: risk of loss of documentation, reduction of paperwork thus simplifying the work.[1]

It was created through contributions from different Health System authorities that have intervened during the care path [3].

The EHR enables the numerous healthcare systems deployed across a nation to communicate, to share and transfer data collected in various healthcare facilities and to gather them together in a single file. The success of EHR is due to the accuracy and synthesis of the data, especially in Northern European countries.

The research question is: "How are electronic instruments, especially the Electronic Health Record, used in some European countries?"

There are too many differences concerning the introduction of the Electronic Health Record and its implementation across the various countries such as timetable, mode of operations and procedures that require standardization and the aim of the European program is to establish common guidelines for implementing specific systems for administrative information [3].

2   The History of the Electronic Health Record

The digitisation process of hospitals and healthcare services has been introduced in the European countries under study during the last ten years and it is still underway; it has already reached excellent levels in some countries [3], especially in Northern Europe which are those that first took advantage of the opportunity and promptly developed their own national model. The European Board included a specific

---

[1]"The Electronic Health Record: national guidelines", Health Ministry, November 2012.

activity called "ICT for health, ageing well, inclusion and governance" in the FP7.[2] The purpose is to use specific ICT instruments to improve health care and to promote the development of new services that can assure customized healthcare to patients [4, 5].

The various information systems must have common semantics and activities to change and to share information [6]. Health Level Seven (HL7) is the major intraoperative system, introduced in the USA in 1987 and used today in 55 countries to change, share, complete and recover electronic health information [7].

HL7 is a useful tool for facilitating the transmission of Electronic Medical Records or Electronic Health Records; it establishes specific guidelines, especially for the EHR:

- it is possible to access and extract information regarding a patient's health in real time in order to complete the medical record;
- the EHR is the main reference and supports a patient's medical care;
- improvement of medical teams due to the opportunity of accessing previous medical data;
- it is possible to define and redefine the use of resources and to plan health services;
- it is possible to carry out research on the state of health and implement and promote public health initiatives [7].

2.1   The Italian Context

Introducing EHR in Italy is one of the objectives of the "Italian digital programme", which originated from one of the EU strategic directives called "the action plan for Europe 2020". In 2010 the Italian Ministry of Health established the EHR guidelines aimed at implementing their use and aligning the Italian context with the international scenario.

The purpose of thee-health information strategy is to develop a harmonious, coherent and sustainable local information system to support the care of patients by increasing the levels of cooperation.

In Italy, there are three levels in the health system: national, regional and local; the EHR is used effectively in only five Regions (Lombardy, Emilia Romagna, Tuscany, Sardinia and the autonomous province of Trento) while it is still under experimentation and in the planning or implementation phase in the other regions (Piedmont, Liguria, Marche, Veneto, Abruzzo, Campania e Basilicata [8]).

---

[2]FP7 is the acronym of the seventh framework programme, the main EU financial tool to incentivize research and development activities.

EHR is useful for ten million people and the laws must support the introduction of an integrated digital health system and safeguard the health of Italian citizens at the same time.

2.2 The UK Context

EHR was introduced in the UK in different phases and periods of time.

In 1997 the British government began transforming the National Health Service (NHS) in England with the aim of creating a "person-based" health care system.

The citizen is at the heart of the public health system and becomes the main health care player; physicians invite him/her to take part in relevant discussions and to assume a decision-maker role. For this reason EHR becomes a fundamental instrument; it favours communication, increases the amount of information concerning the patient's state of health and involves him/her in the collection of data [9].

In 2002, the National Programme for Information Technology (NPfIT) was initiated which established the NHS Care Record Service, that is the creation of an electronic medical record for secondary treatment.

In 2010, numerous difficulties arose due to the overambitious objectives of the project; many problems with software, the lack of deadlines and other mistakes and issues (i.e. the analysts, who studied the project, were not health-care professionals and therefore were not aware of hospital issues and procedures), which brought the e-health, program to a halt.

In 2011 the Prime Minister went out of business, but in order to save a part of the money invested, which amounted to over ten billion pounds, the Summary Care Record and the Electronic Prescription Services were maintained in order to improve the security and efficiency of health care [10] and used by approximately 24 million people in 2013. The Ministry of Health negotiated a new agreement with the software suppliers Computer Science Corporation (CSC). In August 2012, a new agreement established the deadline of July 2016 for allowing major flexibility and the possibility of new solutions for providing health care records [11].

Wales is also introducing information systems (NHS Wales Informatics Service—NWIS). It wants to improve the quality of health care quality and maintain technology and information systems updated. In fact rapid and continual changes are being made at present. Since 2010, patients have been able to use online booking services; they can book appointments, request hospital admissions and radiology examinations.

The EHR is only useful at local health unit level; therefore physicians cannot gain access to the electronic record if a patient uses a hospital service out of his/her area of residence. General practitioners can send their information to the hospital by "e-referral" in a safe and standard way.

In Scotland, the introduction of Emergency Care Summary started in 2004; a national information system records the main communications made by general practitioners: personal data, medicines prescribed, allergies etc. Health organizations can communicate and exchange information by means of the National Information Systems Group known as the Scottish Care Information Gateway (SCI Gateway).

In 2012, the Key Information Summary was introduced to allow information to be shared among health workers, doctors, ambulance crews, off-duty doctors, hospitals, pharmacies and treatment centres. In October 2013, Scotland won the "Excellence in Major Healthcare IT Development" at the Health Insider Awards 2013[3] used by over 60 % of clinics [12].

Northern Ireland has the Emergency Care Summary Record, which is a system with the same characteristics and functions as the Scottish and the Northern Ireland Electronic Care Record (NIECR). After various pilot projects, the latter was completed with success in 2009 and in use at Belfast City Hospital, Ulster Hospital and all over Northern Ireland in 2010.[4]

2.3 The Northern European Context

In Denmark, Finland and Sweden, the state system was fundamental for the information systems. The public model equalized the investments made for information technologies, in contrast with what occurred in other countries with a mixed contribution system [13]. These countries have promoted EHR strategies and plans of action ever since the beginning of the 1990s; they are experts in Health ICT and the first to use these technologies in health services and the first in the cost-of-health/PIL ratio.

In Denmark, the main support came from the state government; since the 1990s, it has defined four standards to digitalize the health service [14]. The aim of the "Danish Action Plan for EHR" was to support the application of EHR and define some guidelines regarding regulations, information, safety, organization and implementation. In the 2000s the Health Ministry continued the Plan with the "National Strategy for IT in the Hospital sector", in order to prioritise the actions in IT for the health plan. The SDSD[5] was created to establish some common guidelines for the development of her, which became part of the national project called BEHR, Basic Electronic Health Record [15] which defines the reference model of EHR. At the end of 2010 there were five systems of EHR, one for every Danish region; a cross consultation of data was not sufficient.

In Finland, there was no centralized health service therefore it was necessary to connect the various territorial frameworks. In order to secure the future of healthcare, the National Health Care program attempted to conciliate financial problems and the increasing demand of health services which together with the National

---

[3]www.alliance-scotland.org.uk.

[4]www.healthcareitnews.com.

[5]SDSD is the acronym of "Sammenhængende DigitalSundhed i Danmark"; it is Connecting Digital Health.

Table 1 The different stories of electronic health record

Historical characteristic	Italy	UK	Northern Europe
1. Promoter of introduction of EHR	Health Ministry	Government	Health Ministry
2. Period of the first guidelines	2010	2002	1990/2000
3. Purpose	To develop a harmonious, coherent and sustainable local information system in order to improve patients' healthcare	To give citizens the main role of the public health system; to make patients the main healthcare players	To give patients autonomy, privacy, participation and access to personal information while providing physicians with complete, secure and accessible information at the same time
4. Diffusion (place)	5 completed regions; 7 in experimentation	According to each single nation (e.g. over 60 % of scottish clinics, 100 % of Irish clinics)	According to each single nation
5. Diffusion (people)	Approximately 10 million	Approximately 24 million (England 2013)	Unavailable

strategy was aimed at assuring health care and implementing EHR within 2007 [16]. In order to solve the patients' problems in terms of autonomy, privacy, participation and access to personal information and provide physicians with complete and accessible data, the eHealth Architecture project [17, 18] was implemented, which reduced the huge heterogeneity of hospital information systems and the EHR, and tried to compensate for the lack of the EHR in pharmacy [19]. The county councils are responsible for the development of EHR [13]. In 2008, the National Patient Summary (NPO) was established, which is a system that enables health workers, to gain access to health information everywhere with the consent of the patients [20].

A historical comparison is reported in Table 1, which shows the main key words.

3 The Different Applications of Electronic Health Record

The EHR experience shows that the introduction of a new information system requires some common actions at organizational, human and technological level. They must satisfy the patients' new needs. The organizational intervention has brought some benefits: reduction of waiting time, simplification of procedures, qualitative improvement [4].

At the beginning, the EHR did not have a flexible cataloguing system and the method of research (chronological for subject or procedure) had to be selected in advance.

At present, the three categories are all together in one thus making consultation more simple [21] and therefore both patients and doctors can easily gain access to the information they need.

3.1 The Italian Context

The EHR is the first step and the reference point during the health care process for realizing the e-health project, since it provides a clear picture of a patient's state of health from birth onwards. It consists in a clinical document, digitally stored in repositories with cumulative indexing systems obtained from a full electronic medical record with access to authorized people. The digital information must be available, easily accessible and transferable and conserved yet it must also comply with the legislations concerning patient privacy rights [22]. In fact EHR enables patients to consult and manage their health data online by means of a web page.

This can be done in compliance with the current privacy and safety regulations concerning personal data. If the patient consents to the processing of personal information, both the reading and entering of data and documents that can add to the EHR, he/she can benefit from a better quality of treatment. In fact the completeness and availability of information helps to increase the quality of services and reduce human and clerical errors, waiting times and possible duplications.

Therefore, EHR improves medical and organisational efficiency and the effectiveness of healthcare procedures while reducing the costs deriving from the bureaucratic procedures and disorganisation related to them. One of the most problematic aspects is to make behavioural changes in healthcare operators; the personnel who are involved in this process should modify their work organisation in order to obtain a patient-oriented vision [23, 24].

3.2 The UK Context

The Electronic Health Record is a longitudinal record that describes the patient's complete healthcare history in various clinics, hospitals and centres. It contains the patient's information regarding sporadic or continuous health care entered by physicians, hospitals and other centres.

The EHR is a database application that memorizes and gathers patients' medical records. Its principal purpose is to gather and store patients' health data and information, to process the results and dispatch orders (for example e-prescribing) and to support the decision-making process involving patients and establish the administrative and reporting procedures [25].

In England there are two levels in the EHR system: the Summary Care Record (SCR) in all countries and the Detailed Care Record (DCR) in particular areas such as Greater London [25]. The principal infrastructure is the New National Networking service (N3), which has three national components: electronical booking, electronic prescription transfer and medical record access. Clinical information is always readily available regardless of area of origin [26].

The EHR is a complex database that allows for the integration and online access of data from heterogeneous clinical applications and therefore harmonization at national or regional level is required [26]. It consists in a list of medicines, physical evaluation, lifestyle, clinical history, discharge, diagnosis, test results etc.

Several research studies state that the use of information systems in health care has encouraged a more complete and accurate documentation by health workers [22]. EHR is extremely useful to patients suffering from acute illnesses who need to monitor their disease and treatments, communicate with medical professionals and obtain information easily. In fact EHR improves communication and helps to create a relationship of trust between patient and doctor [27].

One of the most difficult obstacles is the need for structural changes at organizational level since EHR calls for the modification of hospital infrastructures.

The introduction of electronic health records promotes communication and provides patients with more information concerning their state of health in order to involve them in their treatment [9]. Another obstacle arises from the lack of time and the human resources required for patient care; some physicians are against this approach as they believe it to be time consuming.

Younger doctors accept EHR better than older doctors who are more resistant to change and have a different perception of the benefits of the new tool [28] and consequently they do not directly use the EHR system [29]. People's characteristics, approaches and attitudes are fundamental for the success or the failure of the EHR, which can be terribly opposed at times [28].

3.3   The Northern European Context

The success of the Danish health care system probably originates from decentralization and multi level architecture. At the moment, it is important to coordinate physicians and hospital workers at various levels.

There are a lot of differences regarding the respect of the organizational and distributional parameters and the characteristics of the EHR model. In Denmark, there are 60 EHR models; on one hand they show the commitment made to develop and implement this system, but on the other hand it allows for the huge heterogeneity of their content and therefore shows the need for a common framework [15].

The "National IT strategy for the Danish health care service" provides shared guidelines especially regarding the data collection and information system. The patient's privacy is therefore one of the key factors; the information system must share information safely and ensure that it reaches the right people.

In Denmark, the Sundhed portal provides access to health information and uses a system of engineering controls, such as encryption, electronic identification and control registers, in order to ensure privacy and the security of personal medical information. Patients can check who visited their profiles, and can limit access or reading settings to specific data and people.

The excessive regulation to accessibility represents an obstacle for EHR. In fact legislation has frequently changed the criteria for accessing sensitive health information by patients and medical staff in order to make sure that the interventions were shared with the previous regulations.

A research study carried out in 2012 declared Finland to be the leading OECD member in the management of the health system as it achieved the highest values for all parameters analyzed [30]. The Finnish health care system is too diversified; it uses inputs from several sources to support services and medical care.

In Finland, the EHR are obtained from the various systems of local health records, which are not able to communicate with one another; at times the software used is semantically incompatible or not interoperable and limits communication between patients and doctors. Finnish legislation stipulates that it is the responsibility of every public and/or private healthcare organization to store all health information in a single archive by the year 2014 and to maintain parallel management systems within the local EHR.

The introduction of the e-Archive lowers health care costs, allows for the interorganizational consultation of past and present health records, eliminates unnecessary procedures and saves resources, improves the efficiency of services, completeness, integrity and confidentiality of health data accessible to a group of users over an identified period of time [31, 32]. HL7, CDA, R2 and semantically interoperable infrastructures enable users to send, access and use the data contained in the national archive, through EHR systems, pharmaceutical or online portals.

Finland has gone from a localized approach toward a shared national approach in order to maximize the benefits of local ownership and flexibility; on the other hand, Finland operates within a universal structure by sharing and standardizing information. The government is able to systematically monitor its work in real time, with the aim of perceiving the characteristics of current trends and identifying possible scenarios for future development. The main issues are the costs of the information system and the protection of privacy and security of the stored data, considering the ever-growing demand for data.

Sweden uses a decentralized health system; both central and local government authorities are responsible for most of the costs incurred at national level [33]. Regulatory changes promoted the construction of user-friendly systems, to support decision-making by supplying and sharing the required documents with other systems (used by municipalities, regions or individuals). The measures included EHR systems, the prescription systems and the national patient summary [20].

Twelve county councils use a shared EHR system; four are planning a common solution; the last five are integrating existing EHR systems [34].

The Swedish e-health strategy was implemented to create a common information structure; the state implemented many initiatives for the development of ICT healthcare applications and made significant progress in the standardization of EHR [13]. A comparison is reported in Table 2, which shows the main key words.

Table 2 The various applications of electronic health record

Application	Italy	Great Britain	Northern Europe
1. Role of EHR	To realize the e-health project	To gather and memorize patients' health data and information, to process the results, dispatch orders and to support the decision making process, to involve patients, to set up the administrative procedures and reporting	To coordinate doctors and hospital workers at various levels
2. The base of EHR	A clinical document digitally stored in repositorie, cumulative indexing systems and secure access by authorized people	Summary card record, electronical booking, electronic prescription transfer and medical record access	Multiple systems of local health records (over 60 in Denmark alone)
3. Characteristics of EHR information	Available, easily accessible, transfer and conservation; it must respect the legislation concerning patient privacy	Complex database; integrates online access, to data from heterogeneous clinical applications	Uses a system of engineering controls, to ensure privacy and security of personal medical information
4. Advantage coming from EHR use (patients and organization)	Patients are aware of their updated health history since birth; they can consult and manage their health data online by means of a web page in compliance with current privacy and safety regulations. It reduces human and clerical errors, waiting times, duplications; contributes to achieve	Patients can check their disease and its treatment and have more information and communication; improves trust and communication between patients and physicians	Patients can check who visited their profiles, can restrict access settings or reading to specific people or to specific data; lowers health care costs, allows for the interorganizational consultation of past and present health records, eliminates unnecessary procedures and saves

(continued)

Table 2 (continued)

Application	Italy	Great Britain	Northern Europe
	clinical and organisational efficacy and the efficiency of healthcare processes; reduces the health costs deriving from bureaucratic procedures and disorganisation		resources, improves the efficiency of services, completeness, integrity and confidentiality of health data accessible
5. Obstacles hindering the use of EHR	Difficulty in changing the cultural attitude of operators; the people involved in this process should modify their work organisation to have a patient-oriented vision	Structural changes of hospital infrastructures at organizational level; lack of time, issues concerning the human resources required for patient care	Excessive accessibility regulations and too many changes concerning the criteria required for the accessing of sensitive health information by patients and medical staff. The costs of the information system and the protection of privacy and security of the stored data, considering the ever-growing demand for data

4 The Different Future Developments

The HL7 is nowadays the most commonly used standard, the International Standards Organisation (ISO) and the European Committee for Standardization (CEN) developed their own regulatory standard, the CEN/ISO EN13606. The standard, originally developed by the European Committee for Standardization (CEN), received approval as an international standard ISO by expanding its pool of users [35]. Currently HL7 and CEN are trying to harmonize the two standards in order to bring unity to the respective regulatory actions, which, at present, are characterized by large overlapping areas.

4.1 The Italian Context

Italy is one of the countries, which invests less in healthcare; a recent OECD research shows that the Italian health expenditure is below the average of the other countries belonging to the organization [36].

The reduction of health care ICT expenditure reflects the lack of a shared vision of digital innovation, as well as the lack of a systematic approach to investments [37–39]; this situation contributes to the explosion of a lot of isolated investment, which is not integrated in a national system and is not sufficient to guide development [39]. Italy "lacks an overall plan, a shared vision of e-Health".

Indeed, "there are rules but there is no clear division of roles played by the state, regions and individual health authorities and hospitals. We need a real digital healthcare plan, implemented according to a digital health law" [40].

The decree passed on 21th of June 2013 provides some measures to support the complete fulfilment of the law by 31th of December 2014. It provides the regions with a centralized EHR infrastructure in cloud computing.

4.2 The UK Context

Information technology allows for costs saving, improves data exchange and consequently improves the quality and safety of healthcare [28] due to fewer mistakes and faster results; it also reduces waiting times. Another benefit of EHR concerns clinical research; EHR could enhance coordination between healthcare and research environments, thus leading to great improvement.

Patients are worried about the security and confidentiality of electronic records especially with regard to personal data relating to mental and sexual health. Another complication arises when data relating to a patient should be placed in a health folder since a coding system is required in order to standardize the content.

SnoMed is the clinical translation provided by the EHR system and encodes techniques, diseases, treatments, allergies in clinical terminology. Doctors have stated that the system is not always efficient and requires revision and correction and that there are some problems of terminology. The connectivity and usability of the program is a challenge as continuous training is required for users; another issue is system downtime, which causes delays and difficulties in managing work. Another negative consequence of this model is the additional work for physicians, changes in working practices and impact models of professional work [28].

The National Programme for Information Technology in England aims at computerizing the medical records of NHS patients or care providers across the country. The project is characterized by highly complex, extremely demanding deadlines and affects a large number of doctors, managers and administrative staff, therefore people with different needs and expectations [29].

The implementation and development of the system failed, therefore the government drastically reduced its program. One of the biggest mistakes was the project itself; it was too large and too ambitious: it intended to scan the health documents for the entire population over a four-year period.

The program could not live up to these expectations and achieve all the objectives which delayed the project by a few years. Despite all the money allocated to the system, most UK hospitals in 2010 had not yet integrated electronic medical records and it was never developed in the south of England [41]. The main issues that caused the project to be abandoned were the slowdown in software implementation, the lack of deadlines, extra costs and contractual changes.

The National IT Programme also experienced technical barriers and disputes with suppliers. The contract was renewed because cancelling it would have been more expensive than completing the project. The new contract offered an opportunity to combine clinical modules with additional functionalities.

In Scotland, the EHR contains general practitioners' and other doctors' data; the e-Health strategy wants to complete the Emergency Care Summary and the Key Information Summary before the end of 2014.

4.3 The Northern European Context

The EHR was not able to support daily medical procedures due to the excessive restrictiveness of its requirements, the severity required by health workers, the fragmentation of data and the rigidity of the model.

This experience taught us how to develop the following steps: institutions, physicians, health workers and organizations combined their expertise to promote new EHR activities; EHR was actually able to respond to national priorities: continuity of healthcare, information exchange and coordination among medical centres.

The institutional answer was the creation of the National Patient Index, NPI, which is an infrastructure that can aggregate all medical data relating to a specific patient, regardless of origin. The information is taken from heterogeneous databases at national level, even if it is not interoperable, thanks to a single common format [42].

The current strategy, "Making eHealth work", intends to promote more innovative solutions to ensure interoperability, accessibility and security of EHR systems, thanks to the collaboration of multi-level municipalities, regions and government institutions. The plan of action proved to be useful for defining additional targets to be reached between 2013 and 2017 [43]: new methods for providing services, computerization of flows and procedures, better use of data.

In Finland, one of the national eHealth program activities requires that local EHRs, which are located in first and second level structures, collect available information and send them to the eArchive system. The same issue was the subject of a specific legislation, the National EHR project, which defined the main file requirements so that they can be shared by the entire system [30].

The project followed a prototype developed at international level and identified the principal EHR information. The structure, organization and competences of local authorities are currently being redefined to ensure that individual municipalities are capable of ensuring the highest quality of services to citizens. Legislative and organizational actions are the backbone of the Finnish eHealth program; the next strategy will be the creation of the national EHR archive, a complex operation that will require significant changes in technology, organization and legislation.

The Scandinavian model of welfare does not allow for many forms of private insurance, which continues to play an integrative role. However in Denmark, Finland and Sweden, the national institutions are working to promote the development of a type of private health care, professionals and hospitals to complete the existing public organizations [44]. EHR systems are also improved by people's technological capabilities and their positive approach to change.

5 Conclusions

The adoption rate of Electronic Health Record systems is an important indicator of the degree of national e-health [38]. For example, Jha et al. [45] stated that health information technology in general and EHRs in particular, are tools for improving the quality, safety and efficiency of health systems. They observed that UK, Netherlands, Australia, and New Zealand generally used EHRs among general practitioners (each country >90 %); Germany was far behind (40–80 %); and there was a small minority of doctors in the U.S. and Canada who used EHRs (10–30 %). They also explained that it is difficult for hospitals to obtain quality data and that only a small fraction of hospitals (<10 %), of the countries analysed had the key components required by an EHR.

There are some criticalities of an EHR, since it is a basic component of many advanced medical applications and an essential part of any health information system [45].

Countries such as Denmark, Finland and Sweden took the potential of a structured EHR system. They used it as the cornerstone of their own national healthcare model. In fact, the three states paved the way for EHR systems a long time ago even if their development is still underway. The Scandinavian countries are also trying to promote the use of additional computer applications, such as reservation systems, telemedicine solutions, electronic prescriptions and health portals, in order to facilitate the electronic exchange of data.

However, the benefits of EHR are numerous and generally recognized by all European countries since it allows for:

- Better access to medical records with detailed past and present clinical information regardless of space or time in order to support more informed decision-making;
- Improvement of safety: EHR reduces the number of possible medical errors and prevents the loss of documents or the misreading of the entered data;
- Improvement of healthcare quality and access to past and present information therefore reference to a larger number of data which facilitates decision-making and promotes the quality of services;
- Improvement of health care: it optimizes treatments, consolidates and standardizes information, and links together the various areas of the health system

and reduces administrative and management costs. The information is automatically updated and can be promptly obtained by authorized personnel [46].

The most important aspect concerns quality. It allows for the diffusion of EHR, thanks to the improved completeness and precision of information and the safety and the accessibility of data. The success of the EHR depends on the quality of the information collected obtained from documentation.

In general, the success of the instrument and the information system depend on expectations, ease of use, flexibility of connection and communication and the degree of satisfaction perceived by the user.

Despite the many benefits, EHR is not uniformly used for national and international healthcare. In Great Britain, it underwent many changes according to the theories of the various governments. In Italy, IT improvements are delayed due to the lack of a shared vision of digital information.

For various reasons there are obstacles that hinder the implementation of EHR:

- Lack of universal standards or guidelines;
- Difficulty economic return;
- Operational problems (i.e., data input);
- Reluctance to change.

For the system to be successful it is necessary to implement training programs for specialists. Indeed the Electronic health record is one of the most structured paradigms of information systems with potential development. The organizational reluctance to using the system can be changed if management promote it. It is essential to create a culture and an organizational environment to change that is capable of promoting its use [47].

One of the reasons why Denmark, Finland and Sweden have high rates regarding the use of EHR systems may be that health facilities are owned by the government, which is directly responsible for the service and therefore interested in giving the right priority and attention to the investment. The autonomy of local authorities, as in the Finnish case, is one of the reasons that has led to the adoption of inter regional EHR systems over the years, which are often incompatible with one another.

In the future, for the success of the HER, it is important to develop internationally interoperable systems and provide access infrastructures driven by the need to provide value added healthcare services. It should be a priority to have a competitive healthcare system.

This paper is a summary and represents a first step of the study on this topic. In the future, it would be interesting to support this study, mostly based on literature review, with some data that we are collecting in some of the countries under investigation; or it may also be interesting to study and compare other European countries (German, France, Spain and Portugal...) or to carry out a comparison between Europe and United States.

References

1. Sullivan, M., Brown, D., Vetrosky, D.: Physician Assistant: A Guide to Clinical Practice. Elsevier Health Science (2013)
2. Ministero della salute (eng. trad. Ministry of Health): Il fascicolo sanitario elettronico: linee guida nazionali (eng. trad. "The EHR: national guidelines"), Ministry of Health (2012)
3. Rossignoli, C., Zardini, A., Benetollo, P.: The process of digitalisation in radiology as a lever for organisational change: the case of the academic integrated hospital of Verona. In: Phillips-Wren, G, Carlsson S., Respicio, A., Brezillon P. (eds.) DSS 2.0-Supporting Decision Making With New Technologies, vol. 261, pp. 24–35 (2014)
4. Bonomi, S., Zardini, A., Rossignoli, C., Dameri, P.R.: E-health and value co-creation: the case of electronic medical record in an Italian academic integrated hospital. In: Exploring Services Science, pp. 166–175. Springer International Publishing (2015)
5. Ricciardi, F., De Marco, M.: The challenge of service oriented performances for chief information officers. In: Snene, M (ed.) Proceedings of Exploring Service science. Third International Conference, IESS 2012. Geneva, Switzerland, February 2012. LNBIP vol. 103, (pp. 258–270). Springer (2012)
6. Cavallari, M.: A conceptual analysis about the organizational impact of compliance on information security policy. Lecture Notes in Business Information Processing, 103 LNBIP, pp. 101–114 (2012)
7. Health Level Seven International: Introduction to Health Level Seven (2013)
8. Moruzzi, M., Mazzoli, L., Gliglietto, F.: Osservatorio nazionale FSE: il valore della ricerca, Meeting sul Fascicolo sanitario elettronico in Italia. (eng. trad. National Centre of EHR: The value of the research. Meeting on the Electronic Health Record in Italy) (2013)
9. Pelzang, R.: Time to learn: understanding patient-centred care. Br. J. Nurs. **19**(14) (2010)
10. Versel, N.: British Electronic Health Record Collapse Sparks Lawsuit. Information Week Healthcare, May 10th www.informationweek.com (2011)
11. Shadle, J.: CSC Signs Agreement with U.K. National Health Service, www.csc.com (2012)
12. Todd, R.: Scots Deploy Key Information Summary. eHealth Insider, August 15th. www.ehi.co.uk (2013)
13. Atkinson, R.D., Castro, D.: Digital quality of life: Understanding the personal and social benefits of the information technology revolution. SSRN 1278185 (2008)
14. Bhagat, S., Fontaine, D., Gibson, K.: Danish Healthcare Information Technology. An Analytical Study of Consumer Issues. Polytechnic Institute, Worcester (2010)
15. Nøhr, C., Andersen, S.K., Vingtoft, S., Bernstein, K., Bruun-Rasmussen, M.: Development, implementation and diffusion of EHR systems in Denmark. Int. J. Med. Inform. **74**(2), pp. 229–234 (2005)
16. Doupi, P., Renko, E., Hämäläinen, P., Mäkelä, M., Giest, S. and Dumortier, J. (2010). Country Brief: Finland
17. Ruotsalainen, P., Doupi, P. and Hamalainen, P. (2007). Sharing and management of EHR data through a national archive: Experiences from Finland. World Hospitals and Health Services, 43(4)
18. Ruotsalainen, P., Iivari, A.K., Doupi P.: Finland's strategy and implementation of citizens' access to health information. Stud. Health Technol. Inform. **137**, 379–385 (2007)
19. Manninen, P.: National EHR Archive in Finland, Fujitsu Services (2007)
20. Orebro County Council: http://www.regionorebrolan.se/Files-sv/USO/Kliniker_enheter/K%C3%A4rl-Thorax/broschyr_oll_eng.pdf (2007)
21. Latha, A., Murthy, R., Sunitha, U.: Electronic health record. Int. J. Eng. Res. Technol. **1**, 1–8 (2012)
22. Hayrinen, K.: Definition, structure, content, use and impacts of electronic health records: a review of the research literature. International J. Med. Inform. **77**(3), 291–304 (2008) (Elsevier, Ireland)

23. Davis, K., Schoenbaum, S.C., Audet, A.M.: A 2020 vision of patient-centered primary care. J. Gen. Intern. Med. **20**(10), 953–957 (2005)
24. Dulskaia, I., Menshikova, M.: New service development: best practice of the Italian postal sector. In: Proceedings of MCIS 2014, AIS Electronic Library (AISeL). Online: http://aisel.aisnet.org/cgi/viewcontent.cgi?article=1008&context=mcis2014 (2014)
25. Ge, X., Paige, R., McDermid, J.: Domain analysis on an electronic health records system. In: Proceedings of the First International Workshop on Feature-Oriented Software Development, pp 49–54 (2009)
26. Rossi Mori, A., Consorti, P.: Dalla cartella clinica elettronica locale al fascicolo sanitario personale (eng. trad. From Electronic Medical Record to the personal Electronic Health Record), www.uniroma2.it (2003)
27. Pagliari, C., Detmer, D., Singleton P.: Potential of electronic personal health records. Br. Med. J. **335** (2007)
28. Cresswell, K.: Implementing and adopting electronic health record systems how actor-network theory can support evaluation. Br. J. Clin. Gov. **16**(4), 320–336 (2011)
29. Sheikh, A., Cornford T.: Implementation and adoption of nationwide electronic health records in secondary care in England: final qualitative results from prospective national evaluation in "early adopter" hospitals, **343**, d 6054 (2011) www.bmj.com
30. Tchouaket, É.N., Lamarche, P.A., Goulet, L., Contandriopoulos, A.P.: Health care system performance of 27 OECD countries. Int. J. Health Plan. Manag. **27**, 104–129 (2012)
31. Hayrinen, K., Saranto, K.: The core data elements of electronic health record in Finland. Stud. Health Technol. Inform **116**, 131–136 (2005)
32. Cavallari, M., De Marco, M., Rossignoli, C., Casalino, N.: Risk, human behavior, and theories in organizational studies. In: Proceedings of Wuhan International Conference on E-Business, WHICEB 2015, Wuhan, China, AIS, Association for Information Systems, AIS Electronic Library (AISeL), pp. 283–297 (2015)
33. Doupi, P., Renko, E., Giest, S., Heywood, J., Dumortier, J.: Country Brief: Sweden. (2010)
34. Jerlvall, L., Pehrsson, T.: eHealth in Swedish county councils. Inventory commissioned by the SLIT group, CEHIS (swe: Center för eHälsa i Sverige/Eng: Center for eHealth in Sweden) (2012)
35. Sánchez-de-Madariaga, R., Muñoz, A., Cáceres, J., Somolinos, R., Pascual, M., Martínez, I., Monteagudo, J.L.: ccML, a new mark-up language to improve ISO/EN 13606-based electronic health record extracts practical edition. J. Am. Med. Inform. Assoc. **20**(2), 298–304 (2013)
36. ICT Observatory in Healthcare.: ICT in healthcare: why digital should not remain only on the agenda. School of Management of Milan Polytechnic Institute, Department of Management Engineering, May. Italian Republic Ministry of Health: Electronic Healthcare File Guidel (2013)
37. Recker, J.: Scientific research in information systems Elektronische Daten : a beginner's guide (2013)
38. Dameri, R.P.: Defining an evaluation framework for digital cities implementation. In: International Conference on Information Society (i-Society), pp. 466–470. IEEE (2012)
39. Sorrentino, M., De Marco, M.: Implementing e-government in hard times: When the past is wildly at variance with the future. Inf. Polity **18**(4), 331–342 (2013)
40. Del Bufalo, P.: ICT, il risparmio si fa investendo (eng.trad. ICT, the saving should be done by investments) Il Sole 24 Ore (2012)
41. Soumerai, S., Avery, T.: Don't Repeat the UK's Electronic Health Records Failure. The Huffington Post (2010)
42. Olejaz, M., Nielsen, A.J., Rudkjøbing, A., Krasnik, H O.B.A., Her, C.: Danish Denmark health system review—health system in transition, **14**(2) (2012)
43. Danish Government (2013)
44. Magnussen, J., Vrangbaek, K., Saltman, R.: Nordic Health Care Systems: Recent Reforms and Current Policy Challenges. McGraw-Hill International (2009)

45. Jha, A.K., Doolan, D., Grandt, D., Scott, T., Bates, D.W.: The use of health information technology in seven nations. Int. J. Med. Inf. **77**(12), 848–854 (2008)
46. The McGraw-Hill Companies: An Introduction to the Electronic Health Record. The electronic Health Record. McGraw-Hill Companies, New York (2011)
47. Zakaria, N., Affendi S.: Managing ICT in Healthcare Organization: Culture, Challenges and Issues of Technology Adoption and Implementation. University of Wollongong (2010)

The Value of ICT Applications: Linking Performance, Accountability and Transparency in Public Administrations

Danila Scarozza, Alessandro Hinna, Stefano Scravaglieri
and Marta Trotta

Abstract Beginning in 2009, the Italian legislation proposed a convergent action of "programming" "evaluation" and "transparency" to be applied to the administrative processes. Within this framework, the ICT emerges as a key element in order to put the Reform into practice supporting administrations both in measuring and evaluating performance, and in increasing transparency and accountability. In order to understand the expected effects of ICT use on these relevant aspects of the administrative activities and, more in general, to give an interpretation of the role of the ICT in the reform process, the paper presents the results of a content analysis of 198 documents produced by public organizations for whom the Reform was of immediate application.

Keywords ICT · Performance · Accountability · Transparency

1 Introduction

In the last twenty years Public Administrations (PA) have been involved in a process of change which concerns not only their relationship with the environment but also their internal operative systems [1]. In this frame, New Public Management (NPM) [2, 3] and Public Governance (PG) [4, 5] propositions, aiming to achieve a

D. Scarozza (✉) · A. Hinna · S. Scravaglieri · M. Trotta
University of Rome Tor Vergata, Rome, Italy
e-mail: danila.scarozza@uniroma2.it

A. Hinna
e-mail: alessandro.hinna@uniroma2.it

S. Scravaglieri
e-mail: stefano.scravaglieri@uniroma2.it

M. Trotta
e-mail: marta.trotta@uniroma2.it

© Springer International Publishing Switzerland 2016
F. Ricciardi and A. Harfouche (eds.), *Information and Communication Technologies in Organizations and Society*, Lecture Notes in Information Systems and Organisation 15, DOI 10.1007/978-3-319-28907-6_4

certain level of stability of the internal operative systems (NPM) and looking for the participation of different stakeholders and institutions to public sector policy and management (PG), have favoured a systematic application of effectiveness, efficiency, consistency and transparency as main principles in public politics. Based on this background and for the first time in its history, the Italian legislation (Decree 150/2009) has proposed a convergent action of "programming" "evaluation" and "transparency" to be applied to the administrative processes. Theoretically an explosive mixture, which means PA would be under "goal pressure" as happens in private sector organizations, creating conditions whereby it is more difficult for them to "elude" external pressure regarding results. Note that Decree 150/2009 has an international perspective and is in the stream of national intervention based on NPM principles. In this context the paper aims to verify the application of ICT (Information Communication Technology) to the reform process, investigating "if" and "how" ICT could impact on the Italian reform process, especially in connection with performance, accountability and transparency. In particular, the paper aims to investigate the following research questions:

1. How much attention has been paid to ICT in Italian Policy documents?
2. What is the expected effect of ICT use on the performance of public organizations?
3. What is the expected effect of ICT use on transparency and accountability?

To reply to the research questions, a content analysis was carried out on the following documents already produced by Italian PA for whom the Decree was of immediate application[1]:

- the *Monitoring and Evaluation System Plan* (*MESP*) i.e. the document defining the elements and the technical choices available to control the progress of the organization in achieving its targets and, to evaluate results.
- the *Performance Plan* (*PP*), that is the document defining the elements on which each administration will base its program (beginning this year) of measuring and evaluating the process of accountability of the organization and the individual;
- the *Triennial Plan for Transparency* (TP) in which the administrations must specify the method, the time schedule, the resources to be dedicated and the instruments to be adopted to ensure the effectiveness of the initiative and to guarantee access to the community at large of all "public information", a kind of *open government*.

The rest of the paper is organized as follows. First of all, we briefly present the Italian reform. Then we introduce the conceptual framework and the propositions. In the third section the research methodology is described. Finally, the mains results of the research are presented and discussed.

---

[1]The results (but not the specific contents) of such activities have been presented in First Annual Report (March 2011), by the Commission for evaluation, transparency and integrity in Public Administrations (CIVIT) to the Ministry for the implementation of government programs.

2 Public Administrations Reforms and ICT

Since the 1980s public organizations have been attacked for their inefficiency and for the impossibility of measuring performance and holding public officials to account. Following NPM and PG movements, several public reform policies have been drafted in different European countries as a response to new ideas about the organization and the management of PA as well as a reaction to cut-back operations due to public finance issues [6]. Looking at the assumptions behind the public innovations programs which have been formulated in several European countries it is possible to note that both the nature of the societal problems which governments should address and the specific actions and tools that should be implemented in order to meet the desired modernization goals are different from country to country. Particularly, in many policy documents produced in the last decade we see that the use of ICT is very often seen as an important vehicle for modernizations and public innovation. In 2009 the European Commission (Work Programme ICT 2009–2010) maintains that using the tools and systems made possible by ICT help to provide better public services to citizens: an effective introduction of ICT in PA also involves rethinking organisations and processes, and changing behaviour so that public services are delivered more efficiently to the people who need to use them. In this context, it is possible to affirm that technology can stimulate public innovation, especially if we realize that ICT has rapidly penetrated the primary processes of PA. According to Bekkers et al. [6] it could play an important role in the formulation and implementation of public policy processes, in the delivery of public services, in law enforcement, in the redesign of working processes and, moreover, in budgeting and accounting processes, in the relationship within and outside PA. However, research shows that the effects of ICT are limited and context-driven because its introduction in PA is not neutral but an intervention in a specific policy and organizational context. For this reason, this paper aims to investigate the potential role of ICT in the Italian Reform process.

2.1 Italian Reform Process and ICT: Connection with Performance and Transparency

Among the various reforms carried out in Italian PA the Decree 150/2009 reveals elements of noteworthy connection between the structures of public management and public governance theories [1–5] which ask for the introduction both of a system to evaluate and measure organizational and individual performance and of new regulations which guarantee the transparency and accountability of "each aspect of the organization, of the indicators regarding managerial progress, the use of resources for the accomplishment of the institutional functions, the results of the activity of measuring and evaluating [...], with the aim of favouring the diffusion of forms of social control [...]". The analysis of the Italian policy documents reveals that the major aim of reform is to direct PA toward "total transparency", concerning not only performance, but also possible risks, activities for prevention of corruption, and several other topics. The modernization goal of transparency can be considered as a way to guarantee the external and the internal accountability in public organizations [7, 8]. In the legislative document (Decree 150/2009), transparency is mainly associated with the possibility of access to any relevant information for stakeholders, while accessibility is important not only as the right to information but also to support the stakeholders' external control ("social control"). From another perspective, transparency and information on performance results must generate a course of continuous improvement of the said performance.

Starting from these premises and looking to the Decree and the CiVIT's resolutions, it is undeniable that ICT is considered a key element in order to put the reform into practice. First of all, ICT is necessary to the good running of the monitoring and evaluation system. ICT has been defined as a *pivotal point* of this system. However the theme of ICT is only ever referred to indirectly never explicitly. So, even if the impact of ICT on the reform processes is quite broad and concerns different perspectives, we need to analyse these perspectives through the two dimensions of transparency and performance. The impact of ICT on transparency has a strong relation with the theme of external and internal communication since ICT can guarantee better communication within the organisation [6, 9]: in the Decree, transparency is intended as "total access" to all information concerning the action of the organization, as well as by publishing such information on the institutional web sites. From this emphasis both on data accessibility and the communication of performance results the necessity of paying attention to privacy and personal information security arises. Therefore, Decree 150/2009 and CiVIT's resolutions regulated these features and required that Italian PA should be vigilant regarding privacy issues, particularly concerning personal information disclosure. Another goal of Italian reform is to improve the performance of public organizations. On this issue, ICT is linked mainly to managerial and stakeholders' perspectives. From a managerial perspective, ICT has a fundamental impact on the different features of "quality", which is one of the dimensions of organizational performance. This concern, that accessibility to PA services, must be understood in an extended manner. ICT also has an effect on the timeliness of providing product and services. Moreover, ICT should facilitate the integration of all the control functions and all the informative systems already existing. The integration must lead to the convergence of all the financial and accounting systems, management control systems, personnel administration systems, protocol systems, and so on. From this point of view, large PA could probably increase efficiency by establishing ERP systems. From a stakeholders' perspective, finally, ICT has basically the task to ensure compliance, equal opportunities and reliability. In particular, compliance and equal opportunities are related to the continual comparison of the results achieved. Reliability concerns the necessity of maintaining the same level of consistency of products and services and of data and information. ICT is also the main instrument that allows the participation of stakeholders in the phase of planning in the performance cycle and in the phase of control, after the communication of performance results.

3 ICT, Performance, Transparency and Accountability: Conceptual Framework and Propositions

In a nutshell it can be said that Decree 150/2009, as well as all public acts based on NPM and PG principles, aims to increase performance, accountability and transparency of the Italian Public Administration, following a coherent policy based on the international debate on public sector development and innovation. Furthermore, while literature showed that some elements of New Public Management are outdated, the interest in performance, accountability and transparency is still relevant [10].

ICT has a critical role in this framework. Scholars and practitioners agree with the transformative effects of ICT both on reform processes and on the way public organizations operate [11, 12]. Furthermore, ICT supports the promotion and the integration of performance, accountability and transparency [11]. Public sector ICT initiatives and projects represent an essential and critical part for all public sector reform initiatives [12]. Consistently with the mentioned Italian reform, in the more general debate about the *potential* contribution of ICT to public sector reform [12], some scholars [12] suggest that many governments envision the use of ICT as a vehicle to: (a) promote efficiency (ICT can reduce the cost and/or time required for activities and therefore increase process productivity); (b) encourage decentralization (ICT can support decision making at decentralized location and create new information); (c) increase accountability and transparency at the same time (ICT can deliver new accountability information to different stakeholders providing); (d) improve resource management (ICT can create new performance information and deliver it to decision makers providing more managerial control over government resources); (e) support customer orientation (ICT can encourage the delivery of new forms of public services). According to Madon [13] each type of ICT application addresses different aspects of government reform. The implementation of in-house government applications such as the planning and administrative systems is based on the rationale of improving performance. Similarly, the implementation of government-citizen interactions (such as e-government) is based on a rationale of improving the transparency of public organizations over the short term.

3.1 Public Administration Performance and ICT Use: Main Propositions

The attention on performance over the past two decades, since Osborne and Gaebler [1], suggested that public sector organisations must be "performance driven" and not "rule-bound", due to social changes [14] and the general decline in the availability of financial resources [15]. However, some scholars underlined that performance in public management has multidimensional objectives [16], which can be pursued through the improvement of planning and control systems both at organizational and individual level [15, 17], and through the introduction of pay for performance systems [18]. Therefore the implementation of Performance Management Systems in a PA would lead to increased efficiency and effectiveness [5, 17] and, consequently, to a better and faster accomplishment of its mission. Technological systems provide support to organizations in measuring and evaluating performance, promoting productivity and greater profitability, developing work relations and promoting an efficient use of resources [19–21]. Moreover, ICT can also improve the provision of more timely, consistent and formal information and data about performance. According to Heeks [12] only those technologies that provide monitoring, comparison and control mechanisms can be said to truly support organizational performance. Different comparative analysis, in fact, showed that the application of performance systems presents wide diversity, at least in Europe [22]. Several scholars noted that performance systems do not consider sufficiently the difficulty of measuring and evaluating certain kinds of public results. From this perspective, several studies did not find any relationship between ICT and performance [23–26]. Lucas [27] found that the use of ICT did not explain a great deal of variance in performance. Furthermore, as Brynjolfsson and Hitt [28] pointed out, the true cost of such investments in ICT may be underestimated because they do not consider indirect costs (such as labour, training, process reengineering and services) necessary to an effective implementation in daily work within public organizations. If these costs are included, the impact on organizational performance could be modest. It is possible that ICT investment does not have a higher impact on performance.

Accordingly, we propose:

Proposition 1(a) *ICT use in PA is expected to improve the performance of services and programs.*

Proposition 1(b) *ICT use in PA is not expected to improve the performance of services and programs.*

3.2   Public Administration Accountability, Transparency and ICT Use: Main Propositions

ICT is designed to collect and disseminate information, can easily support such processes, can help track behaviour of all types of entities [29] and can also make more transparent the public actions and the decision making processes [30]. In the NPM context, ICT provides support for controlling decision performance, and is intended to assist in the control of that performance [30]. On the other hand, following the PG framework, every democratic government should be accountable to its stakeholders. This is one more reason to search for means of creating accountability and ICT can be one. For the purpose of this paper it is important to distinguish transparency from accountability. Some scholars distinguish between external and internal accountability [7, 8]: the former indicates the account which is given to some other person/body outside the person/body being held accountable, the latter refers to the responsibility of public agents towards citizens. In summary, accountability and transparency are closely linked with performance but refer to different audiences: accountability, taking into account both internal and external dimensions, refers to whole stakeholders, on the other hand, transparency refers to external ones [31, 32].[2] Of course, ICT can support both accountability and transparency, because it can be used, at the same time, to mirror movements of resources, to publish information that allows the citizens to scrutinize the public use of funds, allowing the linking of movements of money to individual actions and thereby identifying good policy [33, 34]. ICT is therefore an instrument with the potential to improve trust in governments through government accountability and to empower citizens and other stakeholders [35, 36]. Asking for new responsibility ascriptions, ICT can become a "contentious" problem for accountability [37]. ICT, in fact, has the potential to undermine the process of accountability and therefore transparency: the advent of technology produces a loss of paper records however, at the same time, it has little effect on data quality [12]. A frequent problem is that technology is used for the express purpose of deflecting accountability and thus responsibility for PA [37]. Barata and Cain [33] discuss this problem with regards to public sector accountability and they state that the relationship between accountability and ICT is often oversimplified, which, in turn, may lead to a decrease of accountability rather than an increase. At the same time, Bannister [38] identifies a number of phenomena which are likely to delimit the usefulness of technology-enabled transparency and, in particular, the risks arising from blame and hassle avoidance strategies; the problems of conformity connected with the political consensus and potential problems of misinterpretation and misunderstanding of information [38]. Finally, concerning the difference between accountability and transparency, a non-correct use of ICT may lead to a shift in focus from the needs of internal stakeholders to only those of the external ones [39]. Internal information needs may be forgotten or be satisfied only in the case of overlapping with the provisions of these external information systems [30]. Moreover, there would be pressures to control the design and implementation of ICT systems. Power in bureaucratic organizations is closely linked to the possibility of controlling areas of uncertainty [40]. Information technology may contribute to reduce that uncertainty and this explains why politicians and top managers want to control the process of planning and implementation of ICT [41]. On this topic, in fact, Heeks [30], identified political infighting as one of the most relevant factors that lead to failure of information system implementation. So, in order to create a virtuous circle

---

[2]For example, in UN Public Administration programs, transparency refers to unfettered access by the public to timely and reliable information on decisions and performance in the public sector. Accountability refers to the obligation on the part of public officials to report on the usage of public resources and answerability for failing to meet stated performance objectives.

between accountability, transparency and ICT, the PA need to identify the better use of ICT in the single public organization and between the different stakeholders. Accordingly, we propose:

Proposition 2(a) *ICT should be adopted by PA for the purpose of increasing accountability.*

Proposition 2(b) *ICT should not be adopted by PA for the purpose of increasing accountability.*

Proposition 3(a) *ICT should be adopted by PA to achieve transparency.*

Proposition 3(b) *ICT should not be adopted by PA to achieve transparency.*

4 Research Design and Method

To reply to the research questions, a content analysis was carried out on the documents (MESP, PP and TP), already produced by the PA in the first year of reform application. Content analysis uses the scientific process to identify messages relevant to a defined or evolving theoretical framework, recode the messages into a quantifiable form using explicit and objective processes, and analyse the messages to draw conclusions that further the understanding of the theory [42–45]. Management research has utilized the content analysis to draw valid inferences from the textual communications [46]. Content analysis in fact is useful, and may be the only research strategy that could be reasonably employed, when there are a large number of messages to analyse. In particular, beginning with the research questions, we first identified a set of categories for analysis (or questions to be asked to text), secondly we read the documents highlighting all text that on first impression appeared to explain the role of ICT, and finally we coded all highlighted passages using predetermined codes. Concerning the sample of our analysis, on a cross section of a total of "131" Administrations involved since 2010 in the reform project, the sample "66[3]" of the Administrations are in a certain sense, the most commendable, having published and sent to CIVIT, at the 14th of December 2011, all three documents. This criterion of selection (the three documents prepared and published) is justified by the need to gather the best practices on the subject and by the structure of these documents edited in a coherent and integrated form, each one defining the parts of the complex system of measuring, controlling and transparency. Using the contents analysis methodology we analysed a total of 198 documents. Based on their "nature", the PA included in the sample may be classified as follow: Research Institute (22,7 %), Park Authorities (18,2 %), Provident

---

[3]Actually the Public Administrations with all three documents I on the CiVIT website are 67 but one of them (the University of Florence) had not produced an MESP but a newsletter recalling an older system of evaluation of individual performance so we decided to exclude the University from the analysis.

and social security institutions (6,1 %), Public Authorities (18,2 %), Ministries (15,2 %) and University (19,7 %).

From the explorative analysis of the policy documents concerning the reform process (the legislative Decree and the CiVIT's resolutions), we have identified the cognitive goals of our analysis: these are the goals of the content analysis as well. Then, we began to form a table of analysis, paying particular attention to the logical sequence of the questions. While in a traditional survey the sequence of the questions could be identified to obtain truthful responses, in content analysis the order of the questions is designed to facilitate the task of the analysts [47]. We divided the analysis table into 4 different areas. The first one contains general information of the PA, while the other three areas are dedicated to an in-depth analysis of the three documents. The table for the analysis was subjected to a pre-test in order to identify missing points (to be added) and/or superfluous points (to be deleted), to identify errors or inaccuracies in the formulation and in the sequence of the points and, for each point, to supply alternative answers and give indications for the eventual "closure" of "open" points. The gathering of the statistical data was carried out jointly. The analysts completed an initial individual analysis, each one compiling his/her own analysis sheet, after which they carried out an analysis to discuss and resolve any differences. This enabled the study of a reliability index for each operation in order to ensure the maximum correspondence between different test results taken by the individual analysts using the same instruments on the same test cases. At the end of the survey, the completed forms were controlled in order to number the valid replies and to examine the "other" replies for an eventual classification, calculate the ratings (in the case of variables constructed with more than one indicator), close the "open" items. And last, we proceeded to structure the coding plan of the variables and then to construct the analysis sheet. We used the informatics support INSERT to extract the statistical data for analysis. In order to have a coherent vision, we analysed the gathered data with programs for statistical analysis used in social science (SPSS). We followed these steps [48]: descriptive analysis of single questions and, when relevant, bivariate descriptive analysis.

5 Results

5.1 Presence of ICT Theme in the Documents

As shown in the following table, the theme of ICT is almost always present: 65 of the 66 administrations tackle it. Looking at each document separately, we observe the same results both for PP and the TP (Fig. 1) while, referring to the MESP, the ICT theme is present in fewer administrations (47 on 66). This result is really unexpected because the MESP should contain the design of the adopted tools to

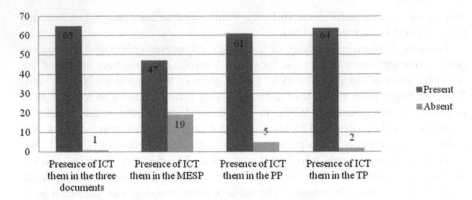

Fig. 1 The presence of ICT theme in the documents (numbers of administration)

manage performance and transparency, among which ICT should be one of the most important tools. We also analysed the documents, with three mutually exclusive responses, looking to the kind of innovation connected with ICT, with a distinction between *incremental*, *radical* and *fully* innovative. In respect of this topic, ICT is associated to the incremental innovation in 93.8 % of cases, radical innovation in 31.3 % of cases, and fully innovative with the creation of ICT infrastructure in 57.8 % of the cases.

In order to obtain a measure of the "centrality" of ICT, we considered the presence of ICT both in a quantitative perspective (how many words are dedicated to the ICT theme) and in a qualitative one (through which keywords). From the number of administrations which consider ICT in their documents, we gathered the number of words dedicated to this issue: the collected data gave us a measure of "how many times it is mentioned". The PP and the TP are the two documents in which ICT is more common. In particular, during the survey, we found that an administration has a whole document attached to the PP, which contains more than 17.000 words, dedicated to the ICT theme. The average number of words focused on the ICT theme is 6.435 for the MESP, 43.708 for the PP and 12.053 for the TP. These values are all above the average for all three documents for administrations that belong to the Provident and social security institutions' category (the average value of numbers words is: 121 in MESP, 4.261 in PP; 161 in TP). In addition, with specific reference to the MESP and TP, and also for the Ministries, the number of words dedicated to the ICT theme is higher than the average (110 words for MESP and 1.869 for TP on average). Moreover, ICT is more often present and connected with the theme of transparency and accountability in the documents of Ministries, Public Authorities and Provident and social security institutions than in Research Institutes, Park Authorities and Universities. To investigate the use and the implications of ICT in the PA' documents, we analysed the main keywords associated with the topic, using a pre-defined set of graphic

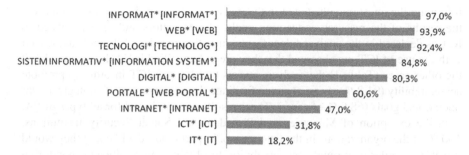

Fig. 2 Percentage of cases in which the keywords have been used at least once in the documents

forms associated with the ICT theme.[4] Starting from these words, we selected from the documents the number of linguistic roots (primary lexical unit of a word associated to a word family) in order to identify the content associated with the semantic content (for ex.: singular and plural name, adjective, etc.).[5]

Figure 2 shows the percentage of cases in which the keywords have been used at least once in the documents and refers to 66 valid cases. In particular, the linguistic root "informat" (that is connected with words as "information", "informatization", "informatics", etc.) and the keywords "web" are used in most parts of the documents we analysed. Furthermore the words related with the linguistic root "technology" (for example: technological, technology, etc.) and "Information System" and "digital" have an high percentage, while the keyword "web portal" in the 60,6 % of cases. However, "ICT" and "IT" are the less common keywords with, respectively, 31,8 and 18,2 % of cases in which these keywords have been used in the three documents analysed. In a nutshell the ICT theme is considerably present in the three types of documents: 65 administrations on 66 tackle the ICT theme, but with different forms and dimensions. ICT is mentioned more in the PP and TP than in the MESP. The ministries, the public authorities and the provident and social security institutions mentioned ICT in connection with performance and transparency, while it happens less in the case of Research Institutes, Park Authorities and University documents.

5.2 ICT Role: Tools, Phase, Actors and Goals

The texts analysis provided an interpretation of both the role and the functions of ICT, in connection with the implementation of the Italian reform. Particularly,

---

[4]The selected graphic forms identify the common words as "Information System", "technology", "intranet", "web", "web-portal", "information", "ICT", "IT" and "digital".

[5]All the documents analyzed are in the Italian language and therefore, in the research, we have considered the Italian linguistic root associated with the selected words.

following the questions illustrated in the method section, in this section we present the results of the research concerning goals, phases, actors and objects related to ICT as declared in the analysed documents. Investigating the main *goals* associated with the use of ICT we observed that they are not specified in 34 documents. In all the other cases (Table 1) the analysis reveals that PA use ICT in order to promote accountability (91,8 % of cases) and to facilitate the achievement of strategic and/or operational goals (68,9 % of cases). These results are confirmed for all types of PA, with the exception of Ministries and Provident and Social Security Institutions. 100 % of the organizations in the latter group, in particular, declare that they would use ICT in order to promote accountability, to obtain a more efficient monitoring system and to facilitate integration with existing systems. In the document published by the Ministries, however, ICT is more often mentioned in reference to the monitoring system, and to the promotion of accountability (80 % of the Ministries declare these two goals) and to the achievement of strategic and operational goals (60 % of the Ministries). Probably, in this case, the different results can be explained by taking into account the previous reforms which involved separately the different types of administrations. It could be a problem of different PA' "starting points". A previous Decree (n. 286/1999, art. 1–2), in fact, obliged only the Ministries to reorganize and to strengthen all the existing mechanisms and tools in order to: (a) ensure legitimacy, regularity and fairness of the administrative action; (b) verify effectiveness, efficiency and economy of the administrative actions; (c) evaluate the public management's performance; (d) verify the congruence between achieved results and defined objectives during the implementation of plans and programs. This implies that the Ministries, unlike the other PA, have already worked on these areas and, consequently, on issues related to ICT, for about a decade. The Research Institutes, however, more than the others declare the use of ICT in order to facilitate integration with existing systems (50 % of cases). Within this percentage of cases we found PA[6] offering particular and more technical services. The research activities and the services adopted by these organizations are characterized by technology-based work processes. Consequently we suppose that their ICT knowledge allows them to take advantage of an integrated technology system. At large, this first section of results seems to confirm that PA' choices follow the direction of the Italian Legislation which proposed the application of an action of "programming", "evaluation" and "transparency" to the administrative processes and activities. The different issues emerging in the "other" sector confirm this idea. In the analysed documents the administrations also affirm the use of ICT in order to ensure customer/citizen satisfaction (6 % of the sample) and to reduce public spending (3 % the sample): these are also, in fact, key drivers of performance in public sector organizations.

---

[6]For example: ASI stands for Italian Space Agency; ENEA stands for Italian National Agency for New Technologies, Energy and Sustainable Economic Development; INGV stands for National Institute in Geophysics and Volcanology; INRIM stands for National Institute for Metrology Research; ISTAT stands for Italian National Institute of Statistics.

Table 1 ICT goals

Goal	Percentage
To promote accountability	91,8
To facilitate the achievement of strategic and/or operational goals	68,9
To facilitate integration with existing systems	45,9
To obtain a more efficient monitoring systems	44,3
Other	18

Table 2 ICT and performance cycles's phases

Phase of performance cycle	Percentage
Reporting	82,5
Organizational performance's measurement evaluation	47,4
Monitoring	45,6
Planning	43,9
Programming	38,6
Budgeting	35,1
Individual performance's measurement evaluation	29,8

In order to understand the relationship between ICT and the performance cycle, we made a more detailed analysis of the mentioned *phases* of the performance cycle, within the document. In 62 documents there is no information about the specific phase of a more "intensive" use of ICT. However, from the other cases (Table 2) it appears that ICT use is more often referred to in the "Reporting" phase (82,5 % of case), to the "Organizational performances' measurement and evaluation" phase (47,4 %), "Monitoring" and "Planning" (respectively in 45,6 % and in 43,9 % of cases).

Despite this general trend, the phases most commonly related to ICT are different across the different administrations. For example, the Ministries declare the use of ICT in the "Programming" phase (100 % of the Ministries), in the "Monitoring" phase (80 %) in the "Planning" phase (70 %) and in 50 % of cases in the "Reporting" phase. Public Authorities affirm the use of ICT more in "Reporting" (100 % of cases) and in the "Monitoring" phase (90 % of cases), than in the "Organizational Performance Measurement and Evaluation" phase (only in 50 % of the cases). Finally, in addition to the "Reporting" phase, Park Authorities announce the use of ICT in "Planning" and "Budgeting" phases (respectively, 75 and 50 % of cases). Of course, in comparison with other administrations, Park Authorities provide different services to the community and their work activities, probably, require a more careful planning and budgeting phase.

Taking into consideration the two phases in which administrations declare the use of more ICT, it seems that the link between performance and transparency is confirmed, because of the use of ICT in both phases. However, the results do not support the strong relationship between organizational performance and individual performance. Probably, if the former influences the latter, PA should use ICT to measure and to evaluate both the organizational and individual performances. Yet this seems to happen only for the Universities: they declare the use of ICT for both levels of performance in the same percentage of cases (27,3 %). As we know, Universities use an evaluation system based more on quantitative targets (i.e. number of publication, impact factor, etc.) than behavioural ones. Therefore, a link between organizational and individual performance may be easier than in other kinds of PA. Using content analysis the "objective" of ICT has been analysed in the plans produced by public organizations. Our interest was in understanding which tools had been considered by administrations in implementing the Reform following CIVIT's suggestions. The documents reveal that Italian public organizations declare the use of more front-end applications such as "Web Portal" (98,5 % of cases) than in-house governments applications such as "Intranet Portal" (41,5 % of cases), "Information protocol" (40 % of cases), "Information System for Planning and Control" (36,9 % of cases) and the "Document Management System" (30,8 % of cases). It is important to point-out that not all the 66 administrations declare in their documents the use of all the tools that CiVIT identified as the most common tools used in the organizations. For example, from the documents it appears that Data System is not used by Research Institutes nor by Provident Institutions and Social Security Institutions; the Universities declare that they do not use ERP System, E-procurement system and Integrated system for Human Resources Management; E-procurement System seems to be used only by Research Institutes, Public Authorities, Provident Institutions and social Security Institutions. Even if in 31 documents there is no information about ICT technology used in public organizations, the analysis reveals that in 13,8 % of cases PA declare the use of tools that we have not identified as common tools such as Technological Platforms, Cloud Computing. Concerning the *actors* connected to ICT, we investigated both "who are people related to ICT" and "what is the role of involved people". Both in establishing and using ICT different actors can perform different roles according to their abilities and skills. On the first point, the analysis shows (Table 3) that the most cited actors in relation to ICT are: "External Stakeholders" (85,7 % of cases), "Civil Servants" (58,7 % of cases), "Public Management" (44,4 % of cases) and Internal Stakeholder (25,4 % of cases) even if the Ministries declare the involvement of "Public Management" more than the Civil Servants.

However, not all the 66 administrations declare the involvement of all the categories of actors in projecting or using ICT: Boards of directors are not related to

Table 3 ICT and actors

Actors	Percentage
External stakeholders	85,7
Civil servants	58,7
Public management	44,4
Internal stakeholder	25,4
OIV	20,6
Board of directors	14,3

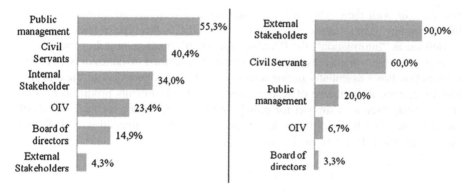

Fig. 3 ICT administrator and users

ICT in "park authorities"; "Internal Stakeholders" are not related to ICT in "provident and Social Security institutions". In 64 documents it has been impossible to obtain information about the type of actors involved.

By studying the actors' role, we analysed the documents to identify the actors involved as designers and administrators of ICT infrastructure and tools, on the one hand, and the actors involved as users of ICT, on the other. The analysis shows (Fig. 3) that "Public Management" (55,3 % of cases), "Civil Servants" (40,4 %), "Internal Stakeholder" (34 %), "OIV" (23,4 %) and "Boards of Directors" (14,9 %) are the actors more involved in ICT design, implementation and management. The Italian administrations prefer to involve only in a few cases (4,3 %) also the "External Stakeholders" in this process. Taking into account the different categories of actors involved as *ICT administrators* for the different types of public organizations we conduct a deeper analysis. Regarding *ICT users* (Fig. 3—on the right), the most common actors are: "External Stakeholders" (90 % of cases), "Civil Servants" (60 % of cases) and Public Management (20 % of cases). It is important to note that, in the documents, administrations do not mention the "Internal Stakeholder" as an ICT user: on the one hand, this result stresses that public organizations want to be accountable to the external community; on the other hand, the non-involvement of the internal actors (i.e. HR Office, Information Systems Unit, etc.) could undermine the goal of internal accountability.

A more in deep analysis reveals also the categories of actors involved in each type of PA. These results allow us to better specify and verify the results obtained by the ICT tools used in public organizations. Even if the web portal is the most used tool evidencing a probable stakeholders-oriented approach, Fig. 3 reveals that ICT is created and managed within the organizations, and rarely involves external stakeholders. Moreover, our analysis shows that only the Ministries (11,5 % of the Ministries) and the Universities (12,5 % of the Universities) involve "External Actors" in ICT implementation and management. We can observe that while the Decree invoked the improvement of transparency and participation of different actors in the life of public bodies, Italian administrations seem to prefer a *one-way relationship* with their stakeholders, assuming a strategy of accountability more than a strategy of transparency. According to the OECD, this type of interaction can be defined as "Information": the PA disseminates information on policy making on its own initiative—or citizens access information upon their demand; in both cases, information flows essentially in one direction, from the government to the citizens. However, even if the theme of ICT is present in the documents produced by PA, ICT is rarely used as a support for policy and decision making. In fact, boards of directors are involved in the role of users only by Universities and Public Authorities (both in 1.7 % of the cases).

6 Discussion

Referring to the *first research question* (How much attention has been paid to ICT in Italian Policy documents?), all the analysed documents demonstrate that ICT could have, (potentially), a strong impact on the reform process: 36 administrations (on 37) tackle the ICT theme even if in different forms and dimensions; a great part of the administrations involved in the research, stated the need to change their ICT systems, pointing out the relevant role that ICT is expected to play in putting into practice the regulatory requirements. Concerning the *second research question* (What is the expected effect of ICT use on public organizations performance?), several results confirm the intention of PA to use ICT in order to improve performance. PP, in fact, is the document in which terms related to ICT are mainly quoted. Italian PA declare that one of the most important goals associated with ICT use is the facilitation of the achievement of strategic and operational objectives. We have also noted some differences in goals depending on the nature of the PA. The analysis of Ministries' documents, for example, shows that ICT is more often mentioned in reference not only to the achievement of strategic and operational goals but also to the monitoring system with great emphasis on the performance theme. The research institutes, instead, declared the use of ICT to facilitate integration with existing systems. Generally we can say that performance and ICT are closely related, but we noted some differences among administrations concerning the use of ICT in achieving performance. All the phases of the performance cycle forecast ICT use: in particular, almost half of the administrations declare the use of ICT in "organizational performance measurement and evaluation", stressing the ICT-performance linkage. This confirms the importance of ICT for the entire cycle and for the performance in itself. Performance, in fact, is not an output of a specific phase but is the result of the whole cycle. Different performance "levels" also need to be considered. Except for the universities, it seems that ICT bears more upon organizational than individual performance. It is possible that PA decided to measure and to evaluate performance without using or without declaring the use of ICT systems. But it may require a more in-depth analysis. The most important categories of ICT administrators declared in the documents are public management, civil servants and internal stakeholders. Probably, the involvement of these categories of actors, more than the others, could offer some benefits in the different phases of the performance cycle (such as setting goals, monitoring, etc.), thus improving its effectiveness. Summarizing the results of this part of the analysis, we can state that the use of ICT can improve performance even if ICT is used in different ways and for different tasks. The results and the discussion allow us to confirm the Proposition 1(a), (*ICT use in PA is expected to improve the performance of services and programs*).

To respond to the *third research question* we have analysed the potential effect of ICT use on public organizations' transparency and accountability. At first sight, ICT seems to have a strong relationship with accountability and transparency. From a quantitative point of view, the average use of terms related to ICT in the TP is very high, while from a qualitative point of view, ICT is associated with several instruments used to favour the correct flow of information from one place to another: such as web, web portal, intranet and informative systems. The goal of promoting accountability is the most cited topic in the documents (almost 92 % of cases). We stated before that ICT is related to all phases of the performance cycle. We showed in the results that the more cited phase is the reporting one. This is coupled with the idea of ICT as a support for transmitting information to relevant internal and external stakeholders. To follow up the discussion, in our conceptual frame we distinguished between transparency and accountability issues and, therefore, we need the same distinction for the rest of the discussions. Indeed the results allow us to think that ICT is a support both to internal accountability and to transparency, but in a different way. In fact, the actors more cited as ICT administrators are all the internal ones: there is a very low percentage of involvement (without any exception in the type of PA) of external players, such as customers. On the contrary, if we consider the ICT users, the most cited are the external stakeholders with a landslide of cases (90 %). The most cited ICT tools are front-end application rather than in-house governments systems. This is particularly related to the goal of promoting the flow of information. We noticed also some differences based on the type of PA, concerning mainly the kind of ICT tool used, the kind of actors involved and some percentages of declaration of use. Anyway, we think that these differences must be coupled with the need to adapt and customize ICT to each PA. Consequently, we can say that ICT, at least at an intentional level, plays an influcntial role in increasing transparency and accountability. So we can confirm proposition 2(a) (*ICT should be adopted by PA for the purpose of increasing accountability*), at least for what concerns internal stakeholders, while we have no evidence to confirm it for external stakeholders. On the contrary, we cannot confirm proposition 3(a) (*ICT should be adopted by PA to achieve transparency*) although we cannot refute it. Summarizing, PA should adopt ICT in response to the needs of the reform. The different use of ICT depends on the perspective of analysis. From the performance perspective, ICT potentially promotes the accomplishment of objectives and facilitates the administration in monitoring and evaluating it, although from a more organizational perspective. From the accountability/transparency perspective, ICT may be used to promote a flow of information towards internal stakeholders, with a goal of internal accountability, and external stakeholders, with a goal of transparency.

7 Conclusion

The encounter between ICT and public organizations generates many questions, inviting both scholars and practitioners to better understand this "relationship". The aim of our research is to explore the intentional use and implications of ICT in supporting the Italian PA reform process. For this reason, we carried out a content analysis on the documents that Administrations have produced in the first year of reform application, to identify "*if*" and "*how*" the ICT theme recurs in these documents. Our research confirms the hypothesis of an important role of ICT in PA reforms. This can be intended from two different points of view: to facilitate the accomplishment of results and to promote the processes of accountability and transparency. These are, at least, the declared intentions of Italian PA. We recognise that effective actions could be different from declared intentions, so we need to verify ex post the eventual gap between these intentions and the real action. We may find, for example, that something that is declared in relation with ICT is pursued without ICT support. Our research, however, concerns primarily the ICT perspective, aiming to understand both what effects Italian PA would realize through the use of ICT and if ICT is among the instruments that should be implemented to meet the desired modernization goals. In this regard, the research revealed some small but significant differences, considering the different types of PA. Several sources contributed to create and to reinforce these differences, such as different starting points (for Ministries in particular), distinct difficulties in measuring and evaluating performance and different "distances" from customers. This demonstrates that the approach to the change can be only situational and not standardized. ICT comprises several actors—political authorities, regulatory bodies, research centres, and for this reason is always ad hoc and changes all the time, thereby needing constant re-conceptualization. Consequently, in order to better understand the roles and the potential of ICT, it is necessary to focus the attention on the context in which ICT is adopted. Moreover, the ambivalent nature of ICT is at the root of the dynamic tension between innovation and conservation that characterizes the organizational culture of public organizations. Any innovation, technical, organizational and socio-cultural, brings about a change in the set of possibilities that defines what can be done and how. All processes of innovation, such as ICT implementation, involve transformations of artefacts, practices and cognitive frameworks. Moving from these considerations, the research in this paper focuses the attention on the use of ICT as a vehicle to support Italian PA reform. This research took place just one year after the implementation of the reform. In order to better understand what really happens "inside" the administrations and not only what they declared, the next step will be to investigate the development in terms of ICT choices and which variables influence these choices.

References

1. Osborne, D., Gaebler, T.: Reinventing government. Addison-Wesley, Reading (1992)
2. Barberis, P.: The new public management and a new accountability. Publ. Adm. **76**, 451–470 (1998)
3. Hood, C., Jackson, M.: Administrative Argument. Aldershot, Dartmouth (1991)
4. Bevir, M., Rhode, R., Weller, P.: Traditions of governance: interpreting the changing role of the public sector. Publ. Adm. **81**, 1–17 (2003)
5. Kettl, D.F.: The global public management revolution. A Report on the Transformation of Governance. Brookings Institution Press, Washington (2000)
6. Bekkers, V.J.J.M., Van Duivenboden, H., Thaens, M.: Information and communication technology and public innovation. New IOS press, Amsterdam (2006)
7. Mulgan, R.: Accountability: an ever-expanding concept. Publ. Adm. **78**, 555–573 (2000)
8. Romzek, B., Dubnick, M.: Accountability in the public sector: lessons from the challenger tragedy. Publ. Adm. Rev. **47**, 227–239 (1987)
9. Boivaird, T.: E-government and e-governance: organisational implications, options and dilemmas. Publ. Policy Adm. **18**, 37–56 (2003)
10. Lapsley, I.: The NPM agenda: back to the future. Fin. Account. Manag. **24**, 77–96 (2008)
11. Bertot, J.C., Jaeger, P.T., Grimes, J.M.: Using ICTs to create a culture of transparency: egovernment and social media as openness and anti-corruption tools for societies. Gov. Inf. Q. **27**, 264–271 (2010)
12. Heeks, R.: The approach of senior public officials to information technology-related reform: lessons from India. Publ. Adm. Dev. **20**, 197–205 (2000)
13. Madon, S.: It-based Government reform initiatives in the Indian state of Gujarat. J. Int. Dev. **18**, 877–888 (2006)
14. Gilbert, N.: Transformation of the welfare state. The Silent Surrender of Public Responsibility. Oxford Press, Oxford (2002)
15. Hood, C.: A public management for all season. Public Adm. **69**, 3–19 (1991)
16. Bouckaert, G., Halligan, J.: Managing performance. International comparisons. Routledge, Oxon (2008)
17. Emery, Y.: Rewarding civil service performance through team bonuses: findings, analysis and recommendations. Int. Rev. Adm. Sci. **70**, 157–168 (2004)
18. Varone, F., Giauque, D.: Policy management and performance related pay: comparative analysis of service contracts in Switzerland. Int. Rev. Adm. Sci. **67**, 543–565 (2001)
19. Devaraj, S., Kohli, R.: Performance impacts of information technology: is actual usage the missing link? Manag. Sci. **49**, 273–298 (2003)
20. Hitt, L.A., Brynjolfsson, E.: Productivity, business profitability and consumer surplus: three different measures of information technology value. MIS Q. **20**, 121–142 (1996)
21. Melville, N., Kraemer, K., Gurbaxani, V.: Information Technology and organizational performance: an integrative model of IT Business Value. MIS Q. **28**, 283–321 (2004)
22. Gualmini, E.: Restructuring weberian bureaucracy: comparing managerial reforms in Europe and the United States Publ. Adm. **86**, 75–94 (2008)
23. Roach, S.S.: Services under siege: the restructuring imperative. Harvard Bus. Rev. **39**, 82–92 (1991)
24. Strassmann, P.A.: The business value of computers: an executive's guide. Information Economics Press, New Canaan (1990)

25. Turner, J., Lucas Jr, H.C.: Developing strategic information systems. In: Guth, W. (ed.) Handbook of business strategy, pp. 1–35. Gorham AND Lamont, Boston (1985)
26. Van Duivenboden, H., Thaens, M.: ICT-driven innovation and the culture of public administration: a contradiction in terms. Inf. Polity. 13, 213–232 (2009)
27. Lucas Jr, H.C.: Performance and the use of an information system. Manage. Sci. 21, 908–919 (1975)
28. Brynjolfsson, E., Hitt, L.M.: Beyond computation: Information technology, organization transformation and business performance. J. Econ. Perspect. 14, 23–48 (2000)
29. Skovira, R.J.: The social contract revised: obligation and responsibility in the information society. In: Azari, R. (eds.) Current security management and ethical issues of information technology, pp. 165–186. IRM Press (2003)
30. Heeks, R.: Reinventing government in the information age. Routledge, London (1999)
31. Gregory, R.: Accountability in modern government. In: Peters, G.G., Pierre, J. (eds.) Handbook of public administration, pp. 339–350. Sage, London (2003)
32. Koppell, J.: Pathologies of accountability: ICANN and the challenge of "multiple accountabilities disorder". Publ. Adm. Rev. 65, 94–108 (2005)
33. Barata, K., Cain, P.: Information, not technology, is essential to accountability: electronic records and public-sector financial management. Inf. Soc. 17, 247–258 (2001)
34. Garson, G.D.: Public information technology: policy and management issues. Idea Group Publishing, Hershey, USA (2003)
35. Demchak, C.C., Friis, C. La, Porte, T.M.: Webbing governance: national differences in constructing the public face. In: Garson, G.D. (ed.) Handbook of public information systems, pp. 179–195. Marcel Dekker, New York (2000)
36. Pina, V., Torres, L., Royo, S.: Are ICTs improving transparency and accountability in the EU regional and local governments? Publ. Adm. 85, 449–472 (2007)
37. Stahl, B.C.: Accountability and reflective responsibility in information systems. In: Zielinski, C., Duquenoy, P., Kimppa, K. (eds.) The information society: emerging landscapes. Springer, New York (2006)
38. Bannister, F., Connolly, R.: The trouble with transparency: a critical review of openness in e-government. Policy Internet 3, 15–32 (2011)
39. Rathore, R.S.: MIS in government environment. In: Kulshreshta, N.K. (ed.) Management information systems, pp. 32–41. SIPA, Jaipur (1977)
40. March, J.G., Simon, H.A.: Organizations. Wiley, New York (1958)
41. Braverman, H.: Labour and monopoly capital: the degradation of work in the twentieth century. Monthly Review Press, New York and London (1974)
42. Krippendorff, K.: Content analysis: an introduction to its methodology. Sage, Thousand Oaks (CA) (2004)
43. Morris, R.: Computerized content analysis in management research: a demonstration of advantages and limitations. J. Manag. 20(4), 903–931 (1994)
44. Williamson, J.B., Karp, D.A., Dalphin, J.R.: The research craft: an introduction to social science methods. Little Brown, Boston (1977)
45. Woodrum, E.: "Mainstreaming" content analysis in social science: methodological advantages, obstacles, and solutions. Soc. Sci. Res. 13, 1–19 (1984)
46. D'aveni, R.A., Macmillan, I.C.: Crisis and content of managerial communications: a study of the focus of attention of top managers in surviving and failing firms. Adm. Sci. Q. 35, 634–657 (1990)
47. Losito, G.: L' analisi del contenuto nella ricerca sociale. Franco Angeli, Milano (1996)
48. Marradi, A.: Concetti e metodo per la ricerca sociale. Giuntina, Firenze (1984)

An Integrated Drugs Logistics Management System: A Case Study in the Healthcare Sector

Roberta Pinna, Pier Paolo Carrus and Fabiana Marras

Abstract The purpose of this work is to analyse the benefits that the healthcare system may enjoy with the adoption of the latest innovations in drug logistics management. In particular the analysis concerns the adoption of the automated cabinet system, ICT solution implemented by an Italian region, and the main organisational implications connected to the use of such a system. The research questions are: Does the automated cabinet system allow the healthcare system to improve the quality of patient care and reduce costs? If so, what are the most important processes and actors in pharmaceutical logistics innovation, and what is their role? The peculiarities detected by this study confirmed that the drug distribution and consumption system solution adopted by the healthcare company has allowed for large savings in terms of cost containment and the traceability of drugs.

Keywords Healthcare logistics management · Healthcare innovation · Logistics management information system

1 Introduction

The aim of this study is to investigate the emerging trends in the pharmaceuticals management and logistics flow redesign. Logistics and supply chain innovation are becoming a highly topical issue in the international research agenda, as well as in practice [1, 2]. The reason is that economic and political factors are raising attention

R. Pinna (✉) · P.P. Carrus · F. Marras
Department of Economics and Business, University of Cagliari, Cagliari, Italy
e-mail: pinnar@unica.it

P.P. Carrus
e-mail: ppcarrus@unica.it

F. Marras
e-mail: fmarras@unica.it

© Springer International Publishing Switzerland 2016
F. Ricciardi and A. Harfouche (eds.), *Information and Communication Technologies in Organizations and Society*, Lecture Notes in Information Systems and Organisation 15, DOI 10.1007/978-3-319-28907-6_5

towards healthcare issues, mainly because of the rapid growth of healthcare costs: the process of local health corporatisation, which involves the introduction of control mechanisms into the National Health System that are similar to competitive market models; the aging of the population; the increasing demand for healthcare services; the rising cost of inpatient and outpatient care; new technologies and new drugs will continue to drive up the total cost of healthcare. Indeed, the limited resources and a steady growth in spending, hence, the need for a public health rationalisation, especially to meet increasingly high quality demands [3–5]. All of this requires a profound transformation that affects not only the processes of diagnosis and treatment, but also those of support; especially logistics, which is essential for the processes of service differentiation, efficiency, quality and safety processes improvement [6].

However, the logistics process of pharmaceutical products in the healthcare sector records a relevant gap compared to other sectors: hospital companies tend to behave like "individual agents" with their own purchasing offices, a pharmacy and an internal distribution system based on an order-delivery process [7]. Additionally, they have to manage very different kinds of goods, taking care of the impact in the process of patient care. Consequently, a large number of transactions sent to different vendors and purchases of large quantities of drugs from individual departments with the resulting generation of high inventory and storage costs. As a natural consequence of this diversity of assets to manage, the organisational responsibility of the logistics function is often fragmented and dispersed across multiple organisational units with clear coordination and integration problems [8].

In order to optimize inventory control and reduce the material handling costs of pharmaceutical products, it is necessary to manage the supply chain in order to obtain an integrated vision that is capable of overcoming the boundaries between professional specialisations and the organisations involved in the implementation of the course of materials from the warehouses to the wards. All of this appeared to be even more important for the Italian National Health Service, where all of the discussions have been concentrated on the fact that the hospitals' costs should be decreased even if the materials managers' duties still have not been defined. Indeed, the state of the art shows that hospital companies, especially in Italy, are in a backward condition from the point of view of materials management from which they have only recently been trying to get out, analyse and rationalize their supply chain processes [4]. Due to the critical role that the supply chain plays in the healthcare sector, cost control and the optimisation of the material flows of the drugs have been the subject of numerous studies, and different approaches and methods have been suggested in the literature [6, 9–11]. However, there is little research on cost containment by applying new management models that are capable of ensuring the maximum efficiency of the care offered by the health system while minimizing the cost of purchasing and management in the Italian healthcare sector. Concerning reengineering the supply chain, the Italian's National Health Plan was developed in 1992 to find solutions that would improve their health services and contain the increase of long-term costs.

In this paper, we explore the possibilities of optimizing the logistics flows in the Italian healthcare sector through the implementation of process reengineering in their supply chain management. The literature review and an in-depth analysis of an Italian healthcare innovation case study help us to explain how changes in the pharmaceutical logistics flow improve efficiency and reduce costs.

The paper is structured as follows: the second paragraph analyses the pharmaceutical logistics process, followed by a description of a Logistics Management Information System; in the third paragraph, the Italian case study is presented; and a final conclusion paragraph identifies the main management implications and an indication of the possible developments.

2　The Pharmaceutical Logistics Process

In healthcare, the term logistics encompasses the set of techniques, methodologies, tools and infrastructure that are used in the management of the physicals flows (such as drugs and surgical medical products), and the associated information flows from the acquisition in the market to the distribution to wards (Fig. 1). The proposed definition allows us to make some important specifications with regards to the *purposes* and *contents*.

With reference to the first aspect, pharmaceutical logistics is the task of placing the right drugs and medical supplies in the right quantities, in the right conditions, at the right health service delivery points, at the right time, for the right patients/users and for the right cost [12]. In other words, logistics seeks to pursue simultaneous efficiency—economical use of resources—effectiveness—service level maximization—and cost-effectiveness—long term capacity to achieve the economic equilibrium. Referring to the content on the other hand, the logistics system is a set of activities (procurement, storage, physical distribution and disposal of expired drugs) that must be managed in an integrated manner.

Fig. 1 The pharmaceutical logistics process

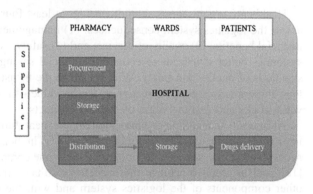

As some authors point out [13], the mains objectives of a good logistics system include:

- Improve information systems for the accurate collection and reporting of data when and where it is needed.
- Improve forecasting/procurement.
- Improve distribution activities.
- Obtain clean, secure and organised storage.

The increased complexity that characterises the management of logistics flows within the healthcare companies is linked to different aspects:

1. The healthcare companies manage at least three broad categories of goods (drugs, surgical medical products and economic goods) characterised by markedly different physical, logical and managerial requirements with important problems of storage space.
2. Logistics organisational responsibility is often fragmented and dispersed among several organisational units with the obvious problems of coordination and integration.
3. The healthcare companies treat patients, and this introduces elements of natural variability.
4. Last but not least, logistics has an important impact on the processes of care that is on the quality and safety of the care provided to patients. When healthcare actors communicate and share information, they are more likely to improve the quality in terms of patient safety, cycle time reduction and operational efficiency [14–17]. The safety of the patients is the top priority in healthcare, and pharmaceutical managers play a crucial role in protecting their interest: their biggest responsibility is to ensure that the products purchased for clinical use are good quality ones. This can be achieved by developing a product evaluation system that consists of well-defined parameters to guarantee that only approved products can enter a hospital's stockroom. Additionally, a timely placement factor is probably not as crucial in any other field as it is in healthcare delivery, where a delay of a few seconds can cost a life.

Healthcare organisations should consider at least four dimensions of analysis to assess the logistics system consequences: (1) management costs; (2) economic and financial benefits; (3) quality of service; and (4) safety. At the same cost, a logistics system is better if it leads to economic-financial savings and ensures the highest standards of quality and safety. With regard to the measurable benefits, there are at least three areas of possible recovery: (i) the value of inventories, (ii) the value of ward stocks and (iii) the value of expired products.

Above all, technological innovation in the near future will enable significant improvements in efficiency, quality and safety in healthcare logistics; but it is necessary to emphasize that technology is only one component of a logistics system [18], and in order to achieve the expected results, it must be consistent with the other components of the logistics system and with the overall corporate strategic plan.

2.1 Pharmaceutical Logistics and Information Systems

The main problems related to the traditional system of drug management are related to: the high value of a ward's fixed deposits; difficulties in controlling the drug consumption at the ward level; the high risk of product obsolescence; the staff time devoted to administrative and pharmaceuticals management; the wards stocks location; the unpredictability of requests from wards and the frequency of urgent requests; the risk of failure in the early stages of patient care; preparation, administration and the manual prescriptions transcription from paper medical records to the nursing register paper [19]. These problems create inefficiencies that result, directly or indirectly, in a lower level of service and higher costs for the hospital [4]. These key logistical activities are required to be integrated because managers operating in the pharmaceutical logistics process face many problems related to data quality: there are various products and they are constantly changing, and this results in product data that is often inaccurate and obsolete; furthermore, product identification codes may not be consistent between hospitals in the same network or even between the floors of the same hospital. The effects of poor data quality are widespread throughout the healthcare supply chain: incorrect product data leads to increased costs due to pricing errors, and this results in wasted time and work for managers as they try to resolve rebate, return and credit issues with suppliers. In addition, the quality of healthcare can be adversely impacted, because data problems can result in healthcare procedure delays due to necessary products not being on hand [20].

Central to collaboration is the exchange of large amounts of information along the logistics process including planning and operational data, real time information and communication. Numerous researchers have found that when the actors communicate and share information they are more likely to improve the quality of their services; cycle time reduction; reduce the costs of protecting against opportunistic behavior and improve cost savings through greater product design and operational efficiencies [14–17, 21].

The optimisation of information storage and its use requires that the organisation and storage of data throughout the supply chain is consistent, so that all of the data is accessible to multiple entities at different levels. The results are well coordinated movements of inventories, products that are delivered quickly and reliably when and where they are needed, as well as a high responsiveness to short lead times [21]. A solution is given by implementing a Logistics Management Information System (LMIS): managers gather information about each activity in the system and analyse that information to coordinate future actions. The LMIS provides a method of feedback for [22]:

- Tracking the storage and movement of goods at every level within the supply system in order to obtain stocks ready for use in healthcare structures.
- Ensuring proper stock rotation so that items of the earliest expiry dates are used first.
- Enabling managers to know the total amounts of commodities that are within the supply and where they are located.

Table 1 Types of LMIS data items

Stock on hand	Quantities of usable stock available at all levels of the system
Rate of consumption	An average of the stock that is dispensed to users during a particular period of time
Losses	Including the quantity of stock that was removed for any reason other than consumption
Adjustments	They are created when quantities are issued to, or received from, other facilities at the same level

The purpose of LMIS is to collect, organise and report the logistics data in order to improve customer service by improving the quality of the management decisions [23]. A well-functioning LMIS provides decision makers with accurate, timely and appropriate data for managing and monitoring the flow of supplies, accounting for products, reducing supply imbalances and improving cost-effectiveness. There are four essential data items in any LMIS (Table 1).

This data must be available for every product, at every level and at all times. The additional data item is known as service statistics, and it may be added depending on the needs of the users. It helps logistics managers to evaluate the success of health programmes. Essential data can be recorded through three different recording systems:

1. The stock keeping records, which keep the quantity of stock to hand, and the quantity of losses information about products. They are completed by anyone who receives or issues stocks from storage, or who takes a physical inventory of stock.
2. The transaction records, which keep information about the movement of stock from one storage facility to another and are prepared by the warehouse personnel or nurses at both the issuing and receiving facilities when a facility issues or requests supplies [19].
3. The consumption records, which keep information about the quantity of each item that is dispensed to the customer (dispensed-to-user data). They are completed by the service personnel at the service delivery point whenever supplies are dispensed to the customers. Only the transaction records move from one facility level to another with the product, while both stock keeping and consumption records remain where they are prepared.

At the end of a certain period, particularly monthly or quarterly, reports should be prepared and sent to the higher levels in the logistics systems for decision making, policy making and planning. Reports are used to move the essential data to the logistics decision makers and the data should be available to the managers in a form suitable for decision making. For this reason, the literature suggests six "rights" for LMIS data: the managers must receive the right data (essential data), in the right time (in time to take action), at the right place (where decisions are made), in the right quantity (having all of the essential data from all of the facilities), in the right quality (correct or accurate) and for the right cost (not spending more to collect information than spending on supplies).

Additionally, the summary report contains all of the essential data items for a specific facility and for a specific time period (usually monthly or quarterly) in the form of a simple report, aggregate summary report and request report. The feedback report informs the lower levels about their performance and even informs the higher level managers about how the system is performing.

3 Research Method

The case study [24] of this contribution regards the introduction of the automated cabinet system solution in the Sardinian Healthcare System, which was one of the first Italian Regions to adopt this innovative system. As [25] states: "data about the innovation process are obtained by synthesizing the recallable perceptions of key actors in the innovation process, written records of the organization adopting, and other data sources". The data mainly consists of primary data collected through qualitative explorative and semi-structured interviews. Secondary, we analysed official documentation, regional laws, archives, historical data and organisational plans provided directly by the organisation, scientific journals and local newspapers.

Face to face qualitative interviews were conducted. The interviews lasted about 2 h; all of the interviews were recorded and fully transcribed. The respondents had to be involved in the automated cabinet system implementation at a top management level. The interview questions were open-ended. Although the number of interviews may be considered small, they were related to the key role that the respondents had in the planning and development of this innovation, which gives a higher level of reliability and validity to the research findings. In order to increase the validity, the article was presented and discussed with a manager of a Sardinian healthcare company.

3.1 Case Study: The Application of the Automated Cabinet System in Healthcare

In recent years, the Italian government has conducted numerous investigations into the Sardinian healthcare system, as well as in other Italian regions. This took into consideration the relevance of the expenditure required for drug-health goods and its significant impact in the regional budget: the need is to monitor its trend to favour the progressive rationalisation and containment/reduction. In particular, with regard to the process of distribution and consumption of drugs in the Sardinian healthcare system, in 2011 the following criticalities were highlighted:

- The absence of adequate procedures of paper or computerised data collection that allow information on a ward's inventories to be obtained.
- Inventories were detected by the management of the hospital pharmacies warehouses.
- Within the Local Healthcare Company (ASL) 8, a computerised drug request was operative, but this flow of information only indicated the amount of drugs distributed to wards by the pharmacy.
- The requests for personalised drugs were not computerised and the traceability of the information flows of health goods were not provided.
- The procedures for the financial flows of data collection were limited to the the flow of drugs that were dispensed by pharmacies to hospital wards and operative structures.

In order to overcome the above criticalities, the Sardinian Region started a project for the implementation of an Integrated Healthcare Information System (SISaR) in 2008 with the following objective: to provide a uniform system for the administrative management of healthcare companies; to support the control of healthcare expenditure; to provide data to the health information system to be forwarded to the Ministries in charge; to allow the health activities dematerialisation process; and to facilitate the citizens' access to healthcare services. Based on these objectives, the Sardinian Region has implemented the automated cabinet system, which supports all of the distribution and the consumption process of drugs within hospitals. In particular, the management information flow covers the monitoring of handling in medicinal products delivered by hospital pharmacies to business units and departments. This e-solution allows the following:

- Automated management and control of the movement of drugs in loading and unloading.
- Obtain reports about the consumption of wards and stocks.
- Automated management of the drug stocks in the wards.
- Efficient and integrated management of the entire procurement process of pharmaceutical goods.

3.2   Analysis and Results

The SISaR application automated cabinet was gradually installed and made operative in almost all of the wards of the Regional Healthcare System Companies. According to the data (Table 2), there were 839 automated cabinet applications activated within the 11 Local Healthcare Companies of Sardinia during the month of January 2013. The number of automated cabinets actually used was very low compared to the number of automated cabinets that was activated. On average, about a quarter (24.08 %) of activated automated cabinets within the hospitals were not operative. The incidence of non-operating automated cabinets appeared

Table 2 Report—January 2013

	Activated cabinets	No. loading operations	No. unloading operations	No. cabinets that have not made loadings	No. cabinets that have not made unloadings	Incidence of cabinets operating only in loading (%)	Incidence of cabinets actually operating in loading and unloading (%)	Incidence of cabinets not operating (%)
ASL 1	122	21,000	35,011	14	31	88.52	74.59	11.48
ASL 2	62	7427	2679	10	33	83.87	46.77	16.13
ASL 3	122	14,024	9688	18	63	85.25	48.36	14.75
ASL 4	19	2201	3410	2	11	89.47	42.11	10.53
ASL 5	98	7557	1105	38	80	61.22	18.37	38.78
ASL 6	20	3450	1	8	20	60.00	0.00	40.00
ASL 7	58	8014	13,326	4	7	93.10	87.93	6.90
ASL 8	117	17,804	13,056	12	80	89.74	31.62	10.26
AO Brotzu	98	10,264	10,567	8	30	91.84	69.39	8.16
AOU Sassari	58	1947	349	52	57	10.34	1.72	89.66
AOU Cagliari	65	8028	12,072	36	37	44.62	43.08	55.38
SARDINIA	839	101,716	101,264	202	449	75.92	46.48	24.08

Source Court of auditors elaboration—Sardinia control section on Sardegna IT data

particularly critical for the Hospital University Company (AOU) of Sassari (89.66 %), for the Hospital University Company (AOU) of Cagliari (55.38 %), for the Local Healthcare Company 6 of Sanluri (40.00 %), as well as for the Local Healthcare Company 5 of Oristano (38.78 %). The situation appears to be in an overall improvement during 2013: in the month of December 2013 (Table 3), the number of automated cabinets installed was 889. The number and the incidence of automated cabinets not used decreases (from 24 to 11.4 %); on the other hand, the number of applications used not only for the loading, but also for the unloading of the ward's actual consumption increased (from 46.5 to 79.6 %).

The incidence of automated cabinets never used either for the loading or the unloading is significantly reduced in almost all of the companies, going from 202 to 101 automated cabinets (loading) and from 449 to 181 automated cabinets (unloading). In all of the Regional Healthcare Companies the impact of the automated cabinets actually operating both in the loading and in the unloading phases increases (loading: from 75.92 to 88.64 % from the Pharmacy to wards; unloading: from 46.48 to 79.64 % with respect to ward consumption/structure). During 2013, the percentage of automated cabinets operating in the loading process is equal to 95.9 %; the proportion of those operating in loading and unloading is approximately equal to 88 %. The degree of utilisation improves significantly compared to the data of the beginning of the year: the overall incidence of non-operating automated cabinets (or never used in the entire year) is equal to 4.14 %.

The described tools above allow the enjoyment of several benefits, some of which are more difficult to be assessed in terms of money, although equally relevant [26, 27]. Based on the interviews with healthcare managers and on the reports, the two main benefits have emerged as:

Table 3 Report December 2013

	No. activated cabinets	No. cabinets that have not made loadings	No. cabinets that have not made unloadings	Incidence of cabinets operating only in loading (%)	Incidence of cabinets actually operating in loading and unloading (%)	Incidence of cabinets not operating (%)
ASL 1	122	9	13	92.62	89.34	7.38
ASL 2	71	6	19	91.55	73.24	8.45
ASL 3	129	16	23	87.60	82.17	12.40
ASL 4	28	5	5	82.14	82.14	17.86
ASL 5	91	16	22	82.42	75.82	17.58
ASL 6	22	1	8	95.45	63.64	4.55
ASL 7	59	3	3	94.92	94.92	5.08
ASL 8	127	13	32	89.76	74.80	10.24
AO Brotzu	102	12	15	88.24	85.29	11.76
AOU Sassari	66	13	25	80.30	62.12	19.70
AOU Cagliari	72	7	16	90.28	77.78	9.72
SARDINIA	889	101	181	88.64	79.64	11.36

Source Court of auditors elaboration—Sardinia control section on Sardegna IT data

Table 4 Hospital pharmaceutical expenditure 2011/2013—distribution by ASL

	Year 2011	Year 2012	Deviation (2012–2011) (%)	Year 2013	Deviation (2013–2012) (%)	Deviation (2013–2011) (%)
ASL 1	11,889,857.89	8,921,293.46	-24.97	8,467,304.61	-5.09	-28.79
ASL 2	6,349,722.70	5,685,109.53	-10.47	5,811,264.54	2.22	-8.48
ASL 3	8,208,745.15	7,034,677.39	-14.30	5,571,298.26	-20.80	-32.13
ASL 4	1,393,286.07	1,296,456.57	-6.95	1,197,867.46	-7.60	-14.03
ASL 5	5,281,001.41	5,754,402.79	8.96	5,344,497.68	-7.12	1.20
ASL 6	2,326,998.07	1,627,722.57	-30.05	1,727,690.92	6.14	-25.75
ASL 7	4,576,768.80	3,982,826.14	-12.98	3,780,345.04	-5.08	-17.40
ASL 8	28,011,461.13	23,974,825.59	-14.41	25,131,798.09	4.83	-10.28
AO BROTZU	6,164,205.42	5,564,820.05	-9.72	6,228,260.69	11.92	1.04
AOU SS	6,791,787.93	3,924,145.93	-42.22	4,219,439.36	7.53	-37.87
AOU CA	6,477,192.68	6,004,080.54	-7.30	5,749,782.22	-4.24	-11.23
SARDINIA	87,471,027.24	73,770,360.56	-15.66	73,229,548.87	-0.73	-16.28

Source Regional health department

- An Increased process efficiency, as a consequence of the reduced time needed to communicate and interact with all of the actors of the logistics process.
- A greater transparency, traceability and expenditure control, as a consequence of:
- Complete information about the drugs distributed by the ward's pharmacy, the ward's consumption, stocks, expired and returns.
- The information stored in the e-distribution and consumption platform has also allowed for the improvement of budgeting and control tools.
- A reduction of medication sanitary goods distributed, consumed and in stock in hospital wards.

Thanks to the diffusion and implementation of the automated cabinet, it was possible to reduce the hospital's expenditure by about 15.66 % (Table 4).

4 Discussion, Conclusions and Limitations

This paper has presented the preliminary results of a case study about an e-solution healthcare system. To summarise, we found that the analysis of the distribution and consumption processes is preliminary to any monitoring initiative for healthcare expenditure for a possible rationalisation and reduction. The most important actors in this project are the Sardinian Region, healthcare companies and ward staff. The Sardinian Region has played an essential role in the promotion of actions favouring the installation of the necessary computerised procedures. In this perspective, the application of the automated cabinet system has been progressively installed and operationalised in the departments of the various companies.

Within the pharmaceutical department and wards, major organisational change has also been observed. In terms of human resource, it has been found that the introduction of the automated cabinet system required, on the one hand, the training and assistance of the personnel both in hospitals and in the pharmacies of the individual departments in the innovative process, on the other hand, the use of this e-distribution and consumption solution has led to a new configuration of the process and the activation of reports for the monitoring of the processes of distribution and consumption of the pharmaceutical goods.

Furthermore, the utilisation in the treatment of such computerised procedures will help to facilitate the implementation of policies to control and contain regional health expenditures. In fact, there are obvious benefits that can be insured due to the use of automated cabinet in the direction of adequate information on the distribution flows and consumption that are allowed to govern the evolution of the consumption of health goods over time. To contain and reduce the costs of health goods, it is essential to know, with precision, the actual consumption, monitor inventories and the volume of expired goods. In other words, achieve a significant degree of certainty about the fact that everything that is bought is administered to patients and not forgotten about in some warehouse until the inevitable deadline.

This research represents a first attempt to explore the latest innovation in favor of healthcare rationalization and optimization. Literature and practice show many important experiences that can offer interesting ideas to be explored in order to improve an area as fundamental as health. It is therefore desirable that future research will address more and more attention to this important issue, focusing on the various possibilities offered by the Information and Communication Technology in favor of patient quality care.

Acknowledgement Fabiana Marras gratefully acknowledges Sardinia Regional Government for the financial support of her PhD scholarship (P.O.R. Sardegna F.S.E. Operational Programme of the Autonomous Region of Sardinia, European Social Fund 2007–2013—Axis IV Human Resources, Objective 1.3, Line of Activity 1.3.1).

References

1. Ivan Su, S.I., Gammelgaard, B., Yang, S.L.: Logistics innovation process revisited: insights from a hospital case study. Int. J. Phys. Distrib. Logistics Manag. **41**(6), 577–600 (2011)
2. Lee, S.M., Lee, D., Schniederjans, M.J.: Supply chain innovation and organizational performance in the healthcare industry. Int. J. Oper. Prod. Manag. **31**(11), 1193–1214 (2011)
3. Chunning, Z., Kumar, A.: JIT application: process-oriented supply chain management in a health care system. In: Proceedings of the 2000 IEEE International Conference, vol. 2, pp. 788–791 (2000)
4. Cagliano, A.C., Carcangiu, C.E., Pilloni, T., Rafele, C.: Supply chain Ospedaliere: Esperienze a Confronto. In: Proceedings XXXVI Convengo Nazionale Ingegneria e Impiantistica Italiana, 11–12 June 2009, Roma, Italia (2009)
5. Bensa, G., Giusepi, I., Villa, S.: Riprogettare la logistica nelle aziende sanitarie: esperienze a confronto. In: Anessi Pessina E., Cantù, E. (eds) L'aziendalizzazione della sanità in Italia, Egea, Milano, vol. 36(2), pp. 331–366 (2009)
6. Colletti, J.J.: Health care reform and the hospital supply chain. Hosp. Mater. Manag. Q. **15**(3), 28–35 (1994)
7. Dameri, R.P., Benevolo, C., Rossignoli, C., Ricciardi, F., De Marco, M.: Centralization vs. decentralization of purchasing in the public sector: the role of e-procurement in the Italian case. In: Contemporary Research on E-Business Technology and Strategy. International Conference on iCETS 2012. Tianjin, China, August 2012. Revised Selected Papers, pp. 457–470. Springer
8. Cavallari, M.: Human-computer interaction and systems security: an organisational appraisal. In: Interdisciplinary Aspects of Information Systems Studies: The Italian Association for Information Systems, pp. 261–267
9. Ross, A.D., Jayaraman, V.: Strategic purchases of bundled products in a healthcare supply chain environment. Decis. Sci. **40**(2), 269–293 (2009)
10. Kazemzadeh, R.B., Sepehri, M.M., Jahantigh, F.F.: Design and analysis of a health supply chain environment. Decis. Sci. **40**(2), 269–293 (2012)
11. Smith, B.K., Nachtmann, H., Pohl, E.A.: Improving healthcare supply chain processes via data standardization. Eng. Manag. J. **24**(1) (2012)
12. Pinna, R., Carrus, P.P., Marras, F.: The drug logistics process: an innovative experience. TQM J. **27**(2), 214–230 (2015)
13. Chikumba, P.A.: Application of geographic information system (GIS) in drug logistics management information system (LMIS) at district level in Malawi: opportunities and

challenges. In: Villafiorita, A., Saint-Paul, R., Zorer, R. (eds.) E-Infrastructures and E-Services on Developing Countries, pp. 105–115. Springer, BerlinHeidelberg (2010)

14. Carr, A.S., Pearson, J.N.: Strategically managed buyer–supplier relationships and performance outcomes. J. Oper. Manag. **17**(5), 497–519 (1999)
15. Kotabe, M., Martin, X., Domoto, H.: Gaining from vertical partnerships: knowledge transfer, relationship duration, and supplier performance improvement in the US and Japanese automotive industries. Strateg. Manag. J. **24**(4), 293–316 (2003)
16. Prahinski, C., Benton, W.C.: Supplier evaluations: communication strategies to improve supplier performance. J. Oper. Manag. **22**(1), 39–62 (2004)
17. Giunipero, L., Handfield, R.B., Eltantawy, R.: Supply management's evolution: key skill sets for the supply manager of the future. Int. J. Oper. Prod. Manag. **26**(7), 822–844 (2006)
18. Ricciardi, F., De Marco, M.: The challenge of service oriented performances for chief information officers. In: Snene, M. (ed.), Exploring Service science. Proceedings of Third International Conference, IESS 2012. Geneva, Switzerland, February 2012. LNBIP, vol. 103, pp. 258–270. Springer (2012)
19. Bonomi, S., Zardini, A., Rossignoli, C., Dameri R.P. et al.: E-health and value co-creation: the case of electronic medical record in an Italian academic integrated hospital. In: Exploring Services Science. Springer International Publishing, pp. 166–175 (2015)
20. Pinna, R., Carrus, P.P., Pettinao, D.: Supply chain Coordination and IT: the role of third party logistics providers. In: D'Atri, A., De Marco, M., Braccini, A.M., Cabiddu, F., (eds.) Management of the Interconnected World, pp. 299–306. Springer (2010)
21. Dulskaia, I., Menshikova, M.: New service development: best practice of the Italian postal sector. MCIS 2014. In: Proceedings, AIS Electronic Library (AISeL). Online: http://aisel. aisnet.org/cgi/viewcontent.cgi?article=1008&context=mcis2014 (2014)
22. Roy, S., Sivakumar, K., Wilkinson, L.F.: Innovation generation in supply chain relationships: a conceptual model and research propositions. J. Acad. Mark. Sci. **32**(1), 61–79 (2004)
23. Casalino, N., Buonocore, F., Rossignoli, C., Ricciardi, F.: Transparency, openness and knowledge sharing for rebuilding and strengthening government institutions. In: Klement, E.P., Borutzky, W. (eds.) Proceedings of Web-based Education—WBE 2013 conference
24. Yin., R.: Case Study Research: Design and Methods. Sage, Markus, Thousand Oaks (2014)
25. Rogers, M.: The Definition and Measurement of Innovation. Melbourne Institute of Applied Economic and Social Research, Parkville (1998)
26. Dameri, R.P. Defining an evaluation framework for digital cities implementation. In: International Conference on Information Society (i-Society), pp. 466–470. IEEE (2012)
27. Fahringer, T., Hamza, M.H., Uskov, V. (eds.), IASTED-ACTA Press Zurich, pp. 11–13 febbraio, Innsbruck, Austria

Smart City and ICT. Shaping Urban Space for Better Quality of Life

Renata Paola Dameri

Abstract Smart City is a recent topic, but it is spreading very fast, as it is perceived as a winning strategy to cope with some severe urban problems such as traffic, pollution, energy consumption, waste treatment. Smart city ideas are the merge of some other more ancient urban policies such as digital city, green city, knowledge city. A smart city is therefore a complex, long-term vision of a better urban area, aiming at reducing its environmental footprint and at creating better quality of life for citizens. Mobility is one of the most difficult topic to face in metropolitan large areas. It involves both environmental and economic aspects, and needs both high technologies and virtuous people behaviours. Smart mobility is largely permeated by ICT, used in both backward and forward applications, to support the optimization of traffic fluxes, but also to collect citizens' opinions about likeability in cities or quality of local public transport services. The aim of this paper is to analyse the Smart Mobility initiatives as part of a larger smart city initiative portfolio, and to investigate about the role of ICT in supporting smart mobility actions, influencing their impact on the citizens' quality of life and on the public value created for the city as a whole.

Keywords Smart city · Digital city · Quality of life · Smart city performance

1 Smart City: A Strategy for Better Quality of Life in Urban Areas

Smart city is a topic that increased its importance all over the world during the latest ten years [1]. The main reasons are to be found in the urbanization interesting all the countries and continents, and the continuous increasing of the number of people living in urban areas. The urban population in 2014 accounted for 54 % of the total global population, up from 34 % in 1960, and continues to grow. It is estimated that

R.P. Dameri (✉)
Department of Economics and Business Studies, University of Genova, Genoa, Italy
e-mail: dameri@economia.unige.it

© Springer International Publishing Switzerland 2016
F. Ricciardi and A. Harfouche (eds.), *Information and Communication Technologies in Organizations and Society*, Lecture Notes in Information Systems and Organisation 15, DOI 10.1007/978-3-319-28907-6_6

by 2017, even in less developed countries, a majority of people will be living in urban areas (Global Health Observatory). Projections show that urbanization combined with the overall growth of the world's population could add another 2.5 billion people to urban populations by 2050, with close to 90 % of the increase concentrated in Asia and Africa (UN World Urbanization prospects).

Managing urban areas has become one of the most important development challenges of the 21st century. Success or failure in building sustainable cities will be a major factor in the well being of people all over the world. If well managed, cities offer important opportunities for economic development and for expanding access to basic services, including health care and education, for large numbers of people. Providing public transportation, as well as housing, electricity, water and sanitation for a densely settled urban population is a need to be accomplished, but taking concurrently into account the impact of human activities on the environment [2].

Figure 1 shows the present distribution of people living in cities and the larger cities in the five continents.

Cities are therefore places where economic development and cultural richness, but also traffic, congestion, difficulty to access to public services and pollution coexist, impacting both positively and negatively on the quality daily life of citizens.

Smart city is considered as a crucial urban strategy to face these problems, preventing pollution and congestion and supporting innovation, economic development and inclusion in the meantime [3]. Even if till now a shared and consolidated definition of smart city doesn't exist, we can describe a smart city using its components, which are: urban area, environment, technology, and people. Indeed, a

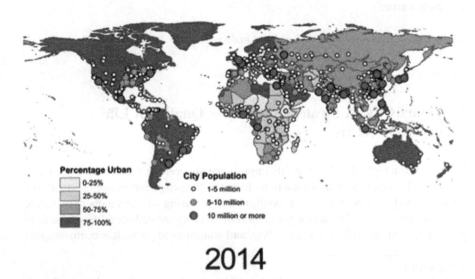

Fig. 1 % People living in cities and the larger cities in the five continents

smart city is a city that uses innovative technologies and especially ICT to prevent and reduce pollution, preserving the environment, and to enhance the quality of life of all its citizens, aiming at economic development and social inclusion. City is the subject, high technologies are the instruments and people and the environment are the addressers of strategy acting with a very large scope, including mobility, urban infrastructure, social policies, culture, economic development and so on [4].

Even if the roots of smart city are faraway in the time, only from 2010 the topic had a boom [5]. We can find the reason of this explosion of interest in several causes, such as: the increasing urbanization, the diffusion of smart phones and other smart devices that support a wired city, the EU funding for research and pilot projects aiming at using the most innovative technologies to reduce the urban footprint on the environment and the CO_2 gases emission.

This high interest regards both the theoretical studies and the real implementation of smart cities all over the world. A survey about scientific papers indexed on Scopus shows that:

- papers with the words "smart city/ies" in the title in 2014 accounted for 280, up from 1 in 1994 when we found the first paper about this topic, but also up from 15 in 2010: it means that the number about this topic has been increasing of 18 times in only five years;
- papers with the words "smart city/ies" in the abstract in 2014 accounted for 464, up from 33 in 2010.

The survey shows also that papers about smart cities are published in academic and scientific journals of all the human field of knowledge [6]: Life sciences, Health sciences, Physical sciences, Social sciences (as classified by Scopus); it is because smart city is a cross topic regarding not only one subject, but almost all the aspects of the human life.

Also the number of implemented smart cities is continuously increasing. Even if we haven't a complete survey about the smart cities all over the world, we can find some figures supporting this fact. For example, the ICF—Intelligent Community Forum names each year the Intelligent Community of the Year, selected amongst 21 nominated cities or metropolitan areas. The ICF nomination is awarded to communities or regions with a documented strategy for creating a local prosperity and inclusion using broadband and information technology to attract leading-edge businesses, stimulate job creation, build skills, generate economic growth, and improve the delivery of government services. The ICF web site lists all the cities nominated from 2006 till now. Figure 2 shows the world map with these cities: it clearly appears that are spread all over the world, with a higher density in Europe, North America and Far East.

The EU Parliament has recently published a detailed report studying the smart city phenomenon in Europe [7]. The researchers examined all the 468 EU cities with population over 100,000 inhabitants within the EU28. Applying the EU definition of the smart city, they found 240 smart cities, that is, 51 % of the sample. It means that more than half cities in Europe are somewhat smart. Even if the report outlines that often these cities are simply implementing one or more smart

Fig. 2 Awarded intelligent cities. *Source* ICF

initiatives, lacking of a veritable strategic plan for becoming smart in all the aspects of the urban life, this percentage reveals that smart cities are a pervasive trend regarding all Europe. EU funding are certainly strongly supporting the implementation of smart initiatives, especially during the economic crisis that prevent local bodies to invest high amount of money in smart projects from their poor budgets. But the EU support has not only a financial role: supporting smart initiatives, EU Commission is also spreading all over the European countries, regions and cities the awareness of better metropolitan areas, based on the three pillars of inclusion, economic development and environment preservation.

Even if the technology is the core component of a smart city, a strategic vision of the city of future including environment preservation, social inclusion, citizens' democratic participation is the critical success factor for improving the quality of life in ever larger and complex cities [8]. Smart cities are therefore not only a technological project, but also a cultural program for livable cities all over the world.

2 Smart City and Digital City: Two Faces of the Same Coin

As already said, even if smart cities are spreading all over the world, a shared smart city definition has not been written till now [9]. However, it is possible to look at the most cited scientific paper about smart city to investigate about this concept and its constitutive components. This survey permits also to investigate about the role

Table 1 Most cited smart city definitions

Smart city definition	Author	Year
A city that monitors and integrates conditions of all of its critical infrastructures, including roads, bridges, tunnels, rails, subways, airports, seaports, communications, water, power, even major buildings, can better optimize its resources, plan its preventive maintenance activities, and monitor security aspects while maximizing services to its citizens	Hall	2000
A city to be smart when investments in human and social capital and traditional (transport) and modern (ICT) communication infrastructure fuel sustainable economic growth and a high quality of life, with a wise management of natural resources, through participatory governance	Caragliu	2009
Smart City is a city in which it can combine technologies as diverse as water recycling, advanced energy grids and mobile communications in order to reduce environmental impact and to offer its citizens better lives	EU-SETIS	2012
A smart city is a well-defined geographical area, in which high technologies such as ICT, logistic, energy production, and so on, cooperate to create benefits for citizens in terms of well-being, inclusion and participation, environmental quality, intelligent development; it is governed by a well-defined pool of subjects, able to state the rules and policy for the city government and development	Dameri	2013

and influence of ICT in building a smarter city. Table 1 shows the most cited smart city definitions used by the author to build a present vision of the smart city concept.

As previously noted, smart city is a recent topic with ancient roots. In 2000 Hall [10] studied the smart city especially focusing on two aspects: city infrastructures and services for citizens. In this work by Hall, the city is seen like a body that should monitor all the physical and environmental resources to improve and preserve them, aiming at satisfying the citizens supplying them the best services, both in quality and in quantity. At that time, Hall already settled the basis of the smart city phenomenon: a crossing of material conditions and citizenship. Differently think other cited authors, such as Hollands [11] focusing more on cultural aspects of a smart city such as entrepreneurship, innovation and intelligence; or Bowerman et al. [12] focusing on the green aspect of a smart city, careful towards the environment and its preservation.

In 2009 Caragliu et al. [4] wrote a very interesting paper analysing smart cities in Europe. Their aim was not to individuate all the smart cities, nor to rank them, but to understand their roots and their characteristics. Also in this work the authors focus on the two core components of a smart city, infrastructures and people. But in this definition several aspects are clearer and better defined. Infrastructures explicitly refer to both traditional, physical artefacts and innovative technology, and the authors recalls ICT like one of the fundamental components of a smart city. People are not simply citizens, but their knowledge potential, that if well managed could create a veritable human and social capital. Smart city aims are multidimensional and include economic development, social inclusion, environment preservation and democratic government. Similarly think also other most cited authors: Nam and Pardo [13] outline the crucial components of a smart city, that are technology, people and institutions; also Giffinger et al. [14] describe a smart city like the interrelationship between multidimensional factors such as economy, people, mobility, government; Paskaleva [15] links the smart city effectiveness to the progress of e-government best practices; Chourabi et al. [16] evidence that the smart city is the synergy between various disciplinary areas and identify eight critical factors of smart city initiatives: management and organization, technology, governance, policy context, people and communities, economy, built infrastructure, and natural environment; Lombardo et al. [17] offer a profound analysis of the interrelations between smart city components connecting the cornerstones of the triple helix, involving firms, public administration and universities or research bodies.

Along with the deep and extensive academic research about the topic, also several international political institutions have been studying this phenomenon. Especially the EU Commission concentrates its funding on the smart city program: EU sees a smart city like an instrument to reduce the environment footprint of large industrialised cities in Europe, through very specific initiatives regarding green mobility, building efficiency, renewable energy sources and low emission cooling and heating. In supporting this vision of a smart city, EU Commission has also contributed to shape a different idea of a smart city, most focused on technology than on people.

However, a smart city is something more than a sum of innovative technologies: it is a large urban strategy interesting a well defined territory, all the infrastructures lying on this territory, citizens and the government and governance of all the city components [18]. A strong strategic vision should support a long term smart program, aiming not only at preserving the environment or at increasing technological innovation, but concretely aiming at improving the citizens' quality of daily life.

In this comprehensive vision of a smarter city, ICT plays a central role. Not only the smart city has its root in the digital city, but also the digital city has becoming the core part of the smart city; ICT is somewhat innerving a smart city in all its aspects. Table 2 shows the most cited definitions of Digital city.

Three are the aspects to be considered.

For the first, several aspects of the Digital city are the same in the Smart city: the territory to be linked, the role of people and government, the aim to improve the quality of life offering public and private services to citizens, as it emerges from the definitions listed in Table 2 [19–23]. Second, the number of studies regarding the digital city has not being increasing from 2010, as it appears absorbed in the smart city field of studies [5]. Third, a deep analysis of most cited papers about smart city reveals that the ICT component is often at the centre of smart projects or of the comprehensive smart strategy for the urban area. For example, Nam and Pardo [13] referring to technology implicitly recalls ICT; Karnouskos and De Hollanda [24] focus their idea of smart city on software components; Su et al. [25] refer to a smart city based on the digital city; Schaffers et al. [26] link the smart city success to the Internet; and the list could continue.

Table 2 Most cited digital city definitions

Digital city definition	Author	Year
A digital city is substantively an open, complex and adaptive system based on computer network and urban information resources, which forms a virtual digital space for a city. It creates an information service marketplace and information resource deployment center	Oi and Shaofu	2001
The concept of Digital City is to build an arena in which people in regional communities can interact and share knowledge, experiences, and mutual interests. Digital City integrates urban information (both achievable and real time) and create public spaces in the Internet for people living/visiting the city	Ishida	2002
A Digital City has at least two plausible meanings: (1) a city that is being transformed or re-oriented through digital technology and (2) a digital representation or reflection of some aspects of an actual or imagined city	Schuler	2007
Digital city denotes an area that combines broadband communication infrastructure with flexible, service-oriented computing systems. These new digital infrastructures seek to ensure better services for citizens, consumers and business in a specific area	Komninos	2008

Therefore, a smart city is strongly based on ICT and the aim to improve the citizens' quality of life is mainly pursued by using ICT in all the multidimensional aspects of a smarter city.

Figure 3 explains how ICT is not a separated dimension of a smart city, but a pervasive element of all the smart city dimensions, regarding transport and mobility, energy, buildings. New research questions therefore emerge from this framework: how and how much ICT contributes to improve the citizens' quality of life in smart city programs? How is it possible to assess and measure this contribution?

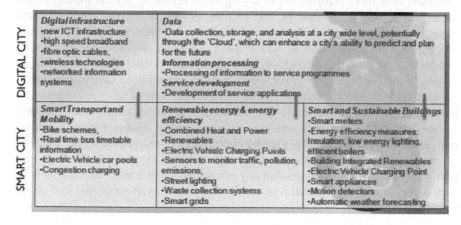

Fig. 3 Digital city pervades smart city

ICT impact evaluation and measurement of ICT contribution in smart projects are central not only to understand the relationship between smart aims and digital components, but also to support political and business decisions in choosing, prioritizing and better planning smart initiatives [27].

3 Evaluating ICT Role and Impact in Smart City Initiatives

Given the pivotal role of ICT in realizing smart city projects and initiatives, a deeper analysis should understand how and how much ICT contributes in differently shaping citizens' daily life in cities, improving their well being. These arguments need to be studied separately. Indeed, one thing is to speak about the role of ICT in defining a smarter city, and how and how much ICT is the leading technology in smart projects rather then the pervasive and supporting technology in projects regarding different aspects of a smart city: such as a smart mobility program using ICT to govern public transport networks, or a smart energy projects using ICT to govern energy smart grid.

Another thing is to speak about how and how much ICT plays its role in generating public and private instruments, artefacts or services able to change the daily life of people living in cities, generating benefits and finally a higher well being.

3.1 Understanding and Assessing the ICT Role and Pervasiveness in Smart City Initiatives

The most of authors studying smart city agree in involving several aspects of the urban life in this large topic [4, 13, 14]. Smart city is a cross urban strategy, regarding both physical components of a city and human and political aspects [15, 16, 28]. Till now, almost all the European smart cities have been implementing their own smart initiatives without a comprehensive strategic plan, but simply putting in their agenda some projects with a smart content especially responding to EU requirements and obtaining EU funding. Also solutions vendors and consultants have been supporting the smart city wave, driving urban innovation especially focused on some topics such and e-government, public administration digitalization, green energy. The result is a strong bottom-up movement producing a plethora of projects often incoherent each other and collected in non-formalised project portfolio. The analysis of these smart city portfolios, when realised and available, is very useful to understand what a smart city includes into its scope and how many projects are pervaded by ICT.

Fig. 4 Smart and digital
projects taxonomy

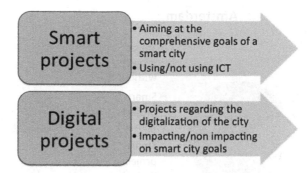

To analyse smart city portfolios, a framework has been defined; it supports the analysis aiming at discovering the role and weight of ICT in smart city. Figure 4 explains the criteria adopted for this survey.

All the projects have been classified as:

- smart projects, when aim that at some typical smart goals such as reducing greenhouse gases, improving building energy efficiency, improving the use of renewal energy sources; smart projects are further classified in using or not using ICT: for example, a solar energy smart grid can use ICT to govern the best energy production and delivery, planning a new park in the city centre positively impact on the environment without using ICT;
- digital projects, aiming at the digitalization of the city; digital projects are further classified in projects impacting or not impacting on smart goals: for example, an app on smart phone informing trucks about the traffic around the city centre impacts on smart goals, the digitalizazion of internal processes of the Municipality doesn't impact on the smart goals of the city.

This framework has been applied on the smart city project portfolio on two amongst the most relevant smart cities in Europe: Amsterdam and Genova. Amsterdam is universally recognised as the first smart and digital city in the world. Genova is the city winning the highest number of EU calls about smart city programs.

In Fig. 5 we can see the results of our portfolio analysis.

It emerges that ICT is an important technology embedded in smart projects or at the core of smart projects, but also that cities are implementing smart projects based on other technologies or without technology at all, only based on changing the behaviour of people [29] or acting on the environmental aspects of the city [30].

The same facts emerge also from the analysis of the international ranking, evaluating the smartness of a city in an international benchmark, applying several smart indicators counting the city equipment in terms of smart artefacts or intangible resources. Three are the main ranking to be considered:

1. the Giffinger ranking of European medium cities [14];
2. the Smart City Wheel [31];
3. The EU Parliament survey on smart cities in EU28 [7].

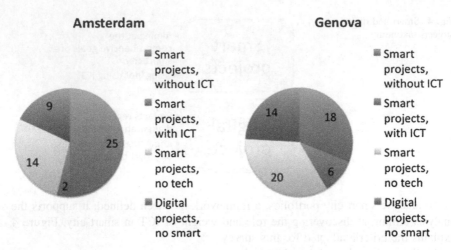

Fig. 5 The portfolio composition of Smart city Amsterdam and Smart city Genova

Each of these rankings considers a different set of indicators; therefore the obtained results are relative, as they depend on the selected indicators, but also the affordability of collected data or their updating. But it is interesting to outline that ICT indicators count only for a partial part of the ranking. For example, Fig. 6 shows the Smart City Wheel model. The red circles evidence the indicators measuring digital equipments in a smart city. It is evident that they are only a small part about all the measured aspects.

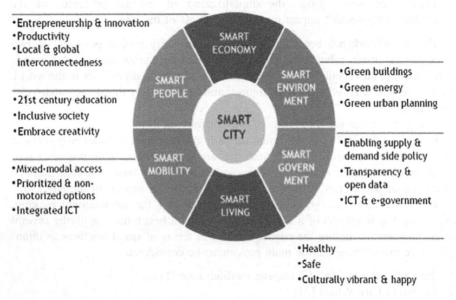

Fig. 6 The smart city wheel model

Therefore we can conclude that:

- the role of ICT in smart cities is important, but not exclusive;
- ICT is assessed both for itself and as a technology supporting smart aspects such as mobility, government and so on;
- ICT weight in smart city depends on the ranking system selected,;
- ICT role in a smart city implementation depend on specific choices of each city and its strategic vision about which type of smart city it wants to implement: digital, green, cultural, or a mix of all of them, and which mix exactly.

3.2 Evaluating the ICT Role and Weight in Improving the Citizens' Quality of Life in Smart Cities

The final aim of a smart city strategy is to pursue the citizens well being and to improve their quality of daily life. But what is well being? And is it possible to measure it?

Several models have been studied to measure people well-being all over the world. A lot of them are specific of one country or geographical area and are therefore not suitable to measure the quality of life in smart city in different countries.

In 2014 OECD designed a framework called Better Life Index, aiming at measuring the citizens' well-being in all OECD countries. This model considers both material and immaterial life conditions, both short term horizon and the future long term horizon of time.

This model could be used to find cause-effect relationships between smart city projects—and also their ICT content—and the impact they exercise on the material and immaterial life conditions. For example, an app informing users of waiting time for a train could improve the quality of life, saving time not wasted in wait but used for doing somewhat else (also having a coffee). The value is then influenced by some dimensions such as:

- readiness of the city, depending on the infrastructure supporting the service and the areas in which the service is available;
- intensity, that is, the number of users capable to access at the service (for example the number of users having a smart phone);
- impact, that is, how much the service is able to influence the daily life of the citizens.

This evaluation is very useful especially a priori. Indeed, when choosing if or what project to implement in a complex smart city program, to be able to estimate the public value it creates is crucial to choice the best projects for the citizens, and not the most innovative but not really impacting on people daily life. For example, to implement bike sharing could be a smart ideas if available bikes are numerous (readiness), people in city are especially students and tourists (intensity of use) and the city is flat, permitting an easy use of bikes for going to work or school (impact on the daily life).

4 Conclusions

Smart city and digital city are not the same thing, even if smart city has its roots in digital city and digital city is finally a core component of a smart city. However, to simply consider ICT an essential facility of smart strategies is not enough for understanding the role and weight of ICT in shaping a better life for citizens in urban areas. On the contrary, the real capacity of ICT to produce public value when implemented in a large smart initiative depends on a well conceived strategic plan connecting the ICT implementation with a smart vision that links each project with the citizens' well being.

To estimate the awaited value from ICT-based smart projects, it is necessary to take into consideration the city readiness, the intensity of IT use by citizens, and the impact of ICT on citizens' daily life. Without this a priori evaluation, it may be impossible to implement smart projects that will really produce better quality of life in urban spaces, as smart city strategies are expected to.

References

1. Cocchia, A.: Smart and digital city: a systematic literature review. In: Dameri, R.P., Rosenthal-Sabroux, C. (eds.) Smart City. How to Create Public and Economic Value with High Technology in Urban Space, pp. 13–43. Springer, Berlin (2014)
2. OECD.: Green Cities Programme (2010). Retrieved from http://www.oecd.org/gov/regional-policy/49318965.pdf
3. Dameri, R.P.: Comparing smart and digital city: initiatives and strategies in Amsterdam and Genoa. Are they digital and/or smart? In: Dameri, R.P., Rosenthal-Sabroux, C. (eds.) Smart City. How to Create Public and Economic Value with High Technology in Urban Space, pp. 45–88. Springer, Heidelberg (2014)
4. Caragliu, A., de Bo, C., Nijkamp, P.: Smart cities in Europe. J. Urban Technol. 18(2), 65–82 (2011)
5. Dameri, R.P., Cocchia, A.: Smart city and digital city: twenty years of terminology evolution. In: ItAIS 2013, X Conference of the Italian Chapter of AIS
6. Ricciardi, F., Za, S.: Smart city research as an interdisciplinary crossroads: a challenge for management and organization studies. In: Mola, L., Pennarola, F. (eds.) From information to smart society: environment, politics and economics. Lecture Notes in Information Systems and Organisation, vol. 5, pp. 163–171. Springer, Berlin (2014)
7. European Parliament.: Mapping smart city in the EU, (2014). Brussels. Retrieved from http://www.europarl.europa.eu/thinktank/en/document.html?reference=IPOL-ITRE_ET%282014%29507480

8. Ricciardi, F., Rossignoli, C., De Marco, M.: Participatory networks for place safety and livability: organisational success factors. Int. J. Networking Virtual Organ. **13**(1), 42–65 (2013)
9. Neirotti, P., De Marco, A., Cagliano, A.C., Mangano, G., Scorrano, F.: Current trends in smart city initiatives: some stylised facts. Cities **38**, 25–36 (2014)
10. Hall, P.: Creative cities and economic development. Urban Studies **37**(4), 633–649 (2000)
11. Hollands, R.G.: Will the real smart city please stand up? Intelligent, progressive or entrepreneurial? City **12**(3), 303–320 (2008)
12. Bowerman, B., Braverman, J., Taylor, J., Todosow, H., Von Wimmersperg, U.: The vision of a smart city. In: 2nd International Life Extension Technology Workshop, Paris, Sept 2000
13. Nam, T., Pardo T.A.: Smart city as urban innovation: focusing on management, policy, and context. In: Proceedings of the 5th International Conference on Theory and Practice of Electronic Governance. ACM (2011)
14. Giffinger, R., Fertner, C., Kramar, H., Kalasek, R., Pichler-Milanović, N., Meijers, E.: Smart cities: ranking of European medium-sized cities. Centre of Regional Science (SRF), Vienna University of Technology (2007)
15. Paskaleva, K.A.: Enabling the smart city: the progress of city e-governance in Europe. Int. J. Innovation Reg. Dev. **1**(4), 405–422 (2009)
16. Chourabi, H., Nam, T., Walker, S., Gil-Garcia, J. R., Mellouli, S., Nahon, K., ... Scholl, H.J.: Understanding smart cities: an integrative framework. In: 2012 45th Hawaii International Conference on System Science (HICSS), pp. 2289–2297. IEEE, Jan 2012
17. Lombardi, P., Giordano, S., Farouh, H., Yousef, W.: Modelling the smart city performance. Innovation Eur. J. Social Sci. Res. **25**(2), 137–149 (2012)
18. Dameri, R.P.: Defining an evaluation framework for digital cities implementation. In: 2012 International Conference on Information Society (i-Society), pp. 466–470. IEEE (2012)
19. Qi, L., Shaofu, L.: Research on digital city framework architecture. In: IEEE International Conferences on Info-Tech and Info-Net, vol. 1, pp. 30–36
20. Ishida, T.: Digital city of Kyoto. Magazine Commun. ACM **45**(7), 76–81 (2002)
21. Schuler, D.: Digital cities and digital citizens. In: Tanabe, M., van den Besselaar, P., Ishida, T. (eds.) Digital Cities II: Computational and Sociological Approaches, pp. 71–85. Springer, Heidelberg (2002)
22. Komninos, N.: Intelligent Cities and Globalization of Innovation Networks. Routledge, London (2008)
23. Ricciardi, F., De Marco, M.: The challenge of service oriented performances for chief information officers. In: Exploring Service Science. Third International Conference, IESS 2012. Geneva, Switzerland, pp. 258–270. Springer, Berlin, Feb 2012
24. Karnouskos, S., De Holanda, T.N.: Simulation of a smart grid city with software agents. In: Third UK Sim European Symposium on Computer Modeling and Simulation, 2009, EMS'09, pp. 424–429. IEEE, Nov 2009
25. Su, K., Li, J., Fu, H.: Smart city and the applications. In: 2011 International Conference on Electronics, Communications and Control (ICECC), pp. 1028–1031. IEEE, Sept 2011
26. Schaffers, H., Komninos, N., Pallot, M., Trousse, B., Nilsson, M., Oliveira, A.: Smart cities and the future internet: towards cooperation frameworks for open innovation. In: Domingue, J. et al. (eds.) Future Internet Assembly, pp. 431–446. LNCS 6656 (2011)
27. Ferro, E., Sorrentino, M.: Can intermunicipal collaboration help the diffusion of e-government in peripheral areas? Evidence from Italy. Government Inf. Q. **27**(1), 17–25 (2010)
28. Dulskaia, I., Menshikova, M.: New service development: best practice of the Itaian postal sector. In: MCIS 2014 Proceedings, AIS Electronic Library (AISeL) (2014). Online: http://aisel.aisnet.org/cgi/viewcontent.cgi?article=1008&context=mcis2014
29. Uskov, V., Casalino, N.: New means of organizational governance to reduce the effects of european economic crisis and improve the competitiveness of SMEs. Law Econ. Yearly Rev. J., Queen Mary University, London, UK, **1**(1), 149–179

30. Za, S., Marzo, F., Marco, M.D., Cavallari, M.: Agent based simulation of trust dynamics in dependence networks, Lecture Notes in Business Information Processing, 201, pp. 243–252 (2015)
31. Hodgkinson, S.: Is your city smart enough? Digitally enabled cities and societies will enhance economic, social, and environmental sustainability in the urban century (2011)

Part II
ICT, Innovation and Organizational Change

Part II

A Framework of Mechanisms for Integrating Emerging Technology Innovations in IT Services Companies

Nabil Georges Badr

Abstract This paper focuses on a systemic issue in IT organizations of companies in the sector of IT services. These organizations are often asked to be both the IT providers for the internal customers (i.e. employees) and the solutions and service providers for the firm's external clients. In order to innovate their business models, these companies often rely on emerging technologies in IT (EIT). The disruption introduced by EIT affects the stability of IT services and the ability of IT organizations to sustain continuity of services required by the business. Therefore, IT organizations are reluctant to act quickly to integrate EIT. Through in-depth case studies in IT services companies, field interviews and focus group discussions, the study brings forth mechanisms that may serve as guidance to develop organizational capabilities for IT-based business model innovation projects.

Keywords IT organizational capability · IT innovation capability · IT governance · IT strategy · Emerging technology integration

1 Introduction

Innovations based on IT depend greatly on the combination of the technology, the organization's technical expertise, and the organization's ability to make effective use of the new capabilities [1]. IT organizations must be able to identify the applications required to support the business strategy and search for innovative uses of technology to transform the business model [2–6]. Challenges of disruption,

N.G. Badr (✉)
Lebanese Association of Information Systems, Beirut, Lebanon
e-mail: nabil@itvaluepartner.com

© Springer International Publishing Switzerland 2016
F. Ricciardi and A. Harfouche (eds.), *Information and Communication Technologies in Organizations and Society*, Lecture Notes in Information Systems and Organisation 15, DOI 10.1007/978-3-319-28907-6_7

101

displacing existing technologies [7] raise an uncertainty and emphasize the ensuing operational risks on IT services.[1]

The resistance to take risks in a fast decision making environment [8] impacts the firm's ability to implement technological innovation [9]. The speed in adopting new technologies is compounded by the rapid change in emerging technologies in IT (EIT) which hinders the capabilities of IT organizations [10]. Chief Information Officers (CIO) are challenged to maintain the necessary balance between technology innovation effectiveness and operational effectiveness [11]. Hence, in the practitioner circles, IT organizations are perceived as *a hindrance* rather than *an enabler* to innovation.[2] This study examines practices used in removing barriers to integration of emerging technologies. The observations and learning from this study are expected to provide guidance for IT organizations in the integration of EIT. A framework of mechanisms for integrating emerging technologies innovations in IT services companies is proposed.

2 Theoretical Background

2.1 Capabilities of IT Organizations

Generally, IS research on resource-based view (RBV) delineates resources as physical capital (e.g. *property*, *plant*, etc.), human capital (e.g. *people*, *experience*, *relationships*, etc.), and organizational capital (e.g. *organizational structure and processes*, etc.) [12]. Competencies are built by combining such resources [13] leading to the ability "*to conceive, implement, and exploit valuable IT applications*" [14, p. 491]). In a dynamic environment, organizational capabilities encompass a set of interrelated operational and administrative routines that evolve based on feedback from organizational performance [15, 16]. These dynamic capabilities [17] yield adjustments to the strategy and resources in order to sustain competitive advantage [18]. Recent empirical studies [19, 20] showed that firms or business units with stronger exploration and exploitation capabilities outperform others. Though both capabilities could be conceived as theories for learning [20], *exploration* capabilities are aimed at discovering new possibilities for innovation while capabilities of *exploitation* are intended to invest old knowledge [21] to realize operational effectiveness.

---

[1]The top 10 risks and opportunities in the light of the current economic environment Ernst and Young|EYG no. AU1132.
[2]Global Innovation Survey, Cap Gemini Consulting, December 2010.

2.2 Consequences of Technology Adoption, Diffusion and Integration

Research on innovation supports innovative characteristics of EIT [22–25] and the associated disruption introduced into the IS operation [26, 27]. The competence of IT leadership and organization is challenged [28]. Research has found that concerns of technical compatibility, technical complexity, and relative advantage (perceived need) are important antecedents to the adoption of innovations [29]. In more recent publications, data privacy was a major concern for Bradford and Florin [30] in their study of accounting software implementation. Some theories support practices adapted to particular adoption contexts such as propagating institutions that may have an effect on lowering the knowledge barriers of adoption [31].

In an advanced stage of the adoption process, diffusion theory deals with how an innovation is assimilated [32]. Academics have thoroughly studied diffusion theories [33]. They identified organizational factors affecting innovation diffusion [34] and disruption impacts on organizations [35], processes [36], and projects [37].

Shin and Edington [38] presented a comprehensive framework for contextual factors affecting IT implementation: those spanned project and resources related factors, end user participation, organizational structure and commitment, IT and CIO competency, and complementary investments.

Taylor and Helfat [39] focused on organizational issues related to changes in the transition in their core technologies. Benamati and Lederer [40] discussed mechanisms for organizations to cope with the ensuing change. Mechanisms that foster an innovative culture in organizations were found likely to facilitate the introduction, adoption and diffusion of innovations with a resulting effect on firm performance [41].

At the strategic level, Luftman et al. [42] and practitioners agree that IT reliability and efficiency as a top management concern. The continuous need for IT assessment and introduction practices [43], due to the uncertainty in the technology, changes the implementation strategy roadmaps [44]. Lu and Ramamurthy [45] suggest that firms that aim to cope with rapid and uncertain changes in order to thrive in a competitive environment need to "*develop superior firm-wide IT capability to successfully manage and leverage their IT resources*" [45, p. 931].

2.3 Research Question

The review of the MIS literature evidenced that IS research has neglected to relate potential implications in form of organizational willingness to implement risky IT innovations (Fig. 1).

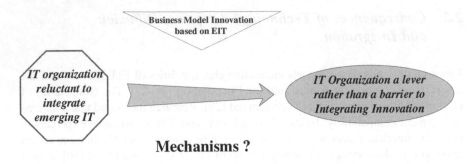

Mechanisms ?

Fig. 1 Research question

Q: What mechanisms could be employed to reduce the reluctance of IT organizations to integrate EIT, thus transforming the IT organization to a lever rather than a barrier to integrating innovation based on emerging technologies in IT?

3   Conceptual Framework

3.1   Exploitation Capability in Managing Uncertain IT Investments

Historically, practitioners encouraged IT managers to plan for uncertainty.[3] In the midst of a rapidly changing environment, the investments required to motivate IT organizations to lessen the reluctance to integrate EIT are complicated by the risks of EIT integration [46].

Key Resources and Partnerships. Key resources such as applications, information, infrastructure, tools and people are needed to execute on the operational objectives and IT innovation strategies. Gatignon et al. [47] have explained how competence-destroying innovation obsolesces and overturns existing competencies, skills, and know-how which may require the retraining and retooling of IT resources. Research illustrates dynamic resource models to represent the infusion of intellectual capital [48] putting the required resources at the right levels in order to address operational and innovation integration initiatives [49]. Additionally, key partnerships with external resources contributed to the success of the innovation effort. External resources such as consultants, suppliers and propagating institutions for capability augmentation [31, 49].

Key Activities. Through suggested **key activities** of assessments and experimentation [50], IT organizations invested initial trials to generate interest with a testing and phased deployment necessary to validate the technology prior to complete rollout testing [29]. IT development and acquisition projects focus on

---

[3]Kaplan, J. (2002). Success strategies for 2003. Network World, 19(50), 47.

costs and firm level risks excluding the relationship between uncertain investment and the abilities exhibited by the resources in IT [51]. MacMillan et al. [52] suggested mechanisms of *"feeling out"* the value added technology through three pilot projects in order to make the informed decisions. In contrast, *"Discovery-driven plans"*[4] were recommended in order to progress uncertain investments in IT into implementation in a step by step approach.

Thus, for the framework, **exploitation capabilities** are operational level capabilities that reflect an ability to perform routine and required activities [53] within the IT function. Such activities would include the review of potential business impact of changes to IT services in order to maintain the platform for business continuity [54].

3.2 Exploration Capability of Learning and Innovation

Exploration capabilities are centered on (1) *learning capability*, including the notion of absorptive capacity [50], and (2) *innovation capability* [10].

Learning capabilities facilitate the creation and modification of dynamic capabilities [55] relying on repetition and experimentation [56]. These exploration capabilities rely on information acquisition and transformation to collective knowledge assets [44, 57]. The absorptive capacity of IT organizations [50] constitutes a foundation for innovation integration [58]. Organizational units operating in a dynamic setting were found to improve their performance by increasing their skills, expertise, and potential absorptive capacity [50]. This dynamic capability provides these organizational units with strategic advantages [17], such as greater flexibility in reconfiguring resources, and effective timing of knowledge deployment at lower costs. Ko et al. [59] assert that antecedents of communication and motivation are important for the transfer of knowledge. The internal collaboration of distributed innovation groups [60]; technology gatekeepers [61], and cross-functional teams [62], facilitate the participative decision making [62], thus increasing IT-business knowledge. The interaction with the external environment [63] was shown to positively associate with the introduction of novel product innovations in firms. Researchers position knowledge as a *"baseline for the serviceability* and the *maintainability"* [64] of the components and systems involved in providing IT services in line with the current and planned business requirements. COBIT[5] advocates capabilities related to the organizational understanding of the

---

[4]McGrath, R.G. (2009). A Better Way to Plan Your Next IT Innovation. Ivey Business Journal Online, 1.

[5]COBIT (Control Objectives for IT) is an IT governance framework and toolset that allows managers to bridge the gap between control requirements, technical issues and business risks. "COBIT emphasizes regulatory compliance, helps organizations to increase the value attained from IT, enables alignment and simplifies implementation of the enterprises' IT governance and control framework." *Source* http://www.isaca.org/Knowledge-Center/COBIT/Pages/Overview.aspx.

requirements, the level of use of best practices and standards and the use of integrated tools for detecting and controlling exceptions.[6] This knowledge is important to reinforce implementation success of an IT innovation [65] and fundamental in ensuring the availability of the services in line with the current and planned business requirements [64].

Innovation Capabilities. Harnessing the competence base, capabilities for innovation [10] leverage an organizational intelligence [66] useful to manipulate information and reduce the inherent uncertainty and ambiguity of innovation [9]. Organizations leverage their innovation capability through their IT team's involvement in decision making [10]. This involvement contributed to the transformation of new knowledge [63] through the sharing of new insights and ideas.

Hence, the conceptual framework incorporates essential components of **IT capabilities of exploration**. These capabilities are indicated by **learning capabilities** to build the organizational knowledge competency and **innovation capabilities** to participate in generating new ideas for the business. Sustained by funding channels, firms appoint innovation champions [61] and devise a reward system to drive innovative behavior and encourage creativity [9].

3.3 Strategic Planning and IT-Business Alignment

The conceptual framework depicts strategic planning mechanisms as enablers to business model innovation based on innovations in IT. Strategic goals for IT should highlight the importance of both exploration and exploitation capabilities of the organization; define roles that specifically focus on exploration, exploitation and the coordination between the two capabilities; in the same way implement technologies that support both exploration and exploitation; and reward on performance for both capabilities [67]. IT leadership participates in the business setting in order to communicate infrastructure requirements for the availability, continuity and recovery specifications ensuring alignment of key IT services with the business strategy [68]. With an awareness of the required service levels from the IT strategy related to business continuity plans [54], the business and IT therefore participate in building the organizational awareness for adoption [69]. Inputs from innovation strategy to fulfill business model innovation objectives are expected from IT architecture on technology policies and specifications [60]. The framework incorporates concepts of IT architecture that pave the way for the next stage of integration and define inputs for IT service continuity with resiliency principles embedded by design [70].

IT Governance. Previous studies considered change management as a complementary investment likely to increase the success of implementation [71]. Concerned with organizational or technical change [72], input from the change

---

[6]COBIT 4.1—the "Work", 2007—DS4 Ensure Continuous Service.

management strategy maintains business requirement for IT in alignment with the business strategy, in an effort of reducing solution and service delivery defects and rework. Sometimes referred to as a capability of IT organizations [73], governance (i.e. *IT governance*) is conceived as a higher level construct for the framework underscoring an enabler role in reducing the risk of integration. Issues of security and governance [74], reliability of the technology, support for current and future business processes and operations are perceived as important with respect to integrating EIT into the corporate strategy. The integration of innovation into an environment, presents a risk on existing infrastructure [75]. Attention to governance, change leadership and program management ensures that complex initiatives are coordinated in objectives, resources, and interdependencies [60]. Xue et al. [76] reinforced governance in IT investment decision processes. Business continuity

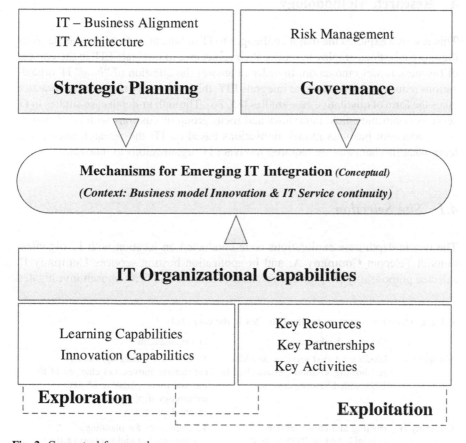

Fig. 2 Conceptual framework

plans outline the level of organizational understanding of the risks [77], vulnerabilities and threats to IT operations or the impact of loss of IT services to the business [78, 79]. Thus, governance reviews are required: namely, an assessment of the responsibilities, and reporting and a review of operational processes [80]. Structural and relational mechanisms were studied as antecedents to IT governance in a high-velocity environment riddled with technological turbulence [81].

These theories bring together a basis for the conceptual framework (Fig. 2).

The proposed framework delineates mechanisms for an ambidextrous IT organization [82] that could balance between *exploration capabilities* to learn and innovate and *exploitation capabilities* to implement and execute [83, 84] with a keen interest in maintaining IT Service Continuity.

4 Research Methodology

This research explores the major challenges to IT organizations and the mechanisms these organizations employ to reduce their reluctance to integrate EIT in the context of business model innovation. In order to answer the question of "*how*" IT organizations reduce their reluctance to integrate EIT, this exploratory research into practice takes the form of qualitative case studies [85, 86]. Through in-depth case studies in IT services companies, field interviews and focus group discussions with practitioners who underwent business model innovations based on IT, the research attempts to learn what mechanisms are required motivate IT organizations to innovate.

4.1 Site Selection

The two in-depth case explorations were conducted on location with IT organizations in Telecom **Company A**, and in application hosting services **Company B**, selected purposefully [87] for this research (Table 1). The firms chosen investigated

Table 1 Overview summary for the two sites in the case study

	Company background	IT organization
Company A	Leading internet services provider and hosting solutions, established in 1995 with 130+ employees	15 members managing security credentials, moves and changes of the internal users; planning of new technology deployment; internal and external customers
Company B	Hosting and cloud services, re-established in 2006 with 42 employees	12 employees for planning, implementation and support of the internal infrastructure with a service desk attending to escalated customer calls

IT is not just a tool to support business processes or to enable business model innovation, but for both. In these two companies, IT is the product of the business processes, and this influences all the decision variables (from the skills of the employees to be hired to the choice of IT vendors). This is still of value as a research as it treats a systemic issue in IT organizations of companies in the IT industry: These organizations are often asked to be the internal IT provider for the internal customers (i.e. employees) and external solutions and service providers for IT clients (i.e. customers).

The similarities in the sites selected reinforce the findings by adding depth into the discovery; similarities to note are of industry context [58], culture [88], international presence [89], with a centralized management model [90] for IT and a collective decision making [91]. These sites also present complementarities that may shed a light on some cross case observations further enriching the empirical study. The sites differ in organization size [92] and maturity [34], employed different mitigation measures in their scope of integration of EIT [93].

4.2 Data Collection and Analysis

The data collection activity combined interviews and brainstorming sessions [94]. Focus group workshops [95] were conducted due to the nature of the topic that requires stimulation and interaction. The specific goals of these focus group discussions were to gather collective knowledge on the topic and stimulate the organizational memory of the specific concepts involved then develop, in detail, the surrounding thoughts with a distance from potential individual bias [96]. Secondary data was collected from organizational charts, process maps, available company reports, and PowerPoint presentations, review the company's and IT organizational structure, roles and responsibilities and identify stakeholders for the data collection stages. Workshop participants were chosen to constitute a homogeneous management team with line managers and participants contributing application ideas to the strategy objectives. These workshops recorded all the participants' input while probing for details; where possible, using illustrative examples [87] to help establish neutrality in the process. In total data collection involved 15 informants chosen from the two companies.

Case summaries and cross-case comparison were compiled in a tabular summary [97], in the form of interview transcripts, field notes from observations, and relevant exhibits (e.g. organizational structures). The data analysis investigated the data correlation through a predefined coding system [98] in order to organize the data and provide a means to introduce the interpretations [99]. A step by step 'Key Point' coding technique [100] was applied to the interview transcripts [101], and relevant concepts are identified. The coding exercise allowed the emergence of a new key concept [100] useful as a refinement of the conceptual framework. These concepts were categorized as "**Key Concepts**" represented by the conceptual framework components. A summary table of key concepts is offered in the Appendix (Table 2).

Table 2 Key concepts or codes used for the data analysis

Seed concept	Key concepts or codes—separated by ";"
Strategic planning	Awareness and communication & management commitment [68]; Budgeting [114, 115]; Timing of introduction-decision [116]
IT—business alignment	IT—Business Alignment [60] IT and business leadership involvement [68]
Architecture	Architectural review [60]; redundancy (resilience) by design [70]
Governance	Change reviews[a]; Business and uptime requirement definition [72]; Compatibility with current systems [78], [79]; review of operational processes [77]; Create and maintain documentation [80]; Risk management [75]
Key activities	Change management[a]; continual maintenance[b,c] Compatibility and impact assessments [23, 78, 79] Project management[d] *Release management <emergent concept>*
Key partnerships	Supplier relationships and joint R&D with key partners [31, 49, 116]
Key resources	Infusion of intellectual capital [48] Human resource allocation [49] Tools[e]
Collaboration with Customers <emergent concept>	*Customer involved in testing; involve employees in projects; include the customer in the assessment of risk; learning workshops at customers; customer involved in planning and implementation*
Knowledge acquisition	Training; knowledge sharing; seek external knowledge; or acquire knowledge internally [108] Knowledge transfer [57] Participation in decision-making [76]
Testing and R&D	Implementation roadmaps [44] *Testing environment; testing; joint R&D with suppliers; <emergent concept>* research activities and feasibility of technology [29, 50, 52]
IT skills and competence	Consultancy skills of engineers [10, 28] IT leads technology evolution/IT leads business process innovation [60]
Incentives and rewards	Incentives and rewards programs [10]

[a]COBIT 4.1—the "Work", 2007—AI6 Manage Changes
[b]COBIT 4.1—the "Work", 2007—AI3.3 Infrastructure Maintenance
[c]COBIT 4.1—the "Work", 2007—AI2.10 Application Software Maintenance
[d]COBIT 4.1—the "Work", 2007—PO10 Manage Projects
[e]COBIT 4.1—the "Work", 2007—DS4 Ensure Continuous Service

5 Empirically Refined Framework

The empirical study was successful in enriching the conceptual framework. The resulting empirically refined framework (Fig. 3) conceptualizes these findings into *mechanisms for enabling IT capability* and *mechanisms for developing IT organizational capabilities*.

5.1 Mechanisms for Enabling IT Capability

Mechanisms for enabling IT capability were identified by the study as mechanisms of strategic planning and governance: strategic planning with IT-business alignment mechanisms and the leadership role in maintaining the connection between IT and

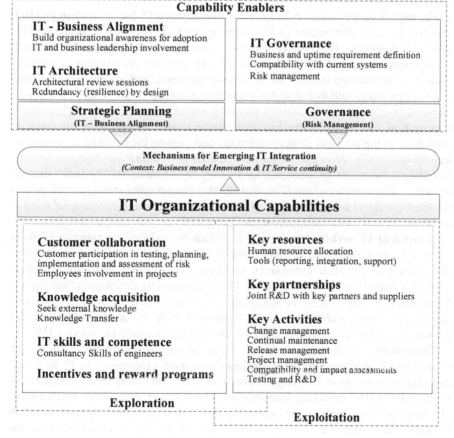

Fig. 3 Empirically refined framework

the business were stated to enable IT organizations. In addition to IT governance mechanisms (e.g. risk management) that prepare IT organizations to integrate EIT, hence reducing the reluctance of IT organizations to integrate "risky" emerging technologies.

5.2 Strategic Planning with a Resilient IT Architecture

Strategic planning was key for integrating and aligning IT resources, otherwise they are likely to end up with fragmented, ineffective and dysfunctional systems [102]. Strategic planning empowered IT organizations and narrowed the IT-business relationship gap. **In both companies**, IT leadership had a clear role in the business initiatives of the company. IT organizations previewed the benefits of applying a new technology. They participated in the choice of technology for the business, established a proper planning for technology and the best way to implement it.

Findings from this research endorse a well-integrated IT-Business strategy [103] enriched by the collaboration of IT leadership with the business executives. This concept is echoed by Bergeron et al. [104] who suggested that, in time of change in the business environment, the redesign of the IT structure and strategy is eminent. Though a documented strategy for IT was not provided, both companies leveraged cross-organization collaboration for collective planning [105]. The business participated in a collective IT activity planning exercise [106]. Reciprocally, the IT organization was aware of the business direction and business plans in order to participate in the business strategy definition and prepare the business for emerging technologies. *"Our IT organization participated in building the business strategy including advantages of emerging technology to influence the business strategy makers ... The member of the IT organization, engineers and managers felt part of the strategic trend setting capacity of the organization which encouraged them to embrace the new deployment (A—Director of IT)"*.

A resilient IT architecture helped to reduce the risks of emerging technology integration. In the study, IT organizations emphasized architectural review sessions [60], aimed to establish redundancy (resilience) in systems architecture and in implementation [70]. This prepared the IT organization by developing *"the correct IT architecture, with a fit in the needs and a flexibility in the features (A—General Manager)"*. These architectures were developed with the assistance of external consultants as key resources in order to insource the required knowledge [59].

Governance mechanisms keep the focus on service continuity [79]. In the context of IT services companies, findings also show governance in IT as a fundamental mechanism in avoiding the obstacles and in preparing the IT organization to integrate "risky" emerging technologies. The required governance mechanisms, of change reviews, business and uptime requirement definition [72] participated in reducing the reluctance. An *"accurate definition of the potential risks in the implementation"* performed by the project manager at **Company B** was echoed by "*a process of continuous review of the requirements and of the specifications of the emerging technology*" was revealed by the director of IT in **Company A**.

5.3 Developing IT Organizational Capabilities of Exploration

The Confluence of Knowledge. Identified as a key **exploration capability** [21], *knowledge acquisition and knowledge transfer* provided IT organizations with greater flexibility in reconfiguring resources and effective timing of knowledge deployment [107]. This was accomplished namely through training, and seeking external knowledge [108]. Knowledge was acquired, shared and transferred: (1) within the IT organization, (2) internally between the business and the IT organization, and (3) between the IT organization and the customer of the IT services (internal and external).

Essential to preparing IT organizations, knowledge acquisition was achieved through extensive training and knowledge building programs. Integration working groups made up of cross organizational members and representations of IT in the business facilitated the knowledge transfer. "*The IT support team meets with the IT infrastructure team regularly to review the customer issues, build the knowledge base and solicit the collaboration of ideas across the technical team internal and external (B—Deputy GM/Operations Director)*". External knowledge was sought through "*the engagement of consultants to provide workshops for requirements definition and draft an initial plan to implement these requirements (Company A)*", "*joint R&D activities with key providers and partners, and peer organizations (Company B)*". These testing and R&D activities, individual skills of the employees, and their accumulated experience increased organizational knowledge.

Knowledge transfer to internal customers was assured through user training sessions and users' manuals. "*This helped the organization overcome users' resistance*" *(Company B)*. IT members "*shared the lessons learned from solving customer issues with the business. This worked as a feedback into the business of the issues facing IT which may in turn drive a business solution or potentially a new service*" *(B—General Manager)*. **Company B** included "*knowledge management systems in their toolset as part of their knowledge sharing strategy*". Thus, in addition to establishing ties with external sources of new knowledge, cross-functional teams and internal collaboration motivated the IT teams to interact and share knowledge [109]. **Company B** were able to assimilate new external knowledge, transform it and exploit it successfully in order to create value from their absorptive capacity [50].

Customer Collaboration. This study sanctions the potential added value of the organizations that **collaborates with the customer of the services**, thus exploiting the tacit knowledge of the customer into the delivery of the new services. The empirical data supports the concept of "*IT-Customer collaboration in project* *execution, in testing and in the assessment of risk in order to gain the customer perspective on the required continuity parameters" (Company B).* A clear suggestion that collaboration would likely ease the adoption obstacles of the new service (*especially for the internal customer of the IT organization*), and prepare IT organizations for the potential risk induced by the emerging technologies to the external customer. The director of IT of **Company A** *"had to iteratively align the implementation of the project to their (Customer) expectations"*, and *"... conduct workshops at their customers"*. On the other hand, the Deputy GM/Operations Director also in charge of IT for **Company B** observed specified that their *"IT team scouts for opportunities at the customers' base and brings forth recommendation to drive more business out of the market share"*: and added that *"... [customers] drive us to provide ancillary services in our data centers to either secure them, backup the data, report on the performance"*. Through this collaboration, IT organizations are hence empowered to deliver a better quality product bringing forth a value proposition to the company (*internally*) and a greater competitive value (*externally*); an acquired organizational ambidexterity that focuses on the "customer intimacy, operational excellence and product leadership as the fundamental value disciplines" [105].

Skills, Competence Building Practices and Incentives. Skills, competence building practices and incentives were necessary to establish IT as a lever to innovation. In order to lead the innovation initiatives in their respective companies, **both IT organizations** increased their focus on knowledge acquisition practices, building the skills and competence of their human resources and aligning IT with the business. For **Company A** the IT organization was *"able to introduce process automation initiatives and be a leader in the company's business process innovation (A—General Manager)."* The IT team of **Company B** *engages in the sales process from the presales activities and close the loop in the post-sales support with the customers"* in order to *"provide consultancy services that drive business revenue (B—General Manager)"*.

Business savvy IT leaders collaborated with IT aware business leaders in order to steer the company towards successful business innovation based on IT. With a strong initiative to embrace new technology, the leadership of the IT organization of **Company B** provided IT team members with a suitable working environment, education and incentive programs. Encouraging the participation of the IT organization in the innovation of the business [110]. *"A reward program is in place to encourage the participation of the IT organization (B—General Manager)"*. Additionally, *"team building activities (events, etc.) were effective incentives in building personal bridges between the business members and the technical IT staff. This facilitated the collaboration and the information sharing (B—General Manager)"*.

Project performance indicators [111], financial and non-financial incentives were introduced. Key competencies of the team in the technology verticals (specific applications with a specific objective) were linked to the revenue from each vertical.

5.4 Developing IT Organizational Capabilities of Exploitation

The *exploitation capabilities* of IT organizations define the ability of the organizations to deliver the services required for effectively executing on the IT strategy [21] and maintain the required level of services to the customer of those services (*internal or external*).

Key Resources. Mechanisms associated with *key resources* support the exploitation capabilities of IT organizations. The required financial resources were secured through "*costing and budget reallocation in order to enable the IT function in the strategic planning process.* Through our s*taff augmentation practices we recruited eager human resources into the IT organization (A—MIS/IT Manager)*". Some were dedicated to R&D to drive the risk out of the emerging technology and promote the innovation capability of the organization [10], "*subject matter experts (technology champions) participated in professional services functions, facing the customer*", and acquiring external knowledge the disseminating it back as new knowledge [107] internally. For these IT organizations tooling was primary investment to prepare the organization. This included tools for learning, reporting and integration, and tools for support. **Company A** provided their IT organization with tools for "*monitoring and troubleshooting, to gain visibility into the customer experience and measure the service health (A—Director of IT)* and **Company B** "*needed to retool the team to adapt the knowledge and develop it forward,* so they "*implemented knowledge management systems in their toolset (B—Deputy GM/Operations Director)*".

Key Partnerships. **Company B** collaborated with their customers and both companies formed key partnerships with their suppliers in order to avoid the obstacles and to motivate IT organizations to integrate EIT. **Company A** often outsourced some functions to a "*supplier resource in order to implement the technology.* Then this subject matter expert was *asked to transfer the knowledge* to the team internally" (A—Director of IT). Similarly, **Company B** "*setup R&D efforts with peer organizations, key partners and suppliers, that helped them acquire the knowledge internally and reduce the reliance on suppliers*". They built connections with multiple suppliers in order to reduce the risk of reliance on one supplier for the implementation and support of EIT.

Key Activities. The study uncovered adjustments required to rapid implementations in order to reduce the potential risk to the delivery and support of IT services. At the top of the list, rigorous change management activities were suggested by **both organizations**, with "*roll back plans developed with the customer (A—Customer Support Manager and B—IT Project Manager and Team Leader)*" then complemented by "*required actions in release management (A), trying alternative configurations (A) and dividing projects into phases (B—Customer Support Manager) especially in order to reduce the obstacles to integrating emerging technologies*". "*On new deployments, a feasibility study is a must (B—Deputy GM/Operations Director)*" for the IT organization of **Company B**.

Agreeing, the IT director of **Company A** asserted that "*... at a certain time even a proof of concept is required in order to place the technology contextually in our environment*". In addition to testing and R&D activities, IT organizations engaged in other key activities of "*compatibility and impact assessments (A—Director of IT)*" with "*effective change management, definition of change, establish change review boards, implement change and document results (B)*" as they transitioned the IT services based on EIT into operation.[7] The formalization of activities with project management tactics, "*continual maintenance (A)*" tasks and were also specified. The focus on key activities such as release, change, and project management evolved both IT organizations' capabilities of exploitation and prepared IT organizations to confidently integrate of emerging technologies.

6 Managerial Implications

The findings of this research have the potential of transforming the IT organizations in IT services companies. These IT organizations would have the prospect to reduce their reluctance to integrate EIT following the guidance from this study. They would need to become ambidextrous organizations, leading internally and externally as a lever of IT innovations, reconfiguring key activities and resources, and exploiting the tacit knowledge of their customers (internal and external). Their leadership would focus on fostering IT-Business alignment, building the IT skills and competence of IT organizations and raising the "confidence" of the IT organization and the business in capabilities of the IT organization.

As such, this study offers guidance in the form of mechanisms and best practices which could empower IT organizations to confidently integrate innovation. These mechanisms emphasize four approaches:

- **IT strategy with a resilient architectural foundation**: Confident IT organizations implement IT innovations through an IT strategy with a resilient architectural foundation. They collaborate with the business to align objective of IT and the business (both ways).
- **IT Governance to manage and avoid risks**: They also apply effective IT governance to manage and avoid risk. They develop well-defined expectation of SLAs with the business and the customer base. Risk evaluations are performed continually and include assessment of critical operational systems and the impact of the potential innovation on these systems.
- **Dynamic organizational capabilities**: IT leadership of confident organizations develop dynamic organizational capabilities of exploration and exploitation, emphasizing the confluence of knowledge. They apply the investments required to build IT skills and competence, muster key resources, and formalize key activities. They motivate their IT organizational learning capabilities, and

---

[7]ITIL 3.1—Service Transition.

reinforce their analytical capabilities. IT leadership of confident organizations demonstrate leadership competence, encourage the adoption of standards and networking with peers. Furthermore, innovative IT organizations develop key partnership with suppliers and peers, and exploit the tacit knowledge of the customer.

- **Rewards and incentive supported by effective metrics**: They implements rewards and incentives tied to metrics to motivate the organization. These metrics monitor the success of the mechanisms and report the value of the IT function to the business.

7 Academic Contribution

The empirical study was successful in enriching the conceptual framework expounding its concepts into mechanisms for IT capability enablement and mechanisms for developing IT organizational capabilities. From in depth case studies, this study combines the new knowledge acquired from the research in a form of a framework of mechanisms that empower IT organizations in innovations based on emerging technologies. Thus this framework goes further extending such studies with an answer to the question of *"How IT organizations reduce the reluctance of IT organizations to integrate emerging technologies in order to successfully innovate the business model based on emerging technologies in IT"*. This new knowledge may be a seed for a new stream of literature focused on producing theories for the empowerment of IT organization to drive innovation.

7.1 Limitations and Opportunity for Further Research

The principles outlined herein are collected from peer IT organizations in IT services industry who successfully motivated their IT organization's resources to maintain the level of capabilities required to confidently integrate EIT. Although the research has reached its aim, some unavoidable limitations can be noted. Limitations related to case study research the research and other contexts such as culture, organizational context and industry can be recognized. Thereby, the outcome of the study is expected to be centered on companies within IT services.

Thus, the indicated limitations of this study could offer opportunities for follow on research. The proposed conceptual framework could be examined through further in-depth case studies in different company models and industries in order to establish potential variations to the framework based on a certain industry context [58] i.e. whether *IT is the core business* (internal supplier of IT Products and services) or *IT as a supporting function* in an organization of users of IT products and services. Additional field work possibly in the form of wider focus groups, with

CIOs, IS professionals and consultants [112] would test the applicability of the framework at other cultural, organizational and other contexts and in order to strengthen the practice implications of the framework introduced by this research [113]. Clearly, this will require further research to validate the proposed mechanisms in different context.

8 Conclusion

In conclusion, the conceptual framework is supported by the empirical study. The paper exhibits a broad context ranging from IT governance and strategy to customer collaboration and risk management, however it focuses on IT capabilities within this context. This study produced a set of capability enabling mechanisms in the strategic planning process connecting IT-business alignment elements with IT architecture and governance guidelines, in order to reduce the present obstacles and prepare IT organizations. For practitioners, this study has brought forth concepts of implementation that may serve as guidance to develop organizational capabilities for IT based business model innovation projects. Capabilities enabled an alignment with business and innovation strategies, collaboration with the intended customers, with proper governance practices to reduce the ensuing risk. With a focus on exploration and exploitation capabilities, key activities, key resources and key partnerships these mechanisms are recommended by the empirical study to establish the IT organization as an internal and external leader in business model innovation based on IT.

Appendix

See Table 2.

References

1. Peppard, J., Ward, J.: Unlocking sustained business value from IT investments. Calif. Manag. Rev. **481**, 52–70 (2005)
2. Kraemer, K., Dedrick, J., Yamashiro, S.: Refining and extending the business model with information technology: dell computer corporation. Inf. Soc. **16**, 5–21 (2000)
3. Wang, J.: Economies of IT systems at WAL-MART. An historical perspective. Acad. Inf. Manage. Sci. J. **9**(1), 45–66 (2006)
4. Edvardsson, B., Enquist, B.: The service excellence and innovation model: lessons from IKEA and other service frontiers. Total Qual. Manag. Bus. Excellence **22**(5), 535–551 (2011)
5. Amit, R., Zott, C.: Creating value through business model innovation. MIT Sloan Manage. Rev. **53**(3), 41–49 (2012)

6. Fitzgerald, M.: Inside Renault's digital factory. MIT Sloan Management Review, pp. 1–4 (2014)
7. Christensen, C.M.: The Innovator's Dilemma: when new technologies cause great firms to fail. Harvard Business School Press, Boston, MA (1997). ISBN 978-0-87584-585-2
8. Eisenhardt, K.M.: Making fast strategic decisions in high-velocity environments. Acad. Manag. J. **32**, 543–576 (1989)
9. Saleh, S.D., Wang, C.K.: The management of innovation: strategy, structure, and organizational climate. IEEE Trans. Eng. Manage. **40**(13), 21 (1993)
10. Lawson, B., Samson, D.: Developing innovation capability in organizations: a dynamic capabilities approach. Int. J. Innov. Manag. **5**(3), 377–400 (2001)
11. Santa, R., Ferrer, M., Bretherton, P., Hyland, P.: The necessary alignment between technology innovation effectiveness and operational effectiveness. J. Manage. Organ. **15**(2), 155–169 (2009)
12. Barney, J.B.: Firm resources and sustained competitive advantage. J. Manag. **17**(1), 99–120 (1991)
13. Grant, R.M.: The resource-based theory of competitive advantage: implications for strategy formulation. Calif. Manag. Rev. **33**(3), 114–135 (1991)
14. Mata, F.J., Fuerst, W.L., Barney, J.B.: Information technology and sustained competitive advantage: a resource-based analysis. MIS Q. **19**(4), 487 (1995)
15. Zollo, M., Winter, S.G.: Deliberate learning and the evolution of dynamic capabilities. Organ. Sci. **13**(3), 339–351 (2002)
16. Varis, M., Littunen, H.: Types of innovation, sources of information and performance in entrepreneurial SMEs. Eur. J. Innovation Manage. **13**(2), 128–154 (2010)
17. Teece, D.J., Pisano, G., Shuen, A.: Dynamic capabilities and strategic management. Strateg. Manage. J. **18**(7), 509–533 (1997)
18. Wade, M., Hulland, J.: Review: the resource-based view and information systems research: review, extension, and suggestions for future research. MIS Q. **28**(1), 107–142 (2004)
19. Gibson, C., Birkinshaw, J.: The antecedents, consequences, and mediating role of organizational ambidexterity. Acad. Manag. J. **47**(2), 209–226 (2004)
20. He, Z.L., Wong, P.K.: Exploration vs exploitation: an empirical test of the ambidexterity hypothesis. Organ. Sci. **15**, 481–494 (2004)
21. March, J.G.: Exploration and exploitation in organizational learning. Organ. Sci. **2**(1), 71–87 (1991)
22. Buyya, R., Shin Yeo, C., Venugopal, S., Broberg, J., Brandic, I.: Cloud computing and emerging IT platforms: vision, hype, and reality for delivering computing as the 5th utility. Future Gen. Comput. Syst. **25**(6), 599–616 (2009)
23. Huff, S.L., Munro, M.C.: Information technology assessment and adoption. MIS Quarterly, pp. 327–340 (1985)
24. Agarwal, R., Prasad, J.: The role of innovation characteristics and perceived voluntariness in the acceptance of information technologies. Decis. Sci. **28**(3), 557–582 (1997)
25. Swanson, E.B.: Information systems innovations among organizations. Manage. Sci. **40**(9), 1069–1092 (1994)
26. Bower, J.L., Christensen, C.M.: Disruptive technologies: catching the wave. Harvard Bus. Rev. (1995)
27. Bhattacherjee, A.: Management of emerging technologies: experiences and lessons learned at US West. Case Stud. Inf. Manage. **33**(5), 263–272 (1998)
28. Duncan, N.B.: Capturing flexibility of information technology infrastructure: a study of resource characteristics and their measure. J. Manage. Inf. Syst. **12**(2), 37–57 (1995)
29. Cooper, R.B, Zmud, R.W.: Information technology implementation research: a technological diffusion approach. Manage. Sci. **36**(2), 123–139 (1990)
30. Bradford, M., Florin, J.: Examining the role of innovation diffusion factors on the implementation success of enterprise resource planning systems. Int. J. Acc. Inf. Syst. **4**(3), 205–225 (2003)

31. Swanson, E.B., Ramiller, N.C.: The organizing vision in information systems innovation. Org. Sci. **8**(5), 458–474 (1997)
32. Fichman, R.G., Kemerer, C.F.: The illusory diffusion of innovation: an examination of assimilation gaps. Inf. Syst. Res. **10**(3), 255–275 (1999)
33. Cavusoglu, H., Nan, H., Yingjiu, L., Dan, M.: Diffusion with influentials, imitators, and opponents. J. Manage. Inf. Syst. **27**(2), 305–334 (2010)
34. Grover, V., Goslar, M.D.: The initiation, adoption, and implementation of telecommunications technologies in U.S. organizations. J. Manage. Inf. Syst. **10**(1), 141–163 (1993)
35. Boynton, A.C., Zmud, R.W., Jacobs, G.C.: The influence of IT management practice on IT use in large organizations. MIS Q. **18**(3), 299–318 (1994)
36. Lyytinen, K., Rose, G.M.: The disruptive nature of information technology innovations: the case of inherent computing in systems development organizations. MIS Q. **27**(4), 557–595 (2003)
37. Wu, W.W., Rose, G.M., Lyytinen, K.: Recognizing and managing innovation points in large IT projects. MIS Q. Executive **10**(3), 121–132 (2011)
38. Shin, N., Edington, B.H.: An integrative framework for contextual factors affecting information technology implementation. JITTA: J. Inf. Technol. Theory Appl. **8**(4), 21–38 (2007)
39. Taylor, A., Helfat, C.E.: Organizational linkages for surviving technological change: complementary assets, middle management, and ambidexterity. Organ. Sci. **20**(4), 718–739 (2009)
40. Benamati, J., Lederer, A.L.: Managing the impact of rapid IT change. Inf. Resour. Manage. J. **23**(1), 1–16 (2010)
41. Uzkurt, C., Kumar, R., Kimzan, H.S., Eminoglu, G.: Role of innovation in the relationship between organizational culture and firm performance. Eur. J. Innovation Manage. **16**(1), 92–117 (2013)
42. Luftman, J., Zadeh, H.S, Derksen, B., Santana, M., Rigoni, E.H. et al.: Key information technology and management issues 2011–2012: an international study. J. Inf. Technol. **27**(3), 198–212 (2012)
43. Bendoly, E., Citurs, A., Konsynski, B.: Internal infrastructural impacts on RFID perceptions and commitment: knowledge, operational procedures, and information-processing standards. Decis. Sci. **38**(3), 423–449 (2007)
44. Legris, P., Collerette, P.: A roadmap for IT project implementation: integrating stakeholders and change management issues. Project Manage. J. **37**(5), 64–75 (2006)
45. Lu, Y., Ramamurthy, K.: Understanding the link between information technology capability and organizational agility: an empirical examination. MIS Q. **35**(4), 931–954 (2011)
46. Benaroch, M.: Managing information technology investment risk: a real options perspective. J. Manage. Inf. Syst. **19**(2), 43–84 (2002)
47. Gatignon, H., Tushman, M.L., Smith, W., Anderson, P.: A Structural approach to assessing innovation: construct development of innovation locus, type, and characteristics. Manage. Sci. **48**(9), 1103–1122 (2002)
48. Chaharbaghi, K., Lynch, R.: Sustainable competitive advantage towards a dynamic resource based strategy. Manag. Decis. **37**, 45–50 (1999)
49. Naghavi, A., Ottaviano, I.P.G.: Outsourcing, Complementary Innovations, and Growth. Ind. Corp. Change **19**(4), 1009–1035 (2010) (Advance Access published January 21, 2010)
50. Cohen, W.M., Levinthal, D.: Absorptive capacity: a new perspective on learning and innovation. Adm. Sci. Q. **35**, 128–152 (1990)
51. Schwartz, E., Zozaya-Gorostiza, C.: Investment under uncertainty in information technology: acquisition and development projects. Manage. Sci. **49**(1), 57–70 (2003)
52. MacMillan, I.C., van Putten, A.B., Rita, G.M., Thompson, J.D.: Using real options discipline for highly uncertain technology investments. Res. Technol. Manage. **49**(1), 29–37 (2006)
53. Collis, D.J.: Research note: how valuable are organizational capabilities?'. Strateg. Manag. J. **15**, 143–152 (1994)

54. Arduini, F., Morabito, V.: Business continuity and the banking industry. Commun. ACM **53**(3), 121–125 (2010)
55. Eisenhardt, K.M., Martin, J.K.: Dynamic capabilities: what are they? Strateg. Manag. J. **21**, 1105–1121 (2000)
56. Bowman, C., Ambrosini, V.: How the resource-based and the dynamic capability views of the firm inform corporate-level strategy. Br. J. Manag. **14**, 289–303 (2003)
57. Alavi, M., Leidner, D.: Review: knowledge management systems: conceptual foundation and research issues. MIS Q. **25**(1), 107–136 (2001)
58. Miles, R.E, Snow, C.C., Miles, G.: TheFuture.org, Long Range Planning, **33**(3), 300–321 (2000)
59. Ko, D.G., Kirsch, L.J., King, W.R.: Antecedents of knowledge transfer from consultants to clients in enterprise system implementations. MIS Q. **29**(1), 59–85 (2005)
60. Cash, J.I., Earl, M.J., Morison, R.: Teaming up to crack innovation and enterprise integration. Harvard Bus. Rev. **86**(11), 90–100 (2008)
61. Tidd, J., Bessant, J., Pavitt, K.: Managing innovation: integrating technological, market and organisational change (3rd ed.). (2005). ISBN: 978-0470093269
62. Hansen, M.T.: The search-transfer problem: the role of weak ties in sharing knowledge across organization subunits. Adm. Sci. Q. **44**, 82–111 (1999)
63. Jansen, J.J., Van den Bosch, F.A.J., Volberda, H.W.: Managing potential and realized absorptive capacity: how do organizational antecedents matter? Acad. Manag. J. **48**(6), 999–1015 (2005)
64. Lim, J., Stratopoulos, T.C., Wirjanto, T.S.: Path dependence of dynamic information technology capability: an empirical investigation. J. Manage. Inf. Syst. **28**(3), 45–84 (2011) (Winter 2011–12)
65. Pozzebon, M., Pinsonneault, A.: The dynamics of client-consultant relationships: exploring the interplay of power and knowledge. J. Inf. Technol. **27**, 35–56 (2012)
66. Glynn, M.A.: Innovative genius: a framework for relating individual and organisational intelligences to innovation. Acad. Manag. Rev. **21**(4), 1081–1111 (1996)
67. Sherif, K., Tsado, L., Zheng, W., Airhia, B.: An exploratory study of organization architecture and the balance between exploration and exploitation of knowledge. VINE **43**(4), 442–461 (2013)
68. Peppard, J., Edwards, C., Lambert, R.: Clarifying the ambiguous role of the CIO. MIS Q. Executive **10**(1), 31–44 (2011)
69. Rai, A., Patnayakuni, R.A.: Structural model for case adoption behavior. J. Manage. Inf. Syst. **13**(2), 205–234 (1996)
70. Paschke, A., Schnappinger-Gerull, E.: A categorization scheme for SLA metrics, multi-conference information systems (MKWI06). Passau, Germany (2006)
71. Sherer, S., Kohli, R., Baron, A.: Complementary investment in change management and IT investment payoff. Inf. Syst. Res. **5**(3), 321–333 (2003)
72. Markus, M.L., Benjamin, R.I.: Change management strategy. MIS Q. **20**(4), 385–407 (1996)
73. Williams, H., Shah, B.: Administering information technology capabilities in competitive global business by preventing replication of technology portfolio. Int. J. Innov. Manage. Technol. **4**(6), 619–624 (2013)
74. Cegielski C.G., Reithel, B.J., Rebman, C.M.: Emerging information technologies and IT strategy. Commun. ACM **48**(8), 113–117 (2005)
75. Merton, R.C.: Innovation risk. Harvard Bus. Rev. **91**(4), 48–56 (2013)
76. Xue, Y., Huigang, L., Bolton, W.R.: Information technology governance in information technology investment decision processes: the impact of investment characteristics, external environment, and internal context. MIS Q. **32**(1), 67–96 (2008)
77. Schwarz, A., Hirschheim, R.: An extended platform logic perspective of IT governance: managing perception and activities of IT. Comput. J. Strateg. Inf. Syst. **12**(2), 129–166 (2003)
78. Vaid, R.: How are operational risk and business continuity coming together as a common risk management spectrum? J. Bus. Continuity Emerg. Plann. **2**(4), 330–339 (2008)

79. Ward, C.C., Agassi, S.S., Bhattacharya, K.K., Biran, O.O., Cocchiara, R.R., Factor, M.E., Wolfsthal, Y.Y.: Toward transforming business continuity services. IBM J. Res. Dev. **53**(6), 7:1–7:15 (2009)
80. Ferguson, C., Green, P., Vaswani, R., Wu, G.: Determinants of effective information technology governance. Int. J. Auditing (2012). doi:10.1111/j.1099-1123.2012.00458
81. Bradley, R., et al.: An empirical examination of antecedents and consequences of IT governance in US hospitals. J. Inf. Technol. **27**(2), 156–177 (2012)
82. Tushman, M.L., O'Reilly III, C.A.: Ambidextrous organizations: managing evolutionary and revolutionary change. Calif. Manag. Rev. **38**(4), 8–30 (1996)
83. Lavie, D., Stettner, U., Tushman, M.L.: Exploration and exploitation within and across organizations. Acad. Manage. Ann. **4**, 109–155 (2010)
84. Bocanet, A., Ponsiglione, C.: Balancing exploration and exploitation in complex environments. VINE **42**(1), 15–35 (2012)
85. Eisenhardt, K.M.: Building theories from case study research. Acad. Manage. Rev. **14**(4), 532–550 (1989)
86. Yin, R.K.: Case study research: design and methods, 4th edn. Sage, Newbury Park, CA (2009). ISBN 978-1-4129-6099-1
87. Patton, M.Q.: Qualitative evaluation and research methods, 2nd edn. Sage Publications, Newbury Park, CA (1990)
88. Kwon, T.H.: A diffusion of innovation approach to MIS infusion: conceptualization, methodology, and management strategies. In: Proceedings of the Tenth International Conference on information Systems, pp. 139–146. Copenhagen, Denmark (1990)
89. Zmud, R.W.: Diffusion of modern software practices: influence of centralization and formalization. Manage. Sci. **28**(12), 1421–1431 (1982)
90. Damanpour, F.: Organizational innovation: a meta-analysis of effects of determinants and moderators. Acad. Manage. J. **34**(3), 555–590 (1991)
91. Rogers, E.M.: Diffusion of innovations. Free Press, New York (1962)
92. Fichman, R.G., Kemerer, C.F.: The assimilation of software process innovations: an organizational learning perspective. Manage. Sci. **43**(10), 1345–1363 (1997)
93. Kwon, T.H., Zmud, R.W.: Unifying the fragmented models of information systems implementation. In: Boland, R.J. Hirschheim, R.A. (eds.) Critical Issues in Information Systems Research, pp. 227–251. Wiley, New York (1987)
94. Hargadon, A.B., Sutton, R.I.: Technology brokering and innovation in a product development firm. Adm. Sci. Q. **42**, 716–749 (1997)
95. Stewart, D.W., Shamdasani, P.N., Rook, D.W.: Focus groups: theory and practice. Sage Publications, Thousand Oaks, CA (2007)
96. Eisenhardt, K.M., Graebner, M.E.: Theory building from cases: opportunities and challenges. Acad. Manag. J. **50**(1), 25–32 (2007)
97. Creswell, J.W.: Qualitative Inquiry and Research Design: Choosing Among Five Traditions. Sage, Thousand Oaks, CA (1998)
98. Miles, M., Huberman, A.M.: Qualitative Data Analysis: A Sourcebook of New Methods. Sage Publications, Newbury Park, CA, USA (1991)
99. Strauss, A., Corbin, J.: Basics of Qualitative Research. Sage Publications, Newbury Park, CA (1990)
100. Allan, G.: A critique of using grounded theory as a research method. Electronic J. Bus. Res. Methods **2**(1), 1–10 (2003)
101. Douglas D.: Inductive theory generation: a grounded approach to business inquiry. Electron. J. Bus. Res. Methods **2**(1), Article 4, Academic Conferences International Limited, (2003)
102. Bradley, R.V., Pratt, R.M.E., Byrd, T.A., Simmons, L.L.: The role of enterprise architecture in the quest for IT value. MIS Q. Executive **10**(2), 19–27 (2011)
103. Broadbent, M., Kitzis, E.: Linking business and IT strategies together: four factors for success. Ivey Bus. J. **69**(3), 1–6 (2005)
104. Bergeron et al: Ideal patterns of strategic alignment and business performance. Inf. Manag. **41**(8), 1003–1020 (2004)

105. Tallon, P.P.: A process-oriented perspective on the alignment of information technology and business strategy. J. Manage. Inf. Syst. **24**(3), 231–272 (2008)
106. Kearns, G.S., Sabherwal, R.: Strategic alignment between business and information technology: a knowledge-based view of behaviors, outcome, and consequences. J. Manag. Inf. Syst. **23**(3), 129–162 (2007)
107. Zahra, S.A., George, G.: Absorptive capacity: a review, reconceptualization, and extension. Acad. Manag. Rev. **27**, 185–203 (2002)
108. Roberts, N., Galluch, P.S., Dinger, M., Grover, V.: Absorptive capacity and information systems research: review synthesis, and direction for future research. MIS Q. **36**(2), 625–648 (2012)
109. Tsai, W.: Knowledge transfer in intra-organizational ntworks: effects of network position and absorptive capacity on business-unit innovation and performance. Acad. Manag. J. **44**, 996–1004 (2001)
110. Westerman, G., Curley, M.: Building IT enabled innovation capabilities at Intel. MIS Q. Executive **7**(1), 33–48 (2008)
111. Sabyasachi, M., Sambamurthy, V., Westerman, G.: Measuring IT performance and communicating value. MIS Q. Executive **10**(1) (2011)
112. Rosemann, M., Vessey, I.: Linking theory and practice: performing a reality check on a model of IS success. In: Bartmann, D., Rajola, F., Kallinikos, J., Avison, D., Winter, R., Ein-Dor, P., Becker, J., Bodendorf, F., Weinhardt, C. (eds.) Proceedings of the 13th European conference on information systems, pp. 26–28. Regensburg, Germany (2005)
113. Rosemann, M., Vessey, I.: Toward improving the relevance of information systems research to practice: the role of applicability checks. MIS Q. **32**(1), 1–22 (2008)
114. Armstrong, C.P., Sambamurthy, V.: Information technology assimilation in firms: the influence of senior leadership and IT infrastructures. Inf. Syst. Res. **10**(4), 304–327 (1999)
115. Bajwa, D.S., Lewis, L., Pervan, G., Lai, V.S., Munkvold, B.E., Schwabe, G.: Factors in the global assimilation of collaborative information technologies: an exploratory investigation in five regions. J. Manage. Inf. Syst. **25**(1), 131–165 (2008)
116. King, J.L., Gurbaxani, V., Kraemer, K.L., McFarlan, F.W., Raman, K.S., Yap, C.S.: Institutional factors in information technology innovation. Inf. Syst. Res. **5**(2), 139–169 (1994)

Relating ICT to Organizational Change in Research and Practice

Moufida Sadok and Peter Bednar

Abstract The topic of ICT-enabled organizational change has been a focus of attention in information systems (IS) research for decades. Besson and Rowe (J Strateg Inf Syst 21:103–124, 2012 [17]), however, have identified a lack of description and conceptualization of the transformation process in the main stream of IS research. This paper discusses key IS paradigms in some of the content of commonly and available well established IS academic text books and research so that it can then be more obvious in how they address the transformation process. We therefore highlight original differences between two dominant IS paradigms and we consider that the distinction between IS as a data processing system and IS as a human activity system provides a frame of reference to explain the reasons why the gaps in understanding the transformation process continue to be relevant issues to explore in IS research. We also extend the debate as to how IS as a discipline should provide guidance on the process and practice of organizational change in order to prepare students to keep up with the complexity and requirements of real world businesses.

Keywords Organizational change · Socio-technical analysis · Technological determinism · Contextual dependencies · ICT

M. Sadok (✉)
Higher Institute of Technological Studies in Communication in Tunis, Tunis, Tunisia
e-mail: moufida.sadok@port.ac.uk

P. Bednar
School of Computing, University of Portsmouth, Portsmouth, UK
e-mail: peter.bednar@port.ac.uk

P. Bednar
Department of Informatics, Lund University, Lund, Sweden

© Springer International Publishing Switzerland 2016
F. Ricciardi and A. Harfouche (eds.), *Information and Communication Technologies in Organizations and Society*, Lecture Notes in Information Systems and Organisation 15, DOI 10.1007/978-3-319-28907-6_8

1 Introduction

The topic of ICT-enabled organizational change has been a focus of attention in information systems (IS) research for decades. Numerous and diverse concepts, theories, methods and designs have addressed the relationships nature between the two variables. Besson and Rowe [17], however, have identified a lack of description and conceptualization of the transformation process in the main stream of IS research. This paper discusses key IS paradigms in some of the content of commonly and available well established IS academic text books and research so that it can then be more obvious in how they address the transformation process. We therefore highlight original differences between two dominant IS paradigms and we consider that the distinction between IS as a data processing system and IS as a human activity system provides a frame of reference to explain the reasons why the gaps in understanding the transformation process continue to be relevant issues to explore in IS research.

In view of IS as a data processing system, efforts for developing IS have been oriented to the design of effective artefacts and a number of structured and formal methods in IS methodologies have been developed. Hard systems approaches have been applied with a focus on the efficacy and internal consistency of systems specifications and their development. In this perspective, the development and implementation of an IS are considered as a driven and results of organizational change. This stream of IS research is pervasive and prevalent in the higher education of future practitioners and academics as well as in the highly ranked IS journals.

Considering IS as human organized activity, the transformation process is described as an emergent learning process based on the exploration and understanding of contextual dependencies and supported by a number of methods and techniques. The socio-technical (ST) systems design literature put forward evidence of the relevance of contextual analysis within which emphasis is placed on human and technical dependencies in the context of an evolving organizational environment. This stream of IS research continue to be poorly referenced and ignored even though the pioneers of this stream have been active and contrarian researchers since the early era of IS history.

The two alternatives paradigms are essential to a discussion about the transformational effect of IS. Reflection upon the impact of each of these paradigms in relation to organizational change led to identify two perspectives within which IS-enabled organizational change is debated through two lenses: deterministic and dialectic views. The former view is underpinning the ICT driven change approach. The later is focusing on the process enabling the change through exploration, development of contextual understanding and problem solving activities.

The "technological imperative perspective" considers technology use as a result of technology determining behavior. By regarding implementation as an isolated achievement, the focus is on implementing technological solutions and infrastructures as a result of change. Adopting such a perspective means that people will by default use technology for intended purposes once it is available to them.

This perspective is widely claimed in available IS references. In this paper, it is explored and applied throughout the particular cases of ERP implementation and IS security policies.

A further perspective rejects the deterministic link between technology and organization (e.g., [28]). By considering the human activity systems as a point of reference rather than a variable IS development design is regarded as an emergent learning process of organizational change. From a socio-technical perspective, it is claimed that a viable system would be more user-centric by accommodating and balancing human processes rather than entertaining an expectation of a one sided change of behavior of the end user. Thereby, the "dialectic perspective" considers the use and adoption of technology as an emergent result of socio-cultural processes, availability of technology and individual contextual dependencies. We argue in this paper that this perspective has attempted to describe and conceptualize the organization transformation process and has dealt with the "routinization" of practices after change. Examples from ST literature will be used for illustration.

Consequently, the objectives of this paper are twofold. Firstly, we explore the key questions emerging from the dialectic relationship between IS and organizational change and put forward several examples to compare and contrast two alternative perspectives that may be applied in forming ICT-enabled organizational change views. Secondly, we highlight and extend the debate as to how IS as a discipline should provide guidance on the process and practice of organizational change in order to prepare students to keep up with the complexity and requirements of real world businesses.

The remainder of the paper is organized in three sections. The first section describes a stream of IS research which have viewed ICT as the core of IS as a discipline and as a practice. We also provide in the same section examples addressing organizational change according to a deterministic approach. The second section illustrates the contribution of ICT to organizational change according to an emergent approach. Finally, concluding remarks are presented in the third section discussing challenges facing academia to revise and adapt curricula design and IS research methodologies.

2 ICT-Enabled Organizational Change: A Deterministic View

The conceptualizations of IT artefact in IS research has been dominated by a computational view which underpins the assertion that once the computational capabilities of the technology have been properly programmed and modelled the usefulness and usability of the technology would necessarily be guaranteed [54]. This view is associated to the computer science approach with an inherent focus on artefact development and presupposes deterministic relationships between technologies and organizations.

2.1 IS as a Data Processing System

The definition of an IS as a system in which data is processed to achieve efficiently organizational goals is commonly accepted. Table 1 presents a selection of IS definitions from the widely used books in higher education for future practitioners in the area of IS design and management. Efforts for developing IS have been oriented to the design of effective artefacts that meet the information needs and requirements of top management. Waterfall, prototyping and prescriptive approaches for IS design (e.g. [62]) as well as a number of structured and formal methods in IS methodologies such as SSADM (Structured Systems Analysis and Design Method and Business Development Method) have been proposed and applied.

Hard systems approaches have been harnessed based on the hypothesis that systems exist in the real world and can be identified and "engineered".

Table 1 IS definitions and concepts in widely used academic text books

Reference	IS definition/concepts/components
[6]	"An IS in an organization provides processes and information useful to its members and clients. These should help it operate more effectively"
[37]	"IS are developed for different purposes, depending of the business"; "Process: The activities that transform or change data in an IS"; "System: a collection of subsystems that are interrelated and interdependent, working together to accomplish predetermined goals and objectives. All systems have input, processes, output and feedback"
[55]	"A computer-based set of hardware, software and telecommunication components, supported by people and procedures, to process data and turn it into useful information"
[44]	"Computer-based IS use computer technology to process raw data into meaningful information"…"An IS can be defined technically as a set of interrelated components that collect (or retrieve), process, store and distribute information to support decision making and control in an organization"…"By information we mean data that have been shaped into a form that is meaningful and useful to human beings"
[40]	"A group of components that interact to produce information… computer, hardware, software, data, procedures and people. These five components are present in every IS, from the simplest to the most complex"
[66]	"Any IS consists of three parts: an external shell through which users interact with the system; an internal or physical design from whose presence users are shielded; and a conceptual model which represents the business requirements, and upon which the internal design is based"
[61]	"Within the system boundary, information is transmitted, stored and transformed in electronic form. At the system boundary are the interfaces between the computer and its environment—the human world, in which information is stored in words, numbers and pictures, and transformed orally and visually"
[57]	"A collection of interrelated components that collect, process, store, and provide as output the information needed to complete a business task"

Consequently, the system objectives can be defined in advance and alternative means of achieving them can be modeled. Considering only one point of view as objective and correct (e.g. software developer perspective), the focus is more on how to do things in certain and precise situations.

Alter [4] however emphasizes a need for IS field to address the whole context within which IT-reliant work system is designed, developed, implemented and maintained. He states that the use of IT to support IS activities does not require IT artefact to be the primary subject focus of IS field. Furthermore, although systems development can be conceived as an integrated process, in practice attempts to standardize the steps and techniques involved have led to less, rather than more, comprehension among the various communities of practice seeking to establish the meanings of these aspects. For example, within an overall context of 'Application Lifecycle Management' different providers have generated a range of different interpretations of what is supposed to be a standardized process [7]. In the discipline of IS, this can be observed in the many efforts to create standardized languages, methods and techniques intended to support complex communication and interaction between different stakeholders in a systems development project. Markus et al. [48] argued that existing IS development methodologies focus on structured or semi-structured decision processes.

Another aspect comes out from Table 1 is the confusing use of data and information as interchangeable terms in most of the references. Reflecting on the nature of IS, Langefors [42, 43] suggests that those people who are to interpret data in order to inform themselves must be viewed as part of the system. He demonstrates this using the infological equation $I = i (D, S, t)$ where "I" is the information (knowledge) produced by a person from data "D" in conjunction with pre-knowledge "S", by an interpretation process "i", during time interval "t". Meaning (information or knowledge) is thus created by each individual. Pre-knowledge "S", here, is considered to be created through the entire lived experience of the individual concerned.

2.2 Organizational Change as a Consequence of ICT Implementation

In this perspective, a deeply taken-for-granted assumption that the IS implementation is intended to has a significant impact on the shape of an organization and its job definitions. Some methodological approaches to systems development discuss 'implementation' as a late stage in the total process, linked to effective change management (e.g. [16]). The implementation of application software packages requires adaptation in terms of revision and development of organizational procedures, business practices and users training both in the new procedures and in the new IT application [25, 29, 45]. The use of technology is assumed to be a "natural" consequence. The IS implementation is expected to produce a change in organizational practices and users need to be educated. The terminology used to describe the technological perspective in IS research often includes adoption, adaptation, acceptance, training and intention to use in order to facilitate software implementation.

In the literature of ERP system use for example, the adoption and implementation issues have remarkably received much attention. A number of models, frameworks and guidelines have been proposed in order to identify critical success factors in the implementation of ERP system. It is noticeable that there is a difference in interests between companies who ask for personalized business applications and ERP providers who design a generic commercial offer. Researchers have recommended that organizations change business processes to match the standardized business processes embedded in the ERP software [15, 30, 32]. In effect, Aloini et al. [3] argue that a key risk factor contributing to high failure rate of ERP project implementation is an inadequate change management. As the ERP implementation involves business process change and organizational adaptation to the package, it's crucial to understand the attitudes toward change [41], to assess the organizational fit of the target ERP system before its adoption [32] and to consider the fit between organizational structure and ERP package characteristics [50].

If such view is taken, then consideration of personal views of users might be postponed to an extent which would be disadvantageous [12]. To develop models of human behavior based on description of organizational activity and without understanding the consequences of a potential misfit between the design of the system and the organized activity will have little real world significance as can be seen through the history of IS development failures.

Continuing this discussion in IS security (ISS) area, the implementation of a security policy is also expected to change organizational procedures and practices as well as to shape and monitor the behavior of employees, through education and training, to ensure compliance with security requirements. However, the specific security methods and standards are generally speaking structured, descriptive and often fail to provide practical guidelines to plan, apply, and maintain security processes [58]. Various studies have argued for practice-based organizational frameworks of security policies and controls. The issues explored in this stream of studies cover the influence of the contextual factors such as national culture [68], organizational structure and culture, management support, training and awareness, users' participation in the formulation process, business objectives, legal and regulatory requirements [35, 38]. Another focus of attention of ISS researches has been the compliance of employees to security procedures and guidelines viewed from behavioral perspective and applying socio-cognitive theories [31, 34, 65]. Although understanding how organizational and environmental factors as well as compliance behavior may affect the efficient use of security controls questions about the relevance of security policies and measures are not addressed. The proposed models and frameworks focus more on the application of security policies, consider the need to change the behavior of employees to ensure compliance with security procedures. The data centric focus in ISS frameworks influences work practices and creates unintended consequences and changes in a human activity design instead of being a part of its design. A conceptual approach focusing on rational and formal descriptions leads work intended to cater for ISS in practice to almost solely focus upon data systems security.

Misleading assumptions about rational and irrational behavior of users may explain many security measures failure. If security policy was developed as an add-on to the real world business practices it is quite possibly the case that breach of security policy may in some instances be necessary as in practice it might be the only way for an employee to do a good job. To request people to change behavior is to try to change organizational practices without understanding the effective behavior of the involved stakeholders in the first place. This leads to a lack of compatibility between the real behavior of professional stakeholders and any requested formal changes are likely to lead to security failures in context. In the case study conducted by Kolkowska and Dhillon [39], the workers noted that "The checks and balances that have been built into the system are not necessarily the way in which any of the case-workers operate". Albrechtsen [1] has furthermore identified that an increased security workload might create difficulties for work functionality and efficiency. The author also noticed a trivial effect of documented requirements of expected information security behavior and general awareness campaigns on user behavior and awareness. Albrechtsen and Hovden [2] discussed ways in which security awareness and behavior may be improved and changed through dialogue, participation and collective reflection.

The weakest link is not necessarily in the (technical) system itself but the difference between the formal model of usage and real usage of system content (data) as such in a human activity system. This realization leads Tryfonas et al. [63] to propose an interpretive framework for expanding and incorporating the security functions in the whole IS development. A systemic and value-focused view of security would result in a better understanding of organizational stakeholders of the role and application of security functions in situated practices and an achievement of contextually relevant risk analysis [13, 27, 56]. The study of Spears and Barki [59] provides a particular application of this view in the context of regulatory compliance and confirms the conclusion that the engagement of users in ISS risk management process contributes to more effective security measures and better alignment of security controls with business objectives.

3   ICT-Enabled Organizational Change: A Dialectic View

Langefors [43] discussed the role of organizational IS and considered that, in order to manage an organization, it would be necessary to know something about the current state and behavior of its different parts and also the environment within which it is interacting. These parts would need to be coordinated and inter-related, i.e. to form a system. Thus, means to obtain information from the different parts of a business would be essential and these means (information units) would also need to be inter-related. Since the effectiveness of the organization would depend upon the effectiveness of the information units, an organization could be seen as crucially 'tied-together' by information. For Langefors, therefore, the organization and its information system could be viewed as one and the same.

3.1 Considering Human Activity in IS Design and Implementation

In the IS academic field ever since its official inception as a specific area of interest at the IFIP (International Federation for Information Processing) conference in New York in 1965, questions in multidisciplinary contexts—such as systems thinking, structuring uncertainty, defining and managing wicked problem spaces, socio-technical systems, human activity systems and inquiry systems have been addressed. Based on the review of literature by Hirschheim and Klein [33], Table 2 presents the pioneers of this stream of IS research in the first era (mid-1960s to mid-1970s) of IS history. Despite the considerable number of publications from the sixties to currently, the ST and soft systems approaches continue to be marginalized and underestimated in the higher education of future IS practitioners and academics.

Holistic IS methodologies such as Effective Technical and Human Implementation of Computer supported Systems (ETHICS) by Mumford [52], Soft Systems Methodology (SSM) by Checkland [19], Client-Led Design by Stowell and West [60], Object Oriented Analysis and Design (OOAD) by Mathiassen et al. [49] and approaches such as the Strategic Systemic Thinking (SST) framework by Bednar [11] support analysis into any relevant aspect of IS analysis and development and deal with complex organizational issues.

Recently, Baxter and Sommerville [9] propose a framework for ST systems engineering that combine ST systems design approaches to systems engineering and improve the communication and interaction between system development and organizational change teams by means of two types of activities: the sensitization and awareness and the constructive engagement. The former activities aim to enhance the awareness of system stakeholders about ST issues that have the potential to significantly influence the design and use of the system. The later activity deals with the use of ST system design methods to problem definition, solution construction and evaluation of the deployed system.

Table 2 The ST and soft systems design, adapted from Hirschheim and Klein [33]

Original schools of thought	Concept of IS
[42]	Infological equation
[22]	Inquiry systems
[28, 51, 53]	Socio-technical systems
[19, 20]	Human activity systems

The SSM supported by a multitude of concepts and techniques (such as CATWOE technique Customers, Actors, Transformation process, Worldview, Owners, Environmental constraints) is used for modelling purposeful human activity system through exploration, sense making, and definition of multiple views of problem situations. In Mathiassens et al.'s OOAD several techniques from methodologies such as ETHICS and SSM are transformed, changed and incorporated with an object oriented focus (with tools such as the FACTOR analysis for example). The SST framework includes several techniques and modelling support for analysis especially aimed at inquiries into uncertain and complex problems spaces (incorporating para-consistent logic, techniques for structuring uncertainty from multiple systemic perspectives and including techniques for modelling diversity networks). Additionally these methodologies include critically informed discussions supporting "problematization" of analytical process and enquiry.

3.2 Organizational Change as an Emergent Process

According to this school of thought, the consequences of any IT-reliant IS development efforts are very contextually dependent (e.g. discussions in [10, 43]). In fact, the IS universe is more and more characterized by the growth in number of stakeholders, the quality and the quantity of the different users influencing the design and implementation of IS projects as well as the successes and failures of such projects [26]. IS development process as an ongoing contextual inquiry [11] is characterized as an emergent socio-technical change process conducted through sense making and negotiations among stakeholders [46, 47]. As Checkland and Holwell point out [18], organizational change is only likely to result in success if the individual actors are engaged with that change. It is thus likely that any change imposed from above is likely to result in failure.

The key underpinning to this perspective is that rational model for organizational problem resolution practice is unsatisfactory ever since the foundation for any assumption of complete analytical knowledge of future developments was refuted by the acknowledgement of open systems thinking; the works of Langefors [42, 43], Bateson [8], Churchman [23], Argyris [5], Weick [67] and Ciborra [24] are representative of this paradigm. As such any problem space is unequivocally intertwined with the unique problem solving activity of the specific professional stakeholder working in the organisational context in focus. As pointed out by Ulrich [64] in his discussion of boundary critique perception of a system varies with the stance of the observer, i.e. this differentiates between an observer's and an actor's picture of reality, which means that anyone wishing to inquire into IS use must continually align themselves with actor perspectives.

By way of a narrative and storytelling that draws on the author's own experiences applying ETHICS in many companies in Europe and the United States, Mumford [52] discussed how her research perspective in relation to socio-technical philosophy can be applied in managing change with the introduction of a new work systems or a new technology as a part of the change process. The case studies described in her book offer examples of organizational design activities and assessments to illustrate how the suggested method, based on a participative design, can provide support to problem solving and change process management. One case study for example addresses the design and implementation of an expert system to assist the sales force of a large American enterprise. The sales force are skilled in sales and business knowledge but they had low computer confidence. The new project manager for the development of the expert system, who also will play the role of a facilitator, decided to use the ETHICS methodology to involve the future users in the design process of the software. He created a design group from the technical project team and from the sales staff to integrate organizational, human, technical and task-related factors into the development process. The sales force identify their needs and requirements and the technical group translate these needs in a working system. It is for example necessary to understand according to a sale force perspective the meaning of a helpful and/or useful system. Mumford describes the stress and anxiety of the project manager before the start of design process, because he had doubts about the adhesion of the sales force to the use of the new system since it might be in dissonance with the principle of "selling". He also had concerns about the use of ETHICS methodology as it might be perceived as complicated. Mumford also provides details about the whole experience of the project development including the multiple meetings of the design group, the enthusiastic and difficult steps of a participative design experience and the successful implementation of the new expert system. She describes how during the different meetings the involved team discusses the problems of existing system, future needs and potential benefits of a new system. Questions about the reasons of change, system sustainability and boundaries are also addressed. The "routinization" meetings cover the implementation diagnosis, the realization of benefit management analysis and the evaluation and self-reflective element in terms of improved efficiency and job satisfaction.

In Checkland and Scholes [21], the authors use creation rather than design to describe the process of information system development. Such process requires a deep understanding of how a particular actors attribute meanings to their perceived world and how the purposes assigned to the IS are perceived to be "truly" relevant within this world. It follows that a dialogue in which management can explore the values, goals and preferences of individuals during the process of IS development must be desired. The application of SSM in the UK's National Health Service (NHS) is a particular case study where techniques such as CATWOE analysis and rich pictures are deployed to support the participation of all stakeholders in complex problem situations. One of the main features of this organization is the absence of unitary power structure because the provision of health care in the UK is based on a complicated network of autonomous and semi-autonomous groups. This leads to consideration of further key problems in NHS projects: identification of relationships in the network subject of change, exploration of the impact of change on existing relationships according to multiple perspectives.

In Client led Information System Design, Stowell and West [60] put the client(s) in control of the whole Information System Development process and apply a set of techniques to support the appreciation process of a problem situation and to enable communication between information system professional and client(s). A case study of a medium sized manufacturing company is given to display the practical use of the aforementioned framework. To cope with increasingly competitive dynamics the reappraisal of the commercial activities has been achieved to consider how the use of IT could help to improve the operating efficiency. The board of this company decided to employ a consultant with multidisciplinary background (combination of business and IT) capable to deal with transversal problems within the Commercial Department uttered by the managing group. A number of techniques and diagrams such as spray diagrams, system map, decision tree, Black box diagrams, Rich pictures, and activity models have been used to consider and represent the information systems processes and activities in the clients' perspectives. These techniques used as a mean of communications support a learning process through which the involved group develops a contextual understanding and awareness of the potential changes and related problems in working practices implied by the developing information system. In this case study, such discussion has revealed the use of a parallel and personal information system by some sales staff to process orders bypassing the formal working procedures. The involvement and commitment of clients is also pursued in the technical specification and implementation phases of the new information system. From a "routinization" perspective, the clients agree about the implementation of the changes arising from the incorporation of IT into the information system which might induce new needs in training and skills development as well as the setup of new working practices.

4 Conclusion

This paper aimed to shed light on key IS paradigms in relation to the contribution of ICT in organizational change. The deterministic or dialectic perspectives offer alternatives descriptions for the design, implementation and use of ICT supporting organizational IS. However, the continuous lack of description of organizational transformation issues requires consideration of ways of teaching and research in IS area. This would include discussions about the content and ways of teaching IS units as the education of the future practitioners and academics is influencing their view and understanding of IS as a discipline and IS as a practice. Kawalek [36] for example pointed out a gulf between IS as a discipline and IS as a practice and argued that IS as a discipline should help students critically reflect on how they develop organizational problem solving skills for holistic understanding of the link between ICT and organizational change. Beyond technological determinism or a dialectic relationship students should be aware of the consequences including human and organizational strategies of each account. It is equally relevant to explore issues and address critical problems that have arisen in companies' practices acting in their immediate environment.

In this perspective, Bednar et al. [14] introduced a teaching experience of IS analysis and design unit based on a ST toolbox that has been developed and used in practice by students in many different types of organizations over a period of approximately ten years. Drawing upon and extending methods and techniques from a collection of a number of contemporary ST methodologies, the toolbox deals with 8 themes supporting the application of ST tools for systems analysis in practice and organized in a particular order for pedagogical purposes. They are: change analysis, system structure definition, system purpose, system perspectives, system priorities, desirable system, system action and system for evaluation and engagement. Every student applies ST toolbox in a real life business in the setting of the realization of a final year project. Mainly the involved organizations are small and local businesses but at times they can also be smaller departments or sections within large organizations (not necessarily always local). These projects give students real world experience of real world business practices, issues, processes and provide opportunities to create a stimulating learning environment. At the same time the projects help involved businesses to develop new insights and understandings of key features of their own work practices, in support of their business development. Given the complexity of business analysis, students require analytical and problem-solving techniques for identifying and evaluating organizational and technical consequences of design and implementation of the proposed system. The work can be described as a form of action research. The analyst (investigator/researcher) engages with a real world problem situation in a business. The project would normally involve three employees per case organization, typically representing three different jobs in the same section or department. The engagement is based on reflection and the methods used include observation, participatory observation, interviews and questionnaires. Typically for dialogue and reflection purposes techniques such as Mind-Mapping and Rich Pictures would be used regularly by the analyst both to support a dialogue about understanding the problem situation between the analyst and the interviewee and as a tool for reflection by the analyst. The typical inquiry would consist of at least six main interviews per employee, regular observation of work activities (typically twice a month) and questionnaires (initially one ST questionnaire with sixty questions per employee). Additionally to this there would also be a small number (usually four or five) of open ended conversations and meetings with relevant line managers. The analyst would normally keep a research journal from which excerpts were used to support the analyst description and documentation of conclusions of the inquiry itself. The main aspects of the analysis and inquiry practice were documented in specific templates which are part of the ST Toolbox.

References

1. Albrechtsen, E.: A qualitative study of users' view on information security. Comput. Secur. **26**, 276–289 (2007)
2. Albrechtsen, E., Hovden, J.: Improving information security awareness and behaviour through dialogue, participation and collective reflection. An intervention study. Comput. Secur. **29**, 432–445 (2010)
3. Aloini, D., Dulmin, R., Mininno, V.: Risk management in ERP project introduction: review of the literature. Inf. Manag. **44**, 547–567 (2007)
4. Alter, S.: 18 reasons why it-reliant work systems should replace "the IT artifact" as the core subject matter of the IS field. Commun. Assoc. Inf. Syst. **12**, 365–394 (2003)
5. Argyris, C.: Overcoming Organizational Defenses: Facilitating organizational Learning. Prentice Hall, New Jersey (1990)
6. Avison, D.E., Fitzgerald, G.: Information Systems Development, 4th edn. McGraw-Hill Companies, UK (2006)
7. Baer, T.: So many paths to Nirvana. The Register (2007). Retrieved from http://www.regdeveloper.co.uk/2007/11/28/automating_application_lifecycle/
8. Bateson, G.: Mind and Nature: a Necessary Unity. 5th edn. Hampton Press (2002)
9. Baxter, G., Sommerville, I.: Socio-technical systems: From design methods to systems engineering. Interact. Comput. **23**, 4–17 (2011)
10. Baskerville, R.L., Land, F.: Socially self-destructing systems. In: Avegerou, C., Ci-borra, R., Land, F. (eds.) The Social Study of Information Systems and Communication Technologies, pp. 263–285. Oxford University Press, Oxford (2004)
11. Bednar, P.M.: A contextual integration of individual and organizational learning perspectives as part of IS analysis. Informing Sci. J. **3**(3), 145–156 (2000)
12. Bednar, P., Welch, C.: IS, process, organizational change and their relationship with contextual dependencies. In: Proceedings of 13th European Conference on Information Systems: Information Systems in a Rapidly Changing Economy. Regensburg (2005)
13. Bednar, P.M., Katos, V.: Addressing the human factor in information systems security MCIS2009. In: Poulymenakou, A., Pouloudi, N., Pramatari, K. (eds.) 4th Mediterranean Conference on Information Systems. Athens, Greece, 25–27 Sept (2009)
14. Bednar, P.M., Sadok, M., Shiderova, V.: Socio-technical toolbox for business analysis in practice. In: Caporarello, L., Di Martino, B., Martinez, M. (eds.) Smart Organizations and Smart Artifacts: Fostering Interaction between People, Technologies and Processes, vol. 7, pp. 219–228. Lecture Notes in Information Systems and Organisation, Springer, Berlin (2014)
15. Benders, J., Batenburg, R., van der Blonk, H.: Sticking to standards: technical and other isomorphic pressures in deploying ERP-systems. Inf. Manag. **43**(2), 194–203 (2006)
16. Bennett, S., McRobb, S., Farmer, R.: Object Oriented Systems Analysis and Design. McGraw Hill, New York (2002)
17. Besson, P., Rowe, F.: Strategizing information systems-enabled organizational transformation: a transdisciplinary review and new directions. J. Strateg. Inf. Syst. **21**, 103–124 (2012)
18. Checkland, P., Holwell, S.: Information, Systems and Information Systems. Wiley, Chichester (1998)
19. Checkland, P.: Systems Thinking, Systems Practice. Wiley, Chichester (1981)
20. Checkland, P.: Towards a systems-based methodology for real-world problem-solving. J. Appl. Syst. Eng. **3**(2), 87–116 (1972)
21. Checkland, P., Scholes, J.: Soft Systems Methodology in Action. Wiley, Chichester (1990)
22. Churchman, C.W.: The Design of Inquiring Systems. Basis Books, New York (1971)
23. Churchman, C.W.: The Systems Approach and Its Enemies. Basic Books, New York (1979)
24. Ciborra, C.: From Control to Drift: the Dynamics of Corporate Information Infrastructures. Oxford University Press, Oxford (2000)
25. Cooper, R.B., Zmud, R.W.: Information technology implementation research: a technology diffusion approach. Manage. Sci. **36**(2), 123–139 (1990)

26. D'Atri, A., De Marco, M.: Interdisciplinary Aspects of Information Systems Studies. Springer, Heidelberg (2008)
27. Dhillon, G., Torkzadeh, G.: Value-focused assessment of information system security in organizations. Inf. Syst. J. **16**, 293–314 (2006)
28. Emery, F., Trist, E.: The causal texture of organizational environments. Human Relat. **18**, 21–32 (1965)
29. Gattiker, T.F., Goodhue, D.L.: Understanding the local-level costs and benefits of ERP through organizational information processing theory. Inf. Manag. **41**(4), 431–443 (2004)
30. Hammer, M., Stanton, S.: How process enterprises really work. Harvard Business Review, Watertown (1999)
31. Herath, T., Rao, H.R.: Encouraging information security behaviors in organizations: role of penalties, pressures and perceived effectiveness. Decis. Support Syst. **47**, 154–165 (2009)
32. Hong, K.-K., Kim, Y.-G.: The critical success factors for ERP implementation: an organizational fit perspective. Inf. Manag. **40**(1), 25–40 (2002)
33. Hirschheim, R., Klein, H.K.: A glorious and not-so-short history of the information systems field. J. Assoc. Inf. Syst. **13**(4), 188–235 (2012)
34. Ifinedo, P.: Understanding information systems security policy compliance: an integration of the theory of planned behavior and the protection motivation theory. Comput. Secur. **31**, 83–95 (2012)
35. Karyda, M., Kiountouzis, E., Kokolakis, S.: Information systems security policies: a contextual perspective. Comput. Secur. **24**, 246–260 (2005)
36. Kawalek, J.P.: Rethinking information systems in organizations: integrating organizational problem solving. Routledge, UK (2008)
37. Kendall, K.E., Kendall, J.E.: Systems Analysis and Design. Pearson Prentice Hall, Upper Saddle River (2005)
38. Knapp, K.J., Morris, F., Marshall, T.E., Byrd, T.A.: Information security policy: An organizational-level process model. Comput. Secur. **28**, 493–508 (2009)
39. Kolkowska, E., Dhillon, G.: Organizational power and information security rule compliance. Comput. Secur. **33**, 3–11 (2013)
40. Kroenke, D.M.: Using MIS. Pearson Education Limited, New Delhi (2013)
41. Kwahk, K.-Y., Ahn, H.: Moderating effects of localization differences on ERP use: a socio-technical systems perspective. Comput. Hum. Behav. **26**, 186–198 (2010)
42. Langefors, B.: Theoretical Analysis of Information Systems. Studentlitteratur, Lund (1966)
43. Langefors, B.: Essays on Infology, Summing up and Planning for the Future. Studentlitteratur, Lund (1995)
44. Laudon, K.C., Laudon, J.P.: Essentials of Business Information Systems. Pearson Prentice Hall, Upper Saddle River (2007)
45. Lucas, H.C., Walton, E.J., Ginzberg, M.J.: Implementing packaged software. MIS Q. 537–549 (1988)
46. Luna-Reyes, L.F., Zhang, J., Gil-Garcıa, J.R., Cresswell, A.M.: Information system development as emergent socio-technical change: a practice approach. Eur. J. Inf. Syst. **14**, 93–105 (2005)
47. Luna-Reyes, L.F., Zhang, J., Gil-Garcıa, J.R., Cresswell, A.M.: Information system development as emergent socio-technical change: a practice approach. Eur. J. Inf. Syst. **14**, 93–105 (2005)
48. Markus, M.L., Majchrzak, A., Gasser, L.: Design theory for systems that support emergent knowledge processes. MIS Q. **26**(3), 179–212 (2002)
49. Mathiassen, L., Munk-Madsen, A., Nielsen, P.A., Stage, J.: Object Oriented Analysis and Design. Marko, Aalborg (2000)
50. Morton, N.A., Hu, Q.: Implications of the fit between organizational structure and ERP: a structural contingency theory perspective. Int. J. Inf. Manag. **28**, 391–402 (2008)
51. Mumford, E.: Computer systems and work design: problems of philosophy and vision. Personnel Rev. **3**(2), 40–49 (1974)
52. Mumford, E.: Redesigning human systems. IRM Press, London (2003)

53. Mumford, E., Henshall, D.: A participative approach to the design of computer systems. Associated Business Press, North-Holland, London (1978)
54. Orlikowski, W.J., Iacono, C.S.: Research commentary: desperately seeking the "IT" in IT research—a call to theorizing the IT artifact? Inf. Syst. Res. **12**(2), 121–134 (2001)
55. Oz, E., Jones, A.: Management Information Systems. Cengage Learning EMEA, Boston (2008)
56. Salmela, H.: Analysing business losses caused by information systems risk: a business process analysis approach. J. Inf. Technol. **23**, 185–202 (2008)
57. Satzinger, J.W., Jackson, R.B., Burd, S.D.: Object-Oriented Analysis and Design with the Unified Process. Thomson Course Technology (2005)
58. Siponen, M., Willison, R.: Information security management standards: problems and solutions. Inf. Manag. **46**, 267–270 (2009)
59. Spears, J.L., Barki, H.: User participation in information systems security risk management. MIS Q. **34**(3), 503–522 (2010)
60. Stowell, F., West, D.: Client-led design: a systemic approach to information systems definition. McGraw-Hill, London (1994)
61. Stumpf, R.V., Teague, L.C.: Object-Oriented Systems Analysis and Design with ULM, 428p. Pearson Prentice Hall, Upper Saddle River (2005)
62. Teichroew, D.: Improvements in the System life Cycle. Information Processing, p. 74. North-Holland (1974)
63. Tryfonas, T., Kiountouzis, E., Polymenakou, A.: Embedding security practices in contemporary information systems development approaches. Inf. Manag. Comput. Secur. **9** (4), 183–197 (2001)
64. Ulrich, W.: Critical Heuristics of Social Planning. Wiley, Chichester (1983)
65. Vance, A., Siponen, M., Pahnila, S.: Motivating IS security compliance: insights from habit and protection motivation theory. Inf. Manag. **49**, 190–198 (2012)
66. Weaver, P., Lambrou, N., Walkley, M.: Practical Business Systems Development Using SSADM—A complete Tutorial Guide. Pearson Education Limited, New Delhi (2002)
67. Weick, K.: Sense-Making in Organizations. Sage, Thousand Oaks (1995)
68. Yildirima, E.Y., Akalpa, G., Aytacb, S., Bayramb, N.: Factors influencing information security management in small- and medium-sized enterprises: a case study from Turkey. Int. J. Inf. Manage. **31**, 360–365 (2011)

e-Business Assimilation Levels in Lebanon

Mary Ann B. El Rassi and Antoine Harfouche

Abstract Developing countries are a potential growth site for e-business expansion and adoption. But despite this promising opportunity, Lebanon has been slow to adopt e-business and the gap between initial and advanced adopters (routinizers) is significant. This paper investigates the factors that explain the differences in e-business assimilation levels. The Perceived e-Readiness Model was adopted and then adapted to fit the Lebanese context. Quantitative data were collected from a large sample of 171 executives from three different industries: banking, retailing, and tourism. While comparing initial adopters to routinizers, our results have shown that routinizers choice to adopt e-Business was based on strategic planning, while initial adopters were mimetic followers.

Keywords e-Business assimilation · IDT · Perceived e-Readiness · Initial adopters · Advanced adopters

1 Introduction

E-business can bring positive potentials to developing countries in addition to making businesses more competitive by offering new opportunities and possibilities for development [1, 2]. According to [3], "by reducing information asymmetry, the Web can increase market efficiency. By lowering intermediation costs, it increases transactional and operational effectiveness. By delinking the storage, processing and ferrying of information from location, it makes distance largely irrelevant,

M.A.B. El Rassi (✉)
Université Saint Joseph, Beyrouth, Lebanon
e-mail: maryann.barbourrassi@usj.edu.lb

A. Harfouche
Université Paris Ouest Nanterre La Défense, Paris, France
e-mail: antoineharfouche@icto.info

© Springer International Publishing Switzerland 2016   141
F. Ricciardi and A. Harfouche (eds.), *Information and Communication
Technologies in Organizations and Society*, Lecture Notes in Information
Systems and Organisation 15, DOI 10.1007/978-3-319-28907-6_9

thereby multiplying the scope and scale of services delivery. Lastly, it is an enabling tool which people can use for increasing productivity."

By using the Web, firms in developing countries have an equal opportunity to access the global markets easily, operate more efficiently, and compete fairly [4]. There has been increased interest recently in online startups that hold promise for different industries, including banking, tourism, retail, education and government. Despite many efforts to capitalize on this growing field, e-business activities in Lebanon do not offer much to the economy.[1] This is due to many reasons that hamper its growth including the weak presence of governmental programs to promote the benefits of e-business [5, 6] and the lack of regulatory supports [7].

However, despite the importance of this topic, there has been very little systematic investigation in Lebanon about why some firms succeed in assimilating e-business while others do not. By assimilation we mean, "to which extent the information and communication technology (ICT) diffuses along the organization's processes and to which extent it becomes integrated in the related activities within the organization" [8].

This paper aims at identifying the factors that affect e-business assimilation in Lebanon. The Perceived e-Readiness Model (PERM model), developed by Molla and Licker [9], was used and then adapted to fit the Lebanese context.

The research methodology was based on a survey conducted to collect. Quantitative data from a large sample of 171 executives. The sample was randomly selected from three specific industries: banking, retailing, and tourism. The data collected were Analyzed using the techniques of Structural Equation Modeling (SEM).

This research reflects our concern ro investigate the factors that can help in attaining the different stages of e-business assimilation in developing countries (DC). Why and how do firms implement ICT have always been the researchers interest in Information System. Therefore, we will discuss the major theories concerning e-business assimilation, then we will present our research model, methodology and results.

2 e-Business Assimilation Theory

Assimilation is a vital construct that can be observed starting from the firm's adoption of ICT till its impact on the organizations' business performance. Purvis et al. [10] define the assimilation processes as "the extent to which the use of technology diffuses across the organizational work processes and becomes routinized in the activities of those processes".

Furthermore, in the literature, most of the studies were based on Rogers' model in conceptualizing innovation adoption as a process through which individuals and

---

[1]http://www.wamda.com/2013/02/overview-of-the-e-commerce-scene-in-lebanon.

other decision makers would pass from first knowledge of a certain innovation to another phase. According to Rogers, the first phase starts by forming a certain attitude towards innovation, then taking the decision whether to adopt or reject the implementation of a new idea and then confirmation of such a decision. Rogers clearly argues that innovation's characteristics are a result of the adopters' perceptiveness of such an innovation. He states that "subjective evaluation of an innovation, derived from individuals' personal experience and perception and conveyed by interpersonal networks, drives the diffusion process" [11].

Furthermore, the theory of Innovation Assimilation also distinguishes between the adoption and assimilation processes. While the adoption process refers to spreading the technology across the organization and among its population, Zhu et al. [12] define e-business assimilation as a series of stages from a firm's initial evaluation of e-business at the pre-adoption stage (initiation), to its formal adoption and finally to its full- scale deployment at the post-adoption stage. During the routinization stage, the e-business becomes an integrated part of the value chain activities.

In this paper, we adopt Zhu et al.'s definition of e-business assimilation that consists of three stages: initiation, adoption, and routinization. The second and third stages of assimilation (adoption and routinization), that describe different levels of e-Business, have particular relevance to our study.

2.1   The Initiation Phase

The first phase "amounts both to identifying and prioritizing needs and problems on one hand and to searching the organization's environment to locate potential solutions that can meet the organization's problems" [11]. Kwon and Zmud [13] argue that the pressure to adopt innovation can derive either from the organizational pressure and needs (pull), or from the technological innovations (push), and/or sometimes from both. This first phase is similar to stages 1–3 in Rogers' model (Figs. 1, 2).

2.2   The Adoption Phase

After making the decision to adopt the new technology, its acceptance or rejection within the organization becomes crucial. This stage is represented by Stages 4 and 5 in Rogers' model (Fig. 1). After initial adoption, the firm and its members usually do not have sufficient knowledge to leverage the system, and often misalignments occur between the new technology adoption and the user's environment [12]. Therefore, the use of resource allocation in this phase can help spreading e-business assimilation in the advanced phase [8].

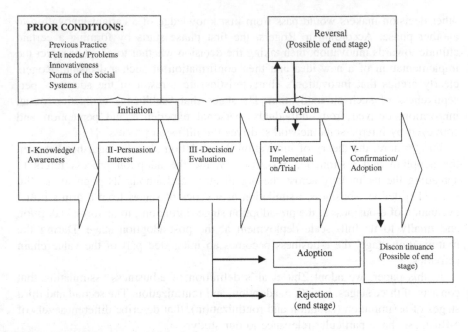

Fig. 1 Rogers' five stages model of adoption

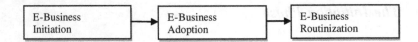

Fig. 2 e-Business assimilation process

2.3 The Routinization Phase

The e-business routinization is identified as the phase where e-business is broadly used as an essential part of the organization's value chain [12]. At this level, the innovation becomes integrated within the company's business activities.

For the purpose of our research, we omit the initiation phase and only consider the last two phases: adoption and routinization. Indeed, our decision is based on the fact that we aim at investigating e-business assimilation among firms that have already decided and started to adopt e-business and identifying the factors that might hinder the assimilation phase in adopting e-business and reaching a full routinization.

Our definition focuses on the firm's relative success in integrating the web technologies in e-business strategies. e-Business assimilation is considered as the result of a set of structures and human behaviors that adopt Web technologies to enhance their business strategies and improve their customer relationship management.

3 Antecedents of e-Business Assimilation

Many theoretical frameworks were developed to investigate the factors that influence the e-business assimilation. Amongst the most widely cited, we may state: (1) the Diffusion of Innovation Theory, (2) the Technology-Organizational-Environmental Framework, and (3) the Institutional Theory, and (4) the Perceived e-Readiness Model. For the context of our research, we will review these four theoretical models and compare them accordingly as they explain the e-business assimilation in organizations.

3.1 The Diffusion of Innovation Theory (DOI)

Rogers [11], in his 1995 research study, builds up a new model called Organizational Innovation Diffusion Theory. In this model, he identifies the variables related to the firms' innovation adoption decisions. He argues that the innovation diffusion process in an organization is influenced by individual's characteristics, as well as external and internal factors. Indeed, he states that the leader's attitude towards change weighs heavily on the overall decision. In addition to this, he considers the centralization of the decision, the complexity that refers to the employees level of expertise and knowledge, the formalization that refers to which extent the organization would push their employees to follow regulations and procedures within the system, the interconnectedness that refers to the extent to which the departments are connected within each other inside the organization, and last, the firms' size. Rogers also takes into consideration the system openness as an important antecedent of the innovation assimilation.

3.2 The Technology–Organization Environment Theory (TOE)

Tornatzky and Fleisher's [14] TOE model considers three different organizational characteristics that may have an impact on the way the company adopts e-business: Technological, organizational and environmental. The technological framework takes into consideration the external and internal factors that are relevant to the organization, such as availability of equipments and technologies. The organizational framework takes into consideration the size, structure and capacity of an organization. While the environmental framework depends on the environment where the organization conducts its business such as the competition, the industry type and the existing governmental support and rules etc...

3.3 The Institutional Theory (IT)

The Institutional theory accentuates the fact that the external environment has a very strong effect on the organization's behavior. It has been adopted in the is research to study antecedents of ICT assimilation in organizations. According to this theory, organizational goals are not always driven by efficiency but can sometimes be influenced by external environmental factors [15]. Research results on IT assimilation [10, 16, 17] show that organization's predisposition for assimilation is influenced by three major factors: Mimetic, coercive and normative institutional pressures. The mimetic pressures are detected when the organization imitates other organizations in its environment [18]. The coercive pressures are the informal or formal pressures that are being exerted on the company by other organizations [15]. The normative pressures are the result of dyadic relationships between organizations. When the organization shares direct or indirect bounds (rules, norms and information) with other organizations, it will learn from the other's experience.

The main limitation of the IT is that it only considers the influence of external factors.

3.4 The Perceived e-Readiness Model (PERM)

The previous listed theories have had much empirical support in the literature, and based on them, many models have been developed to study different angles and perspectives of e-business adoption and assimilation (see Table 1). While some models have only examined the external environmental factors [16], some others have considered only the technological factors [19].

Furthermore, most of these studies were built up for the case of developed countries. But developed countries differ from developing countries in terms of environmental factors, such as the delivery and payment systems. Therefore, we will adopt a model developed specifically for developing countries: The Perceived e-Readiness Model (PERM) that was proposed by Molla and Licker [9]. This model recognizes numerous organizational and contextual factors that might influence e-Business assimilation in developing countries. It includes two major constructs that assess endogenous and exogenous factors: Perceived Organizational

Table 1 Major studies based on previous stated theories

Theoretical model	IT Adoption	Authors
DOI	Material requirements planning (MRP)	[8]
DOI	e-Business	[12]
TOE	e-Business initiation, adoption and routinization	[12]
TOE	e-Business Usage	[7]
TOE	Deployment of B2B e-Commerce firms versus non B2B firms	[17]
TOE and IT	Electronic procurement systems (EPSs)	[18]

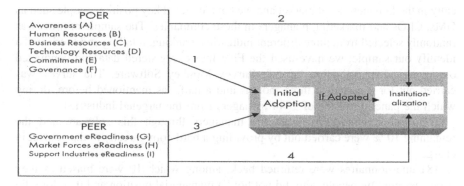

Fig. 3 The PERM model [9]

e-Readiness (POER) and Perceived External e-Readiness (PEER). Both of these constructs take into consideration managers' perception of internal and external factors affecting the e-Business assimilation level. The POER describes managers' perception of the extent to which they believe that their firm is aware of the potential benefits, has the adequate resources and commitment, and the organization's governance to implement e-Business [9]. While the PEER construct describes managers' perception as well as their assessment of the extent to which they believe that external market forces, government e-readiness, and other supporting industries could encourage their organization to assimilate the e-Business activities (Fig. 3).

4 Research Methodology

The goal of our research is to investigate the factors affecting assimilation of e-business in Lebanon by comparing the initial adopters with the advanced adopters in order to understand further the assimilation process and how these factors may have differential effects in different industries. Indeed, our research methodology

Table 2 The response rate distributed over the three sectors

Industry type	Response rates		
	Sample	Response group	Response rate (%)
Banking	249	45	18
Retailing	530	80	15
Tourism	265	46	17.35
Total biased responses		10	0.95
Total number of responses	1044	181	17.33

was based on a survey conducted to collect quantitative data from a large sample of executives that were chosen from click and mortar organizations operating physically in the Lebanese local market and we have targeted key position people such as GMs, CEOs and marketing managers in these companies. The sample of firms was randomly selected from three different industries: banking, retailing and tourism. To identify our sample, we have used the Five Index[2] registered data and conducted our empirical investigation through Survey Monkey Software. The survey was carried out for a period of three months and a half,[3] as mentioned before, during which the panel consisted of 1044 managers from the targeted industries.

We reached almost 90 % of the managers through this software and the remaining 10 % were carried out by providing a hard copy directly to the contact in charge.

181 questionnaires were returned back, among which 10 were biased as they were answered by people who did not hold a managerial position and therefore did not have enough experience in the field. The remaining 171 questionnaires were useful and the response rates are presented in Table 2. These companies are divided into two groups: initial adopters and routinizers according to their level of e-Business assimilation.

Data collected were analyzed using the techniques of structural equation modeling (SEM). These methods are widely accepted in IS especially when it comes to testing complex causal models with many latent variables. The estimation procedure we adopted was the Partial Least Squares Path Modeling (PLS). Data was processed using the software SmartPLS [20].

---

[2]The 5 index is a comprehensive database consisting of an electronic search engine that includes fundamental information about businesses operating in the Lebanese market.

[3]Giving the fact that most our respondents are busy professional people with a very tight schedule, the choice of the survey and the circumstances was limited to 47 questions that took an average of 27 min to be filled out over the internet. This had allowed us to avoid offending busy executives with long questionnaires and face to face interviews.

5 Research Model

We adopted the Perceived e-Readiness Model in Developing Countries (PERM). This model proposes the "e-Business Adoption Level" as a dependent variable that is composed of two different levels: (1) Initial adoption of e-business and (2) institutionalization of e-Business in addition to two major constructs: perceived organizational e-readiness (POER) and perceived external e-readiness (PEER).

POER is defined as managers' perception to which they believe that their organization has the awareness, commitment, governance and resources to adopt e-Business. For example, Awareness refers to the organization's ability to perceive and comprehend any potential benefits, opportunities, and threats of adopting e-business.

Resources refer to the human, technological and business resources level in the firm. Commitment refers to the management's support, especially from the upper management, in an effort to champion e-business projects.

Governance refers to the tactical, strategic and operational model that identifies the way the organizations structure their operations to set up objectives, search up for resources and make decisions.

While the PEER is defined as managers' perception to which they believe that market forces e-readiness, government e-readiness, and supporting industries e-readiness are ready to support organization's e-Business implementation.

Government e-Readiness refers to the important role that government can play in encouraging the adoption of e-business in DC [21]. Market Forces e-Readiness refers to the market environment. Indeed, organizations are mostly influenced by their market environment, such as: competitors, suppliers, and clients [15]. Supporting Industries e-Readiness refers to the development of support to e-Business in a given industry such as having the right e-payment systems available and at an affordable cost.

The model and its constructs reasonably cover several characteristics and contexts that previous studies had identified as important determinants of innovation adoption.

Furthermore, as we have adopted the PERM original scales, it was important to measure the quality of the selected scales in our research specific context. We did it in two steps: (1) Exploratory factor analysis and (2) Confirmatory factor analysis.

5.1 Exploratory Factor Analysis

The exploratory factor analysis has been done through a principal component analysis (PCA). We did one PCA for the external variables and another one for the internal variables. We started the verification process by validating the Kaiser–Meyer–Olkin's measure and the Bartlett's test. Both internal and external factors show a very good test of Kaiser–Meyer–Olkin measure (with 0.827 and 0.941 much higher than the minimum of 0.40 requested) and a significant Bartlett's test (sig < 0.05).

Then, we checked the variables' commonality that estimates the percentage of each item that will be covered by their factors. None of the items showed any communality less than 0.50, so none of the items was eliminated.

To determine the number of factors to be retained, we adopted the Kaiser's method that proposes to keep only factors with eigenvalues greater than 1. In the case of external factors, only the first three factors or components had an eigenvalue >1. In our model we also have three latent variables that resume the external forces (Government e-Readiness, Supporting Industries e-Readiness, and Market Forces e-Readiness). In the internal factors, only the first four factors had an eigenvalue >1. But in our model, we have seven latent variables (Awareness, Commitment, Governance, Human Resources, Business Resources, Technological Resources, and Level of e-Business adoption). Therefore, a new construct called e-Business Assimilation Level (e-BAL) was created by combining the four variables related to the firm's resources (Human, Business, and Technological) with the level of e-Business adoption.

5.2 Confirmatory Factor Analysis

The reliability test was conducted with a confirmatory factor analysis (CFA). The validation was done through two elements: (1) the convergent validity, and (2) the internal validity.

Thus, we first verified that all items actually converge to their respective variable. As shown in Table 3, the CFA confirms the results of the exploratory factor analysis for the latent variables: Government e-Readiness, Supporting Industries e-Readiness, Market Forces e-Readiness, Awareness, Commitment and Governance. Indeed, all their items show a loading greater than 0.7 ($\lambda > 0.7$). Nevertheless, the new construct that we have called Level of e-Business Assimilation has some items that do not fully converge to the construct. Indeed, the CFA showed that we need to eliminate HR2 ($\lambda = 0.46$), TR4 ($\lambda = 0.57$), BR1 ($\lambda = 0.68$), BR3 ($\lambda = 0.67$), and BR5 ($\lambda = 0.58$) as their respective loadings do not meet the minimum value required ($\lambda > 0.7$).

After conducting a bootstrap, we found that all the items have a t >|1.96| and a p < 0.05 except BR2 that has a t = 1.955 and p = 0.051; Therefore we will also eliminate this item. The convergent validity per latent variable was then measured using the Average Variance Extracted (AVE) where, as shown in Table 4, AVE are all greater than 0.5 (AVE > 0.5).

Then, we verified the internal validity or consistency of each latent variable. The internal validity confirms that the chosen items capture the essence of the variable. The Cronbach's alpha is used as an indicator to measure the reliability and to ensure that all the variable's items are compatible.

Table 3 Item to construct correlation

	GeR	MFR	SIeR	A	C	G	e-Business assimilation
GeR1	**0.80**	0.21	0.31	−0.04	0.10	0.14	0.03
GeR2	**0.92**	0.11	0.40	−0.06	0.12	0.13	−0.04
GeR3	**0.90**	0.19	0.41	−0.08	0.16	0.14	0.00
GeR4	**0.84**	0.13	0.42	−0.07	0.10	0.08	−0.03
MFR1	0.18	**0.92**	0.28	0.22	0.15	0.19	0.04
MFR2	0.15	**0.90**	0.31	0.25	0.14	0.13	0.16
SIeR1	0.25	0.26	**0.72**	0.09	0.16	0.22	0.18
SIeR2	0.32	0.32	**0.78**	0.22	0.25	0.31	0.20
SIeR3	0.27	0.39	**0.74**	0.12	0.24	0.19	0.15
SIeR4	0.19	0.25	**0.76**	0.07	0.16	0.19	0.11
SIeR5	0.28	0.29	**0.70**	0.13	0.33	0.32	0.25
SIeR6	0.26	0.34	**0.75**	0.23	0.32	0.37	0.32
A1	−0.04	0.38	0.20	**0.84**	0.18	0.19	0.32
A2	−0.07	0.38	0.20	**0.89**	0.16	0.18	0.28
A3	−0.05	0.37	0.12	**0.84**	0.07	0.30	0.29
A4	−0.07	0.37	0.15	**0.84**	0.27	0.13	0.19
A5	−0.03	0.37	0.17	**0.86**	0.19	0.21	0.20
A6	−0.07	0.25	0.09	**0.82**	0.02	0.22	0.36
A7	−0.13	0.34	0.15	**0.75**	0.19	0.06	0.27
C1	0.11	0.41	0.27	0.26	**0.85**	0.16	0.16
C2	0.03	0.43	0.23	0.26	**0.82**	0.19	0.17
C3	0.13	0.43	0.25	0.27	**0.89**	0.14	0.17
C4	0.21	0.36	0.33	0.14	**0.74**	0.17	0.15
C5	0.11	0.33	0.26	0.17	**0.84**	0.20	0.16
G1	0.04	0.34	0.29	0.16	0.12	**0.83**	0.16
G2	0.11	0.34	0.36	0.26	0.17	**0.85**	0.17
G3	0.20	0.25	0.35	0.36	0.17	**0.84**	0.17
G4	0.08	0.34	0.30	0.16	0.17	**0.87**	0.17
G5	0.09	0.34	0.28	0.16	0.17	**0.86**	0.16
G6	0.12	0.24	0.31	0.15	0.17	**0.81**	0.16
G7	0.20	0.33	0.26	0.14	0.16	**0.79**	0.16
G8	0.07	0.24	0.15	0.25	0.16	**0.73**	0.26
HR1	−0.04	0.14	0.10	0.15	0.15	0.15	**0.73**
HR2	−0.24	0.20	−0.08	0.23	0.25	0.22	**0.46**
TR1	0.05	0.32	0.24	0.15	0.16	0.26	**0.70**
TR2	0.05	0.28	0.26	0.16	0.16	0.16	**0.75**
TR3	−0.08	0.33	0.18	0.16	0.15	0.25	**0.72**
TR4	0.05	0.25	0.14	0.14	0.14	0.14	**0.57**
TR5	0.06	0.26	0.21	0.14	0.15	0.25	**0.75**

(continued)

Table 3 (continued)

	GeR	MFR	SIeR	A	C	G	e-Business assimilation
TR6	0.00	0.38	0.23	0.16	0.16	0.26	**0.80**
Adoption Level	0.09	0.38	0.24	0.14	0.15	0.25	**0.70**
BR1	−0.15	0.29	0.11	0.15	0.14	0.15	**0.68**
BR2	−0.06	0.26	0.10	0.15	0.15	0.15	**0.71**
BR3	0.05	0.26	0.17	0.15	0.15	0.15	**0.67**
BR4	−0.05	0.43	0.29	0.16	0.17	0.27	**0.72**
BR5	−0.24	−0.02	−0.05	0.09	0.02	0.03	**0.58**
BR6	0.03	0.32	0.25	0.15	0.16	0.26	**0.76**

The bold is due to standards in the representation of statistical results

Table 4 Convergent and discriminate validity

	AVE	Composite reliability	R square	Cronbachs alpha	Convergent validity	Discriminant validity
A	0.70	0.94	0.18	0.93	VC	VC
C	0.69	0.92	0.48	0.89	VC	VC
e-Business-assimilation	0.57	0.92	0.69	0.90	VC	VC
G	0.68	0.94	0.73	0.93	VC	VC
GeR	0.75	0.92	0.00	0.89	VC	VC
MFeR	0.83	0.90	0.17	0.79	VC	VC
SIeR	0.55	0.88	0.20	0.84	VC	VC

VC Validity is confirmed

As shown in Table 4, all the latent variables have a Cronbach's alpha greater than 0.7. The index of Composite Reliability of Dillon and Goldstein will also be used to validate the reliability of the latent variables by checking the internal consistency of each block of indicators. Based on Nunnally and Bernstein [22], we will adopt 0.70 as an acceptable level of Dillon and Goldstein's Rho. As shown in Table 4, all latent variables have a great Composite Reliability higher than 0.88.

6 Research Results

The research model (Fig. 4) consists of three levels: (1) The external variables level: Government e-Readiness, Supporting Industries e-Readiness and Market Forces e-Readiness; (2) the managerial and strategic level: Awareness, Commitment, Governance; and (3) the e-Business Assimilation level.

This model will be estimated for two segments: initial adopters and routinizers.

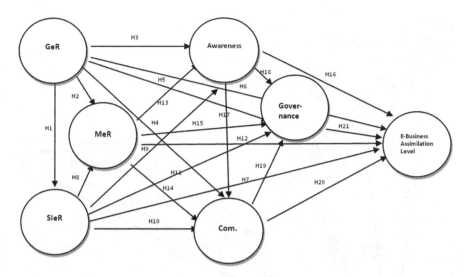

Fig. 4 The research model

6.1 Comparison Between Initial-Adopters and Routinizers

6.1.1 Initial Adopters: Mimetic Behavior

In the initial adoption stage, the e-Business Assimilation process starts with the external forces with a negative but significant impact from the Government e-Readiness towards Awareness, Commitment and Market Force e-Readiness (GeR -> MFeR path value = , t = −0272, t = 3.9746; GeR -> C path value = 0.4778, t = 4.8946; GeR -> A path value = −0.4105, t = 5.03).

We also notice that e-Business Assimilation is the direct result of four latent variables among them three show a statistically strong and direct relationship with e-Business Assimilation (MFeR -> e-BAL path value = 0.3655, t = 5.65; C -> e-BAL path value = 0.3542, t = 3.345; and SIeR -> eBAL path value = 0.6792, t = 5.0649) while Governance shows a negative but significant direct relationship with e-Business Assimilation Level (G -> e-BAL path value = −0.4479, t = 3.8398). Thus, e-Business Assimilation Level is 78.3 % explained by those four latent variables (R2 = 0.783).

Another interesting point is the lack of support and relationship from Awareness towards Governance and e-Business Assimilation Level (Fig. 5).

At this point, the results of the structural model show that there is a positive relation between the External Forces (SIeR and MFeR), Awareness and Commitment, but the decision to adopt the right Governance is a direct result of the Commitment only (R2 = 0.48) rather than the Awareness (no link between Awareness and Governance). Those results lead us to conclude that initial adopters are adopting e-business due to External Pressure with no strategic vision to reach a

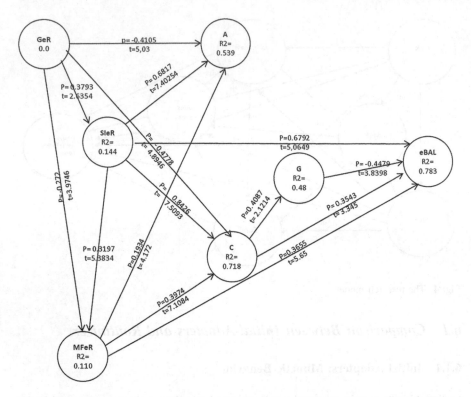

Fig. 5 The initial adopters model estimated with path coefficient values and t values (see Appendix A)

higher Assimilation Level. Organizations lack a strong commitment and absence of Awareness which is reflected in a weak Governance to support a high level of e-Business assimilation. Thus, the low Assimilation Level can be due to imitation factors as the investment in e-Business is not based on Awareness of the potential benefits. This refers us back to the mimetic isomorphism of IT where DiMaggio and Powell [15] state: "when goals are ambiguous, or when the environment creates symbolic uncertainty, organizations may model themselves on other organizations as a method for dealing with uncertainty".

6.1.2 Advanced Adopters: Strategic Adoption

The external pressure starts form GeR with two relationships that show to be negative but significant (GeR -> MFeR path value = −0.2722, t = 4.0672; GeR -> C path value = −0.1425, t = 2.6071), while Market Force e-Readiness has a positive and significant influence on the organizations' strategies (MFeR -> A path value =

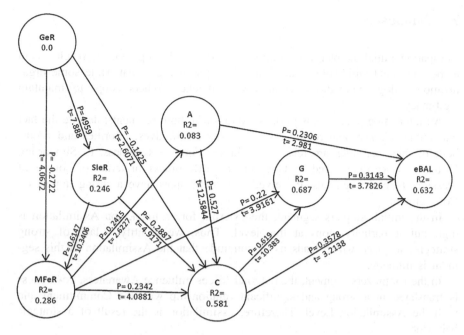

Fig. 6 The routinizers model estimated with path coefficient values and t values (see Appendix B)

0.2415, t = 2.6227; MFeR -> C path value = 0.2342, t = 4.0881; MFeR -> G path value of 0.22, t = 3.9161).

E-Business Assimilation is the direct result of all three latent variables: Awareness, Commitment and Governance with an R squared value of 0.632 (A -> e-BAL path value = 0.2306, t = 2.981; C -> e-BAL path value = 0.3578, t = 3.2138; G -> eBAL path value = 0.3143, t = 3.7826) (Fig. 6).

This model is different from the initial adopters' model by having only the organizational strategies such as Awareness, Commitment and Governance explaining 63.2 % of the e-Business Assimilation Level. The role of the Governmental Support towards Market Force e-Readiness and Commitment differs also shows a negative but significant relationship. This can be explained by the fact that advanced adopters are aware of the potential benefits and therefore strongly committed to adopt e-Business and look forward for having a stronger Governmental Support, such as laws and regulations, that would encourage them to be more committed and therefore pressure the market environment to positively influence their commitment.

The high assimilation level is the result of a strong organizational strategy that is influenced by their market environment and those organizations expect a stronger support from the government as well.

7   Conclusion

Comparing initial adopter with routinizers (advanced adopters), the results seem to be consistent with Tolbert and Zucker [23] who argue that while some organizations adopt innovations to improve efficiency, others adopt to maintain legitimacy.

An interesting point seems to be in common in both segments: despite the fact that initial adopters and routinizers have different motives, priorities and needs, both of their activities are related to Market Force e-Readiness, to Supporting Industries e-Readiness and to Government e-Readiness in terms of source of pressure. In both segments, Perceived External Forces have a strong impact on Commitment.

In the initial adopters segment, the external forces impact on Assimilation is high but it partially stops at this level. Thus, we identify a lack of strong strategies in place which leads us to conclude that the Assimilation in this segment is mimetic.

In the routinizers segment, the external forces influence Awareness. Awareness is translated in a strong and significant relationship with the Commitment and with the Assimilation Level. Therefore, assimilation is the result of a strategic behavior.

This research is particular somehow in its content and results. Indeed, we adopted a model that was already tested before in Developing Countries and we adapted it to our current context. However, we propose future tests and refinement for our proposed models that would seem to be useful and helpful in advancing knowledge in this field.

Some of the limitations that are present in this research are related to the data while others are related to the study by itself. Given the fact that our study was based in a country that counts less than 53 % of Web users [24] and given that the study covered the three major industries, the number of respondents would have been recommended to be larger. Indeed, if the size of the sample of initial adopters fell within the accepted margins, it was nevertheless inadequate to produce the ideal statistical results when it comes to analyzing each industry by itself and comparing initial to advanced adopters per industry.

An interesting further research in this area would be to develop a larger sample that includes not only the stated three industries but to also include all related industries in Lebanon to obtain a robust result for this model if possible. Furthermore, and because our research was a Cross-sectional study, a further Longitude study is recommended to observe the same variables over a longer period of time.

Appendix A

Hypotheses		Path coefficient	Value t (≥2.02)	Results
Hypothesis 1 GeR -> SIeR	Government e-Readiness → supporting industries e-Readiness	0.3793	2.6354	H1 validated
Hypothesis 2 GeR -> MFeR	Government e-Readiness → market Force e-Readiness	−0272	3.9746	*H2 non validated but significant*
Hypothesis 3 GeR -> A	Government e-Readiness has a positive impact on organization's awareness	−0.4105	503	*H3 non validated but significant*
Hypothesis 4 GeR -> C	Government e-Readiness has a positive impact on organization's commitment	−0.4778	4.8946	*H4 non validated but significant*
Hypothesis 5 GeR -> G	Government e-Readiness has a positive impact on organization's governance	0.0137	0.0849	H5 non validated
Hypothesis 6 GeR -> e-Business assimilation level	Government e-Readiness has a positive impact on the level of e-business assimilation	−0.1606	1.6602	H6 non validated
Hypothesis 7 SIeR -> MFeR	Supporting Industries e-Readiness is positively related to market force e-Readiness	0.3197	5.3834	H7 validated
Hypothesis 8 SIeR -> A	Supporting Industries e-Readiness has a positive impact on Awareness	0.6817	7.4025	H8 validated
Hypothesis 9 SIeR -> C	Supporting industries e-Readiness has a positive impact on commitment	0.8426	7.5093	H9 validated
Hypothesis 10 SIeR -> G	Supporting Industries e-Readiness has appositive impact on governance	0284	0.81	H10 non validated
Hypothesis 11 SIeR -> e-Business Assimilation Level	Supporting Industries e-Readiness has a positive impact on the level of e-business assimilation	0.6792	5.0649	H11 validated
Hypothesis 12 MFeR -> A	Market Force e-Readiness has a positive impact on awareness	0.1934	4172	*H12 non validated but significant*
Hypothesis 13 MFeR -> C	Market Force e-Readiness has a positive impact on commitment	0.3974	7.1084	H13 validated
Hypothesis 14 MFeR -> G	Market Force e-Readiness has a positive impact on governance	0.0185	0.1782	H14 non validated
Hypothesis 15 MFeR -> e-Business assimilation level	Market Force e-Readiness has a positive impact on the level of e-business assimilation	0.3655	5.65	H15 validated
Hypothesis 16 A -> C	Awareness is positively related to commitment	−0.2249	186	H16 non validated

(continued)

(continued)

Hypotheses		Path coefficient	Value t (≥2.02)	Results
Hypothesis 17 A -> G	Awareness is positively related to governance	0.0913	0.4801	H17 non validated
Hypothesis 18 A -> e-Business assimilation level	Awareness has a positive impact on the level of e-Business assimilation	0.0051	0.0504	H18 non validated
Hypothesis 19 C -> G	Commitment is positively related to governance	0.4087	2.1214	H19 validated
Hypothesis 20 C -> E-business assimilation	Commitment has a positive impact on the level of e-business Assimilation	0.3542	3345	H20 validated
Hypothesis 21 G -> E-business assimilation level	Governance has a positive impact on the level of e-business assimilation	−0.4479	3.8398	H21 non validated but significant

Appendix B

		Path coefficient	Value t (≥2.02)	Results
Hypothesis 1 GeR -> SIeR	Government e-Readiness → supporting industries e-Readiness	0.4959	7.8888	H1 validated
Hypothesis 2 GeR -> MFeR	Government e-Readiness → market Force e-Readiness	−0.2722	4.0672	H2 non validated but significant
Hypothesis 3 GeR -> A	Government e-Readiness has a positive impact on organization's awareness	−0.0558	0.6571	H3 non validated
Hypothesis 4 GeR -> C	Government e-Readiness has a positive impact on organization's commitment	−0.1425	2.6071	H4 non validated but significant
Hypothesis 5 GeR -> G	Government e-Readiness has a positive impact on organization's governance	0.0789	1.7504	H5 non validated
Hypothesis 6 GeR -> e-Business assimilation level	Government e-Readiness has a positive impact on the level of e-business assimilation	−0.0969	1.7665	H6 non validated

(continued)

(continued)

		Path coefficient	Value t (≥2.02)	Results
Hypothesis 7 SIeR -> MFeR	Supporting industries e-Readiness is positively related to Market Force e-Readiness	0.6147	10.3406	H7 Validated
Hypothesis 8 SIeR -> A	Supporting industries e-Readiness has a positive impact on awareness	0.0865	0.0931	H8 non validated
Hypothesis 9 SIeR -> C	Supporting Industries e-Readiness has a positive impact on Commitment	0.2887	4.9171	H9 Validated
Hypothesis 10 SIeR -> G	Supporting industries e-Readiness has appositive impact on governance	−0.0356	0.6001	H10 non validated
Hypothesis 11 SIeR -> e-Business assimilation level	Supporting industries e-Readiness has a positive impact on the level of e-business assimilation	0.0026	0.3806	H11 non validated
Hypothesis 12 MFeR -> A	Market force e-Readiness has a positive impact on awareness	0.2415	2.6227	H12 Validated
Hypothesis 13 MFeR -> C	Market force e-Readiness has a positive impact on commitment	0.2342	4.0881	H13 Validated
Hypothesis 14 MFeR -> G	Market Force e-Readiness has a positive impact on Governance	0.22	3.9161	H14 Validated
Hypothesis 15 MFeR -> e-Business Assimilation Level	Market Force e-Readiness has a positive impact on the level of e-business Assimilation	−0.0475	0.7641	H15 non validated
Hypothesis 16 A -> C	Awareness is positively related to commitment	0.0527	12.5844	H16 Validated
Hypothesis 17 A -> G	Awareness is positively related to governance	0.1299	1.6326	H17 non validated
Hypothesis 18 A -> e-Business assimilation level	Awareness has a positive impact on the level of e-business assimilation	0.2306	0.2981	H18 validated
Hypothesis 19 C -> G	Commitment is positively related to Governance	0.0619	10.383	H19 validated
Hypothesis 20 C -> e-Business assimilation level	Commitment has a positive impact on the level of e-business assimilation	0.3578	3.2138	H20 validated
Hypothesis 21 G -> e-Business assimilation level	Governance has a positive impact on the level of e-business assimilation	0.3143	3.7826	H21 validated

References

1. Paré, D.J.: Does this site deliver? B2B e-Commerce services for developing countries. Inf Soc **19**(2), 123 (2003)
2. Kannabiran, G., Narayan, P.C.: Deploying Internet Banking and e-Commerce—case study of a private-sector bank in India. Inf Technol Dev **11**(4), 363–379 (2005)
3. Chaudhuri, A.: ICT for development: solutions seeking problems & quest. J Inf. Technol. **27**(4), 326–338 (2012)
4. Heeks, R.: IT innovation for the bottom of the pyramid. Commun. ACM **55**(12), 24 (2012)
5. Charbaji, A., Mikdashi, T.: A path analytic study of the attitude toward e-Government in Lebanon. Corp. Gov. Int. J. Effective Board Perform. **3**(1), 76–82 (2003)
6. Harfouche, A., Robbin, A.: Inhibitors and enablers of public e-Services in Lebanon. J. Org. End User Comput. **24**(3), 45–68 (2012)
7. Zhu, K., Kraemer, K.L.: Post-adoption variations in usage and value of e-Business by organizations: cross-country evidence from the retail industry. Inf. Syst. Res. **16**(1), 61–84 (2005)
8. Cooper, R.B., Zmud, R.W.: Information technology implementation research: a technological diffusion approach. Manage. Sci. **36**(2), 123–139 (1990)
9. Molla, A., Licker, P.S.: e-Commerce adoption in developing countries: a model and instrument. Inf. Manag. **42**(6), 877–899 (2005)
10. Purvis, R.L., Sambamurthy, V., Zmud, R.W.: The assimilation of knowledge platforms in organizations: an empirical investigation. Organ. Sci. **12**(2), 117–135 (2001)
11. Rogers, E.M.: Diffusions of Innovations, 4th edn. Free Press, New York (1995)
12. Zhu, K., Kraemer, K.L., Xu, S.: The process of innovation assimilation by firms in different countries: a technology diffusion perspective on e-Business. Manage. Sci. **52**(10), 1557–1576 (2006)
13. Kwon, T.H., Zmud, R.W.: Unifying the fragmented models of information systems implementation. In: Critical Issues in Information Systems Research, pp. 227–251. Wiley, New York (1987)
14. Tornatzky, L.G., Fleischer, M.: The Process of Technological Innovation. Lexington Books, Lexington, MA (1990)
15. DiMaggio, P.J., Powell, W.W.: The iron cage revisited: institutional isomorphism and collective rationality in organizational fields. Am. Sociol. Rev. **48**(2), 147–160 (1983)
16. Chatterjee, D., Grewal, R., Sambamurthy, V.: Shaping up for e-Commerce: institutional enablers of the organizational assimilation of web technologies. MIS Q., **26**(2), 65–89 (2002)
17. Teo, T.S.H., Ranganathan, C., Dhaliwal, J.: Key dimensions of inhibitors for the deployment of web-based business-to-business electronic commerce. IEEE Trans. Eng. Manage. **53**(3), 395–411 (2006)
18. Soares-Agular, A., Palma-Dos-Reis, A.: Why do firms adopt e-Procurement systems? Using logistic regression to empirically test a conceptual model. IEEE Trans. Eng. Manage. **55**(1), 120–133 (2008)
19. Claycomb, C., Iyer, K., Germain, R.: Predicting the level of B2B e-Commerce in industrial organizations. Ind. Mark. Manage. **34**(3), 221–234 (2005)
20. Ringle, C.M., Wende, S., Will, A.L Smart PLS 2.0. Hambourg (2005)
21. Vatanasakdakul, S., D'Ambra, J.: A conceptual model for e-Commerce adoption in developing countries: a task-technology fit perspective. Int. J. Inf. Technol. Manage. **6**(2–4), 1 (2007)
22. Nunnally, J.C., Bernstein, I.H., Berge, J.M.T.: Psychometric Theory, vol. 226. McGraw-Hill, New York (1967)
23. Tolbert, P.S., Zucker, L.G.: Institutional sources of change in the formal structure of organizations: the diffusion of civil service reform, 1880–1935. Adm. Sci. Q. **28**(1), 22–39 (1983)
24. Internet World Stats, Usage and Population Statistics. http://www.internetworldstats.com/stats.htm

Supply Chain Management and the Role of ICT: DART-SCM Perspective

Lucia Aiello, Iana Dulskaia and Maria Menshikova

Abstract Information technology infrastructure has a crucial role in improving Supply Chain Management (SCM) capability and in supply chain strategy. The increase in the use of Information Communication Technologies (ICT) reduce interaction and transaction costs and has an influence on logistics, procurement, vendor relationship management, and customer relationship management. In this perspective, the e-tools have stimulated and changed the supply chain. The paper in a first phase analyses the main literature on Service Dominant Logic and Dialogue-Access-Risk Benefits-Transparency (DART) framework in order to investigate how the academics and practitioners put this framework in action in the international scenario in Supply Chain Management. The last phase discloses a case study where the ICT are pervasive, the approach of the procurement process has changed. Through a case study focalized on e-procurement in a multinational enterprise that operates in the chemical-pharmaceutical sector, the research aims to highlight the coherence of e-tools with DART perspective.

Keywords Supply chain management · Service dominant logic · DART-SCM · E-procurement · E-tools

L. Aiello (✉)
Universitas Mercatorum, Rome, Italy
e-mail: l.aiello@unimercatorum.it

I. Dulskaia · M. Menshikova
Sapienza University of Rome, Rome, Italy
e-mail: iana.dulskaia@uniroma1.it

M. Menshikova
e-mail: maria.menshikova@uniroma1.it

© Springer International Publishing Switzerland 2016
F. Ricciardi and A. Harfouche (eds.), *Information and Communication Technologies in Organizations and Society*, Lecture Notes in Information Systems and Organisation 15, DOI 10.1007/978-3-319-28907-6_10

1 Introduction

There has been a great rise in interest in supply chain management (SCM) because of its innovative approach to business and competitive advantage [1]. The field of SCM has evolved rapidly. Formerly focused on internal integration [2] and then concentrated on supplier [1] and customer [3] to achieve optimal levels of performance. A Closer relationship with the customer provides higher SCM performance for the company [4]. Information system capability and advanced information technology infrastructure can be crucial tools in improving SCM capability [5, 6]. Information system (IS) capability is arising as an important characteristic of supply chain strategy. The use of IS significantly reduces interaction and transaction costs and has an influence on logistics, procurement, vendor relationship management, and customer relationship management [6, 7]. Application of information systems in SCM is referred to the use of inter-organizational systems for information sharing and/or processing across organizational boundaries [8]. The possibility that modern information and communication technologies provide, give an idea of the entire supply chain and how to redesign and manage it in order to satisfy an increasingly cost- and value-conscious customer who is demanding more, varied, often individualized value from the supply chain [9]. The great demand variety, uncertainty, costs, distances, and time lags on a global scale require all these chain processes to be realized more efficiently and effectively. Therefore, the focus shifted from the firms' competitive advantage to competitive advantages of the entire supply chains. According to [10] many researches demonstrate that ICT has a positive effect on performance either directly or indirectly via SCM. Progressive use of Information Communication System (ICT) can crucially change the supply chain's cost and value equation and can also provide the modern supply chain with the ability to respond to a greater uncertainty of demand and variety of the service and product, and give the supply chain the possibility to have much shorter response times or cycle times at the lowest possible cost.

In this study we concentrate our attention on the chemical-pharmaceutical sector, where the role of suppliers and relationships with them are crucial. Thus, the need for further research and understanding of the impact of ICT from the supply chain perspective become vital. This paper adapts the Dialogue-Access-Risk Benefits-Transparency (DART) framework proposed by Prahalad and Ramaswamy [11] to conceptualize one of the supply chain practices that is the procurement process.

The research questions of this study are (1) to analyze the automation development of procurement function by means of ICT, (2) to verify if the procurement automation and the e-tools are coherent with the spread of DART practices.

The structure of this paper is organized in the following way. Firstly, the SCM concept was observed and the relevant literature in this scientific area was reviewed. Secondly, the previous findings on the service dominant logic in SCM were analyzed. Thirdly, the DART concept in supply chain management and its implementation in ICT were described. Fourthly, a case study about the procurement process change in the chemical-pharmaceutical sector was studied in order to verify how the ICT is integrated in the supply chain from the DART point of view. Finally, the managerial implications of the findings and the possibilities for future studies were discussed.

2 DART-SCM Perspective

2.1 Theoretical Background

In spite of the widespread popularity of the term supply chain management, both practitioners and scholars have noticed the considerable confusion of its meaning. Some scholars define SCM in operational terms considering the flow of materials and products, others regard it as a management philosophy, and some consider it in terms of a management process [12]. Other authors identify the supply chain as a network of organizations. Supply chain management has been defined as «the systemic, strategic coordination of the traditional business functions and the tactics across these business functions within a particular company and across businesses within the supply chain (that consists of multiple firms), for the purposes of improving the long-term performance of the individual companies and the supply chain as a whole» [13]. SCM is known as a holistic approach to demand, sourcing and procurement, production and logistics process management [14]. It is a network that consists of different parties involved directly or indirectly which include manufacturer, supplier, retailer, customer and so forth, in producing and delivering products or services to ultimate customers both upstream and downstream [12] through physical distribution, flow of information and finances [15]. As SCM is undergoing a major transformation [16] and evolving rapidly; modern SCM concept in the new economy incorporates strategic differentiation, value enhancement, operational efficiency improvement, cost reduction [17], supply chain integration and collaboration, operational excellence and virtual supply chains [14]. The future and success of SCM as a system depends on how the companies can develop certain capabilities and competitiveness such as the ability to create a trusting relationship with its suppliers, look for total supply chain coordination, increase communication to reduce uncertainty and inventory levels, ensure on-time delivery of high quality goods and services at a reasonable cost, and the involvement of the right business partners [2, 18]. Lambert [19] identified supply chain management as the integration of key business from end user to original suppliers that provide products, services, and information that add value for customers and other stakeholders. Recently, managers have attempted to implement business processes and integrate them with various key members of the supply chain [20–22]. Integrated value in supply chain management relies on the usage of information about and by all business functions to facilitate the flow of goods and services through the supply chain [23].

Figure 1 demonstrates the supply chain network structure of a manufacturer with two tiers of suppliers, the information and product flows, and the supply chain management processes that should be implemented within organizations across the supply chain. All the processes are cross-functional and cross-firm. Each organization in the supply chain requires being included in the implementation of the same eight processes, but corporate silos and functional silos within companies are barriers to this integration. Successful management of the supply chain requires the involvement of all the corporate business functions. However, an "industry standard" does not exist that deals with business process in the context of supply chain management, all the members of the supply chain decide for themselves how to carry out the business process. The supply chain management processes are identified by Global Supply Chain Forum and as shown in Fig. 1 are as follows:

- Customer Relationship Management
- Supplier Relationship Management
- Customer Service Management
- Demand Management
- Order Fulfilment
- Manufacturing Flow Management
- Product Development and Commercialization
- Returns Management

Each supply chain management process has both strategic and operational sub-processes. As shown on Fig. 1, information flow has a great influence on all the

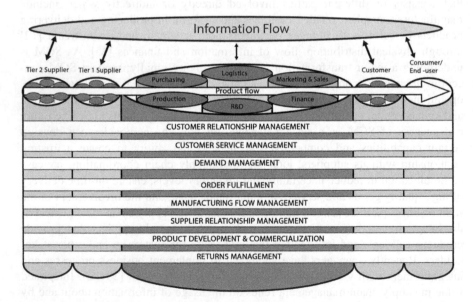

Fig. 1 Supply chain management: integrating and managing business processes across the supply chain (*Source* Adopted from [19])

processes of the supply chain. The complexity of SCM has forced companies to go for online communication systems. Supply chain management emphasizes the long-term benefit of all parties of the chain through cooperation and information sharing that confirm the importance of IT in SCM [24] and making them a crucial part of a successful business performance.

According to [9] «on the supply side, the availability of modern information and communication technologies (ICT) makes it possible to obtain an overview of the entire supply chain and to redesign and manage it in order to meet this demand» [9: p. 59]. The value chain is amply integrated through the ICT, the managers can obtain a better overview, thus they can redesign and manage the process of value co-creation in order to involve all stakeholders (suppliers, customers, others). In the following paragraphs, after the introduction of the S-D logic, the DART-SCM will be studied considering the fact that ICT have a huge impact on SCM. This practice, in our opinion, is more afferent to analyze the supply chain management and the role of ICT.

2.2 Service Dominant Logic as a Reference Point

There is a shift towards a service-oriented perspective and the understanding of value-creation [25]. This shift is focused on the identification and development of main competences in order to achieve a competitive advantage which is directed at enhancing relationships with key actors who can derive benefits from each other's value propositions and competences [26]. Benefits that derived from the specialized competences can be used by suppliers and customers in the value-creation processes, thus, positioning these actors as co-producers of value and thereby assuming an active role in the "relational exchanges and coproduction" [27]. This arising consideration is referred to as a service dominant logic and it is thought to have strong potential in explaining purchasing and supply chain phenomenon [28, 29]. Within the marketing literature a rapidly developing and integrated body of thought centered on service-dominant logic (S-D logic) has particular relevance to SCM as it seeks a more transcending perspective [27, 30–33]. S-D logic argues that service is the basis of economic activity. This logic focuses on the process of service versus a goods-dominant or manufacturing logic that focalizes on the production and provision of outputs. S-D logic replaces the concept of a supply chain with a network concept that is referred to as a service ecosystem. A service ecosystem is a spontaneously sensing and responding spatial and temporal structure of largely coupled value proposing social and economic actors interacting through institutions and technology, to: (1) co-produce service offerings, (2) exchange service offerings and (3) co-create value. A supply chain is oriented on the service ecosystem [34]. In order to develop and maintaining relationships in the supply chain the managers need to focus on helping customers to achieve their objectives, which require a service dominant logic [35]. The relationship marketing is focused on the customers, looking downstream in the supply chain. Nevertheless, the development and maintenance of relationships with key suppliers should be based on the same principles, in order to allow suppliers to be profitable. In other words, organizational success is based on relationship management with both suppliers and customers in the lens of S-D logic.

2.3   DART Framework

In order to have a better understanding in a set of SCM practices that may be useful in value co-creation, we would like to pay attention to the work of [11]. These scholars point out that there has been an emergence of "connected, informed, empowered, and active..." network partners challenging the traditional perspective and participating into increased value co-creation. Prahalad and Ramaswamy [11] used the term "consumers" to indicate the buyers in the market who rapidly showed interest in interacting with the supplying firm and hence co-creating value in course of their transactions; thus, redefining the very nature of the buyer-supplier interaction and redefining the new worship of value "co-creation" instead of regular "creation" and the processes associated with it. These scholars demonstrated a framework referred to as the DART framework (D-A-R-T stands for dialogue, access, transparency, and understanding of risk-benefits), which enables the co-creation and co-extraction of value [36]. As can be seen in Fig. 2, value co-creation (VCC) is located at the center of the S-D logic principle.

The first measurement of DART stands for dialogue, which is significant for any exchange of information in order to be successful and to establish fruitful relationships. The latest studies conducted by [37, 38] demonstrated the necessity of a more detailed attention to the need for a managerial dialogue, performed as a discourse between two or more network partners, that can lead to mutual learning, deep understanding and consensus for a better collaborative consciousness and action. Moreover, [39] highlight that "dialogue is more than listening... It entails empathic understanding built around experiencing... and recognizing the emotional, social and cultural context of experience" [39: 23]. Research conducted by Levine et al. [40] conceptualized the network environment (i.e. the market) as "sets of conversation" between the buyer and the supplier. This conceptualization can be also applied to B-2-B business between a buying firm and its suppliers.

The access dimension of DART framework represents a critically important practice in the supply chain. Access signifies the availability and reach of information and knowledge existing in the network and the following transactions between the network actors in order to achieve better understanding of the associated risk and benefits of actor exchanged decisions [11]. Moreover, these scholars showed conceptualization of "access" centered primarily on a downstream perspective (with the customer base), but the literature in SCM illustrates that access is also an important measurement in upstream practices. In a recent study it is argued that "the goal of consumers is access to desirable experience (...)" [39: 25] through on-demand tools and resources such as computing.

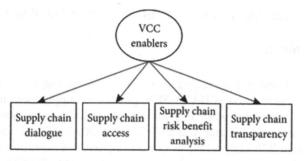

Fig. 2 Enablers of value co-creation (*Source* Adopted from [54])

The third DART argument is analysis of risk and benefit as the parameter with which network actors are able to assess the consequences of their decisions to cooperate [11, 41–43]. According to [41] this kind of interaction decision could also include their decision to take a part in any purchasing group alliance and most importantly to impact on the type of relationship practices, in order to involve the upstream supply partners and downstream customers. Some researches have demonstrated concerns that deal with the risk associated with the sharing of procurement of information with such alliances taking into consideration the loss of confidentiality with competing firms as well as proportion of gain, perceived by different sizes of the firms at different stages of the purchasing group [44]. The ultimate dimension of the DART framework is transparency [11]. A primary aim of the procurement function is interaction transparency, this is the extent to which network actors demonstrate trust, and reveal their true motivations, goals, and agenda gain importance and this has been the basis of the concentralization of SC transparency [45–47]. The study of [48] empirically proved the key role that transparency plays in enhancing supply chain partnerships. S-D logic gives the ability of the creation of a purchasing platform where clarity takes place and the goals of all the actors are equal [49]. This relationship helps to achieve a globally optimized supply chain and network-wide trust among all the actors. Global thinking affects business processes, thus, transactional and relational approaches allow to implement benefits for SCM. Transactional efficiency requires information technology (IT). IT has changed the way companies do business and adapt their organizations to new environments. IT provides up-to-date information to geographically dispersed managers working in different functions. IT facilitates the implementation of cross-functional teams and can be used to support relationships with key members of the supply chain. The management of inter-organizational relationships with members of the supply chain involves people, organizations, and processes [8, 50–52]. The ability to manage inter-organizational relationships «may define the core competence of some organizations as links between their vendors and customers in the value chain» [50: 152].

3 Case Study: An Analysis of the Procurement Process

3.1 Methodology

The objective of this paper, according to the main literature on supply chain management, is the revision of DART-SCM practice in supply chain management. This practice is performed when ICT has a strategic role. Information and communication technologies in supply chain management are self-evident today. The implementation of ICT along all the supply chain processes requires a shift towards a new perspective that gives the opportunity to put the DART-SCM practice into action. The design of the case study is divided in the following steps that were proposed by Yin [53]: the research questions, the study propositions, the unit of the case analysis, the linking data to propositions, the criteria for the interpretation of the results. The case study describes the DART-SCM practice in one of the supply chain parts, that is procurement, in an enterprise of the chemical-pharmaceutical sector.

The questions that were identified inside the case study are: In which way is the automation of procurement function actually developing? Is the diffusion of e-tools coherent with DART-SCM practice? The units of the case analysis are team members of procurement function of the organization. The study recommends the proposition of DART-SCM practice thanks to Information Communication Technology. The linking data to propositions is DART-SCM practice application to the case study. The criteria for the results interpretation is the vision of e-tools inside the procurement process through the DART-SCM lens.

The company, that has been chosen as the object of the present study is a multinational operator of the chemical-pharmaceutical sector, which produces and enters to the market products in various therapeutic areas: anesthesia, diabetes, neonatal care, diagnostic tools etc. The name of this company was not mentioned in accordance with the rules of the privacy policy.

3.2 Description and Objectives

In the present case study we focus on the analysis of a part of the Lambert model that was proposed in the literature review (Fig. 3). We attempt to investigate the role of the inclusion of some ICT tools in the process of supply and creation of relationships with suppliers. Hence, we concentrate on the study of competitive advantage development that has been defined by Vargo [50] also as core competence creation, thanks to the effective management of inter-organizational relationships, in this case between the purchasing department and its direct and indirect suppliers. Furthermore, in this part of the paper we seek to determine the relevance and appropriateness of ICT tools to the main concepts of the DART.

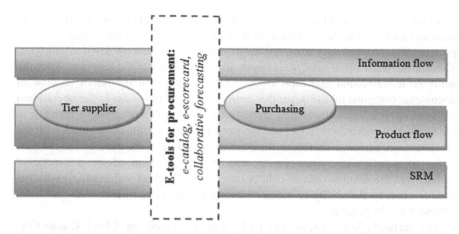

Fig. 3 Focus of the case study: e-tools for procurement. *Source* Adopted from [19]

The present paper describes the application of new technologies and their role for the purchasing department, which turns out to be quite complex in the case of company under analysis. This department controls extremely critical supplies, both to ensure compliance with the rules of the Quality Assurance of all the Countries in which the product is marketed, and to ensure the continuity of production, including the need for efficient performance, even on the side of indirect purchases—in other words, all purchases that are not directly related to the pharmaceutical product. In order to manage all procurement processes better, the purchasing function of the studied company has recently initiated the road of e-procurement with a structured program that is now emerging in a comprehensive way.

To discover the motivations of managers for this organizational change and to detect all the peculiarities of the processes included in this electronic mode of supply, we visited the company and observed the different stages and functions of the e-procurement. Moreover, we conducted several interviews with managers and employees from the department in order to gain more knowledge about these concepts and receive more detailed information.

Within the purchasing area of this complex reality, there are two fundamental structures: "International Purchasing" and "Strategic Sourcing". "International Purchasing" is responsible for all the products of global interest and it integrates the needs of different plants. "Strategic sourcing", instead, finds alternative sources of supply in the global market. The purchasing department of the analyzed company is integrated in the framework of "Supply Chain Operations", which includes logistics, operational planning, customer care, business development and control of industrial management. Moreover, the department is divided in direct purchases (raw materials/ingredients and packaging) and indirect ones (utilities, technical purchasing, services, stationery and office supplies).

In the conversation with members of the department team we revealed different reasons that have led the organization to a transition from the traditional forms of procurement to completely managed for of procurement through new technologies. The starting point was to analyze in depth all the processes of the function. After the analysis, it was found that most of the activities required the intensive flow of documents compiled by the buyer that employs a lot of resources in the operational activities, hence, low-value-added. In addition, there was a progressive increase in the number of orders to manage, and the need for close continuous contact with the most strategic partners. Therefore, the primary objective of the transition to the new forms of supply chain management was the optimization of the transactional activity and the development of collaborative tools (internal and external) with the goal of creating the ability to communicate with suppliers in particular and local communities in general.

The technological choices, i.e. tools that are based on Cloud Computing, Software as a Service have some advantages: the simplicity of use, the light-weight impact on technological infrastructure of the company and the ability to support the whole cycle of supply chain processes. These advantages allow the company integration with all strategic suppliers of production, perfectly corresponding to the DART-SCM logic, will be described in more detail below.

The system adopted by the company has permitted the creation an extranet that is a Web space, in which the community created by the company and its supplier effectively manages all the operations related to the supply chain. The features of Cloud Computing have satisfied the need for constant collaboration, mutual learning and deep understanding between the company and its main suppliers. These have also become strategic partners with whom it is possible not only to establish the business relationship of the transaction, but also to develop the relations of value co-creating for end-users, that require more attention and product customization according to their particular needs. Furthermore, this technology allows activation of the dialogue that checks the attitude of suppliers towards the sustainability and social responsibility to which the analyzed company pays the most attention. In this way the need for the use of Cloud Computing technologies, in our opinion, determines the importance of the first component defined in the perspective of the DART-SCM as "dialogue".

3.3 Discussion

3.3.1 E-Catalogs in the Perspective of DART-SCM

One of the approaches of Application Service Providing use is the creation of electronic catalogs (e-catalogs) that have defined the first step in the development of the e-procurement system by the analyzed company. The stationery was the object of the first catalog. Both the cost of the items and the standardization of the catalog were traded with suppliers. Obviously, it was also an opportunity to rationalize purchases: from the overall offer of the supplier only articles that are actually required for the performance of daily activities were selected. The availability of the items that can be ordered is reduced from several thousand to just over 500 codes. The most significant and very appreciated by the users aspect is the significant reduction of the processing times of the order. In fact, thanks to easy selection of articles directly from PC, to the approval via email and the availability of the material within 24 h, it has shifted from two weeks to two days. From the formal point of view the Internet process is identical to the traditional one: the approval work-flow of purchase requests that is demanded by local and international policy was rebuilt on the platform.

The users that have a password can make a direct request for the articles they need; after the request follows the authorization process. The person who should approve the new request receives a notification by e-mail and then he/she connects to the portal to view this request in more detail (thanks to a link in the email). The process concludes with the automatic transmission to the supplier that guarantees delivery within 24 h. In this way, apart from the periodic revision of the catalog for item and costs, the purchasing department intervenes only in cases when problems occur, offering users the highest level of transparency and the possibility to access to all the necessary information about the order and its verification.

Furthermore, the purchase system via e-Catalog has been extended to more complex categories of products such as computing consumables; in this case the authorization process is realized by the IT department.

The catalogue related to the laboratorial materials deserves special attention which is an extremely critical category of commodities for two reasons: great connection with quality control laboratories, large number of suppliers (about 40).

The first step was to single out one supplier that would be able to act as a central player. The choice was made on the basis of skills and scientific competences of the supplier. His/her function is not only to be able to execute the orders, but also to monitor the market, to scout and to suggest products and sources of alternative supply. The supplier, receiving orders, checking from time to time other offers and providers, pointing out new opportunities. Certainly, an important actor in this process is the function of Quality Assurance, which reviews and approves the supplier's recommendations. Only at the end of this process the new item is loaded in the catalog.

Therefore, the company activates continuous dialogue with the strategic supplier, giving him the utmost confidence and integrating him in the process of value co-creation.

After the implementation of the electronic catalog, introduced as a simple tool for the issuing of orders, the process has been further optimized by means of a tool that allows monitoring of the status of an order moving to the direction of more efficient information exchange with a supplier.

In fact, the "collaboration" program was developed and introduced that offers the possibility to have the feedback about product availability and delivery time, as well as notifications about executed dispatch that guarantees the maximum transparency of information and the simplicity of access to it.

3.3.2 E-Management of the Suppliers' Qualification Process for Risk-Benefits Understanding

The second step of e-procurement integration is the digital portal usage in the purchasing performance in order to realize the document exchange aimed at the qualification and the maintenance of suppliers.

We have to keep in mind that the typical qualification process in the pharmaceutical industry, in particular for direct materials, is extremely complex, because it has to take into account the Quality Assurance (QA) rules in the country where the process of production takes place and the rules of QA in all countries where the products will be marketed. Moreover, issues related to the environment and safety should be taken into consideration that will allow understanding of risks and benefits that may be present in the relationship with a single supplier.

Recently, the company carried out the studies of a digital portal development in order to create a quick and efficient exchange of the necessary information for a supplier's qualification/requalification, with the additional benefit that allows the tracking of the qualification process: it is possible to control which documents were delivered and by whom, what is missing, etc.

Another important factor is that all the files will be stored in a repository through the Cloud technology. This virtual library can be accessed by all the users.

Additionally, the advantage was achieved by the automation of many aspects: the responses to the questionnaires will be processed automatically for the creation of vendor's evaluation. This assessment will also be automatically compared with the annual evaluations of performance in order to update the points obtained from each supplier.

Each potential supplier will have a password to enter the portal and to respond to the prequalification questionnaire. Obviously, the questionnaires will be different, and the responses weighted differently depending on the product category. If the supplier is considered suitable at the first examination, the company requests the essential documentation and possible inspections. From that moment the qualification is achieved with a scorecard that was created on the basis of the chosen key performance indicator (KPI).

According to the policy of the analyzed company, all the suppliers of direct materials need to be upgraded every two years. Thus, the new e-tool can support the staff of the purchasing department and the QA. This allows not only to understand the risks and the benefits from the collaboration with a certain type of supplier and store the documentation, it also gives an opportunity to suppliers access to the information about decisions on the choice of a supplier that can be viewed by all users of the digital portal.

3.3.3 The Collaborative Forecasting as an Attribute of the Maximum Transparency

The third step towards the system of e-procurement is defined as Collaborative Forecasting or VMI (vendor managed inventory). In this case, the production's needs of the company become absolutely visible to suppliers. In this way, connecting to the digital portal, the supplier will have access both to the data related to the short-term needs, and to forecast needs related to its supply, with obvious benefits for both parties; the supplier will be able to plan production in line with the actual consumption and the needs of the prospective customer; this will reduce their inventory through the supply line with the use.

In its more advanced version, the VMI provides the transmission of the responsibility related to management, accounting and inventory of the material from the customer's location to supplier's one, amplifying the benefits of the previous point.

The Collaborative Forecasting consists of two phases: start-up phase, phase of enlargement/maintenance.

The first phase includes the implementation of the model and the solution test, which will involve 2 suppliers that are representative of mapped processes.

The second phase provides the extension of the application to all providers of interest and the maintenance of the platform that ensures maximum integration with the supplier and transparency towards them.

4 Conclusion and Managerial Implication

Nowadays, information and communication technologies ICT are thought to play a key role in the coordination and integration of SCM activities. Supply chain management in a dynamic, demand-driven environment requires ICT-enabled connectivity, cooperation, and coordination between actors within an industry (horizontal coordination) and across industry and firms (vertical coordination). Global market and its high competitiveness highlight such parts of relationships with stakeholders as a global outsourcing and partnership and these signify the usage of ICT-integrated SCM. The supply chain managers in order to have a successful business take into consideration a shifting focus from the traditional tangible aspects of skills, knowledge and information power towards more coherent intangible aspects involving interactivity, connectivity and building relationships with up and downstream stakeholders which leads to a service dominant logic. S-D logic concerns a concept of value co-creation, which is created within a supply chain network. In order to provide a more profound vision on a value co-creation aspect, the DART framework was implemented in supply chain management with ICT perspective.

Having analyzed the current activity and e-tools used by the studied company, we can arrive at the conclusion by considering the recent changes in the management of many organizational processes (in this specific case, the operation of the entire purchasing area), caused mainly by the development of ICT that are based on the principles of maximum interactivity and dialogue [55]. In our opinion, it would be appropriate to consider the management of the supply chain from the viewpoint of DART-SCM with its 4 indispensable pillars: "dialogue", "access", "risk/benefit understanding" and "transparency".

The present study evidences the necessity of paying detailed attention to concepts of DART in the development of the relationships with main stakeholders by managers of the enterprises in order to achieve the fruitful process of co-creation value combining the basic building blocks of DART concept in different ways. The greatest attention to these aspects should be paid by the enterprises that operate in the virtual environment or those that seek to automate some SCM process by means of new technologies.

The limitation of this research consists of the consideration of only one part of the supply chain management that is the procurement process. Moreover, the collected data did not allow the conduct of in-depth study of the advantages and disadvantages of DART and comparing them with other concepts of SCM.

Future studies could focus on a comparative analysis of the DART frame with other approaches of supply chain management in order to analyze the strengths and weaknesses and to identify appropriate applications of each approach. Another direction of research development could be the study of other business processes across the supply chain and other sectors in the DART-SCM perspective.

References

1. Chin, T.A., Hamid, A.B.A., Rasli, A., Baharun, R.: Adoption of supply chain management in SMEs. Procedia Social Behav. Sci. **65**, 614–619 (2012)
2. Monczka, R., Handfield, R., Guinipero, L., Patterson, J.: Purchasing and supply chain management, 5th edn. Cengage Learning, USA (2011)
3. Lagrosen, S.: Customer involvement in new product development: a relationship marketing perspective. Eur. J. Innov. Manage. **4**(8), 424–36 (2005)
4. Thoo, A.C., Huam, H.T., Yusoff, R.M., Rasli, A., Bakar, A.H.A.: Supply chain management: success factors from Malaysian manufacturer s perspective. Afr. J. Bus. Manage. **17**(5), 7240–7247 (2011)
5. Sahay, B., Cavale, V., Mohan, R.: The Indian supply chain architecture. Supply Chain Manage. Int. J. **2**(8), 93–106 (2003)
6. Depaoli, P., Za, S.: Towards the redesign of e-business maturity models for SMEs. In: Baskerville, R., De Marco, M., Spagnoletti, P. (eds.) Designing organizational systems, pp. 285–300. Springer, Heidelberg (2013)
7. Fasanghari, M., Habibipour, F., Roudsari, Chaharsooghi, S.: Assessing the impact of information technology on supply chain management. World Appl. Sci. J., **1**(4), 87–93 (2008)
8. Pinna R., Carrus P.P., Pettinao D.: Supply chain coordination and IT: the role of third party logistics providers. In: Management of the interconnected world, pp. 299–306 (2010)
9. Kumar, K.: Technology for supporting supply chain management: introduction. Commun. ACM **6**(44), 58–61 (2001)

10. Zhang, X., van Donk, D. P., van der Vaart, T.: Does ICT influence supply chain management and performance?: a review of survey-based research. Int. J. Oper. Prod. Manage. 11(31), 1215–1247 (2011)

11. Prahalad, C.K., Ramaswamy, V.: Co-creation experience: the next practice in value creation. J. Interact. Market. 3(18), 5–14 (2004)

12. Mentzer, J.T., DeWitt, W., Keebler, J.S., Min, S., Nix, N.W., Smith, C.D., Zacharia, Z.G.: Defining supply chain management. J. Bus. Logistics 2(22), 1–25 (2001)

13. Mentzer, J.T., Min, S., Zacharia, Z.G.: The nature of interfirm partnering in supply chain management. J. Retail. 4(76), 549–568 (2000)

14. Chow, W.S., Madu, C.N., Kuei, C.-H., Lu, M.H., Lin, C., Tseng, H.: Supply chain management in the US and Taiwan: An empirical study. Int. J. Manage. Sci. 36, 665–679 (2008)

15. Stock, J.R., Boyer, S.L.: Developing a consensus definition of a supply chain management: a qualitative study. Int. J. Phys. Distrib. Logistics Manage. 8(39), 690–711 (2009)

16. Melnyk S.A., Lummus, R.R., Vokurka, R.J., Burns, L.J., Sandor, J.: Mapping the future of supply chain management: a Delphi study. Int. J. Prod. Res. 16(47), 4629–4653 (2009)

17. Bidgoli, H.: The handbook of technology management: supply chain management, marketing and advertising, and global management, vol. 2. Wiley, New Jersey (2010)

18. Acharyulu, G., Shekbar, B.: Role of value chain strategy in healthcare supply chain management: an empirical study in India. Int. J. Manage. 1(29), 91–97 (2012)

19. Lambert, D.M. (ed.) Supply chain management: processes, partnerships, perfomance. Supply Chain Management Inst., Sarasota (2008)

20. Lambert, D.M., García Dastugue, S.J., Croxton, K.L.: An evaluation of process oriented supply chain management. J. Bus. Logistics 1(26), 25–51 (2005)

21. Dameri, R.P., Perego, A.: Translate IS governance framework into practice: the role of IT Service Management and IS performance evaluation. In: Proceedings of the 4th European conference on information management and evaluation: Universidade Nova de Lisboa, Lisbon, Portugal 9–10 Sept. 2010, p. 53. Academic Conferences Limited (2010)

22. Vom Brocke, J., Simons, A., Sonnenberg, C., Agostini, P.L., Zardini, A.: Value assessment of enterprise content management systems: a process-oriented approach. In: D'Atri, A., Saccà, D. (eds.) Information systems: people, organizations, institutions, and technologies. Springer, Physica-Verlag HD, pp. 131–138

23. Lusch, R.F.: Reframing supply chain management: a service dominant logic perspective. J. Supply Chain Manage. 1(47), 14–18 (2011)

24. Yu, Z., Yan, H., Cheng, T.E.: Benefits of information sharing with supply chain partnerships. Indus. Manage. Data Syst. 3(101), 114–121 (2001)

25. Metters, R., Marucheck, A.: Service management—academic issues and scholarly reflections from operations management researchers. Decis. Sci. J. 2(38), 195–214 (2007)

26. Vargo, S., Akaka, M.: Service-dominant logic as a foundation for service science: clarifications. Serv. Sci. J. 1(1), 32–41 (2009)

27. Vargo, S.L., Lusch, R.F.: Evolving to a new dominant logic for marketing. J. Market. 1(68), 1–17 (2004)

28. Caldwell, N.D., Roehrich, J.K., Davies, A.C.: Procuring complex performance in construction: London heathrow terminal 5 and a private finance initiative hospital. J. Purchasing Supply Manage. 15, 178–186 (2009)

29. Schmenner, R.W., Van Wassenhove, L., Ketokivi, M., Heyl, J., Lusch, R.F.: Too much theory, not enough understanding. J. Oper. Manage. 5(27), 339–343 (2009)

30. Vargo, S.L., Lusch, R.F.: Service-dominant logic: continuing the evolution. J. Acad. Market. Sci. 1(36), 1–10 (2008)

31. Lusch, R.F., Vargo, S.L.: Service-dominant logic: reactions, reflections and refinements. Market. Theory 3(6), 281–288 (2006)

32. Lusch, R.F., Vargo, S.L., O'Brien, M.: Competing through service: insights from service-dominant logic. J. Retail. 1(83), 5–18 (2007)

33. Ricciardi, F., De Marco, M.: The challenge of service oriented performances for chief information officers. In: Snene, M. (ed.) Exploring service science. third international conference, IESS 2012. Geneva, Switzerland, February 2012. Proceedings, pp. 258–270. LNBIP, vol. 103. Springer, Berlin
34. Lusch, R.F., Vargo, S.L., Tanniru, M.: Service, value networks and learning. J. Acad. Market. Sci. 1(38), 19–31 (2010)
35. Hunt, S.D., Madhavaram, S.: The service-dominant logic of marketing. The service-dominant logic of marketing: dialog, debate, and directions, vol. 67 (2006)
36. Callaway, S., Dobrzykowski, D.: Service-oriented entrepreneurship: service-dominant logic in green design and healthcare. Serv. Sci. 4(1), 225–240 (2009)
37. Raelin, J.A.: The manager as facilitator of dialogue. Organization 6(20), 818–839 (2013)
38. Gambetti, R.C., Giovanardi, M.: Re-visiting the supply chain: a communication perspective, Corporate Communications. Int. J. 4(18), 390–416 (2013)
39. Prahalad, C.K., Ramaswamy, V.: The future of competition: co-creating unique value with customers. Harvard Business Press, Cambridge (2013)
40. Levine, R., Locke, C., Searls, D., Weinberger, D.: The clue-train manifesto: the end of business as usual. Perseus Publishing, Cambridge, MA (2001)
41. Hu, Q., Schwarz, L.B., Uhan, N.A.: The impact of group purchasing organizations on healthcare-product supply chains. Manuf. Serv. Oper. Manage. 1(14), 7–23 (2012)
42. Tummala, R., Schoenherr, T.: Assessing and managing risks using the supply chain risk management process (SCRMP). Supply Chain Manage. Int. J. 6(16), 474–483 (2011)
43. Chen, I.J., Paulraj, A.: Towards a theory of supply chain management: the constructs and measurements. J. Oper. Manage. 22, 119–150 (2004)
44. Essig, M.: Purchasing consortia as symbiotic relationships: developing the concept of "consortium sourcing". Eur. J. Purchasing Supply Manage. 1(6), 13–22 (2000)
45. Handfield, R.B., Bechtel, C.: The role of trust and relationship structure in improving supply chain responsiveness. Indus. Market. Manage. 4(31), 367–382 (2002)
46. Fawcett, S.E., Magnan, G.M., Williams, A.J.: Supply chain trust is within your grasp. Supply Chain Trust Manage. Rev. 2(8), 20–26 (2004)
47. Lamming, R., Caldwell, N., Phillips, W.: Supply chain transparency. In: New, S., Westbrook, R. (eds.) Understanding supply chains: concepts, critiques and futures, pp. 191–214. Oxford University Press Inc., NewYork (2004)
48. Su, H.Y., Fang, S.C., Young, C.S.: Influences of relationship transparency from intellectual capital reporting on supply chain partnerships with suppliers: a field experiment. Supply Chain Manage. Int. J. 2(18), 178–193 (2013)
49. Dobrzykowski, D., Hong, P., Park, J.: Building procurement capability for firm performance: a service-dominant logic view. Benchmarking Int. J. 4–5(19), 567–584 (2012)
50. Vargo, S.L. (ed.) The service-dominant logic of marketing: dialog, debate, and directions. ME Sharpe (2006)
51. Mola, L., Rossignoli, C., Rigodanza, A.: ICT and Procurement: the E-sourcing systems of an Italian Bank Group. In: Management of the interconnected world, pp. 465–472. Physica-Verlag HD
52. Pinna, R., Carrus, P.P., Marras, F.: The drug logistics process: an innovative experience. TQM J. 27(2), 214–230 (2015)
53. Yin, R.K.: Case study research. Design and Methods. SAGE Pubblications, USA (2014)
54. Chakraborty, S., Dobrzykowski, D.D.: Examining value co-creation in healthcare purchasing: a supply chain view. Bus Theory Practice/Verslas: Teorija ir Praktika, 15(2), 179–190 (2014)
55. Cavallari, M. Analysis of evidences about the relationship between organisational flexibility and information systems security. Information Systems: crossroads for organization, management, accounting and engineering: ItAIS: The Italian Association for Information Systems, pp. 439–447 (2013)

How Subjective Age and Age Similarity Foster Organizational Knowledge Sharing: A Conceptual Framework

Alessandra Lazazzara and Stefano Za

Abstract The demographic changes occurring in the workforce and the risk of losing critical knowledge when older workers make the transition to retirement have turned knowledge sharing into a crucial asset for companies aiming to remain competitive. However, a failure to consider how individual or situational characteristics influence knowledge sharing has led to inconclusive research outcomes and pointed up the need for new lines of enquiry. In this paper, we review the literature on knowledge sharing, examining the influence of subjective age (how young or old people perceive themselves to be) and age-similarity within the work context. In conclusion, we propose a conceptual framework that highlights how subjective age and age similarity may affect (i) the extent to which the people in an organization are inclined to share and (ii) the knowledge-sharing route they prefer.

Keywords Knowledge sharing · Subjective age · Age-similarity · Knowledge management systems

1 Introduction

Knowledge is often recognized as a valuable resource for organizational growth and sustained competitive advantage, particularly for organizations acting and competing in uncertain environments [1, 2]. In such a scenario, digital technology can play a key role in managing and exploiting this value [3, 4]. However, the "socio-technical

A. Lazazzara (✉)
Department of Educational Human Sciences, University of Milano-Bicocca, Milan, Italy
e-mail: alessandra.lazazzara@unimib.it

S. Za
Research Center on Information Systems (CeRSI), Luiss Guido Carli University, Rome, Italy
e-mail: stefano.za@uniecampus.it

S. Za
eCampus University, Novedrate, Italy

© Springer International Publishing Switzerland 2016
F. Ricciardi and A. Harfouche (eds.), *Information and Communication Technologies in Organizations and Society*, Lecture Notes in Information Systems and Organisation 15, DOI 10.1007/978-3-319-28907-6_11

systems" perspective suggests that organizations are composed of both social and technical elements [5, 6], which should be jointly taken into account when managing knowledge.

According to Alavi and Leiner [3], "Knowledge management systems (KMS) refer to a class of information systems applied to managing organizational knowledge", in terms of capturing, storing, sharing and using this knowledge [7]. Indeed, KMS are aimed at "creating, gathering, organizing and disseminating organizational knowledge" [8].

The information systems literature classifies digital applications for organizational knowledge management projects into three main categories [3]: (1) the coding and sharing of best practices, such as internal benchmarking designed to promote the transfer of internal best practice; (2) the creation of corporate knowledge directories mapping internal expertise; (3) the creation of knowledge networks, aimed at bringing the experts together so that key knowledge is shared and expanded.

The focus of the current paper is the last-mentioned class of applications, that is to say, those supporting knowledge sharing and/or transfer processes [9]. Knowledge sharing is defined here as the "willingness of individuals in an organization to share with others the knowledge they have acquired or created" [10], and knowledge transfer is a particular knowledge sharing process in which both source and recipient are identified [11, 12].

Following the "socio-technical systems" perspective, when developing new systems, the social component of systems design should be taken into account in addition to technical factors [13]. This is relevant to KMS in that knowledge management is not only technology-driven [10]. Given that knowledge sharing is a "socially complex process that involves a variety of actors with different needs and goals" [2], the adoption of knowledge management systems that support knowledge sharing does not of itself guarantee that knowledge sharing will take place [8, 14]. Indeed, the interpersonal context as well as the individual characteristics influencing knowledge sharing tend to be underestimated [15]. For example, few research contributions have analysed the influence of age, a factor that is relevant to knowledge sharing [16], or interpersonal aspects such as social network composition. Overall, social network theories have been underutilized in knowledge sharing studies [17].

This paper seeks to conceptually analyse how two particular social/individual characteristics, such as age and age-similarity can contribute to the occurrence of knowledge sharing. In particular, we analyse how these two aspects affect (i) the extent to which the people in an organization are inclined to share and (ii) the knowledge-sharing route they prefer. The aim of this paper is twofold: (i) to provide a theoretical contribution prompting and guiding future research on how chronological and subjective age, as well as social network structure, influence knowledge sharing among employees (ii) to guide practice by offering a conceptual framework to inform managerial decisions about the adoption of a KMS that draws attention to the combined effects of these two aspects on the knowledge sharing process.

The paper is structured as follows. First, we provide an overview of knowledge sharing and age-related constructs including subjective age. Then, we outline how social dynamics, namely perceived age-similarity within the work group and age-related changes in social behaviours, influence knowledge sharing, in terms of both "what" and "how" to share. Finally, we propose and discuss a conceptual framework that outlines how subjective age and age-similarity within the work group affect each other, resulting in four different attitudes towards knowledge-sharing.

2 Theoretical Background

In a context characterized by high uncertainty and dynamism, knowledge is becoming a crucial organizational resource for gaining competitive advantage [7, 18]. Indeed, the aging of the European workforce, coupled with a skills shortage in some sectors (e.g. information and communication technology, engineering), makes ensuring that knowledge and skills acquired are retained and passed on effectively to newer workers a critical strategic issue for human resource management. Although organizational knowledge is an organizational attribute involving the collection of knowledge and experience and their incorporation into procedures, routines and rules [19–23], in many cases knowledge resides in specific individuals, who are recognized as experts on particular issues or aspects. Many of these are senior members of the baby boomer generation and are soon due to exit the labour market. As the baby boomers retire, companies need to address the issue of knowledge sharing in terms of intervening to retain critical knowledge [24].

Employees who are close to attaining retirement criteria and will exit the labour market over the coming years could take with them a huge amount of knowledge based on years of practical experience and the accumulation of know-how, especially in the area of technical-specialist knowledge that is difficult to transmit and replace. This raises a number of uncertainties, in relation to both the management and retention of knowledge, particularly practical knowledge, which is most at risk in that it is often only formally documented and shared in part. This shortfall could cause serious difficulty for companies do not take preventive measures, undermining their ability to innovate, their efficiency and the quality of their products and services [24, 25].

2.1 Knowledge Sharing

Most of the research on knowledge management has originated within the fields of information technology or information systems [26, 27]. However, given the key importance of knowledge management skills and knowledge sharing for the transfer of knowledge among employees, there is growing interest in the role of individuals in knowledge management processes [28–30]. This people-centred perspective stems from the notion that, within organizations, individuals are repositories of knowledge [31] that needs to be moved to the levels of the group and the organization as a whole for the expected outcomes to be reached [32]. Nonaka and Takeuchi [18] were among the first to recognize the role of individuals in the knowledge creation process, arguing that when there is a low level of knowledge sharing among employees, knowledge creation is unlikely to occur.

Knowledge sharing consists of making knowledge available to others within the organization and it is the process by which knowledge held by individuals is shaped in a way that can be understood, absorbed and used by other individuals. According to Lowendhal and colleagues [33], the types of individual knowledge that have an impact on the organizational effectiveness are: know-how, know-what and dispositional knowledge. Know-how refers to experience-based knowledge that is subjective and tacit and requires interpersonal interactions in order to be shared or transferred. Know-what includes task-related knowledge and is objective, and easily stored and transferred. Dispositional knowledge is personal knowledge that includes talents, aptitudes and abilities and cannot be shared. Moreover, knowledge sharing opportunities may be both formal and informal. Formal opportunities include training sessions, structured work teams and technology-based systems [34, 35] that ensure the distribution of knowledge though mainly of the procedural and task-related kind. In contrast, informal opportunities include personal relationships and social networks that can be effective in promoting socialization but may not necessarily lead to the broader dissemination of knowledge [36].

Nevertheless, a prerequisite for successful knowledge sharing is that knowledge owners have the willingness to share it and that knowledge receivers are inclined to internalizing knowledge. Indeed, Hendriks [37] argued that knowledge sharing is based on two sub-processes. First, it presumes an act of "externalization", which may either be conscious or unconscious, on the part of those who own knowledge Second, it involves an act of "internationalization" by those seeking to acquire knowledge. Unfortunately, there are barriers that can restrict or prevent this exchange process. In particular, because knowledge only exists within a specific organizational and interpersonal context, the context can affect the way in which knowledge is perceived and used. If employees view knowledge as a source of power within their organization, they may be less motivated to share it, because they are concerned that they may lose their value and/or be exploited. They will therefore be more reluctant to get involved in knowledge sharing activities [38, 39]. This could be the case, for example, when an employee has the perception that the company is discriminating against him/her to benefit a younger colleague. While on one hand, it has been claimed that diversity on work teams leads to opportunities for synergistic knowledge and information sharing, a more pessimistic view contends that diversity only offers advantages under certain conditions [40]. The recent demographic changes have increased not only the degree of age diversity present in most organizations, but also the urgent need for knowledge sharing among the different age groups. Theoretical and research effort have not yet cleared up what types of diversity influence knowledge sharing in work context, so the effect of age diversity on knowledge sharing is uncertain and more research is needed to fill this gap.

2.2 Subjective Age

The growing focus on aging within organizations has led many researchers to investigate the effect of age at work by focusing on chronological age. However, they have mainly taken chronological age as a proxy for the meanings associated with age [41], without taking into account other conceptualizations of age or the influence of the context in which the age variable is investigated.

Age may be conceptualized in many different ways, as for example in Sterns and Doverspike's [42] taxonomy of chronological age, performance-based or functional age, psychosocial age, organizational age, and life-span age (Fig. 1). This classification rests on the idea that there is an underlying continuum between, at one extreme, age understood as an individual characteristic and, at the other, age interpreted as a characteristic of the environment. At the mid-point of this continuum, we find a conceptualization of age as a function of the interaction between person and environment [43]. Chronological age refers to one's calendar age and is the primary conception of age. Functional or performance-based age is related to variations in a worker's performance underpinned by their level of health and by physical decline over time. Psychosocial or subjective age is based on self- and social perceptions of age and refers to attitudes, expectations, and norms about the behaviours, lifestyles and characteristics appropriate to different ages. Organizational or job age refers to job tenure and, finally, life-span age emphasizes the influence of the life cycle on behavioural changes given the variations in family life and economic constraints experienced at different life stages [42].

This paper focuses on the construct of subjective age, which is based on the idea that there is often a difference between the objective and subjective experience of age. Individuals of the same chronological age may in fact attribute different meanings to their age, as for example in the case of two persons aged 26 years, one still enrolled on a university course and the other employed as a group leader in a company. Subjective age is commonly defined as how old or young individuals experience themselves to be [44]. It is related to age group identification and implies a feeling of solidarity with age peers [45].

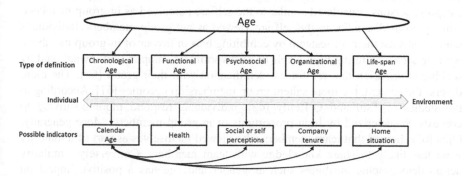

Fig. 1 Possible definition of "age" (Adapted from de Lange et al. [50])

This also occurs in the workplace, although little research has focused on the role of subjective age in work contexts [46–49]. Workers more frequently report feeling, looking, acting, and preferring to be younger than their chronological age, while employees that feel older than their chronological age experience more job-related strain [47].

More research is needed to fully understand the relationship between age and the work attitudes of employees. Furthermore, following Shanahan and co-authors' [51] finding that subjective age varies with social context and considering that other researchers [41, 52–54] have indicated that studies on aging should take into account the characteristics of the context in which a person operates, it is imperative that social interactions within an organization be included in analyses of age in a work context.

3 Social Dynamics of Knowledge Sharing

3.1 The Role of the Context: Age-Similarity

Workforce diversity has received considerable attention in the managerial and organizational literature, revealing that demographic diversity can foster knowledge sharing only if it exposes group members to unique and new sources of work-related knowledge [55, 56]. The relational demography perspective is based on the idea that individual demographic characteristics, as well as perceived demographic similarity or dissimilarity within a group, have an impact on individual work experience [57]. In particular, research has indicated that those perceiving themselves as similar to the other members of their work context have more positive work attitudes and experience better relationships at work than those who are demographically dissimilar [56, 57]. The framework of relational demography largely builds on ideas from social identity [58] and self-categorization theories [59]. These theories postulate that people tend to classify themselves and others into social groups, using personally meaningful dimensions that can include demographic categories such as gender, age, race, etc. In relation to a specific social category, persons considered similar to the self are perceived as in-group members, while persons dissimilar to the self are viewed as out-group members. Individuals tend to enhance their self-esteem by exhibiting bias in favour of in-group members, who are seen as offering high levels of trustworthiness, support and reward, and by seeking information that reinforces identification with their group [60]. The more diverse the context, the more salient group membership becomes [61]. According to the studies of Tsui and O'Reilly [62], individuals respond more positively to contexts characterized by high proportions of in-group members. More generally, Ojha [63] showed that team members who viewed themselves as part of a minority were less likely to share knowledge with team members. Conversely, similarity across demographic attributes such as gender and age has a positive impact on group processes such as communication and knowledge sharing [64].

According to the similarity attraction paradigm [65], people like and are attracted to others who are similar, rather than dissimilar, to themselves, especially when it comes to sharing similar attitudes. This means that people will display high level of interpersonal attraction to those who are demographically similar to them because they perceive them as having the same life experience, values and beliefs [66]. With regard to age similarity, it is expected that when coworkers' age is perceived as similar to one's own, both age group identification and identification with coworkers will be enhanced [60].

Research has also suggested the importance of visible categories as a basis for identification and network formation, in that people tend to interact with similar others [67]. This is known as the "homophily proposition" [68, 69]. It is important to point out that within an organizational context people develop both informal and formal ties. Formal ties are strictly work-related (colleagues) and provide instrumental resources (e.g. sponsorship, work-related advice, etc.). Informal ties (friendship) in contrast, provide emotional resources and support. Because they are compulsory, formal ties are characterised by a greater degree of heterophily, while informal ties are more likely to be characterized by homophily. Studies of close work and friendship ties consistently show that individuals tend to create bonds with others sharing similar demographic attributes such as education, gender, age and ethnicity [67, 70, 71]. Specifically, people tend to develop strong friendship ties in a work context characterized by age similarity [60]. Indeed, age is the second most important demographic driver of social network homogeneity and friendship dyads are usually characterized by people of similar ages [72].

3.2 Motivations for Knowledge Sharing and Subjective Age

When discussing knowledge sharing, it is crucial to analyse the motives that lead people to interact with their social partners. Furthermore, social interaction and reasons for knowledge sharing change throughout the life-cycle [73, 74].

According to socioemotional selectivity theory—SST—[73, 74], a life-span theory focused on the causes of age-related changes in social behaviour, two of the primary goals of social interaction are the acquisition of information and the regulation of emotion. The acquisition of information is a primary activity throughout life, and for young people at the beginning of their career in particular all social interaction is likely to result in information gain. People at this life stage are characterized by knowledge acquisition goals such as learning about new elements of the environment, analysing information and incorporating it into their job performance and career advancement activities [75]. However, as time horizons shrink, as they typically do with age, people become increasingly selective in interacting with social partners and invest greater resources in emotionally meaningful goals and activities, while their interest in acquiring new knowledge diminishes [73, 74]. It is though they prefer to preserve the quality of their relationships at the expense of the number. In other words, people at these life stages aim to find meaning in life, establish intimacy with others and develop a sense of belonging to their social environment [75]. Therefore, as people get older they tend to have less contact with those individuals previously considered as utilitarian sources of information and tend to engage more with social partners that satisfy their emotional needs such as friends and relatives [76].

SST suggests that behavioural goal changes are associated with shifts in perspectives on time, as people consciously and subconsciously monitor how much longer they perceive will live [77]. Therefore, the origin of this goal shift is not age itself, but rather an age-associated shift in time perspective [78]. In this sense, because subjective age is perceptual in nature, SST seems particularly useful for explaining the relationship between subjective age and a range of job attitudes.

4 Discussion and Preliminary Results

The above-mentioned lines of research suggest that further attention should be directed to how individual and situational factors, in particular subjective age and age-similarity among co-workers, can influence attitudes towards knowledge sharing. First, it should be noted that age similarity positively affects willingness to share and the quality of knowledge shared among employees, given that greater age similarity enhances the likelihood that employees will engage in knowledge sharing. This is due to the fact that, according to the relational demography perspective [62], those perceiving themselves as similar to the other members of their work context, especially in relation to outwardly evident traits such as age, have more positive work attitudes and experience better relationships at work than those who are demographically dissimilar [56, 57]. People respond more positively to contexts characterized by high proportions of in-group members [62]. Conversely, the more dissimilar the context, more salient group membership becomes [61]; it follows that people will be less likely to share knowledge with others considered dissimilar, resulting in poorer knowledge sharing in terms of both frequency of interaction and kind of knowledge. This is because according to the "homophily proposition" [68, 69], people tend to interact with similar others and establish more informal ties with them. Informal ties provide emotional resources and support, while formal ties are strictly work-related and provide instrumental resources that, in turn, can offer advantages in terms of career advancement or sponsorship opportunities. Therefore, perceived age similarity enhances the creation of informal ties that implies a higher willingness to share knowledge, while perceived age dissimilarity leads to instrumental ties that limits the willingness to share knowledge. Secondly, subjective age negatively affects willingness to share and the variety of knowledge shared among employees. Relying on socioemotional selectivity theory [73, 74], we postulate that individuals share because their main goal is to acquire knowledge that may be functional to reaching professional goals. On the other hand, individuals experiencing themselves to be older than their chronological age are in general less prone to knowledge sharing and more prone to maintaining good relationships with their affective ties, especially because they experience more job-related strain [47].

Based on our analysis to date, we propose a conceptual framework for knowledge sharing processes (Fig. 2) that takes into account how subjective age and perceived age-similarity among co-workers may affect (i) the extent to which the people in an organization are inclined to share and (ii) the knowledge-sharing route they prefer. The horizontal dimension represents age similarity in a work context, which may be either high if employees perceive themselves as similar to their co-workers in terms of age, or low if they perceive themselves as dissimilar. The vertical dimension refers to subjective age, whereby employees can evaluate themselves as younger or older than their actual age.

By crossing these two dimensions, we obtain a matrix with four quadrants showing four possible scenarios resulting from different combinations of age-similarity and subjective age on work teams. The first scenario (Q1) presents a situation in which age similarity is low and employees perceive themselves as younger than their real age. In this situation, according to the SST idea that the perception of having a long time horizon characterising people who feel younger makes them future-oriented and motivated by knowledge-related goals [73, 74], employees will be more prone to interact with colleagues who do not necessarily belong to their own age group in order to obtain procedural or technical knowledge useful for improving their performance and career advancement. They will be likely to engage in instrumental social interaction functional to attaining knowledge-related goals and developing technical skills. On the basis of these assumptions, they will be more inclined to internalize and less inclined to externalize knowledge with those considered out-group members [64]. However, when employees

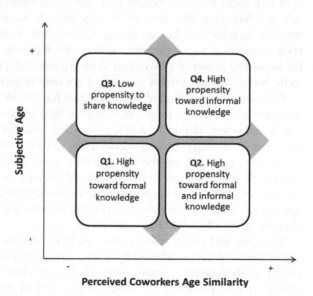

Fig. 2 Organizational knowledge sharing attitudes framework

Subjective Age

Q3. Low propensity to share knowledge

Q4. High propensity toward informal knowledge

Q1. High propensity toward formal knowledge

Q2. High propensity toward formal and informal knowledge

Perceived Coworkers Age Similarity

perceive themselves as younger than their real age and age similarity is high, they will be more inclined both to internalize and externalize knowledge, not only because of their focus on acquiring know-what knowledge [74, 76] but also because of a feeling of solidarity with age peers due to age group identification [45]. Therefore, in this scenario (Q2) employees will be likely to create affective ties and share with them both job-related knowledge and information about themselves and their feelings, in order to receive support and advice.

When people feel older than their real age and their time horizons shrink, they are more selective in interacting with social partners and tend to interact less with those not considered in-group members [73, 74]. Therefore, if they perceive low age-similarity within their work context (Q3) knowledge sharing will be less likely to occur either formally or informally. Alternatively, if they perceive a high level of age similarity (Q4), knowledge sharing will be likely to occur although it will not be primarily aimed at sharing technical information or acquiring new knowledge but mainly oriented towards satisfying emotional needs [76], for example individuals' requirements for support, admiration, gratification and commitment.

5 Conclusion and Next Steps

According to "socio-technical systems" theory, organizations are composed of both social and technical elements [5], hence scholars intending to study these systems need to pay attention to both social and technical factors [6, 13]. Moreover, if technical factors are viewed as artefacts of IT, an information system may also be seen as a socio-technical system [79]. Indeed, in information systems disciplines, scholars following this line of enquiry provide socio-technical principles and research approaches for designing information systems [80–82]. Based on socio-technical design principles, system development should "jointly optimize" the social and technical subsystems of an organization [13], ensuring key attention to the social side of systems design and not only to technical factors.

Following this perspective, the conceptual framework proposed and discussed in the previous section is aimed at shedding light on specific social aspects to be considered when adopting a KMS, particularly dynamics that could affect knowledge transfer among people operating in the same context (e.g. organizational unit, workgroup, etc.) but displaying a certain level of age diversity. Indeed this framework represents an initial theoretical attempt to conceptualize knowledge sharing, while taking into account two understudied dimensions, namely subjective age and age similarity, which are especially relevant today due to the demographic changes taking place within organizations.

Managers and policy makers involved in the design and adoption of KMSs in organizational contexts affected by an increasing level of age diversity can use this conceptual framework to make more reliable decisions that can foster knowledge sharing among employees of different ages and in different contexts. By highlighting the influence of subjective age, one advantage of this model is that of reducing the influence of age-related stereotypes in decision-making processes, and making managers aware of the existence of other relevant age-related constructs. Nevertheless, the influence of the more general context in which this model is applied should be also taken into account. Specifically, managers must be aware whether the prevailing focus of their organization is technical or relational, in order to adopt the most appropriate KMS. As a theoretical contribution, the aim of this paper is to provide insights to guide further research on how chronological and subjective age, as well as social network structure, influence formal and informal knowledge sharing among employees. With this paper, we have only begun to scratch the surface of the challenges associated with workforce aging and its consequences and knowledge sharing. Future research developments will be to empirically test and validate this conceptual framework by taking into account a set of contextual and control variables. Finally, it may also be of value to investigate what characteristics a KMS should have in order to better mitigate the effects of age diversity and foster the knowledge sharing process.

References

1. Kankanhalli, A., Tan, B., Wei, K.: Contributing knowledge to electronic knowledge repositories: an empirical investigation. MIS Q. **29**, 113–143 (2005)
2. Wasko, M., Faraj, S.: Why should I share? Examining social capital and knowledge contribution in electronic networks of practice. MIS Q. **29**, 35–57 (2005)
3. Alavi, M., Leidner, D.: Review: Knowledge management and knowledge management systems: Conceptual foundations and research issues. MIS Q. **25**, 107–136 (2001)
4. Za, S., Spagnoletti, P., North-Samardzic, A.: Organisational learning as an emerging process: the generative role of digital tools in informal learning practices. Br. J. Educ. Technol. **45**, 1023–1035 (2014)
5. Emery, F., Trist, E.: The causal texture of organizational environments. Hum. Relat. **18**, 12–32 (1965)
6. Sorrentino, M., Virili, F.: Socio-technical perspectives on e-government initiatives. Electronic Government. pp. 91–94. Springer, Berlin (2003)
7. Davenport, T.H., Prusak, L.: Working knowledge: how organizations manage what they know. Harvard Business School Press, 2000 (1998)
8. Alavi, M., Leidner, D.: Knowledge management systems: issues, challenges, and benefits. Commun. AIS. **1**, (1999)
9. Zardini, A., Mola, L., Vom Brocke, J., Rossignoli, C.: The role of ECM and its contribution in decision-making processes. J. Decis. Syst. **19**, 389–406 (2010)
10. Gibbert, M., Krause, H.: Practice exchange in a best practice marketplace. In: Davenport, T.H., Probst, B.G.J. (eds.) Knowledge Management Case Book: Siemens Best Practices, pp. 89–105. Publicis Corporate Publishing, Erlangen, Germany (2002)
11. Ko, D., Kirsch, L., King, W.: Antecedents of knowledge transfer from consultants to clients in enterprise system implementations. MIS Q. **29**, 59–85 (2005)
12. Dameri, R.P., Sabroux, C.R., I.S.: Driving IS value creation by knowledge capturing: theoretical aspects and empirical evidences. Information Technology and Innovation Trends in Organizations. pp. 73–81 (2011)
13. Robey, D., Anderson, C., Raymond, B.: Information technology, materiality, and organizational change: a professional odyssey. J. Assoc. Inf. Syst. **14**, 379–398 (2013)

14. Orlikowski, W.: Learning from notes: organizational issues in groupware implementation. In: Proceedings of the 1992 ACM conference on Computer-supported cooperative work. pp. 362–369 (1992)
15. Voelpel, S., Leibold, M., Streb, C.: The innovation meme: managing innovation replicators for organizational fitness. J. Chang. Manag. **5**, 57–69 (2005)
16. Virtainlahti, S., Moilanen, R.: Sharing tacit knowledge in organisations—a challenge in managing young and ageing employees. EBS Rev. **20**, 110–120 (2005)
17. Wang, S., Noe, R.: Knowledge sharing: a review and directions for future research. Hum. Resour. Manag. Rev. **20**, 115–131 (2010)
18. Nonaka, I., Takeuchi, H.: The knowledge creating company: how Japanese companies create the dynamics of innovation. New York (1995)
19. Cyert, R., March, J.G.: A behavioral theory of the firm. Prentice-Hall, Englewood Cliffs, NJ (1963)
20. Levitt, B., March, J.G.: Organizational learning. Ann. Rev. Sociol. **14**, 319–340 (1988)
21. Huber, G.P.: Organizational learning: the contributing processes and the literatures. Organ. Sci. **2**, 88–115 (1991)
22. March, J.G., Schulz, M., Zhou, X.: The dynamics of rules: change in written organizational codes. Stanford University Press, Stanford, CA (2000)
23. Schulz, M.: The uncertain relevance of newness: organizational learning and knowledge flows. Acad. Manag. J. **44**, 661–681 (2001)
24. De Long, D.W.: Lost knowledge: confronting the threat of an aging workforce. Oxford University Press, New York (2004)
25. Lazazzara, A., Bombelli, M.C.: HRM practices for an ageing Italian workforce: the role of training. J. Eur. Ind. Train. **35**, 808–825 (2011)
26. Davenport, T.H., De Long, D.W., Beers, M.C.: Successful knowledge management projects. Sloan Manage. Rev. **39**, 43–57 (1998)
27. Gourlay, S.: Knowledge management and HRD. Hum. Resour. Dev. Int. **4**, 27–46 (2001)
28. Earl, M.: Knowledge management strategies: towards a taxonomy. J. Manag. Inf. Syst. **18**, 215–233 (2001)
29. Stenmark, D.: Leveraging tacit organizational knowledge. J. Manag. Inf. Syst. **17**, 9–24 (2001)
30. Bonomi, S., Za, S., Marco, M. De, Rossignoli, C.: Knowledge sharing and value co-creation: designing a service system for fostering inter-generational cooperation. LNBIP 201—exploring services science. Proceedings of the 6th international conference, IESS 2015. pp. 25–35 (2015)
31. Spender, J.C., Grant, R.M.: Knowledge and the firm: overview. Strateg. Manag. J. **17**, 5–9 (1996)
32. Nonaka, I.: The dynamic theory of organizational knowledge creation. Organ. Sci. **5**, 14–37 (1994)
33. Lowendahl, B.R., Revang, O., Fosstenlokken, S.M.: Knowledge and value creation in professional service firms: a framework for analysis. Hum. Relat. **54**, 911–931 (2001)
34. Ipe, M.: Knowledge sharing in organizations: a conceptual framework. Hum. Resour. Dev. Rev. **2**, 337–359 (2003)
35. Cicotto, G., De Simone, S., Giustiniano, L., Pinna, R.: Psychosocial training: a case of self-efficacy improvement in an Italian school. J. Chang. Manag. **14**, 475–499 (2014)
36. Holtham, C., Courtney, N.: The executive learning ladder: a knowledge creation process grounded in the strategic information systems domain. In: Hoadley, E., Benbasat, I. (eds.) Proceedings of the Fourth Americas Conference on Information Systems. pp. 594–597., Baltimore, MD (1998)
37. Hendriks, P.: Why share knowledge? The influence of ICT on the motivation for knowledge sharing. Knowl. Process Manag. **6**, 91–100 (1999)
38. Alvesson, M.: Management of knowledge-intensive companies. Walter de Gruyer, New York (1993)
39. Empson, L.: Fear of exploitation and fear of contamination: Impediments to knowledge transfer in mergers between professional service firms. Hum. Relat. **54**, 839–862 (2001)

40. Mannix, E., Neale, M.A.: What differences make a difference? The promise and reality of diverse teams in organizations. Psychol. Sci. Public Interes. **6**, 31–55 (2005)
41. Lawrence, B.S.: New wrinkles in the theory of age: demography, norms, and performance ratings. Acad. Manag. J. **31**, 309–337 (1988)
42. Sterns, H.L., Doverspike, D.: Aging and the retraining and learning process in organizations. In: Goldstein, I., Katzel, R. (eds.) Training and development in work organizations, pp. 229–332. Jossey-Bass, San Francisco (1989)
43. Schalk, R., Veldhoven, M.Van, De, A.H., Bertrand, F., Claes, R., Crego, A., Dorenbosch, L.: Moving European research on work and ageing forward: overview and agenda. Eur. J. Work Organ. Psychol. **19**, 76–101 (2010)
44. Montepare, J.M., Lachman, M.E.: "You"re only as old as you feel': self-perceptions of age, fears of aging, and life satisfaction from adolescence to old age. Psychol. Aging **4**, 73–78 (1989)
45. Sherman, S.R.: Changes in age identity: self perceptions in middle and late life. J. Aging Stud. **8**, 397–412 (1994)
46. Barnes-Farrell, J.L., Piotrowski, M.J.: Discrepancies between chronological age and personal age as a reflection of unrelieved worker stress. Work Stress **5**, 177–187 (1991)
47. Barnes-Farrell, J., Rumery, S., Swody, C.: How do concepts of age relate to work and off-the-job stresses and strains? A field study of health care workers in five nations. Exp. Aging Res. **28**, 87–98 (2002)
48. Iskra-Golec, I.: Personal age and assessment of work stress in Polish nurses. Exp. Aging Res. **28**, 51–58 (2002)
49. Rioux, L., Mokounkolo, R.: Investigation of subjective age in the work context: study of a sample of French workers. Pers. Rev. **42**, 372–395 (2013)
50. de Lange, A., Taris, T., Jansen, P., Smulders, P., Houtman, I., Kompier, M.: Age as a factor in the relation between work and mental health: results of the longitudinal TAS survey. In: Houdmont, J., McIntyre, S. (eds.) Occupational health psychology: European perspectives on research, education and practice, pp. 21–45. ISMAI Publications, Maia, Portugal (2006)
51. Shanahan, M.J., Porfeli, E.J., Mortimer, J.T., Erickson, L.D.: Subjective age identity and the transition to adulthood: when adolescents become adults? In: Settersten, R.A., Furstenberg, F.F., Rumbaut, R.G. (eds.) On the frontier of adulthood: theory, research, and public policy, pp. 225–255. University of Chicago Press, Chicago, IL (2005)
52. Cleveland, J.N., Landy, F.J.: The effects of person and job stereotypes on two personnel decisions. J. Appl. Psychol. **68**, 609–619 (1983)
53. Sterns, H.L., Alexander, R.A.: Industrial gerontology: The aging individual and work. In: Schaie, K.W. (ed.) Annual Review of Gerontology and Geriatrics. Springer, New York (1987)
54. Cleveland, J.N., Hollmann, G.: Context and discrimination in personnel decisions: direct and mediated approaches. In: Meindl, J.R., Cardy, R.L., Puffer, S. (eds.) Advances in Information Processing in Organization. JAI Press, Greenwich, CT (1991)
55. Cummings, J.N.: Work groups, structural diversity, and knowledge sharing in a global organization. Manage. Sci. **50**, 352–364 (2004)
56. Williams, K., O'Reilly, C.: Demography and diversity in organizations: a review of 40 years of research. Res. Organ. Behav. **20**, 77–140 (1998)
57. Tsui, A.S., Gutek, B.A.: Demographic differences in organizations: current research and future directions. Lexington Books, Lanham, MD (1999)
58. Tajfel, H., Turner, J.C.: The social identity theory of inter-group behavior. In: S. Worchel, Austin, L.W. (eds.) Psychology of Intergroup Relations. Nelson-Hall, Chicago (1986)
59. Turner, J.C.: Rediscovering the Social Group: A Self-Categorization Theory. Blackwell Publishing, Oxford (1987)
60. Avery, D., McKay, P., Wilson, D.: Engaging the aging workforce: the relationship between perceived age similarity, satisfaction with coworkers, and employee engagement. J. Appl. Psychol. **92**, 1542–1556 (2007)
61. Thompson, V.L.S.: Variables affecting identity salience among African Americans. J. Soc. Psychol. **139**, 748–761 (1999)

62. Tsui, A.S., O'Reilly, C.A.: Beyond simple demographic effects: the importance of relational demography in superior-subordinate dyads. Acad. Manag. J. **32**, 402–423 (1989)
63. Ojha, A.K.: Impact of team demography on knowledge sharing in software project teams. South Asian J. Manag. **12**, 67–78 (2005)
64. Van Knippenberg, D., De Dreu, C.K.W., Homan, A.C.: Work group diversity and group performance: an integrative model and research agenda. J. Appl. Psychol. **89**, 1008–1022 (2004)
65. Byrne, D.: The Attraction Paradigm. Academic Press, New York (1971)
66. Chattopadhyay, P.: Beyond direct and symmetrical effects: the influence of demographic dissimilarity on organizational citizenship behavior. Acad. Manag. J. **42**, 273–287 (1999)
67. Mehra, A., Kilduff, M., Brass, D.J.: At the margins: A distinctiveness approach to the social identity and social networks of underrepresented groups. Acad. Manag. J. **4**, 441–452 (1998)
68. Brass, D.J.: Men's and women's networks: a study of interaction patterns and influence in an organization. Acad. Manag. J. **28**, 327–343 (1985)
69. Lazarsfeld, P.F., Merton, R.K.: Friendship as a social process: a substantive and methodological analysis. In: Berger, M. (ed.) Freedom and Control in Modern Society, pp. 18–66. Van Nostrand, New York (1954)
70. Ibarra, H.: Homophily and differential returns: sex differences in network structure and access in an advertising firm. Adm. Sci. Q. **37**, 422–447 (1992)
71. Lincoln, J.R., Miller, J.: Work and friendship ties in organizations: a comparative analysis of relation networks. Adm. Sci. Q. **24**, 181–199 (1979)
72. McPherson, M., Smith-Lovin, L., Cook, J.: Birds of a feather: Homophily in social networks. Annu. Rev. Sociol. (2001)
73. Carstensen, L.L.: Socioemotional selectivity theory: Social activity in life-span context. Annu. Rev. Gerontol. Geriatr. **11**, 195–217 (1991)
74. Carstensen, L.L.: Motivation for social contact across lifespan: A theory of socioemotional selectivity. In: Jacobs, J.E. (ed.) Nebraska Symposium on Motivation, pp. 209–254. University of Nebraska Press, Lincoln (1993)
75. Ng, T., Feldman, D.: The relationships of age with job attitudes: a meta-analysis. Pers. Psychol. **63**, 677–718 (2010)
76. Carstensen, L.L.: Social and emotional patterns in adulthood: Support for socioemotional selectivity theory. Psychol. Aging **7**, 331–338 (1992)
77. Carstensen, L.L., Turk-Charles, S.: The salience of emotion across the adult life span. Psychol. Aging **9**, 259–264 (1994)
78. Santrock, J.W.: A topical approach to life-span development. McGraw-Hill, New York (2008)
79. Beynon-Davies, P.: Information systems as socio-technical or sociomaterial systems. AMCIS 2009 proceedings, San Francisco, California (2009)
80. Bostrom, B.R.P., Heinen, J.S.: MIS problems and failures: a socio-technical perspective PART 1: The Causes. MIS Q. **1**, 17–32 (1977)
81. Clegg, C.W.: Sociotechnical principles for system design. Appl. Ergon. **31**, 463–477 (2000)
82. Henningsson, S., Rukanova, B., Hrastinski, S.: Resource dependencies in socio-technical information systems design research. Commun. Assoc. Inf. Syst. **27**, Article 42 (2010)

Information Technologies and Quality Management. Towards a New Idea of Quality?

Teresina Torre

Abstract Quality has become one of the most relevant challenges for enterprises that wish to satisfy the needs and expectations of their clients. In this paper, we aim to verify if potentialities of information technologies (ITs) could help to ensure a better quality for enterprises and if and how they influence the concept of quality. In order to pursue this goal, our analysis examines the relationship between technology and quality investigating which of the many ITs, used in enterprises, affects more directly the quality levels and underling the principal effects they produce. Our study considers the specific case of an Italian software house, where it is possible to clarify and understand the role of ITs with regard to our research topic. Therefore, some considerations about the evolution of the classic idea of quality, enabled by technologies, are proposed.

Keywords Information technologies · IT · Quality · Quality management · Business case

1 Introduction

Quality is considered one of the most relevant challenges for enterprises that wish to satisfy needs and expectations of their old and new clients, being—quality—by now a key element in the definition of the enterprise's strategic view and in the organization of its operational programs, required in order to face increasing global competition.

Some scholars argue that 'more' quality asks for a strong will on the part of the management, oriented to focus on this aspect in every process (indeed, total quality management represents the most relevant system supporting quality [1, 2] and top management involvement represents one of the basic values in this field) [3]; others

T. Torre (✉)
Department of Economics and Management, University of Genova, Genoa, Italy
e-mail: teresina.torre@economia.unige.it

© Springer International Publishing Switzerland 2016
F. Ricciardi and A. Harfouche (eds.), *Information and Communication Technologies in Organizations and Society*, Lecture Notes in Information Systems and Organisation 15, DOI 10.1007/978-3-319-28907-6_12

underline the point that commitment and participation of all workers are necessary conditions (i.e. [4–8]. Again, others offer evidence of the fundamental role of the organizational culture and of the structural change, which are able to facilitate attention towards quality [9, 10]; while others emphasize the centrality of cost control (the question has received a particular attention just by the fathers of the quality movement, Juran, Feigenbaum and Crosby; [11, 12]). All these topics have been examined and discussed in detail [13–15] both from the theoretical point of view [16] and from the empirical one [17, 18].

The relationship between information technologies (ITs) and information system and quality management has been studied, as well [19–21]. In this perspective, attention has been focused on two aspects. The first topic consider the point that many enterprises are providing better products through the introduction of ITs: so technology becomes an enabling mechanism for quality. From another point of view, a few contributions have considered how specific IT applications could impact on quality and its management, which rely heavily on ITs: in this case, ITs act as a feedback mechanism and a communicator helper [22, 23].

In this paper, we wish to deepen a specific aspect about the role of ITs with respect to quality, that is: whether they can change the very idea of quality, as traditionally we are used to know it. So, our interest is mainly focused on the concept itself and not on the strategic and operational implications, being their relevance an accepted fact.

In order to pursue our goal, the paper is organized in the following manner. First, we will examine how quality can be attained using technology, starting from the definition of quality according to some of the most important and famous authors, and then examining two complementary dimensions: in brief, the quality of technology (just to remember how this aspect is unavoidable) and, more in depth, how the various typologies of technologies work to favour quality and what kind of changes they produce. In the next paragraph, we will consider a business case to illustrate how the description of the different context of technological applications can find a clear documentation in a particular example of an enterprise, the business of which is exactly to support quality. Finally, we will discuss our question about the evolution of the concept of quality and propose some considerations useful for further researches.

2 Quality Through Technology

According to the definition of some of the most important scholars, quality is essentially what client wants [24] and what he/she thinks it is [25]: Feigenbaum first and Deming after him, they both emphasize this aspect, stressing the importance of translating the future needs of the consumer in measurable characteristics so that the product can be designed and realized with the best conditions to satisfy client and guarantee, at the same time, the efficiency of the enterprise's system. As

Feigenbaum writes 'the interest for quality ends when client has its product and he is satisfied' [25: 77].

Juran [26] clarifies that quality is fitness for use, highlighting the same point of view, from another perspective: the product must be adapted to the expectations even before excellent. Crosby [27] adds that quality is measured in term of conformance to requirements (both the product's and the customer's requirements that often are not the same).

Closely related to this, there is another important element: all these authors consider quality to depend on the integration of the efforts of the various groups of the organization (just as Feigenbaum [25] assert that integration is a key point). Therefore, it can be achieved only with the participation of human resources [24], implying that people are interested in the process of improving quality [26], a prerequisite to total quality [13, 14, 28, 29].

Starting from this point, each scholar underlines different aspects. Deming, for example, emphasises a specialized and technical approach, where competencies are necessary to create quality in accordance with the client's wishes. Crosby [28] stresses the motivational condition requested from all workers, involved in the entire productive process. Juran's method is a process-focused one: so, his idea is near to that of continuous improvement, proposed by Ishikawa and developed first by Japanese industries.

The best-known implication of the quality movement is given by the twisting of Fordist logic, focused on quantity, and by the introduction of new organizational models coherent with the different perspective that the attention to quality opens up (i.e. flat organization, network), putting clients at the heart of the organization [30].

An important role is played by technology in general—that is, each process and equipment useful in transforming an input into an output and then every art practice that affects the organizational structure and the working procedures and practice [31, 32]—and specifically by information technology (IT), the role of which in minimizing uncertainty and reducing complexity is absolutely central. As Delic [21] underline, it is showed that quality management and IT could provide a very useful basis for improving organizational performance [33, 34]. The question is in what way and with what implications it happens.

2.1 The Interaction Between Quality and Technology

In general, the interaction between quality and technology can be examined from two different perspectives [35]: one is focused on the quality of technology; the second considers technology to do quality [36, 37].

Front the first point of view, it is evident that technology—and the tools in which it is absorbed—has a problem of intrinsic quality. In other words, the definition of quality as suitability [26] asks for technologies ready to work with appropriate quality levels, regardless of the type of technology and its refinement. In this context, the evolution in technology from mechanization to automation has introduced a lot of changes: for example, in the work organization according to the different process configurations, in the jobs connected with them and in the skills involved, aligned with new competencies necessary to use new technologies.

At the same time, the requirement of suitability continues to be present like a premise (preliminary conditions to plan the quality of the productive process) and as a result (in term of awaited characteristics of the product). In a way, there is a chain of quality in technology, each link of which contributes—together with human factor, as socio-technical perspective shows [38]—with a high level of interdependence to the quality of the final offer to the customer and with a relevant effect on quality in the field of decision making system [39]. This is one of the key aspects of the total quality approach.

2.2 Technologies for Quality

Even if the quality of technology is important, our interest has been previously focused on how technology can be used for the purpose of seeking out quality and for managing process quality. The information and communication technologies (ICT) systems are normally used by many companies to simplify and optimize their management, to increase their productivity, to reduce their cost levels [36, 40], to hinder the overblown shortening of product lifecycles and extend efficiency in distribution [41], but they are not usually considered for the specific aim to operate 'with more quality' [37]. It is exactly on this question that we wish to focus, examining the different kinds of ICTs which are, by now, more and more diffused in enterprises.

Specifically, we will first examine the topic of integrated information system, that is enterprise resource planning (ERP). Then, we will analyse other system applications created to meet specific information needs that are not adequately covered by ERP; in detail: the system created for marketing interests, that is customer relationship management (CRM); afterwards, the one for planning of products, namely product data management (PDM), the other for e-procurement and finally that for production and distribution of products, known as supply chain management (SCM).

ERP is the principal support to plan and manage in a coordinated way a lot of information and resources present within an enterprise. It consists in 'sets of software modules produced from a single source and operating on a single database properly designed' [42: 85].

In brief, ERP systems present some important features. One concerns the extent of the included areas—dealing with major operational support activities; another affects the hierarchical structure, which becomes leaner as a result of more intense exchange of information. All this makes possible:

- a reorganization in accordance with the logic for processes, which has become one of the principal source for competitive advantage [29, 43];
- an increase in coordination and integration between the flows of activities and organizational units, through the possibility to develop the various activities that make up the process in parallel, encouraging in this way the respect of the scheduling and a greater balance in the allocation of tasks [44];
- a growth in the standardization of the different activities, which makes stable and predictable the outputs of each unit and enlarges the possibility to guide workers' behaviours.

These matters are, indeed, indicated as the principal way of attaining quality. ERP enhances the basic needs of quality, i.e. coordination, integration and exchange of information [45]. So, ERP can be a real support in change in the short term: it helps to map in detail the information flows in order to intervene on the organizational structure, reducing the numbers of levels. Other advantages derive from the possibility of building a network for the exchange of information, both internally and externally, by encouraging knowledge creation and sharing, producing positive effects in the long term on efficiency and effectiveness.

CRM uses technology to manage every process useful to identify, acquire and retain as many consumers as possible, adapting the offer to their changing needs and expectations. It is known that consumers have become more exacting thanks to the increased number of information sources they can use, so their choices are more aware and informed. In this context, enterprises have to face with two different questions: to attract new prepared clients and to sustain their satisfaction during the time, as it has being demonstrated that regaining lost clients is really expensive. CRM applications offer support for three important processes of interaction with clients, which are: sale forces; support and services, and marketing.

In particular, applications of sale force automation serve to make interactions with the customer more effective and efficient, enabling sales forces to use any available information. It is possible to offer proposal on customized products or services, based on the automation of all the systems involved in sales activities. Applications for customer service and support enhance the opportunities for establishing contact with clients to maximize their satisfaction, not only when it is necessary to solve problem with claims, but also to help them to use better the potential of products and to do so in an interactive and continuous way.

Finally, the applications of marketing automation are aimed at improving the planning and the execution of promotional campaigns to better identify markets and new potential customers in a more incisive manner. The fundamental point is the analysis and information processing. For this, new CRM systems employ data mining capabilities, a term which commonly refers to an 'integrated set of analysis techniques designed to extract knowledge not known a priori from large data sets seemingly unrelated' [46: 78] that seems really useful to the development of CRM strategies. In the pursuit of quality, CRM plays an absolutely central role: it helps to put the customer at the heart of the organization, to understand "what he/she asks," and to do develop customization, which represents the highest possible quality according the most appropriate definition in our perspective. In other words, the client can be put in the middle of the organizational system, going beyond the traditional contrast between the classic organizational pyramid and the innovative one, which imagine it overturned just to show the importance of the client. It allows to gain other important goals, over customer retention, for example enlarging clients groups and increasing sales, offering detailed and targeted proposals.

Regarding the service activities, the recent evolution towards web call centres makes more flexible and interactive the relation with clients, extending its duration; these activities may offer new support like page-pushing, co-browsing and application-sharing, in order to assist client in each of his/her questions.

At the same time, it should be underlined that three fundamental aspects have to be well considered in order for the enterprise to focus on ICTs to improve quality in relations to clients; the interactions systems, which ask for a cultural change in the mind of the client, who has to become more proactive; the guidance processes in the relationships with clients; which asks for an effective integration between front office and back office workers, and the knowledge collection, based on structured knowledge management systems.

Briefly, the role of CRM towards quality is absolutely central, especially if we remember Deming's definition and its orientation to future needs.

The role of new technologies is crucial in production area, too. In particular, new requirements for the management of technical data related to the product throughout its life cycle have favoured the development of PDM systems, a recent and richer evolution of CAD system. These are characterised by the ability to manage data associated with the product at all stages, from its creation to its disposal by the consumer: on this basis, many applications have been created. Briefly, we recall:

- the management of data and documents to guarantee the integrity of information assets;
- the classification of the parts of a product, grouped by similarity and, therefore, by replaceable use (with benefits on the efficiency of the production system)
- the configuration of the structure of the product, taking into account the greatest possible number of combinations of elements (forming the basis for customization for the client and, at the same time, allowing the management in an economically favourable manner by the enterprise).

The most obvious consequences are: the increase of productivity of the technical staff, the minimization of errors (in numbers and in relevance) in relation to the number of variants and the number of steps of the completeness of the information and controls (software does it automatically), resulting in a decrease in safety stocks (indispensable for managing according just in time approach). All this is the contribution of the PDM to the orientation towards quality (Figs. 1 and 2).

There are two kinds of implications of the different sequence in the process. The first is on the quality of the production, which also benefits from the sharing of the information base and its digitization—now it is a file that is available to all and shared by all, and not a set of single drawings to coordinate each other. The other concerns the quality of customer service, which becomes more and more tailored to

Fig. 1 The traditional sequence

Fig. 2 The new sequence with PDM

his/her needs: this traditionally and typically handcrafted way may be now offered in the industrial context.

Many of the efforts made with regard to the design and fulfilment of a product would be in vain if the used inputs were not adequate (both in terms of their quality and quantity, than in times they arrive to enter the productive process): the adoption of ICT in the area of supply allows to run more efficiently activities that binds the enterprise to suppliers, that is e-procurement.

The link between e-procurement and quality is not as immediate as it appears among the previously described system, but it does exist and plays an important role in creating favourable conditions. E-procurement systems collaborate to 'co-makership', facilitating the evaluation of suppliers to choose them (for everyone can be easily ready any information on costs, reliability, quality, geographical distance and time to delivery) in order to make possible a real integration with them through the sharing of information and the use of suppliers' competencies to find the best solution to obtain the sought result, indirectly facilitating the internal organization of the supplier itself.

Some specific applications of Supply Chain Management operate in the same direction. For example, with these systems, it is possible to improve coordination between suppliers, productive functions and distribution; in particular, three kinds of implementations are possible:

- supply chain configuration, usually composed of a multitude of knots that form a network, in which the characteristics of different nodes (production units, distribution centre, etc.) and their relationships allow to simulate the various, then the possible, solutions to find the best one;
- supply chain planning, useful to get an effective and efficient production (i.e. balance between what market demands and what can be produced and distributed in the requested time) and support the main processes (demand forecasting, order management, production planning, procurement); this is important when the production system works in order to assemble it as make to order, but also when the system is based on make-to-stock (where the forecast on market evolution is really essential);

- supply chain execution, designed to ensure daily operations, to organize the activities of storage and handling of materials, functional to the management of the physical flows in inbound and in outbound logistics.

As far as e-procurement is concerned, the contribution to the quality of the SCM is not direct, but once again it is essential because it is convenient for ensuring:

- an effective product customization, as the PDM uses information that logistics offers;
- a high reliability and quality of support services (more predictive capabilities, certain times).

We can therefore argued that PDM and SCM enrich and support each other, creating a virtuous circle essential for quality, in all its dimensions, because they are a source of competitive advantage, even if they don't assume a primary role. In a specific way, the possibility to have more personalized products needs of an appropriate back system, composed by an information part and by an organizational one, both promised by our systems.

3   The Business Case: Z-Lab Solutions

Z-Lab is an Italian software house, that has been present for thirty years in the market of computer systems. It operates as a national leader in the development of solutions dedicated to large manufacturing companies—with particular expertise for those operating in the fields of rubber and fuel. Moreover, it has a particular interest in small and medium enterprises (SMEs) [47]—that represent a really important market in Italy and to which it offers a wide range of solutions developed entirely in-house, alongside others realized in partnership with leading companies in the provision of services for business, a strategy that allows to satisfy each need of its specific target.

Its attention to quality problems goes back to the beginning of the last decade, when its management chose this perspective to introduce a differentiation strategy in order to develop its market perspectives.

3.1   Z-Lab Offer

Based on the conviction that the global supply of ICT contained products that were too complex to be used by many enterprises, Z-Lab decided to focus on the development of IT solutions that have to be accessible to those who are not computer science friendly. Currently, its offering consists of over 20 solutions, standard or customized by demand, which comprehensively meet the multiple needs of different types of firms asking for its help in managing ICT. Among these, some, in particular, enable to show how strong the link between ICT and quality is.

Z-Lab main product is composed of a homemade solution refined over the years, which serves as platform for the other modules that can be recomposed and added in accordance with the needs of each enterprise. It is important to underline that our software is developing services through cloud, which has the first and relevant effect to maintain the positive peculiarities of the applications just seen and to use the real innovation introduced by cloud, which is the place wherein information and modules are situated—the cloud—reducing, up to remove, any problem of capacity and storing and of continuous upgrading.

3.2 Different Functions for Different Quality Dimensions

The principal product is represented by Z-Web; its characteristics and functionalities covers the field of ERP systems. The Z-Web is organized as an online multipurpose platform, usable on any device with internet access. It offers a number of key features useful to store, manage and share, in a structured manner, lots of information circulating within the company, so as to facilitate coordination and integration of all employees and an optimal use of their time.

The system helps in managing data and knowledge about clients, both from the inner side (i.e. about their preferences, about the history of the relationship and its evolution and so on; and also by research functions that allow one to find common criteria and elaborate the data themselves in order to plan activities and focused strategies) than in external one towards the client him/herself (i.e. any possible contact for any client with the complete set of means to talk with him/her, always immediately and directly usable through simple links).

Z-Web is an efficient platform, able to favour the complete process management and the processing of all information; so, it is possible to standardize sale and services process and, at the same time, create the necessary base to work with quality.

This characteristic has a good effect on quality of service provided, because it allows to know always the situation of each relevant variable and its history (Fig. 3).

This application is usually associated with the functions of CRM, Z-shop (for supporting online sales), Z-view (for analysing sales data) and PDM-autodata (for designing processes with drastically lower costs).

CRM, as known, is a powerful tool for quality: it allows one to use knowledge to improve the relationship with the customer at every stage. Anyone who has to interact with him/her can have useful elements to run this relation in a short time and in a personalized way and develop it; not only that, the client's supervisor is able to prepare on the best the relationship itself (through improvement or innovation of the product in accordance with the consumer's tastes and his/her behaviour). In the same direction, the other modules work and do it in a simple way. For

Fig. 3 Z-Web, basic script

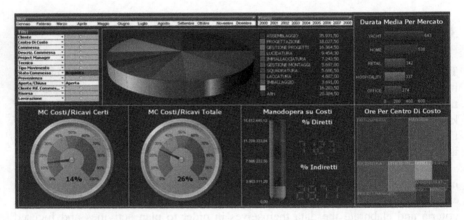

Fig. 4 Z-Web interface

example, Z-Shop offer a simple and easy system to introduce orders by agents working outside or directly by clients. Z-View is a more sophisticated tool to analyse some specific indicators—about sales, purchases, accounting data and orders—producing simple and effective representations (Fig. 4).

As Feigenbaum and others authors underscore, quality of product and service is fundamental, but—and this is particularly true in times of increasing competition— a strong attention to costs is necessary: here, it is exactly the value produced by these systems, which offer contemporary support to work for the present in quality and for the future evolution according to costumer's tastes with a reasonable cost level. The fundamental problem is the correct design of the infrastructure of support, wherein the role of the suppliers of services determines the quality approach and the quality orientation. This is considered by Z-Lab the real benefit of the investment in ITs proposed to its clients and its success on the market shows how this strategy is appreciated.

4 Is It Possible a New Idea of Quality?

On the basis of the arguments presented in this paper, the answer to our question—can ITs change the idea of quality?—is positive. And now we will summarize the most important implications of the developed analysis in order to shed light on the concept of quality and its possible evolution. ITs not only contribute to the process of research and quality management—as any kind of technology has done from the beginning of quality movement; moreover, its development can also influence and change the logic on which quality has been built since its foundation as a key point in the definition of the enterprise strategy.

To recall, quality is based on four pillars:

- the customer, who is at the heart of all activities;
- the integration of the efforts of the various groups in the organization;
- the relationship between quality and costs;
- and, finally, the continuous improvement as a basic condition for better quality, necessary to face with competition [48].

With regard to the first point, ITs—especially ERP and CRM—make use of any information in an easier and faster manner, and then facilitate information translating into explicit knowledge: both these characteristics contribute to intensifying competition among enterprises and to raise its level. Not only does, every employee has all the information he/she needs to quickly decide on what he/she is working, but through information sharing, information and knowledge will continue to grow in value. In addition, technologies also promote communication, dialogue and exchanges between inside and outside the enterprise.

The potential of ERP and CRM is increased by that coming from SCM and PDM systems. The first allows to monitor and effectively to manage the information flow within the supply chain, in order to reduce obstacles, that may appear when enterprises are involved in a unique productive process, and improve the workflow. The second promotes the exchange of data among all those who are concerned with the design and prototyping, so errors are reduced and the time required to engineer a product is shortened. In this way, it is possible to maximize the integration of the efforts of various groups as suggested by Feigenbaum [49]. In addition to this, the dialogue and the parallelism between the activities of employees, the larger and extended coordination of the phases of the supply chain are elements that act positively on the relationship between cost and quality. As Juran argued, it is always necessary to support the cost estimates, in order to prevent all or part of those resulting from excessive or unnecessary controls or by any failures. Moreover, flexibility and adaptability of these technologies foster a real and intense continuous improvement, more and more necessary in dynamic economic conditions, as at present.

All applications allow the management to track down and solve the problems at source, to monitor the results in real time, achieving high degrees of control and, consequently, driving the company towards the highest levels of quality. This is not done in an automatic way, but through commitment for this to happen.

Changes are required in the structural organization, in order to support the flow of information; but also in the case where such changes do not require little effort, these are paid off by the advantages and supports offered by the use of ITs.

Process organization comes out significantly improved, thanks to the coordination and integration of the flow of activities and organizational units, along with the ability to standardize the most monotonous and often repetitive phases. Quality strategy allows one to balance cost leadership and differentiation at the same time. Indeed, through PDM, companies can offer large-scale or unique and tailored products to specific physical and functional characteristics required by the customer.

This imparts dynamism to the concept of quality, making it less necessary to define, and emphasizes the role of the quality of the enterprise and, moreover, of the entire supply network. Quality becomes, from this perspective, an ever-changing state, that overtakes the idea of continuous improvement and strengthens its interactive dimension, facilitating a tailor-made approach in every context [50].

This is so fascinating and so unpredictable, that it is evident that this change has to be carefully monitored; especially, it will be useful to deepen with compared case analysis how quality dimensions are re-configuring.

References

1. Talha, M.: Total quality management (TQM): an overview. Bottom Line 17(1), 15–19 (2004)
2. Yusof, S.M., Aspinwall, E.: Total quality management implementation frameworks: comparison and review. Total Qual. Manag. 11(3), 281–294 (2000)
3. Hellsten, U., Klefsio, B.: TQM as a management system consisting of values methodologies tools. TQM Mag. 12(4), 238–244 (2000)
4. Imai, M.: Kaizen. McGraw-Hill, New York (1986)
5. Lemak, D., Reed, R.: Commitment to total quality management. is there a relationship with firm performance? J. Qual. Manag. 2(1), 67–86 (1997)
6. Agus, A., Hassan, Z.F.: Enhancing production performance and customer performance through total quality management: strategies for competitive advantage. Procedia Soc Behav. Sci. 24, 1650–1662 (2011)
7. Giannini, M.: Politiche della qualità, coinvolgimento del personale e dinamica organizzativa. Giappichelli Editore, Torino (1996)
8. Groth, J.C.: Total quality management: perspective for leaders. Total Qual. Mag. 7(3), 54–59 (1995)
9. Tobin, L.M.: The new quality landscape: total quality management. J. Syst. Manag. 12(3), 343–363 (1990)
10. Fok, Y.L., Fok, W.M., Hartman, S.J.: Exploring the relationship between total quality management and information systems development. Inf. Manag. 38, 355–371 (2001)
11. Schiffauerova, A., Thomson, V.: Managing cost of quality: insight into industry practice. TQM Mag. 18(5), 542–550 (2006)
12. Fawcett, S.E., Calantone, R.J., Roath, A.: Meeting quality and cost imperatives in a global market. Int. J. Phys. Distrib. Logistics Manag. 30(6), 472–499 (2000)

13. Compagno, C.: Il management della qualità. Dagli standard al Knowledge Management. Utet, Torino (1999)
14. Colurcio, M., Mele, C.: Management della qualità: principi, pratiche e tecniche. McGraw-Hill, Milano (2010)
15. Martinez-Costa, M., Martínez-Lorente, A.R.: Does quality management foster or hinder innovation? An empirical study of Spanish companies. Total Qual. Manag. 19(3), 209–221 (2008)
16. Sousa, R., Voss, C.A.: Quality management re-visited: a reflective review and agenda for future research. J. Oper. Manag. 20(1), 91–109 (2002)
17. Baccarani, C. (ed.): I saggi sulla qualità nell'economia di impresa. Cedam, Padova (1995)
18. Binney G., Williams, C.: Making quality work: lessons from Europe's leading companies. The results of a pan European study of the application of quality management principles. The Economist Intelligence Unit, Special Report, Ashridge (1992)
19. Sanchez-Rodriguez, C., Dewhurst, F.W., Martínez-Lorente, A.R.: IT use in supporting TQM initiatives: an empirical investigation. Int. J. Oper. Prod. Manag. 26(5), 486–504 (2006)
20. Khanam, S., Siddiqui, J., Talib, F.: Role of information technology in total quality management: a literature review. Int. J. Adv. Res. Comput. Eng. Technol. 2(8), 2433–2445 (2013)
21. Delic, M., Radlovacki, V., Kamberovic, B., Masimovic, R., Pecujlija, M.: Examining relationship between quality management and organizational performance in transitional economies. Total Qual. Manag. Bus. Excellence 25(4), 367–382 (2014)
22. Kock, N.F.J., McQueen, R.J.: Using groupware in quality management program. Inf. Syst. Manag. 14, 56–62 (1997)
23. Miller, H.: The multiple dimensions of information quality. Inf. Syst. Manag. 13, 79–82 (1996)
24. Deming, W.E.: Out of the Crisis. MIT Press Edition, Cambridge (1982)
25. Feigenbaum, A.V.: Total Quality Control. McGraw-Hill, New York (1961)
26. Juran, J.: Quality Control Handbook. McGraw-Hill, New York (1951)
27. Crosby, P.B.: Quality is Free. McGraw-Hill, New York (1979)
28. Cappelli, L., Renzi, M.F.: Management della qualità. Cedam, Padova (2010)
29. Candiotto, R.: L'approccio per processi e i sistemi di gestione per la qualità. Giuffrè, Milano (2003)
30. Crosby, P.B.: Quality without Tears: The Art of Hassle-Free Management. McGraw-Hill Professional, New York (1995)
31. Ciborra, C.U., Schneider, L.: Transforming the context and routines of management, strategy and technology. In: Adler, P. (ed.) The Future Of Work. Oxford University Press, Oxford (1992)
32. Thompson, J.D.: Organizations in Action. McGraw-Hill, New York (1967)
33. Haley, M.: Information technology and the quality improvement in defense industries. TQM J. 26(4), 348–359 (2014)
34. Dewhurst, F.W., Rafael Martínez-Lorente, A., Sánchez-Rodríguez, C.: An initial assessment of the influence of IT on TQM: a multiple case study. Int. J. Oper. Prod. Manag. 23(4), 348–374 (2003)
35. Schatzberg, E.: Changing meanings of technology before 1930. Technol. Cult. 47(3), 486–512 (2006)
36. Sanchez-Rodriguez, C., Martinez-Lorente, A.R.: Effect of IT and quality management on performance. Ind. Manag. Data Syst. 111(6), 830–848 (2011)
37. Martinez-Lorente, A.R., Martinez-Costa, M.: ISO 900 and TQM: substitutes or complementary? An empirical study in industrial companies. Int. J. Qual. Reliab. Manag. 23(3), 260–276 (2004)
38. Emery, F.E., Trist, E.L.: Analytical model for sociotechnical system. Pasmore, Sherwood (1978)

39. Semenova, E.G., Smirnova, M.S., Tushavin, V.A.: Decision making support system in multi-objective issues of quality management in the field of information technology. Int. J. Appl. Eng. Res. **9**(22), 16977–16984 (2014)
40. Martinez-Lorente, A.R., Sánchez-Rodríguez, C., Dewhurst, F.W.: The effect of information technologies on TQM: an initial analysis. Int. J. Prod. Econ. **89**(1), 77–93 (2004)
41. Mahmood, M.A., Soon, S.K.: A comprehensive model for measuring the potential impact of information technologies on organizational strategic variables. Dec. Sci. **22**, 869–897 (1991)
42. Bracchi, G., Motta, G.: Processi aziendali e sistemi informativi. Franco Angeli, Milano (1998)
43. Flynn, B.B., Schroeder, R.G., Sakakibara, S.: The impact of quality management practice on performance and competitive advantage. Decis. Sci. **26**(5), 659–691 (1995)
44. Kim, D.Y., Kumar, V., Kumar, U.: Relationship between quality management practices and innovation. J. Oper. Manag. **30**(4), 295–315 (2012)
45. Zelnik, M., Maletic, M., Maletic, D., Gomiscek, B.: Quality management system as a link between management and employees. Total Qual. Manag. Bus. Excellence **23**(1), 45–62 (2012)
46. Berry, M.J., Linoff, G.: Mastering Data Mining: The Art and Science of Customer Relationship Management. Wiley, Brisbane (2000)
47. Garengo, P., Biazzo, S.: From ISO quality standard to an integrated management system. An implementation process in SME. Total Qual. Manag. Bus. Excellence **23**(3–4), 310–335 (2013)
48. Walsh, A., Hughes, H., Maddox, D.P.: Total quality management continuous improvement: is the philosophy a reality? J. Eur. Indus. Train. **26**(6), 299–307 (2002)
49. Feigenbaum, A.V.: Total Quality Management. Wiley, New York (2002)
50. Klefsjo, B., Bergquist, B., Edgeman, R.L.: Six Sigma and total quality management: different day, same soup? Int. J. Six Sigma Competitive Adv. **2**(2), 162–178 (2006)

Acquihiring: A New Process for Innovation and Organizational Learning

Roberta Fantasia

Abstract There's a new process, called "acqui-hiring", that is emerging among the largest technology companies, aiming for innovation and a stronger competitive position. In this process, a start-up is bought not just for its assets or patents, but above all for its human capital. In this way, acqui-hiring is becoming an alternative strategy that aims to recruit not just based on individual talent, but on the synergy of entire teams with proven, successful projects. This paper aims to give an academic contribution to a better comprehension of this strategy's success for organizations, in fostering innovation and consolidating a competitive position. This work presents the theoretical background at the basis of the adoption of the acqui-hiring strategy, which includes studies on organizational learning and the dynamic capabilities. The process of acqui-hiring is also described, focusing primarily on the post-acquisition phase, and on some key points from research being conducted on an Italian firm.

Keywords Acqui-hiring · Innovation · Organizational learning · Knowledge management

1 Introduction

Recently, it has become very common to read about operations of acquisition, made by a leading tech company (think about Google, Facebook, etc.) that buy a small business, typically at the first stage of its life cycle. Moreover, the start-up is often not so profitable, and runs a business that is not directly related to the buyer company's activity. It is clear that the purpose of the operation is not to acquire a project or an asset [11]: thereafter, what do these companies aim to accomplish?

R. Fantasia (✉)
Department of Management, Sapienza University of Rome, Rome, Italy
e-mail: roberta.fantasia@uniroma1.it

© Springer International Publishing Switzerland 2016
F. Ricciardi and A. Harfouche (eds.), *Information and Communication Technologies in Organizations and Society*, Lecture Notes in Information Systems and Organisation 15, DOI 10.1007/978-3-319-28907-6_13

To solve this puzzle, we can refer to a very interesting phenomenon that recently has gained the attention of media and managers: it is called "acqui-hiring" and stands between an acquisition operation and a recruiting process [23].

To explain how an "aqui-hiring" operation works, let's think about some well-known stories, such as the acquisition of the start-up Lala by Apple. In 2009, when we read the news on the major newspapers/magazines on the topic, Lala was one of the most used streaming music tool and let the users play their favourite music directly from the web. After one year from the acquisition, Apple decided to say "so long" to Lala, in order to let the team work on a new project "closer" to Apple itself: iCloud.

Another more recent episode is the acquisition of Loki Studios and other start-ups by Yahoo. They were all start-ups operating in the mobile game market, and even if Yahoo did not buy them for their products and technologies, the company clearly stated in a twitter message, at that time: "We recently added 22 entrepreneurs to our growing mobile team".

These and other examples show us that "acqui-hiring" can be considered as an alternative strategy of recruiting talents, engineers, programmers, the best and brightest minds, typically in the ICT environment. All the major operations of start-up acquisition made in 2014, indeed, concerned firms operating in the high tech market: Facebook acquires WhatsApp, the famous mobile messaging app; Google buys Nest Labs, which applies the concept of the internet of things producing software and hardware for home automation; Disney buys Maker Studios, producers of YouTube channels' video. These cases suggest that the phenomenon of acqui-hiring could be considered customary for ICT firms. The fact that in some cases the original project of the startup is discarded, in order to employ the acqui-hired team in a new project, is a clear sign that a company acqui-hires a start-up aiming to the quality of the team of people, beyond the profitability of their actual project.

At this point, we could question: why does a company not hire the single talents, in a more traditional (and less expensive) way? Wouldn't the hiring process be easier without buying the assets of a whole enterprise? To date, the principal sources of information on this topic are blogs, forums, and management magazines specializing in technology and innovation; still, these sources focus on the contractual and financial aspects of acquisitions. Academic contributions are very few and only recently the attention has been driven towards the "acqui-hiring" phenomenon. The principal academic study on the topic has been conducted by Coyle and Polsky [6], two professors working at North Carolina University, who investigated this new process from a legal point of view.

They studied the reasons behind acqui-hiring, and considered a series of criteria (such as reputation, self-image, etc....) as a potential explanation for why young talent prefers being acquired over being hired more conventionally.

A very recent contribution on the topic is from Chatterji and Patro [3] from Duke University. They describe the acqui-hiring operation as an asset orchestration tool, a specific dynamic capability possessed by the acquirer firm aiming for renewing and transforming its human capital. Their work presents some descriptive statistics on this phenomenon, with increasing trends from 2009.

In academic literature concerning dynamic capabilities, the acquisition of a firm is often considered as one of the principal alternatives to acquiring new resources. In these studies, it is not excluded that human capital could be one of the assets sought after. This way, even if it's not defined as "acqui-hiring", this phenomenon could be included among the group of alternative strategies used for acquiring external resources (e.g. alliances, joint ventures, etc.). An example of recent contributions on the topic is presented by Di Stefano et al. [12], which studied Cisco System's strategy of acquisition with an "organizational drivetrain" metaphor. The human resources configuration makes an organization benefit from knowledge flows across and within its boundaries. Ranf and Lord [32] studied acquisitions in high-technology industries and explained that knowledge transfer is more effective for an acquirer company if it is able to retain the key employees from the acquired firm.

With this research in progress we aim to explain the success of acqui-hiring in order to give a contribution to the studies of the phenomenon from an organizational point of view. In particular, this paper describes the acqui-hiring process, offering some conceptual discussion points about its peculiar phases.

The theoretical framework related to acqui-hiring is outlined in this next section, along with a description of the acqui-hiring process and some key points derived from informal discussions with managers working in an Italian firm, experts in innovation and HR management.

2 The Theoretical Background

There are many streams in Firm theory that link the acqui-hiring process to academic organizational literature.

One of the key points within strategic studies is the sustainability of the competitive advantage of a firm, which derives from the ability to put in place a strategy that is not implemented by its competitors and whose benefits are not easily duplicable by others [2]. This does not mean that a competitive advantage is unlimited in time, but it is interesting to observe how in Barney's definition the attention is driven also towards the potential duplicability of a strategy's benefits.

The Resource Based View paradigm is the first to confirm the central importance of resources for a firm, and in particular concerning knowledge [1, 2, 28, 29, 33, 43]. At the roots of this theory there are two key points: the sustainability of the competitive advantage, as defined before, and the heterogeneity of resources [20].

With the development of the Knowledge Theory, however, knowledge has become the critical resource for every organization. Following this view, a company is a cognitive system who generates, elaborates and spreads knowledge and competences with continuing learning processes [4, 15, 17, 19, 25, 31, 37, 38–42]. Knowledge and competences let the firm produce a high value output, thanks to the conversion and the combination of the initial mix of resources. This, however, requires [14]: the implementation of a strategy that benefits from all the key organizational resources and competences; a smart resources consumption and the development of the critical resources within the society. Besides the exploitation of resources, it is important to take into consideration how to manage the existing skill/resource gaps and create the basis for future resources, which will then be the source and the strength of competitive advantage.

Considering what could be the trigger of an acqui-hiring strategy, the management, on the one hand, should be able to understand what resources and skills are necessary for implementing its strategy, which skills and competences the firm needs to internalize or have under its control; on the other hand, the management has to find how to use and capitalize the same resources, with respect to the context in which they were created, processed and metabolized. In other words, the problem is how to turn them into core competencies [34] or strategic capabilities [18] for the organization as a whole. The core competences of a firm derives from tacit knowledge, or skills/resources that a company builds and capitalizes over time [5, 21]. The approach used is thus process-oriented, rather than content-oriented: the imperfect mobility, the inimitability and the non-replaceable qualities of resources which become "core" for the enterprise must be read as the result of the dynamic properties of the systems of knowledge (or resources in general) accumulation [5].

At this point, knowledge and competences belong to the firm as a whole and are part of the so called "background knowledge" of the organizational system [36]; in other words, they become independent from the single people thanks to different processes of communication and social learning [9] that take place throughout what we can define as a learning organization [35]. One of the most famous way to analyze the actual mix of competences in a firm is the chain value, presented by Porter, but also by McKinsey; they both lead to a classification on the basis of the activities of the organization.

Another important contribution is, in evolutionary theories of organization, the study about practices and routines [24], at an explicit and codified level of knowledge, but also at the level of tacit knowledge, although this is unlikely to be formalized in a systematic way. Then there are several interesting considerations on the dynamics of the same resources, not just depending on the variable "time" (dynamic coherence of resources, as defined by [16]). The dynamic capabilities framework, thus, makes the assumption that core competences should be used to improve the short term position of the organization, which is at the roots of the concept of the sustainability of the competitive advantage in the long run.

Also, human management literature is useful for this research, concerning the importance of establishing a human resources program, in order to translate the objectives in a portfolio of strategic skills with well-defined qualitative and quantitative characteristics, and to identify policies to manage and develop these skills [7].

On the basis of the theoretical concepts that have been discussed in this section, in the next paragraph are described some key points, from the study of an Italian firm, operating in the publishing sector, which has adopted the acqui-hiring strategy to foster innovation.

3 The "Acqui-Hiring" Process: Discussion Points

As said before, "acqui-hiring" refers to an operation where a company acquires a small firm, aiming at the quality of its people and how the team members interact with each other as a cohesive group, who has proven cultural fit as well as technical prowess [22].

In this section, a conceptual analysis is presented with some discussion points about the acqui-hiring process. This preliminary consideration emerges from the analysis of field notes and informal discussions with managers working for one of the major Italian multimedia publishing companies, considered experts of innovation and HR management.

Below is a scheme of an acqui-hiring process, following the point of view of the larger company that decides to acqui-hire a smaller firm, with the evidence of three main steps: scouting and targeting, acquisition and integration process (Fig. 1).

In the first stage, the key points for scouting and targeting the start-up to acqui-hire are:

- What skills/competences are effective to the mission of the company? Which is the organizational skills-gap to fill to improve the competitive advantage of the firm?
- How and where can a company find the start-up with the needed competence to acqui-hire?

Concerning the first point, we know that even in a modern society it is not so easy to identify the core competences (as defined in the second paragraph) that are needed by the organization. Keeping the same job descriptions could lead an organization to discover its needs in competences and skills only when they're already facing a difficult/critical situation. This way, an analysis of the organizational skill-gap will help to overcome this risk.

Concerning the second point, it is possible for the company to activate a double channel of scouting: it can contact the start-up directly, perhaps creating a unit/a

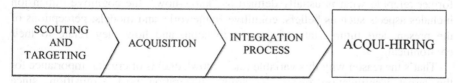

Fig. 1 The acqui-hiring process

professional ad hoc for this task, not necessarily in the human resources area (even if—obviously—strictly related); the same company can also be part of a network involving start-ups, business incubators/accelerators, business angels, universities and all the actors that help the best start-ups to growth and strengthen their position.

Another interesting point is related to the company's dimensions. In fact, even if at the early stage of its lifecycle, a start-up can reach a dimension that makes itself too expensive to acquire; in these cases, there are lots of alternative forms of collaboration and partnership that could be used.

From the news about this kind of operations, enterprises often working in the ICT environment are involved for both the acqui-hirer and the acqui-hired. It is not uncommon for the transfer of high tech knowledge-based resources and soft skills is one of the major issues related to this type of acquisitions. Recent studies [32] confirm that obtaining critical knowledge-based technologies and capabilities from the acquired firms is one of the most critical drivers in choosing a company to acquire.

In the phase of transition (acquisition), the process is very similar to a "traditional" acquisition of a firm. As proved within the project management studies, this kinds of projects are structured as follows: target definition and planning, project execution, monitoring and control of results [9].

The third and last step of the process is probably the most significant for the success of the whole operation. The main points emerged from our interviews are:

- How much autonomy does one grant to an aqui-hired team?
- How does this team interact with the rest of the pre-existent organization?
- What happens to the start-up's products and projects?
- How does the culture of the new team combine with that of the bigger organization?

As said before, the integration post acquisition of an acqui-hiring operation is particularly interesting for the tacit dimension of knowledge; this is because, unlike a traditional policy of recruiting, acqui-hiring has not the aim to hire the individual, but a whole team of people, already established and operating, with its practices, its values and, more generally, its own culture. This aspect, as already explained, is relevant to both identify the start-up to acqui-hire and for sharing/integration of knowledge (that is not codified and standardized) after the operation.

As defined by Polanyi [30], tacit knowledge is the set of rules that an individual considers most correct and therefore enacts when looking for a solution to a problem in a given context. Nonaka and Takeuchi [27], from these concepts, define the two dimensions of tacit knowledge as "technical" and "cognitive". While the former refers to what is usually defined as "know-how", the cognitive dimension includes aspects such as beliefs, cognitive frameworks and models, perceptions of the present and future state of the organization, and how they relate to their environment.

That's the reason why this variable (tacit knowledge) is of crucial importance for the target identification phase. Regarding integration post acquisition, since knowledge is created by individuals, the organization must support creativity and foster an environment that works as a facilitator of the creation and sharing of tacit knowledge, which is the basis of the cultural heritage of the whole organization [26].

The success of an acqui-hiring operation, thereafter, depends on how well the organization is able to define and promote a virtuous cycle of knowledge sharing and creation. The social and organizational context, in fact, should move along three directions [9]: (1) create the right context to promote and facilitate new knowledge; (2) promote conditions and roles to spread implicit knowledge; (3) stimulate debate and openness to new knowledge.

In another study, [13], in order to understand whether the knowledge sharing is dependent from certain events or is endogenous to the same organizational context, consider the connection between sharing context and the role of each individual. If they're coherent with each other, the mutual exchange of knowledge is greater, more effective and coordinated, creating a "collective basis of knowledge".

Regarding the context as facilitator of knowledge creation and sharing, we can also refer to Von Krogh's research [42] about the "care" in the process of knowledge creation. He argues, in fact, that to fully understand this process it is necessary to understand how the participants of an organization are related with each other, if there is a more social than individual orientation.

Nonaka and Takeuchi [27] identify some necessary conditions that make an organizational context able to establish and consolidate dynamically over time the process that they themselves define as "spiral of knowledge". These conditions are: intentionality, autonomy, fluctuation, redundancy and, finally, a minimum required variety. Following what has been said before, the success of an acqui-hiring operation also depends on which among these conditions are respected and why.

4 Conclusions and Next Steps

This paper studies a new strategy that companies, especially in recent times, have used in pursuit of their innovation policies. The acqui-hiring process, halfway between the acquisition of enterprise and hiring human resources [8], has become one of the most used tools by companies that want to innovate and incorporate in their knowledge capital new skills and competences [10], and consolidate their position as market leaders. However, is it a more effective strategy than traditional recruiting policies? Within academic literature, the acquisition of a firm as a strategic operation to acquire new resources is not a new concept; but there seems to be a lack of studies about this specific phenomenon, where the human capital becomes a primary target. Some major scientific contributions are offered by two law professors Coyle and Polsky [6], that study the cultural characteristics and the system of funding start-ups in the Silicon Valley area, California.

To fill the gap in the academic and organizational literature, this article presents some discussion points concerning the acqui-hiring process, derived from research in progress conducted with one of the leading multimedia Italian firm. This article first presented a theoretical framework to explain the phenomenon from an academic point of view. Then the acqui-hiring process was analyzed and dissected into its primary actionable steps, with emphasis on the individual sections that most succinctly characterize the entire operation including the scouting phase, where companies identify a target for acquisition, and the integration phase post-acquisition. While in the first phase, the main problem is to find the right channels to acqui-hire the missing skills for the organization, within the integration phase the creation of a social and organizational context that can facilitate creativity and confidence between individuals is of crucial importance, and that is also characterized by the conditions that in the literature of knowledge management are considered as necessary to trigger a virtuous cycle of creation, sharing and capitalization of organizational knowledge. At a strategic level this strongly influences the skills and the core competencies as the basis of the competitive advantage of the company in the long run.

This paper, as said before, illustrates the first conceptual considerations of a research in progress on the topic. The next step of the research is to go deeper in the study of the key points here presented, in order to verify that an acqui-hiring process is a better alternative to the traditional recruiting policies among the ICT environment. Another interesting point that will be investigated concerns the link between the artifact produced by the acqui-hired start-up and the choice of a target made by the acqui-hirer: could the fact that it is digital, for example, make the start-up a more desirable target for an acqui-hiring operation? Further research will be also directed to the study of organizations as platforms, above all if digital (taking into consideration the fact that acqui-hiring has been implementing primarily by the big tech companies). The feature of modularity that is typical of a platform-based system, indeed, could make an acqui-hiring operation more suitable for a company that is structured with a nucleus of core components on the one hand, and a set of more variable and peripheral components on the other hand. With an acqui-hiring strategy, in fact, a firm modifies, in a dynamic perspective, both its organizational structure and processes, influencing the presence and effectiveness of the characteristics of the social and organizational context, in order to facilitate and promote a virtuous cycle of knowledge sharing and creation.

References

1. Amit, R., Schoemaker, P.: Strategic assets and organizational rent. Strateg. Manag. J. **14**, 33–46 (1993)
2. Barney, J.B.: Firm resources and sustained competitive advantage. J. Manag. **17**, 99–120 (1991)
3. Chatterji, A., Patro, A.: Dynamic capabilities and managing human capital. Acad. Manag. Perspect. **28**(4), 395–408 (2014)
4. Cohen, M.D., Sproull, L.S.: Organizational Learning. Sage Publications, Thousand Oaks (1996)
5. Cohen, W.M., Levinthal, D.A.: Absorptive capacity: a new perspective on learning and innovation. Adm. Sci. Q. **35**, 128–152 (1990)

6. Coyle, J., Polsky, G.: Acqui-hiring. Duke Law J. **63**(2), 281–346 (2012)
7. Costa, G.: Economia e Direzione delle Risorse Umane, Utet Libreria (1997)
8. Costa, G., Gianecchini, M.: Risorse Umane. Persone, Relazioni e Valore. McGraw-Hill, New York (2009)
9. Decastri, M., Paparelli, A.: Organizzare L'innovazione. Guida Alla Gestione Dei Processi Innovativi Aziendali, Editore Ulrico Hoepli (2008)
10. Dewhurst, M., Hancock, B., Ellsworth, D.: Redesigning knowledge work. Harvard Bus. Rev. 58–64 (2013)
11. Dierickx, I., Cool, K.: Asset stock accumulation and sustainability of competitive advantage. Manage. Sci. **35**(12), 1505–1511 (1989)
12. Di Stefano, G., Peteraf, M., Verona, G.: The organizational drivetrain: a road to integration of dynamic capabilities research. Acad. Manag. Perspect. **28**(4), 307–327 (2014)
13. Doz, Y., Santos, J., Williamson, P.: Da Globale a Metanazionale, Il Mulino (2004)
14. Grant, R.M.: L'analisi Strategica nella Gestione Aziendale, Il Mulino (1994)
15. Grant, R.M., Spender, J.C.: Knowledge and the firm. Strateg. Manag. J. **17**, 5–9 (1996). (Special Issue)
16. Itami, H., Roehl, T.W.: Mobilizing Invisible Assets. Harvard University Press, Massachusetts (1987)
17. Kogut, B., Zander, U.: Knowledge of the firm, combinative capabilities, and the replication of technology. Organ. Sci. **3**, 383–397 (1992)
18. Lenz, R.T.: Strategic capability: a concept and framework for analysis. Acad. Manag. Rev. **5**, 225–234 (1980)
19. Levitt, B., March, J.G.: Organizational learning. Ann. Rev. Sociol. **14**, 319–340 (1988)
20. Lipparini, A.: Le Competenze Organizzative, Carocci (1998)
21. Mahoney, J.T.: The management of resources and the resources of management. J. Bus. Res. **33**(2), 91–101 (1995)
22. Makinen, M., Haber, D., Raymundo, A.: Acqui-hires for growth: planning for success. Venture Capital Rev. 31–42 (2012)
23. Nargi, M.: Acqui hire, ovvero la tua idea non mi interessa ma il tuo talent sì. INNOV'AZIONE **19**, 4–5 (2012)
24. Nelson, R., Winter, S.: An Evolutionary Theory of Economic Change. Harvard University Press, Massachusetts (1982)
25. Nickerson, J.A., Zenger, T.R.: A knowledge-based theory of the firm. The problem solving perspective. Organ. Sci. **15**(6), 617–632 (2004)
26. Nonaka, I.: A dynamic theory of organizational knowledge creation. Organ. Sci. **5**(1), 14–37 (1994)
27. Nonaka, I., Takeuchi, H.: The Knowledge Creating Company. Oxford University Press, Oxford (1995)
28. Penrose, E.T.: The Theory of the Growth of the Firm. Wiley, New York (1959)
29. Peteraf, M.A.: The cornerstones of competitive advantage: a resource-based view. Strateg. Manag. J. **14**, 179–191 (1993)
30. Polany, M.: The Tacit Dimension. Anchor Books, New York (1967)
31. Prahalad, C.K., Hamel, G.: The core competences of the corporation. Harvard Bus. Rev. **68**, 79–91 (1990)
32. Ranf, A.L., Lord, M.D.: Acquiring new knowledge: the role of retaining human capital in acquisitions of high-tech firms. J. High Technol. Manag. Res. **11**(2), 295–319 (2000)
33. Rumelt, R.P.: Theory, strategy and entrepreneurship. In: Teece, D. (ed.) The Competitive Challenge, Ballinger, pp. 137–158 (1987)
34. Selznick, P.: Leadership in Administration: A Sociological Interpretation. Harper & Row, New York (1957)
35. Senge, P.M.: The Fifth Discipline: The Art and Practice of the Learning Organization. Doubleday Currency, New York (1992)
36. Spender, J.C.: Making knowledge the basis of a dynamic theory of the firm. Strateg. Manag. J. **17**, 45–62 (1996)

37. Stalk, G., Evans, P., Shulman, L.E.: Competing on capabilities: the new rules of corporate strategy. Harvard Bus. Rev. **70**, 57–69 (1992)
38. Teece, D.J., Pisano, G.: The dynamic capabilities of the firm: an introduction. Ind. Corp. Change **3**, 537–556 (1994)
39. Teece, D.J., Pisano, G., Shuen, A.: Dynamic capabilities and strategic management. Strateg. Manag. J. **18**(7), 509–533 (1997)
40. Ulrich, D., Lake, D.: Organizational Capability. Wiley, New York (1990)
41. Vicari, S.: Conoscenza e impresa. Sinergie **76**, 43–66 (2008)
42. Von Krogh, G.: Care in knowledge creation. Calif. Manag. Rev. **40**(3), 133–153 (1998)
43. Wernerfelt, B.: A resource-based view of the firm. Strateg. Manag. J. **5**, 171–180 (1984)

The Optimization of the HRM at the "LSCA" in an Economy with Delay in Modernization of Systems

Claude Chammaa

Abstract This research aims to shed light on a subject with lack of research in a society that seems modern and open to the world, but simultaneously suffers from perpetual political conflict making any form of modernization impossible. The research uses Lebanon as a context; despite a very difficult economic environment and limited financial flexibility, Lebanese companies are realizing the need to develop their distinctive capabilities Hoftsede (Cultural Tools, Comparison coutr in, [14]) by developing their information resources. Our research focuses on LSCA, an insurance company leader in the Lebanese market. This paper encompasses literature review of development and adaptation of information technology to human resource department. Furthermore, it shows contributions that may result from implementing a new HRIS (Human Resource Information System) in a Lebanese company issues supporting its acquirement despite the costs related, the magnitude of change, the use of its features, and most of all its primary role of decision-making. Finally, it concludes that local communities modernization may be a key factor of the implementation and development of the HRIS in companies, especially the LSCA.

Keywords Human resource management · HRIS · Optimization · ICT · Decision-making · Implementation

1 Introduction

The Lebanese economy has been unstable during the period of internal and external conflicts (1975–1992). Exchanges with the outside were inexistent. Later on, with the advent of peace, promises were launched regarding the efforts of the Lebanese state to restructure the private sector and contribute to its development. Among

C. Chammaa (✉)
Université St. Joseph, Beirut, Lebanon
e-mail: claude.chammaa@hotmail.com

© Springer International Publishing Switzerland 2016   215
F. Ricciardi and A. Harfouche (eds.), *Information and Communication
Technologies in Organizations and Society*, Lecture Notes in Information
Systems and Organisation 15, DOI 10.1007/978-3-319-28907-6_14

these efforts, reforms were made in the telecommunication sector. Unfortunately, these measures have only been in effect in the past three years, which largely affected the private sector and contributed to a decrease of foreign investment in Lebanon.

In a world where people live in perpetual change, fundamental challenges are extant in the traditional techniques adopted by the state. The processes did not evolve with the increased technological development in the world. The "status quo" adopted by the state due to the country's economic instability hardly encourages private businesses to adopt new technologies in order to facilitate common transactions. However, this did not prevent some companies and organizations to modernize their processes in order to communicate with the outside, especially those that are already international firms (LSCA). This study aims to present the role of ICT (Information and Communication Technologies) in the transformation of the human resources department at the LSCA and understanding challenges, and the issues of integrating an HRSI in a firm while it does not constitute a priority in its strategy.

Several questions regarding this issue occurs:

- What major changes and benefits HRIS would bring in formalizing and standardizing activities in LSCA?
- Did the implementation of HRIS meet expectations and HRM (Human Resource Management) goal?
- How can HRIS be a system for decision-making support for managers within the LSCA?
- What are the purposes that would encourage HRM to acquire an HRIS in a country where all procedures are still obsolete?

To provide answers to these questions, we intend initially to recall the main theoretical frameworks of ICT through a literature review. We develop in a second step the methodological approach. Then, we propose to identify the elements that constitute the HRIS and their application in the LSCA, present the contributions of HRIS in terms of measuring capacity, process, and procedural changes, and discuss the results of the study based on the extent of induced change. Finally, we present the findings and conclusion.

2 Towards a Vision of ICTs: Evolution and Role

2.1 ICTs and Their Evolution: A Literature Review

Formerly, the work was done manually and verbal or written communication was subject to protocols and time-consuming procedures. Globalization, with the opening of markets, required the use of communication and information tools that have become inevitable due to their impact on the dynamics of organizations.

Table 1 Evolution of the link between IT and organization

Criteria	1970s	1980s	1990s	2000+
Dominance	IT production "Mainframe"	Personal computing "My computer"	Computer network "Communication"	Computer integrated "Banalization"
Type of organization	Linear	Decentralized	Matrix	Virtual
Management	Hierarchical	Delegation	Local and functional	By project
IT image	Productivity	Cost centers	Strategic	Innovation
Goals	Automate	Reduce costs	Linking SIC processes	Take the "leadership" through SIC
Keywords	Enthusiasm ignorance	Necessary, expensive, heavy	End user, service centre, usability	Competitive advantage: differentiation and globalization
Great ideas for management	Increase productivity	Improve reactivity	Increase competitiveness	Winning the "leadership"
Great ideas for IT	Automate tasks with low added value	Downsizing externalization	Integrated software redesign process	"Daily strategic computing"
Computer scientist	Who knows	Whoever costs the organization	That can establish link organization-SIC	One that can help to generate a competitive advantage

ICT is the result of the combination of IT (Information Technology), technology, Internet, and telecommunications. Karsenti and Lorentz [18] detail the evolution of the link between IT and organization (Table 1).

2.2 The IS: ICT Derivative

According to Reix [22], an information system is a set of elements put together to meet a certain purpose: it is a set of resources (hardware, software, data, procedures ...) to acquire, treat, store, transmit information within and between organizations. Later, Reix et al. [23] defined the information system on several levels: individual, group, organizational and inter-organizational. To be effective, information systems must be used optimally by the stakeholders of the company in order to extract maximum performance. As part of our study, we will try to explore one part of IT and its impact on the management of human resources in particular: HRIS.

2.3 HRIS "LINK" Between HRM and ICT

Nowadays, organizational success depends mostly on the performance of HRM [19–32]. This performance is the result of the adopted work procedures, mainly HRIS. Interpretations of information systems are so varied that we retain those that describes the purpose of our work. This purpose is to better understand the constituent dimensions of an HRIS. Regarding the operational dimension, Tannenbaum [29] defines HRIS as: "a system to acquire, store, manipulate, analyze, retrieve and distribute relevant information regarding human resources of an organization". In this same perspective, it should complete the technical dimension presented by Silva [27]: "The HRIS is a computerized software package that, on one hand, a number of tasks of the different missions of the HR function and, furthermore, their information system". On the other hand, Tixier [31] highlights the identification of the function of the HRIS that is "to help the HRM to identify sites of action, assess the relevance of certain decisions, and anticipate organizational change".

2.3.1 History and Evolving Vision of the HRIS

According to Just [17], the story of HRIS can be followed through two evolutions: The Evolution of Human Resource Management (HRM), and the computerization of the Human Resources (HR) function. We will focus on the evolution of human resources management and information systems adapted by Bencheman and Galindo [6] (Fig. 1).

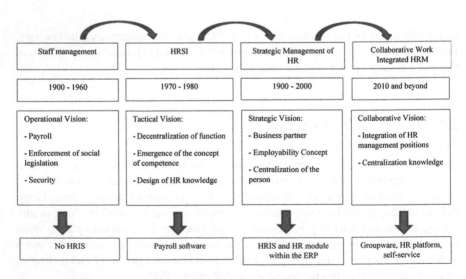

Fig. 1 Evolution of human resource management and information systems

2.3.2 HRIS and Involving Actors

By enabling better access to parameters, HRIS can improve administrative efficiency through faster data processing, improved employee communications, greater
accuracy of information, lower costs and overall improvement of the human
resources productivity [5, 9, 33]. In summary, HRIS is no longer in the heart of the
HRM, but in the heart of the business because it affects and involves all actors of
society [28].

2.3.3 ... A Tool at the Service of the Employees

The implementation of HRIS in HR departments has become a necessity (since the
90s). This automatically generates cost reduction of payroll [12], decreases the risk
of error, standardization of processes and tools, and increases productivity [21].
This information system allows to decentralize the HR function with features of
standardized use, easily manipulated by HR employees.

3 Methodological Approach

Our research is built on a qualitative study in the configuration of a case study [34]
considered a "privileged access to the real strategy" [24]. Different sources were
used to collect information:

- The website of the insurance company,
- External publications,
- Some other website's publications comparing Lebanese insurance companies,
- Two interviews with the HRM,
- Three interviews with employees of the Human Resource Department.

The collection of information was done on the basis of individual interviews and
documentation over a two month period (October–December 2014). An interview
guide with the main themes was developed for this purpose. Each interview was
approximately one hour to one hour and a half and was conducted by the author.
The number of interviews was limited. However, the research objective was based
on an in-depth description of the case. Three interview guides were built (as syn-
thesized in Table 2).

Our major goal was to analyze the reasons that encourage the HRM to make such
an investment. The first interview grid (that was completely exploratory) was carried
out with HRM and two of the employees in the human resources department.

The idea was to understand the organization of the human resources department
and the different steps of implementation. The main subject was expressed without
questions, which allowed us to locate the study and prepare the interviews that
follow.

Table 2 Summary of interview grids

	Interview type	Theme	Questions
Grid 1	Semi-structured	Description, history, and organizational context of the LSCA	Open-ended and close-ended
Grid 2	Semi-structured	Extent of change	Open-ended and close-ended
Grid 3	Structured	Features and advantages of HRIS	Close-ended

A second and a third grid were prepared based on first interviews. At this stage, interviews were administered to the HRM to enrich and complete understanding of the data.

A more detailed quantitative study will be conducted with employees of the LSCA after final adoption of the system in order to determine the impact on the procedures and methods of work, productivity and motivation of the personnel. Our study goes beyond the implementation of HRIS, its functionality and its impact on human resources management in general. It concerns not only the components already mentioned but also their application in a new context and environment: the LSCA insurance company.

4 Implementation of HRIS in the LSCA

4.1 The LSCA, a Pioneer in Insurance Services in Lebanon

Founded in 1959, LSCA has gradually established itself in six countries with over 30 branches. It is part of Delta Near East Holding, pioneers in insurance services in Lebanon, the Middle East, and the Gulf region [13]. The services offered involve individuals and companies with a wide range of products covering all types of insurance. In December 2014, the number of employees in LSCA is esteemed at more than 250 people, which clearly reveals the future plan of an SME (Small and Medium-sized Enterprises) wishing to internationalize.

«The aim of LSCA to expand overseas was born of a desire to cover surfaces that can meet the group size of LSCA».

The GM of LSCA.

4.2 Factors Facilitating the Implementation of HRIS

«Well, it was time to change … not easy to manage 250 employees … Manual methods were becoming too complicated …»

The Director of the HR department

«The main factor is the simplification of work processes and JIT (Just In Time) required by obtaining the ISO 9001 certification in November 2014. The necessity for the establishment of a quality system required the computerization process and management...»

An employee in the human resources department

The major need was to implement a payroll and time management system. Later, other options were integrated constituting the current HRIS (succession, planning, etc.). The implementation of the system meant rethinking processes to optimize and adapt them to new situations.

The HRIS became functional recently, in 2015. A transition period is planned using both systems (manual and HRIS) simultaneously in order to identify differences and flaws. This system will be installed and tested at the headquarters first time for possible future implementation in the branches and overseas.

4.3   Feature Analysis

Several maps of HR processes have been proposed by various researchers. In order to know the structural elements of HRIS in the LSCA, a summary made by Exbrayat et al. [10] was chosen. Based on the survey conducted by "Business and Careers" in 2006 with 69 publishers HR solutions, they were retained in the analysis features of HRIS, cutting into seven thematic HR (recruitment, training, skills and knowledge, time and activities, total compensation, payroll and balanced scorecard) in addition to the administrative management. This map was given to the Director of Human Resources Department of LSCA who selected the exploited features (selected in gray). The eight themes were grouped under two headings: functions related to the administration and payroll, and those related to career management (Table 3).

4.3.1   Decomposing Used Features

The design of functions such as planning, recruitment, selection, evaluation and performance management, reward management, development, health and safety, and labor-management relations [8] is supposed to provide the HRM better opportunity to influence strategic decisions to improve organizational performance [7, 26]. Concerning LSCA, the results of the above table show that the optimal use of HRIS is vested mostly in payroll, total compensation and balanced scorecard (tasks related to administration and payroll) (Table 4).

Table 3 HR themes

Functions related to the administration and payroll	
Payroll	
Countries covered (minimum Lebanon)	Multi-company management
Legal assistance (online or telephone)	Update and automatic update, free legal and contractual developments
Balanced scorecard	
Analysis of payroll	Simulation of the evolution of the wage by incorporating demographic mass
Statistical analysis of social indicators (absenteeism, dismissal, resignation)	Statistical analysis of time and activity
Statistical analysis of training actions	Statistical analysis of recruitment
Administration tool online opinion surveys	
Administrative management	
Managing employee records	Installation of self-service solutions
Annual declarations	Monitoring of medical visits
Managing time and activities	
Clocking	Entering declarative time online
Decentralized management (including validation managers) leave and absences	Time management
Managing modulation of working time	Semi-automatic planning of working times and activities
Interim Management	
Global compensation	
Decentralized management of variable pay	Decentralized management of individual raises
Benefits in kind management	Benefits management
Management profit sharing and participation	Management individualized assessment
Career management-related function	
Recruitment	
AutoPlay papers CV	Application form
Auto entry application forms	Syntax analysis of electronic CV
Behavioral assessment tests	Business assessment tests
Management scoring	Matching management
Candidate relationship management (automated responses, online calendar…)	Bonuses management
Management of internal mobility	Management of the "on boarding"
Management of trainees	Interim Management
Training	
Management of the training plans	Management of tax return
Management of the "individual right to training"	Management of professionalization interviews
Catalog management training	Online management of trainee's enrollment
Online training platform	Courses design tool
Tool design and administration of tests	

(continued)

Table 3 (continued)

Skills and knowledge	
Managing individual interviews	Management of self-assessments
360 feedback management	Behavioral assessment tests
Business assessment test	Management of succession plans
Managing a referential of skills and knowledge	Mapping of knowledge and skills
Syntax analysis of knowledge	Skills and knowledge directory (Who's Who)

Table 4 HRIS utilization rate

General features	% Utilization
Payroll and administration	
Payroll	100
Total compensation	83
Balanced scorecard	85
Administrative management	50
Career management	
Time management	42.5
Recruitment	50
Skills and knowledge	40
Training	11

As emphasized Reix [22], "The observation of an organization shows that its operation is based on making various decisions in both their level (operational or strategic) and frequency (repetitive or exceptional)." In LSCA, missing software features make it less reliable as an effective decision-making tool (candidate selection, compliance with values of group culture, e-HR, training needs according to the indicators, etc.) as "... the provisioning of data as part of an IS ... allows to define uniform criteria for making different processes: recruitment, training, skills management and trades, mobility and career management ..." [2].

4.4 Conversion Phase: Major Impediment

Data conversion was seen by employees of HRM as a major impediment. Therefore, it was necessary to reorganize all data in order to be compatible with the system. Data processing activities were performed in Excel. This software provided digital calculation functions, graphing and data analysis, but its scope was limited. Work on Excel did not guarantee the accuracy, reliability and efficiency of data.

The challenge remained to convert and monitor data by ensuring reliability before final registration in the HRIS.

4.5 The HRIS in the Heart of the LSCA: Impacts and Effects

The implementation of the system will have no adverse effect on employee job situation (hiring or firing), especially those working in the human resources department, but will allow them to devote more time to analysis and that developing their skills by making them more "experts" the social issues [30]. Indeed, as emphasized Allen and Morton [1]: "The success of technology projects depends on Human Resources that should allow for a flexible policy:

- Participating employee in the change processes to integrate information technology;
- Maintaining, if possible collaborators in their jobs so they can easily experiment new ways of working" (Fig. 2).

As shown in the diagram above, the main objective for the acquisition of an HRIS is the need to improve procedures. Once installed, the tool will help to manage all HR processes within the LSCA. This topic will be developed in the next section.

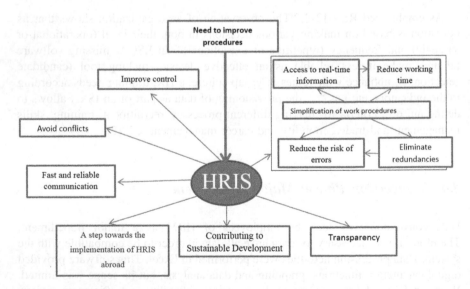

Fig. 2 Mapping HRIS

5 HRIS: Strengths, Challenges and Perspectives

5.1 A Technology to Manage Internal Flows

> ... Four sessions of three hours were enough to convince us to implement a new HRIS. Despite the high cost of its acquisition, developers and consultants have not had many difficulties to convince us of the usefulness of such an operating system ... We had a lot of propositions, much cheaper, but none met our expectations ...

The Director of the HR department

- Formalizing procedures: The change initiated by the introduction of a computer system would make managers less reluctant as they are forced to comply. Thus, managers would be less autonomous since the work would become more formal.
- Reducing working time: All staff requests (certificates, leave, absence, delay, etc.) are subject to a long work routine. The reduction of working time through HRIS would make managers more available. If administrative requests stay without reply, they would be automatically sent to a superior after 48 h. This automated process is expected to significantly reduce conflicts since all applications do not depend on one particular person but on a whole team.
- Transparency and information flow: The majority of the staff will be able to access information each according to his position. However, as mentioned by Imbert [16]: "HR and HRIS should while widely disseminating information, maintain control data and control their privacy." As for payroll, only the CEO (Chief Executive Officer) and CFO (Chief Financial Officer) have access to all information concerning salaries and remuneration of the Board, while the HRM have only access to salaries information of managers (Fig. 3).
- Contribution to Sustainable Development: The operational system would allow LSCA to develop an internal ecology (A new conception of public interest in Lebanon) by reducing paperwork to gain in productivity and provide an environment free of complications. Specifically, all reports would be easily duplicated which would represent a protection against losses and material destruction.
- Control: The HRIS is expected to help promote consistency between the traditional control methods and IT tools by strengthening every step of use. The system would be instrumental in identifying "who does what" and developing balanced scorecards for managers to review.
- Reduced risk of conflict: by the evidence that could be brought forth with each HRIS application on change scheduled shift or work. The slightest delay in response to a notification of an employee would give rise to an escalation to the immediate superior of the department head.

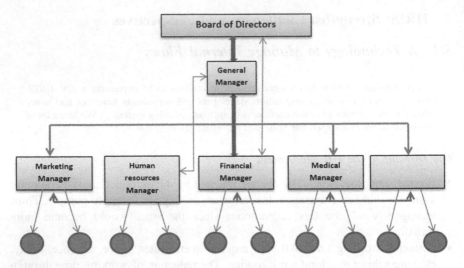

Fig. 3 Circulation of financial information

- Reduced error rates by securing data: The slightest error would be easily
  detectable by the centralization of the main access to interfaces. Access would
  be personal, secure and strictly confidential (e-safe box).

5.2 Towards a Vulnerability of Information Systems

Like any tool, HRIS have limitations. One limitation concerns the flow of information. Over time, they become enormous in terms of data. Another limitation
concerns the overload of features. Ultimately, HRIS would overlook cultural
complexities and psycho social aspects [4] which increases its vulnerability.

6 Nature and Extent of Change

Four employees are mainly affected by the change. However, the 250 employees will
benefit from the functions of system information. Everything that was done manually would be completed in record time by reducing administrative procedures.
(Request and calculations, leave, bonus, transportation, summer schedules, etc.)

With the implementation of HRIS, directors would access all information about
their employees, starting with the morning delays. The software would

automatically calculate the transport allowances at the end of each month and all declarations to the tax service and social security.

6.1   Training

Employees were informed through the intranet (by email). The project plan includes a training by department given the number of people involved. The training is expected to take place in stages and would be provided by the human resources department employees assisted by a delegate of the company in order to add a formal aspect of training and avoid possible non-participation.

6.2   Probable Resistance to Change

The main source of resistance to change lies mainly in changing the system and procedures for the delays and absences. With manual procedures, delays (less than 30 min) were allowed on presentation of proof to the direct supervisor of the person. With the implementation of the new system, any delay would be reported to the corresponding department of employees and the HR department. This situation would bring more rigidity and less flexibility to work schedules.

6.3   Diagnosis and Mapping

Generally, diagnosis and mapping exercises are undertaken in the diagnostic phase of a project to determine the most effective forward action. We chose to conduct it during the transition phase to understand the magnitude of change in LSCA.

To complete the mapping of change, HR manager responded to 16 questions that deal with 16 points changes. Answers to questions are expected to explore changes [3] and rank them according to their importance (1, very important change, 2, moderately significant change and 3, no significant change) (Table 5).

According to the answers received, the conversion rate was calculated by adding the responses that allow to affirm the importance of change. The total is shown in the diagram below (12/16 = 0.75) (Fig. 4).

We clearly discern a high conversion rate that represents a significant change. In such case of major transformation, it is strongly recommended that a change management (communication, training) would be carried through the integration period to moderate resistance as much as possible. This step would begin with an analysis of impacts to build a support plan for change.

Table 5 Mapping changes

Question	Answer	Score
Is the current strategy changed, deleted or replaced?	Replaced	1
Must the corporate culture change significantly?	Yes	1
Will new jobs be created in the company?	Not	3
Does the company introduce new technology?	Yes	1
Will it change the existing process?	Yes	1
Does the hierarchy will sustain changes?	A little	2
Is there going to be creations or deletions process?	Not	3
There will be shifts in the allocation of human and financial resources?	Yes	1
Will employees have to learn new technical skills related to their job?	Yes	1
Will they have to learn new management skills?	Moderately	2
Will employees need to upgrade their computer skills?	Yes	1
Will Employees have to change their behavior?	Yes	1
Must procedures be updated or rewritten?	Yes	1
Will the change affect monitoring tools and performance assessment?	Yes	1
Will it affect methods of communication between employees?	Yes	1
Will it affect operational activity?	Yes	1

Fig. 4 Change rate

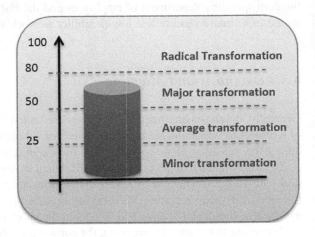

7   Conclusion

Research contribution

Originally, this article targeted the major changes that ICT would bring in formalizing and standardizing activities in LSCA. Our findings confirm the need to acquire such systems in order to ease work and procedures of the HR department. The main contribution of such system implementation would be operational transparency, however, not unique. Feedback from the interviews adds further expected contributions such as reducing the time of operations, costs and contribution to sustainable development.

Consequently, we can conclude that investment in HRIS would help improve the effectiveness of simple procedures within HRM practices by formalizing them to meeting the expectations of the Director of Human Resources. However, despite some studies claiming that "... over-exploitation of the international HR function would be unproductive" [4], it remains important that integrating HRIS "Today" at LSCA may induce concerns on major missing features that could have an impact on the modernization of procedures and general management.

This situation leads us to conclude such impacts on business responsiveness as well as its primary role of decision support features that are primary to the future of the business, improving productivity and employee motivation. The delay in the modernization of systems can lead to a shift on the optimal use of information systems among other decision support tools. This can indirectly affect the decisions of the HR by choosing optimization HRIS that integrates advanced features for managing new recruits (website, intranet, online selection criteria) career (skills that can develop human capital by attending training), talent (recruitment, training, career mobility), objectives, changes in payroll and predictive analysis. Indeed, as stated Hussain et al. [15], HRIS have different impacts on human resources in organizations. In addition to their role as facilitators, they hold a contributing role in the strategic decision-making in companies. Furthermore, the establishment of a historical database would be essential to effective career management, as it becomes a reference for statistical analytics that could influence managerial decisions. (Mobility, career, competency profiling, etc.)

Research limitation
One of the major limitations is the "timing" of the study. It would have been more interesting to revisit this study after effective and widespread use of HRIS in order to identify strengths and weaknesses of the system. Another limitation concerns the narrow number of Lebanese companies implementing an HRIS. Further, it may be interesting to make a comparison between 4 and 5 different systems in order to provide use model HRIS adapted to the country's culture. Another limitation concerns the number of people interviewed

Research extension
After a decade of intensive deployment of IT applications, the complications in the integration of these tools are still numerous today: 30 % of IT projects fail to achieve [20], 66 % exceeded the initial budget, are late or do not implement the features planned in the early stages [11]. The lack of control of outcomes as well as insufficient ownership of the ambition of the project by its actors induce semi-failures that ultimately represent not only a cost but also generate a loss of confidence and motivation of employees of the business.

Within these results, where is the HRIS project the LSCA and what will be its future? Could we say that the implementation of an HRIS at LSCA is an asset to improve its performance and the involvement of its employees [28]? And, if, by optimizing HRIS, profile concepts and experiences could be replaced by those of skill [25]? Since the causes of failure could be multiple, could a lack of communication, non-adherence, and non-understanding of the project be determining reasons for project failure? In response to all these questions, it would be interesting to analyze the post-implementation conditions by an empirical study among employees of LSCA to better understand their behavior in relation to change (proactive or passive opponents), adaptation, and the motivation to use new methods and tools.

References

1. Allen, T.J., Morton, M.S.: Information Technologies and the Corporation of the 1990 's. Oxford University Press. Lucas, H. C, New York (1994)
2. Allègre, C.B. et Andréassian, A. *Gestion des ressources humaines, valeur de l'immatériel.* 1ère édition. Editions De Boeck Université, Bruxelles (2008)
3. Autissier, D., et Moutot, J-M. *La boîte à outils de la conduite du changement.* Dunod, Paris; (2013)
4. Barabel, M. et Meier, O.: *Gestion internationale des ressources humaines.* Dunod, Paris; (2014)
5. Beadles II, N.A., Lower, C.M., Johns K.: The impact of human resource information systems: An exploratory study in the public sector. Commun. IIMS. **5**(4), 39–46 (2005)
6. Bencheman, M. et Galindo, G.: *Memento de gestion des ressources humaines.* Gualino, Paris (2006)
7. Bowen, D.E., Ostroff, C.: Understanding HRM-firm performance linkages: the role of "strength" of the HRM system. Acad. Manag. Rev. **29**, 203–221 (2004)
8. DeCenzo D. et al.: Fundamentals of Human Resource Management, 10th ed. Wiley (2010)
9. Dery, K., Grant, D., Wiblen, S.: Human resource information systems: replacing or enhancing HRM. In: Proceedings of the 15th World Congress of the International Industrial Relations Association IIRA. Sydney, Australia (2009)
10. Exbrayat, G., Fisteberg, N. et Fouesnant, R. Le Système d'Information des Ressources Humaines (SIRH): un atout dans l'optimisation de la GRH au service de l'entreprise. Mémoire, MBA, Dauphine (2010)
11. Gartner.: http://www.gartnergroup.com/. Source: AUTISSIER D., MOUTOT J.-M. *Méthode de conduite du changement,* Dunod, Paris (2010)
12. Gilbert, P.: Les progiciels intégrés et la GRH : quand l'ambiguïté des enjeux est fonctionnelle. Gérer et Comprendre, Annales des Mines (2000)
13. Hawi, R.: Les compagnies d'assurance libanaises tentées par l'étranger... http://www.1stlebanon.net/actufr/archives/resultat.php?id=252&debut=0 (Consulted the 24th of december 2014) (2003)
14. Hoftsede.: Cultural tools, comparison country. http://geert-hofstede.com/lebanon.html (Consulted the 24th of december 2014) (2012)
15. Hussain, Z., Wallace, J., et Cornelius, N.E.: The use and impact of human resource information systems on human resource management professionals. Inf. Manag. **44**(1), 74–89 (2012)
16. Imbert, J.: Les tableaux de bord RH, Eyrolles. Editions d'organisation, Paris (2007)
17. Just, B.: Pas de DRH sans SIRH. Editions Liaisons, Paris (2010)
18. Karsenti G. et Lorentz F, B. La fin du paradoxe de l'informatique. L'heure du retour sur investissement. Editions Organisation, Paris (1999)
19. Lippert, S.K., Swiercz, P.M.: Human resource information systems (HRIS) & technology trust. J. Inf. Sci. **31**(5), 340–353 (2005)

20. People and change.: http://rh.sia-partners.com/20110426/la-conduite-du-changement-concernant-les-systemes-dinformations-est-un-processus-damelioration-continue/ (Consulted the 27th of december 2014) (2011)
21. Reix, R.: Les technologies de l'information, facteur de flexibilité. Revue Française de Gestion. 1999; n. 123 mars mai, pp. 111–119 (2011)
22. Reix, R. Système d'information de l'outil à la stratégie. Economie et management. **116** (2005)
23. Reix, R., et al.: Systèmes d'information et management des organisations. Editions Delavilla, Paris (2011)
24. Roussel, P., Wacheux, F.: Management des ressources humaines: Méthodes de recherche en sciences humaines et sociales. Edition de Boeck, Bruxelles (2005)
25. Satta, J.-M.: *La révolution silencieuse des SIRH*. Delavilla, Paris (2011)
26. Sheehan, C., Cooper, B.K.: HRM outsourcing: the impact of organizational size and HRM strategic involvement. Personnel Review. **40**(6), 742–760 (2011)
27. Silva, F.: Etre e-DRH. Entreprise et Carrières, Paris, Editions Liaisons, Collection (2008)
28. Storhaye, P.Le: SIRH - Enjeux, facteurs de succès et perspectives. Dunod, Paris (2013)
29. Tannenbaum, S.I.: Human Resource Information Systems: User Group Implications. J. Syst. Manag. **41**(1), pp. 27–32 (2005)
30. Thévenet, M., Dejoux, C., Marbot, E. et Normand, E. *Fonctions RH politiques, métiers et outils des ressources humaines.* Pearson Education, Paris (2009)
31. Tixier J.: Système d'informations RH et Gestion du changement. In: Meier, O et al., Gestion du changement, Dunod, Paris (2007)
32. Troshani, I., Jerram, C., Hill, Rao: S. Exploring the public sector adoption of HRIS. Indus. Manag. Data Syst. **111**(3), 470–488 (2011)
33. Wiblen, S., Dery, K., Grant, D.: Transitioning From a Proprietary to Vanilla HRIS: The Resulting Implications for Talent. In: Proceedings of the 3rd European Academic Workshop on Electronic Human Resource Management, Bamberg, Germany, May 20–21 (2010)
34. Yin, R.: Case Study Research: Design and Methods, 4th edn. Sage Publishing, Thousand Oaks (2009)

Part III
Interacting in an ICT-Enabled Relational Landscape

The Brand Website as a Means of Reviving Memories and Imaginary

Imed Ben Nasr, Lisa Thomas, Jean François Trinquecoste
and Ibtissame Abaidi

Abstract The paper explores mental imagery in the consumer online website navigation experience. We examine contributions of experienced mental images on the consumer's post-visit in influencing e-satisfaction and attitude. Combining qualitative and quantitative attributes of mental imagery as influencers of consumers' e-satisfaction and brand attitude we gauge the relative importance of these attributes and illustrate the role of website imageability and consumer familiarity with the brand in influencing consumer mental imagery. With limited prior research in the domain, we contribute to the literature particularly concerning the role played by qualitative aspects of mental imagery in the consumer online experience. Our conceptual model is validated with a quantitative survey methodology using confirmatory factor analysis. Results reveal the preeminent role of website imageability and consumer website familiarity in conditioning all quantitative attributes of mental imagery and selected qualitative attributes generated by the website-visit. Our discussion affords implications both for research and practice.

Keywords Mental imagery · Brand website · E-satisfaction · Brand attitude · Quantitative survey methodology

I.B. Nasr (✉)
La Rochelle Business School, La Rochelle, France
e-mail: bennasri@esc-larochelle.fr

L. Thomas
Neoma Business School, Reims, France
e-mail: lisa.thomas@neoma-bs.fr

J.F. Trinquecoste
IRGO, University of Bordeaux, IV-Montesquieu, Bordeaux, France
e-mail: jean-francois.trinquecoste@u-bordeaux.fr

I. Abaidi
Laboratory of Regards, IUT de Troyes, Troyes, France
e-mail: abaidiibtissame@hotmail.com

© Springer International Publishing Switzerland 2016
F. Ricciardi and A. Harfouche (eds.), *Information and Communication Technologies in Organizations and Society*, Lecture Notes in Information Systems and Organisation 15, DOI 10.1007/978-3-319-28907-6_15

1   Introduction

This study explores the role of mental imagery processing for the consumer website visit experience. It aims to respond to the following questions: Firstly, what is the psychological process that underlies the experience of mental imagery during the brand-website-visit? Secondly, what are the relative contributions of the experienced mental images on the consumer's post-visit in influencing e-satisfaction and attitude? (E-satisfaction refers here to the consumer's affective condition that results from his global evaluation of the brand website [5], and attitude as the consumer's location on the affective dimension vis-à-vis the brand of the website [5]). Finally, the study assesses the role of website imageability and consumer familiarity as contextual constructs in influencing consumer mental imagery.

From a review of the literature in the domain of marketing, it is found that the experiential approach (which is phenomenological in spirit and regards consumption as a primarily subjective state of consciousness with a variety of symbolic meanings, hedonic responses and aesthetic criteria [19]) criticizes the iniquitousness and the partiality of the information processing perspective [which regards the consumer as a logical thinker who solves problems to make purchasing decisions]. Research within the information processing perspective stresses only discursive processing and ignores imagery processing. Consequently, many phenomena of consumer psychology and consumption are neglected [19]. However, the experiential approach emphasizes the polymorphic nature of the consumption experience with its focus on functional and experiential dimensions. As such, this perspective brings to the fore imagery processing as the main means of the subjective consumer experience, for example; enjoyment, escapism, memories and imaginary.

However, the value of the experiential approach to an understanding of mental imagery is less evident in studies in the context of consumer online experiences. Consequently, the role of mental imagery in the consumer experience of online navigation of e-commerce websites and branding appears insufficiently studied [27].

In an attempt to extend the literature, we explore the psychological process that underlies the experience of mental imagery during the brand-website visit. We draw on extant literature which emphasizes the role of mental imagery and explore this role in the consumer online experience. We present and empirically test our conceptual model within the current quantitative study. We follow with a discussion of our results and presentation of the implications of our study for theory and practice.

2   Theoretical Background

Mental images, as a psychological phenomenon, have instigated the interest of psychologists from the early 19th century. Researchers such as Betts [2] evidenced this interest. The role of mental images was also emphasized with the rise of cognitive science and the growing need to understand the dual-task processing of individuals. In this context, authors including Sheehan [26], Paivio [25] and Childers and Houston [12] differentiate two approaches to information processing: discursive processing and imagery processing.

The difference between discursive and imagery processing is based on the way a person represents perceived stimuli in their mind. Generally, in discursive processing, stimuli are represented by words and numbers and in imagery processing, perceived stimuli are represented as multi-sensorial information (visual, auditory, tactile, olfactory or even kinesthetic) commonly named mental images. Imagery processing is defined as "a process by which sensory information is represented in working memory" [22, p. 473].

This multisensory information processing is materialized in the consumer's mind through mental images that are different in their characteristics such as their quantity, vividness, valence, elaboration, content and, sensorial modality. Within the literature, the attribute of quantity refers to the number of mental images that a person experiences when faced with a stimulus while vividness, valence, elaboration, content and sensorial modality refer to the quality of these mental images. Table 1 illustrates definitions and key research conducted in this respect.

The role of mental imagery in the consumption experience was first introduced by Holbrook and Hirschman [19] who discussed the relevance of mental images as a core component of the customer's experience. The authors consider mental imagery as a conscious and intuitive elaboration process, supporting the experience of subjective cognitive and affective reactions during the consumption experience. These reactions are represented in the consumers' mind by mental images that refer to the memories and the images activated by stimuli during the experience. Holbrook and Hirschman [19] ascertain that manipulating the attributes of mental images represents a means of enhancing the consumer experience. This position is also shared by Bourgeon and Filser [8] who argue that mental images play a key role in improving the consumer experience in the form of theatrical representation. Their results evidence the role of mental imagery [and the related mental images] in rendering the influences of for example, a plays' scenario and related feelings on the experienced perceived values.

Table 1 Definitions and key studies in the domain of attributes of mental images

Attributes	Definition	References
Quantity	The number of images that comes to the consumer's mind while processing information	[14, 25]
Vividness	The clarity with which the individual experiences an image	[7, 29]
Valence	The individual's interpretation of the emotional meaning attached to concrete memories	[9, 24]
Elaboration	The extent to which information in working memory is integrated with prior knowledge structures	[4, 27]
Modality	The sensory nature—visually, auditory, gustatory, olfactory and/or tactility—of the mental images	[24]
Content	Mental representations of the mental images	[17]

Within advertising research, mental images are also widely studied [1, 6, 10, 28]. Authors suggest that mental images mediate the influences of the advertisement on consumer cognition, affect and attitude. Babin et al. [4], Burns et al. [10] and Helme-Guizon [17], for example, present the influences of the mental images' attributes on the consumer reactions to the advertisements. However, their results differ as concerns the dimensions involved in this process. For example, for print advertisements, Babin et al. [4] and Burns et al. [10] show that the elaboration of mental images positively influences the consumer's attitude toward the advertisement, the brand and purchase intentions. Helme-Guizon [17], however, puts forward that only the valence of perceived mental images influences the consumer attitudes. Within the context of radio advertising, Bone and Ellen [7] conclude that only the quantity of the mental images plays a key role in impacting the consumer attitudes toward the advertisement and the brand.

Dissimilarities within these results could be explained by the difference in the attributes of the stimuli used in these studies, in particular their imageability and their concreteness. This point is emphasized from the results of Bolls' study [6] which highlights the key role of the advertisement's imageability in enhancing the experience of mental images. The Bolls' [6] results indicate that listening to high-imagery radio advertisements engages visual cognitive resources and thus, enhances the attributes of the perceived mental images. For Walters et al. [28], concreteness of the pictures and the words contained in the advertisement also conditions the experience of mental images, in particular their elaboration and quality. These results suggest that combining instructions to imagine with concrete pictures is the most effective advertising strategy based on mental images.

Moreover, in the context of Internet marketing, the role of mental imagery as a core component of the consumer online experience is stressed by many authors [16, 18, 20, 23, 27]. Hoffman and Novak [18], building on [19] study, suggest that mental imagery represents a core attribute of recreational online behavior. This idea is somewhat shared by Mathwick et al. [23] and Schlosser [27] who consider imagery processing as the experiential facet of the consumer's online experience. Mathwick et al. [23], for example, point out that the experience of mental imagery during the website visit enhances the sensory responses of the consumer and the experienced hedonic values. Additionally, Schlosser [27] demonstrates that imagery processing underlines the mental representations the consumer experiences when manipulating virtually a product and that these mental images, through their vividness, condition the consumer's attitude toward the brand and subsequent purchase intentions.

A review of the marketing literature further reveals that despite consensus concerning the relevance of imagery processing in creating value within the consumer experience, dissimilar results were found concerning the contributions of the dimensions of mental images in this process. Indeed, studies, such as Bone and Ellen's [7], emphasize the relevance of the quantity of mental images in influencing consumer satisfaction and attitude whereas others, like [3] and [10], underscore the key role of the quality of the attributes of mental images; vividness, valence and/or elaboration, in this process.

Additionally, when considering the role of each of the qualitative attributes of mental images in consumer satisfaction and attitude, studies reveal differing findings. Babin and Burns [3], for example, presents valence as the unique dimension of mental images that influences consumer reactions while [17], Schlosser [27] and Lebel et al. [20] state that elaboration of mental images significantly conditions consumer's reactions.

Consequently, this study aims to explore the contribution of both the mental images' quantitative and qualitative attributes as part of the consumers' website navigation experience. This allows the analysis of the specific influences of both quantitative and qualitative attributes in consumer e-satisfaction and attitude toward the promoted brand.

To set our study in context in order to analyse experienced mental images we need to underline factors that condition the process of mental imagery. The literature identifies several conditioning factors leading to experienced mental images. These factors are: the interactivity of the picture, the concreteness and the abstractness of the stimulus, the instruction to imagine, familiarity with the stimulus and the imageability of the stimulus [4, 13]. For the purpose of the current study, we focus on these two latter factors.

The imageability of the stimulus was first introduced by [25] who reveal that stimuli vary in their capability to evoke mental images. Hence, the imageability of the stimulus is defined as the ability of a stimulus to stimulate mental images quickly and spontaneously in the consumers' mind. This idea is supported in the marketing literature by Burns et al. [10] and Babin et al. [4] who confirm that imageability of print and radio advertisements condition the vivacity of the mental images and the consumer attitude toward the brand. Bolls [6] further explains this arguing that listening to high-imagery radio advertisements engages visual cognitive resources suitable for the experience of mental images that in turn influence the consumer's attitude toward the brand.

In the context of website design, the orientation of the website to dominantly pictorial or verbal content could impact the experience of mental images during the website visit [21]. The results of Lee and Gretzel's experiment, for example, put forward the preeminent role of the websites' pictures in impacting the quantity and the modality of the experienced mental images and the resulting consumer attitude toward the website.

Moreover, the role of familiarity with the stimulus in mental imagery processing can be discussed by contending that imagery processing requires some prior knowledge with the stimulus. Babin Burns and Biswas [4] comment that "the more familiar one is with the stimulus object, the richer is the base from which images will spring". This idea was taken up by Danaher et al. [13] who argue that the consumer experiences greater efficiency in their website browsing as experience is gained with the website; ability to review more pages within the same time span and reduction in the time spent per viewed page. Indeed, when the consumer is familiar with the website, they don't need to use discursive processing. As such, imagery processing predominates and results in well scored mental images. We present our conceptual model in what follows.

3 Conceptual Model

In our quest to understand the psychological process that forms the basis of experience of mental imagery during a brand-website visit, our review of the literature
reveals that imagery processing is the means through which the stimuli of the brand
website enhance the consumer online experience and thus, impact e-satisfaction and
attitude [5, 20, 27]. More explicitly, when consumers visit a brand website, their
perception of the website execution attributes (design, colours, interactivity,
usability) and content creates mental images in their mind that are foremost very
personal and intimately related to their past experiences and imagination.
Additionally, these mental images are very specific in their quantity—indicated
through the number of perceived mental images—and their qualities—represented
by the vividness, the valence and the elaboration of these mental images.

Based on our review of the literature, we aim to assess the relative influence of
the quantitative and qualitative aspects of the online experienced mental images in
the consumers' e-satisfaction and attitude. We then explore the role of consumers'
familiarity with the website and website imageability as contextual constructs
which have a potential influence on consumers' mental imagery. Figure 1 represents
our conceptual model. We present our hypotheses in what follows.

3.1 Mental Imagery

Core to our conceptual model is mental imagery. Previous research suggests that the
quantity attribute of mental images has a positive influence on consumer
e-satisfaction where importantly, it is the number of mental images the consumer
experiences which leads to greater e-satisfaction (considered as the consumer's
affective condition that results from a global evaluation of the brand website) [23].
However, simply experiencing numerous mental images doesn't necessarily equate
with good quality mental images [4]. In addition, experience in terms of vividness,

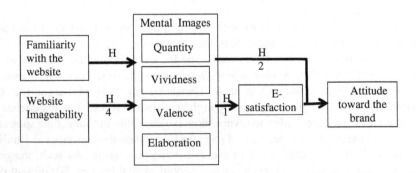

Fig. 1 Conceptual framework

valence and elaboration are revealed as important [4, 7, 29]. Nevertheless, we propose that the number of experienced mental images influences consumer e-satisfaction, yet, in addition we propose that this is less important than the contribution of quality attributes [14]. Thus:

- Hypothesis 1: Quality attributes of mental images in terms of vividness, valence and elaboration experienced by consumers when they visit the brand website have a stronger impact on their e-satisfaction than quantity attributes.

Concerning consumers attitude toward the brand [defined as the consumer's location on the affective dimension vis-à-vis the brand] resulting from a website visit, we propose that, the qualitative aspects of the mental images represent a kind of "fictitious experience" of the brand that provides the consumer with new knowledge about the brand and product. This is due to the sensorial, emotional and symbolic properties of these qualitative attributes. More explicitly, good quality mental images (vivid, clear, elaborated and good valence) arouse in the consumers' mind fictitious scenario of product usage that are sources of subjective knowledge and feelings [27]. These elements would condition the consumer's perception and attitude toward the brand. Thus, they would be a relevant means—more than the quantitative attribute of mental images—in influencing the consumers' attitude toward the brand. This is in line with MacInnis and Prices' [22] and Holbrook and Hirschmans' [19] argument that the more the mental images evoked by the website visit are integrated in the consumer's knowledge structure, the more important they influence attitude toward the brand. In other words, the more elaborated the experienced mental images, the greater their impact on consumer attitude toward the brand. Hence:

- Hypothesis 2: The quality attributes of the mental images (vividness, valence and elaboration) experienced by consumers during a brand-website-visit have a stronger impact on the consumer's attitude toward the brand than the quantity attribute.

3.2 Familiarity with the Website

According to the literature review, familiarity with the website conditions the consumers' website visit and the related imagery processing. Therefore, from a psychological perspective, a consumer familiar with a website is prone to immersion in the website visit and adopts good quality imagery processing i.e. vivid, elaborated and with positive valence—and quantity i.e.—numerous—mental images. The construct of familiarity with the website therefore has a related influence on the consumers' mental imagery. Thus we propose:

- Hypothesis 3: Consumers familiarity with the website enhances the quantity, the vividness, the valence and the elaboration of the mental images experienced during website visit.

3.3 Website Imageability

Website imageability is a further contextual construct within our conceptual model
that has the potential to influence the consumer's mental imagery. Exploring the
role of website imageability provides the opportunity to assert the notion of it being
a reliable means of materialization and quantification of the websites' ability to
evoke mental images in the visitors' mind. The technical and aesthetic aspects of
the website and its content are found to play a key role in the consumer's mental
imagery experience by conditioning the characteristics of the perceived mental
images [21]. In reference to [10] and Lee and Gretzel [21], the imageability of the
website should play a key role in the influence of the attributes of the mental images
experienced by the consumers during their website visit. Thus:

- Hypothesis 4: Website imageability has a positive influence on the quantity and
  the quality—vividness, valence and elaboration—of the mental images evoked
  in the consumers' mind during the website visit.

4 Methodology

We empirically test our hypotheses by employing a quantitative research
methodology. Our respondents included one hundred and ninety-six undergraduate
business students. The study was conducted in a classroom setting where the
subjects were randomly assigned to one of two example cases of car-brand-websites
(BMW, Audi).

The choice of product category within one single industry (automotive industry)
allows the control of potential variability of influences from product category differences—such as consumer involvement, knowledge, engagement and/or attitude
toward the product category—on consumer responses. Whilst acknowledging that a
single product category may limit the external validity and the generalizability of
the findings, it is felt that such an approach helps prevent possible moderation
effects of the product's category and/or the brands' characteristics on the results.

Potential limitations may be levelled at our choice of sampling frame; the student
population. However, we justify our choice by arguing that the student population
has the same attitudes and usages of the Internet as non-students and therefore
represents a homogeneous population for use in studies of Internet usage. During
the study, the subjects were first provided with a hardcopy of the questionnaire.
They were instructed to respond to questions on their familiarity with the respective
case brand. They were then asked to visit the website of their respective case brand
[for ten minutes at least]. This was followed by their completing the rest of the
questionnaire in hardcopy.

The measures used in our questionnaire to study the constructs within our
conceptual model are adapted from existing scales (Table 2 for details).

Table 2 References and CFA results of the measures

Measure scales	References	Reliability Joreskog's Rho	Explained variance (%)	CFA fit indexes
Mental images (8 items)	[4]	0.96	92.49	NNFI = 0.978; CFI = 0.992; RMSEA = 0.055
Familiarity with the website (3 items)	[24]	0.94	91.75	⁻
Website imageability (2 items)	[25]	0.94	93.99	⁻
E-satisfaction (4 items)	[21, 27]	0.85	69.08	NNFI = 0.989; CFI = 0.996; RMSEA = 0.055
Brand attitude (4 items)	[5, 20]	0.95	87.85	NNFI = 1.010; CFI = 1000; RMSEA = 0.000

⁻Not calculated because of the limited number of items

In order to test the reliability of the measures, EFA and CFA were conducted. The results of confirmatory analysis confirm the good fit of the factorial structures of mental images measure scale (NNFI = 0.978; CFI = 0.992; RMSEA = 0.055), e-satisfaction scale (NNFI = 0.989; CFI = 0.996; RMSEA = 0.055) and attitude toward brand scale (NNFI = 1.010; CFI = 1.000; RMSEA = 0.000) to empirical data. All the measures scale items present absolute, comparison and incremental fit indices superior to 0.9 [11, 15] (Table 2). Moreover, the scores of SRMR and RMSEA indicate the absence of approximation and estimation errors for the cited structural factors. The results of the Levene test show no significant differences between the variances of the two sub-samples according to the studied brand, highlighting that the data can be used to analyse the causal model. Additionally, structural equation modelling is used to examine the adjustment of the proposed model and to test the hypothesized relationships between the constructs.

5 Results and Discussion

The goodness-of-fit indices indicate a good fit of the sample data to the research model (Table 3). All the calculated indices respect the recommended fit criteria [11, 15]. For example, the scores of the NNFI (0.966) and the CFI (0.973) were consistent in suggesting that the hypothesized model represented an adequate fit to the data. The RMSEA (0.047) (<0.05) and the related confidence interval ranging from 0.032 to 0.061 indicates a good degree of precision of the RMSEA—and confirm the idea that the hypothesized model fits the data well.

Table 3 Table summary of hypotheses testing

Hypothesis		Standardised β(t)	Decision	Hypothesis		Standardised β(t)	Decision
H1	ImgQtty → E-satf	0.038 (0.402)	Supported	H3	WsFam → ImgQtty	0.012 (0.253)	Partially supported
	ImgVvd → E-satf	0.177 (2.190)			WsFam → ImgVvd	−0.007 (−0.130)	
	ImgVlce → E-satf	0.599 (2.576)			WsFam → ImgVlce	0.366 (2.688)	
	ImgElab → E-satf	0.279 (3.424)			WsFam → ImgElab	−0.027 (−0.436)	
H2	ImgQtty → AttBd	−0.088 (−1.191)	Partially supported	H4	WsIgb → ImgQtty	0.756 (9.544)	Supported
	ImgVvd → AttBd	0.019 (0.244)			WsIgb → ImgVvd	0.549 (6.987)	
	ImgVlce → AttBd	0.341 (1.300)			WsIgb → ImgVlce	0.421 (2.770)	
	ImgElab → AttBd	0.196 (2.309)			WsIgb → ImgElab	0.601 (7.361)	

(S-Bχ^2 = 218.489 (152); NNFI = 0.966; CFI = 0.973; SRMR = 0.048; RMSEA = 0.047, CI: 0.032, 0.061)

Note *WsFam* Familiarity with the website; *WsIgb* Website Imageability; *ImgQtty* Mental images quantity; *ImgVvd* Mental Images vividness; *ImgVlce* Mental images Valence; *ImgElab* Mental images elaboration; $p < 0.05$

The testing of the hypotheses illustrates the nature of the relationship that exist between the characteristics of the mental images and the consumer's e-satisfaction (Table 3). They show that all the qualitative characteristics of the mental images impact significantly consumer e-satisfaction and that the quantity of these mental images doesn't play a relevant role in this process. This result, confirming H1, is contrary to the findings of Bone and Ellen [7] who suggest that quantity of mental image is the most important attribute of the mental imagery process. However, clarity of the mental images, their emotional tone and the extent to which they are integrated with the consumer's prior knowledge structures—*represented here by their vividness, their valence and their elaboration respectively*—appear to be the elements that play a key role in conditioning the consumer's e-satisfaction. Additionally, referring to the standard coefficients, valence of mental images seems to be the attribute that contributes the most in this process ($\beta_{std} = 0.599$). These findings support those of Babin and Burns [3] and Schlosser [27] who report that the emotional tone of the mental images represents the main contributor to consumer satisfaction. Furthermore, these results indicate that emotional reactions could, to some extent, mediate the relationship between the perceived mental images and the consumer's e-satisfaction. This is in line with authors such as Holbrook and Hirschman [19] and Mathwick et al. [23] for example, who emphasize the preeminent role of imagery processing and the resulting mental images being the key route to materializing the experiential and emotional aspects of the consumers' [online and offline] experiences.

Concerning the influences of the attributes of the mental images on the attitude toward the brand, our results partially confirm H2. More specifically, the results indicate that only the elaboration of the mental images significantly impacts the consumer's attitude ($\beta_{std} = 0.196$, t = 2.309). This suggests that the more the mental images evoked by the website visit are elaborated, in terms of memories and imaginary, the more important their influence on the consumer's attitude toward the brand. In other words, the experience of mental images, in terms of their level of integration within the consumers' knowledge structure, promotes a gradual influence on the consumers' attitude toward the brand such that the more the experienced mental images are integrated within consumers' memories and imagination, i.e. long-term memory and subconscious, the more they impact consumer attitude. Indeed, mental images related to memories require an activation of the long term memory and a subsequent effort in retrieving past experiences and memories. Consequently, mental images stimulate the consumer's subconscious and allow fantasies and repressed desires to emerge and to materialize within imagined scenes involving the brand. Consequently, the resulting mental images are very personal and intimate and thus, their influences on the consumer's attitude toward the brand are likely to be significant. Furthermore, our results illustrate the valence of the mental images is significantly related to consumer familiarity with the website ($\beta_{std} = 0.366$, t = 2.688), albeit partially, therefore confirming hypothesis H3. Hence, the consumer who is familiar with the website—and thus has already a knowledge structure related to this website—experiences intense and emotionally charged mental images compared to a consumer who is unfamiliar with the website.

They will likely experience enjoyable, entertaining and valuable mental images. Contrariwise, a consumer unfamiliar with the website will have more difficulty in experiencing pleasant and attractive mental images, because of the prior cognitive load experienced through the exploration and the processing of the website's stimuli and content. Indeed, a consumer who is unfamiliar with the website will adopt discursive processing to elaborate the stimuli and the content of the website; a mode of processing that is not opportune to the experience of mental images as stated by MacInnis and Price [22]. Therefore, as noted by Babin et al. [4], prior knowledge of the website could be considered as a prerequisite to experiencing intense and emotionally charged mental images.

The results reveal that H4 is supported i.e. 'website imageability' is relevant to use in materializing and quantifying how the website arouses mental imagery processing in the consumers mind. The imageability of the website represents to a degree, a reliable quantification of the imagery properties of the website. This finding corroborates Paivio's study [25] as concerns the relevancy of the general notion of stimulus imageability to summarize the imagery abilities of a stimulus. This idea has been successfully evidenced by marketing researchers in their attempts to quantify the abilities of an advertisement to evoke mental images [10, 17].

6 Implications for Research and Practice

The results of this research bring to the fore the role of mental images' attributes in influencing the consumer's online satisfaction and attitude toward the brand. For website managers, such findings point to the need to distinguish between consumers based on their website familiarity and therefore their ability to process the content and components of the website. This underlines the relevance of developing an online strategy which manages and displays website content according to consumer familiarity and prior experiences with the website.

Additionally, for the brand manager, the results highlight the relevance of a website communication strategy based on mental imagery as an alternative to information based websites/webpages in creating value within the consumer's online experience and thereby improving brand perception and attitude. More specifically, the results stress the need for such managers' to consider the attributes of the mental images that fit the brand's image and positioning and to define how to stimulate them in the consumers' mind. From this perspective, to consider simultaneously the website's characteristics (i.e. content, design, usability), its imageability properties and their links with the brand image's attributes is beneficial in establishing a coherent and valuable online communication strategy based on mental imagery stimulation.

Our study is not without its limitations some of which have been briefly mentioned above. Conceptual limitations concern the need to take into consideration variables reflecting consumer psychological characteristics and consumers' prior relationships with the brand and the website. However, in terms of future research in the domain, studies that attempt to ascertain the properties that underlie the specific relationships between the execution and content elements of the website could be insightful. For example, research might explore a website's usability, interactivity, design, text and images and their relationship with its imageability. This will help to determine the nature of the link between the attributes of the website and its imageability. Also, such an approach could reveal the components of the website that may represent leverage for enhancing the mental imagery experience of the consumer and their subsequent reactions vis a vis the website and the brand. Furthermore, future research might be conducted so as to include additional constructs within the conceptual model. For example, constructs which might enhance the consumer's experience of mental imagery might be considered, including content characteristics of the website, aesthetics, interactivity and usability.

Finally, these results mean that emotional reactions could, to some extent, mediate the relationship between the perceived mental images and the consumer's e-satisfaction. This idea, whilst finding support in the existing marketing literature [10], merits further study in the context of online consumer behavior.

References

1. Aydınoğlu, N.Z., Cian, L.: Show me the product, show me the model: effect of picture type on attitudes toward advertising. J. Consum. Psychol. (Elsevier Sci.) 24(4), 506–519 (2014)
2. Baddeley, A.D., Andrade, J.: Working memory and the vividness of imagery. J. Exp. Psychol. 129 (1), 126–45 (2000)
3. Babin, L.A., Burns, A.C.: Effects of print ad pictures and copy containing instructions to imagine on mental imagery that mediates attitudes. J. Advertising 26(3), 33–44 (1987)
4. Babin, L.A., Burns, A.C., Biswas, A.: A framework providing direction for research on communication effects of mental imagery-evoking advertising strategies. Adv. Consum. Res. 19, 621–628 (1992)
5. Ben, N.I.: An analysis of the brand website experience through the benefits it provides and their impacts on the customer's satisfaction and attitude: an application to car brands' websites. PhD dissertation, University of Bordeaux IV-Montesquieu, (2012)
6. Bolls, P.D.: I can hear you, but can I see you? The use of visual cognition during exposure to high-imagery radio advertisements. Commun. Res. 29(5), 537–564 (2002)
7. Bone, P.S., Ellen, P.F.: The generation and consequences of communication-evoked imagery. J. Consum. Res. 19(2), 93–104 (1992)
8. Bourgeon, D., Filser, M.: The contributions of the model of research of experiences to the analysis of the consumer's behavior in the cultural field: a conceptual and methodological exploration. Res. Appl. Mark. 10(4), 5–25 (1995)
9. Bower, G.: Mental imagery and associative learning. In: Gregg, L. (ed.) Cognition in Learning and Memory. John Wiley, New York (1972)
10. Burns, A.C., Biswas, A., Babin, L.A.: The operation of visual imagery as a mediator of advertising effects. J. Advertising 22(2), 71–85 (1993)
11. Byrne, B.M.: Structural Equation Modeling with eqs: Basic Concepts, Applications, and Programming, 2nd edn. Lawrence Erlbaum Associates, Inc. (2006)
12. Childers, T.L., Houston, M.J.: Conditions for a picture-superiority effect on consumer memory. J. Consum. Res. 11, 643–654 (1984)

13. Danaher, P.J., Mullarkey, G.W., Essegaier, S.: Factors affecting web site visit duration: a cross-domain analysis. J. Mark. Res. (JMR) **43**(2), 182–194 (2006)
14. Gavilan, D., Avello, M., Abril, C.: The mediating role of mental imagery in mobile advertising. Int. J. Inf. Manag. **34**(4), 457–6 (2014)
15. Hair, J.F., Black, W.C., Babin, L.J., Anderson, R.E., Tatham, R.L. (eds.). Multivariate Data Analysis, 6th edn. Pearson International Edition (2005)
16. Hall, R.H., Hanna, P.: The impact of web page text-background colour combinations on readability, retention, aesthetics and behavioural intention. Behav. Inf. Technol. **23**(3), 183–95 (2004)
17. Helme-Guizon, A.: Image, imagery and effects of persuasive communication: application to an art work included in an advertisement. PhD dissertation, University of Paris-Dauphine (1997)
18. Hoffman, D., Novak, T.: Marketing in hypermedia computer-mediated environments: conceptual foundations. J. Mark. Res. **60**(July), 50–68 (1996)
19. Holbrook, M.B., Hirschman, E.C.: The experiential aspects of consumption: consumer fantasies, feelings and fun. J. Consum. Res. **9**, 132–140 (1982)
20. LeBel, J., Yanan, Y., akratsas, D., Mukherjee, A., Dube, L.: Delivering differentiated experiential branding in web environments. Adv. Consum. Res. **33**, 302–303 (2006)
21. Lee, W., Gretzel, U.: Designing persuasive destination websites: a mental imagery processing perspective. Tourism Manag. **33**(5), 1270–1280 (2012). doi:10.1016/j.tourman.2011.10.012
22. MacInnis, D.J., Price, L.L.: The role of imagery in information processing: review and extensions. J. Consum. Res. **13** (Mars) (1987)
23. Mathwick, C., Malhotra, N.K., Rigdon, E.: The effect of dynamic retail experiences on experiential perceptions of value: an internet and catalog comparison. J. Retail. **78**(1), 51–60 (2002)
24. Miller, D.W., Hadjimarcou, J., Miciak, A.: A scale of measuring advertisement-evoked mental imagery. J. Mark. Commun. **6**, 1–20 (2000)
25. Paivio, A. (ed.).: Imagery and Verbal Processes. Rinehart & Winston, New York (1971)
26. Sheehan, P.: A functional analysis of the role of visual imagery in unexpected recall. In: Sheehan, Peter (ed.) The Function and Nature of Imagery, pp. 189–221. Wiley, New York (1972)
27. Schlosser, A.E.: Experiencing products in the virtual world: the role of goal and imagery in influencing attitudes versus purchase intentions. J. Consum. Res. **30**(2), 184–198 (2003)
28. Walters, G., Sparks, B., Herington, C.: The effectiveness of print advertising stimuli in evoking elaborate consumption visions for potential travelers. J. Travel Res. **46**(1), 24–34 (2007)
29. Yoo, J., Minjeong, K.: The effects of online product presentation on consumer responses: a mental imagery perspective. J. Bus. Res. **67**(11), 2464–2472 (2014)

Location Privacy Apprehensions in Location-Based Services Among Literate and Semi-literate Users

Wen Yong Chua, Klarissa T.T. Chang and Maffee Peng-Hui Wan

Abstract Personalized services provided by Location Based Services (LBS) are becoming increasingly prevalent to the large population of semi-literate users living in emerging economies due to the low costs and ubiquity. However, usage of LBS is still threatened by location privacy threats as it keeps track of the individuals' location. Studies typically only addressed how to mitigate location privacy apprehensions for the literate users and not the semi-literate users. To fill that gap and better understand location privacy apprehensions among different communities, this study draws upon theories of Restrict Access/Limited Control and Familiarity to identify the antecedents of location privacy apprehensions related to personalized services provided by LBS and user literacy. The proposed research model is empirically tested in a laboratory experiment. The findings show that the different types of LBS do affect the degree of location privacy apprehensions between the literate and semi-literate users. Implications for enhancing usage intentions and mitigating location privacy apprehensions for different types of mobile applications are discussed.

Keywords Location-based services · Personal-subscriber level privacy · Corporate-enterprise level privacy · Location privacy apprehensions · Usage intentions

W.Y. Chua (✉) · K.T.T. Chang · M.P.-H. Wan
National University of Singapore, Singapore, Singapore
e-mail: wenyong@comp.nus.edu.sg

K.T.T. Chang
e-mail: changtt@comp.nus.edu.sg

M.P.-H. Wan
e-mail: diswp@nus.edu.sg

1 Introduction

Usage of low cost smartphone has become prevalent in the developing countries through "technological leapfrogging" [17]. Smartphones are equipped with cellular triangulation and Global Positioning System (GPS) technologies. Developers leveraged on such technologies to obtain user's location so that they can provide personalized services [15]. These applications are known as Location Based Services (LBS). Such applications may be very popular in developed countries around the world but it may not be the case in developing countries, as the semi-literate users do not wish to reveal their information to anyone else. For example, Srinivasan [19] observed that some farmers were reluctant to use the kiosk service because they do not want to release any personal information to the operator. The farmers required assistance from operators as they do not know how to use the computer. Carolyn and Beth [2] has conducted another study in Uzbekistan and found out that people generally minimize mobile phone usage in public areas where another party can see the things that they are doing.

Such apprehensions often arise due to location privacy, which denotes the "ability to prevent other authorized parties from learning ones' current or past location" [11]. While it may be important for developers to leverage on users' location information to provide personalized information for an individual [3], users' might be subjected to location privacy threats [5, 6, 9, 23, 26]. According to Ling [11], location privacy threats are "risks that an adversary can obtain unauthorized access to raw location data, derived or computed location information by locating a transmitting device, hijacking the location transmission channel and identifying the subject (person) using the device". For example, it can be used to stalk the whereabouts of an individual, which may lead to physical harm.

Ling [11] has identified two kinds of location privacy conceived by LBS namely the personal subscriber privacy and the corporate-enterprise level privacy. In order for a corporate-enterprise level privacy to take place, every employee must be willing to reveal their information to their company which might not be a case among the semi-literate users. Studies have shown that semi-literate users living in the developing countries are having apprehensions over releasing their location information [20]. Existing privacy literature typically target at the literate users to explain the impact of control on individuals' location privacy apprehensions.

Motivated by the differences between a literate and a semi-literate user as well as the different kinds of LBS on apprehensions for location privacy, our study aims to answer the following questions:

1. What are the impacts of literacy on location privacy apprehensions?
2. Are location privacy apprehensions related to usage intention?

2 Literature Review

2.1 Literate/Semi-literate Users

Defining literacy can be very problematic as it varies from context to context. It can be generally defined as "the ability to read, write, communicate and comprehend". A literate user is one who "reads and writes easily" and a semi-literate user is one who "reads and writes with difficulty" [21]. Hence, education level is one dimension that separates a literate user from a semi-literate user. Studies have shown that individuals with higher education level have more apprehensions over location privacy than individuals with lower education level [18].

Literacy in the context of information communication technology (ICT) is the "knowledge and ability to use ICT". Knowledge and ability to use ICT is another dimension that differentiates a literate user from a semi-literate user. Literate users are users who can use ICT efficiently. A Semi-literate user is one who has minimal skills with ICT [13].

The familiarity viewpoint is a useful theoretical lens for comprehending the moderating effects of users' expertise on the relationship between the personal subscriber level privacy/corporate-enterprise level privacy and individuals' apprehensions for location privacy. Familiarity is being defined as the individuals' acquaintance of each other with reference to previous interactions, experience and learning of the "what, who, how and when of what is happening" [8]. Therefore, individuals' familiarity with LBS comes with the direct experience of receiving information from LBS. Familiarity eases the uncertainty of an expectation through a better acquaintance of the individuals' experiences with location privacy [12, 24].

Adhering to the lens of familiarity, a literate user will experience a stronger apprehension for location privacy than a semi-literate user if he/she has been exposed to location privacy threats while using mobile applications. On the other hand, a literate user will have a lesser apprehension for location privacy than a semi-literate user if he/she has never been exposed to location privacy threats [18, 25]. With greater acquaintance regarding location privacy threats, the literate users will have a greater apprehension for location privacy. Hence, we hypothesize:

- H1: Literate users will have experience greater apprehension for location privacy as compared to the semi-literate users.

2.2 Restricted Access/Limited Control Theory

The Restricted Access/Limited Control (RALC) theory is built upon three components namely concept of privacy, justification of privacy and management of privacy [10, 14].

Moor [14] has defined the concept of privacy as "An individual or group has privacy in a situation if and only if in that situation, the individual or group or information related to the individual or group is protected from intrusion, observation and surveillance by others." Two categories of private situations can be: naturally private and informatively private. Naturally private situations are situations where individuals are being protected from intrusion or information gathering naturally. In this case, a loss of natural privacy is not an invasion of privacy. However, in the case of informatively private situation, an individual is legally and morally protected. This implies that intruding or gathering information about the individual is morally or legally prohibited.

Control of information is an important aspect in the justification and management of privacy. Justification of privacy is the capability of an individual to decide what benefits to seek and what harms need to be avoided. The management of privacy is done through three ways namely choice, consent and correction. Privacy can be controlled by deciding the situation that gives an individual the desired level of access ranging from total privacy to unabashed publicity. This implies that privacy can be chosen. For instance, an individual can choose to minimize the usage of their mobile phones in public areas if they do not want others to know about their lifestyle. Privacy can also be managed by control through consent. Individuals have the right to restrict or allow access of their location information by third party. Consent is a way of control that manages privacy and justifies what will be an invasion of privacy. Correction of personal information is another manner to manage privacy. It is a means for an individual to control their personal information and suggests a precaution against keeping unsafe inaccurate information that is collected.

Adhering to RALC, we first have to decide if the individuals' location should be granted normative protection. If the individuals are conceiving the personal subscriber privacy, the individuals has been given the liability to opt out of the LBS services. Hence, such situation should be regarded as naturally private situation. In such circumstances, an individual who prefers to have control over their information instead of enjoying the personalized services provided by LBS, will opt out of LBS and not use them.

On the other hand, if the individual is conceiving the corporate enterprise level privacy, the enterprise is liable for controlling individuals' location information. However, if the enterprise did not incorporate good privacy protection measures, there is still a tendency that individuals' location will be lost. Therefore, individual will have apprehensions over how the organization protects their location information. The individual might not corporate with the enterprise to use the services if the individual feels that the enterprise cannot protect their privacy.

Hence, we hypothesize:

- H2: Apprehensions for location privacy will not lead to usage than without.

3 Methodology

3.1 Research Design

To test the hypotheses, we conducted a laboratory experiment with 250 subjects. It was designed with a 2 (personal subscriber level privacy/corporate-enterprise level privacy) by 2 (literate/semi-literate) factorial design. A mobile agricultural application prototype running on the Android platform was developed for the experiment.

3.2 Prototypes of Mobile Application

The application used to conduct this experiment was built using the native Android platform. We simulated an environment that is similar to the actual usage by embedding network connectivity and GPS on the device. This application works on a client-server architecture where the mobile application takes in input from the user and sent it back to the server. The web application that resides on the server processed the request and stored the information into the database.

3.3 Participants

There were a total of 250 literate and semi-literate participants in this experiment. The literate users were undergraduate students in a large university. The semi-literate users were farmers in their home country with an education level of up to high school. Participants were determined if they belong to the literate or semi-literate group though a survey. The survey includes questions to check if they show apprehensions about location privacy. Participants who did not fall into the literate or semi-literate group were removed from the statistical analysis. Participants who did not have any apprehensions for location privacy were also removed. Examples of participants who were removed were farmers who had low level of qualification but they have a high amount of experience with mobile phones. Another example was students who indicated that they did not show any apprehensions about location privacy and had little prior experience with mobile phones. The final sample size included in the statistical analysis was 95 literate and 95 semi-literate users. The demographics of the participants were shown in Table 1.

Table 1 Demographic information of subjects

		Literate	Semi-literate	Total
Gender	Female	51	47	98
	Male	44	48	92
Age	20–24	68	45	113
	25–29	27	22	49
	30–34	0	19	19
	35–39	0	8	8
	40–44	0	1	1
Education	Elementary	0	36	36
	High school	14	59	73
	Bachelor	77	0	77
	Graduate	4	0	4
Prior experience with mobile phones	Less than 1 year	0	38	38
	1–2 years	0	44	44
	3–4 years	40	13	53
	5–6 years	25	0	25
	7–8 years	20	0	20
	9–10 years	10	0	10

4 Procedures and Tasks

The participants were required to complete a survey at the start of each session. The questions in this survey include questions about their demographics, apprehensions about location privacy, experience with mobile phones and mobile applications. Participants were asked take the role of a farmer. As a farmer, the participants registered for an account using their phone number, password and the crop that they grow in the farm.

Participants who belong to the group that experience a personal subscriber level privacy was required to initiate a request for the latest alert that is being send by the other nearby participants. Upon initiating the request, personalized advice on how to manage their crop were given. Participants who belong to the group that experience a corporate-enterprise level privacy will automatically receive a notification whenever other participants in the nearby location have triggered an alert. Personalized advice on how to manage their crop was given in that alert notification.

4.1 Measurements

Usage intention in this study was measured by asking the individuals if they were going to use the application in the future. For example, "I will use this application in the future." We also considered the usefulness as part of usage intention. For instance, "This application is useful for my daily tasks." The questions were being adopted from Angst & Agarval [1] and Venkatesh et al. [22]. Location privacy apprehensions in this study was measured by probing if the individual was worried that the application could track and access their personal information continuously. An example of such question is: "I am fearful when the application keep track of where I am." We also questioned if the individual is worried that the application would disclose their personal information to a third party. An example of such question is: "I am worried over who can see what I have done with the application." The questions were adopted from Dinev and Hart [7] and Xu et al. [25].

4.2 Experimental Manipulation

The corporate enterprise-level privacy channel has been operationalized by retrieving the users' location and time implicitly. The mobile prototype will deliver a notification of the alert that has been sent by other nearby participants at that time. Personalized advice on how to manage the crop was also disseminated. On the other hand, the personal subscriber level privacy has been operationalized by retrieving the users' location only if the individual has request for the notification explicitly. Hence, personalized advice will only be sent to the user if the user has explicitly requested for it. The manipulations of the literate and semi-literate users were accessed through the pre-experiment survey which included questions related to their experience with mobile phones and education level.

4.3 Control Variables

Prior literature have suggested that additional factors that should be incorporated due to their potential impact on usage intention and apprehensions for location privacy. Therefore, in this study, we have controlled the demographics of our subjects. Demographic variance was found to have potential impact on the degree of apprehensions for location privacy.

5 Data Analyses

5.1 Manipulation Checks

The manipulation of personal subscriber and corporate-enterprise levels privacy were accessed based off the presentation on each screen. To evaluate success of the manipulations, we conducted an independent T-Test. The outcomes conclude that the treatments were manipulated successfully. The participants understood that the methods used to deliver the notification to them were different (F = 4.182, t = 1.010, $p < 0.05$).

5.2 Factor Analysis

In this study, we conducted a principle component factor analysis to evaluate the dependability and legitimacy of apprehensions for location privacy and usage intention. Results are shown in Table 2. The eigenvalue for apprehensions for location privacy is 3.90 and the percentage of the variance is 58.2 explained by this factor.

The eigenvalue for usage intentions is 2.34, and percent of the variance is 33.20 explained by this factor. A total of 91.96 % of the variance can be explained by these two factors (see Table 3). Cronbach's alpha coefficients for the constructs far exceeded the threshold introduced by [16] which is 0.70. The measurements for location privacy apprehensions and usage intentions were highly reliable.

5.3 Hypothesis Testing

A two-way ANOVA was conducted in this study to analyze the relations between personal subscriber level privacy/corporate-enterprise level privacy and user group and their impact on apprehensions for location privacy and usage. The two-way

Table 2 Results of factor analysis

	Component	
	Apprehensions for location privacy	Usage intentions
PC1	0.94	0.29
PC2	0.93	0.28
PC3	0.94	0.24
PC4	0.92	0.33
PC5	0.92	0.26
PC6	0.90	0.30
U1	−0.31	0.88
U2	−0.37	0.89
U3	−0.35	0.90
U4	−0.27	0.90
U5	−0.36	0.90
U6	−0.11	0.82

Table 3 Variance explained

Factor	Cronbachs' alpha	Eigenvalue	Variance explained (%)	Cumulative variance (%)
Location privacy apprehensions	0.70	3.90	58.2	47.39
Usage intention	0.70	2.34	33.20	90.38

ANOVA emphasizes on testing the significance of the variations of means in diverse conditions in a between-subject design. It has been widely adopted in experimental studies to reveal the main and interaction effects of the categorical independent variables on interval dependent variables. Therefore, the two-way measure ANOVA is a suitable statistical method to examine the main and interaction effects of personal subscriber/corporate enterprise level privacy and user groups on location privacy apprehensions and usage of mobile applications. Regression was used to inspect the relationship between privacy apprehensions and usage of mobile application.

Location Privacy Apprehensions

Data associated with location privacy apprehensions was analyzed using the two-way ANOVA test with two between-subject factors as independent variables personal subscriber/corporate enterprise level privacy and user group. The mean values and standard deviations are shown in Table 4, while the results of the two-way ANOVA test are presented in Table 5.

Figure 1 shows the interaction effect of personal subscriber level privacy/corporate-enterprise level privacy and user group on location privacy apprehensions. It shows that corporate enterprise level privacy channel triggers a

Table 4 Means and standard deviations for privacy apprehensions

User group	LBS	Location privacy apprehensions	
		Mean	Standard deviation
Semi-literate	Corporate enterprise	4.87	0.21
	Personal subscriber	3.43	0.39
Literate	Corporate enterprise	4.70	0.26
	Personal subscriber	3.30	0.28

Table 5 Results for two-way ANOVA on privacy apprehensions

	F	P-value	Observed power
User group	3.22	0.01	1
LBS	610.76	0.00	1
Group LBS	0.161	0.10	0.068

Fig. 1 Estimated marginal
means of location privacy
apprehensions

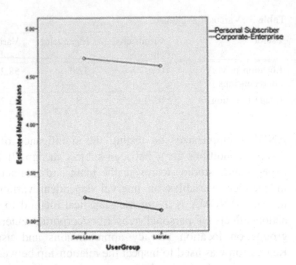

Table 6 Results of regression

Model	Unstandardized coefficients		Standardized coefficients	T	Sig
	B	Std. error	Beta		
(Constant)	7.14	0.15		42.83	0
Location privacy apprehensions	−0.25	0.03	−0.26	−6.53	0

higher privacy apprehension in both the literate and semi-literate users. The results in Table 5 suggest that there is no significant interaction effect between personal subscriber/corporate-enterprise level privacy channel and user group on location privacy apprehension. Hence, H1 is not supported.

Location Privacy Apprehensions and Usage Intention
The relationship between location privacy apprehensions and usage intention needs to be examined to satisfy the independence assumption. Location Privacy Apprehensions negatively influence usage intentions (B = −0.25, $p < 0.05$), as presented in Table 6. Hence, H2 is supported.

6 Discussion

6.1 Key Findings

This study was conducted in a laboratory experiment to examine if a personal subscriber level privacy or corporate-enterprise level privacy has impact on apprehensions for location privacy among the literate and semi-literate. Our findings suggest that personal subscriber level privacy/corporate-enterprise level privacy does have impact on both literate and semi-literate users. The corporate-enterprise level privacy triggers a greater degree of apprehension for location privacy than the personal subscriber level for both groups of user. This is in line with prior research (e.g. [4]) that technologies that conducts surveillance triggers a greater apprehension for location privacy.

The semi-literate users show no significant difference in the degree of apprehension for location privacy from the literate user. This is an interesting finding because previous studies (e.g. [20]) suggests that education level does influence apprehensions for location apprehension. One plausible explanation is that individuals are just coping with the current situation. In fact, the existing privacy literature only carry out their study with the literate users.

6.2 Theoretical Implication

This study focuses on the impact of technological attributes on users' apprehensions for location privacy. RALC was used to examine factors that will affect usage of LBS. It provides empirical evidence on the significance of literacy level and the technological attributes in accessing individuals' apprehensions for location privacy and usage intentions. It is critical for researchers to consider the reasons behind using LBS before designing each system because it will affect the apprehensions that the individual will have which will have a negative impact on individuals' usage behavior.

Secondly, our study examines the effects of the different types of privacies in LBS and individuals' literacy level on the apprehensions for location privacy. Our results suggest that the apprehensions for location privacy have a negative impact on usage intention. It also suggests that usage intention is higher when individuals are given the option to adopt the personal subscriber level privacy. Hence, it is important that developers consider about the personal subscriber level privacy when developing new application.

Third, our study expands the knowledge about apprehensions for location privacy from individual users to user groups.

6.3 Practical Implications

Many developers are leveraging on the ability of mobile devices to obtain users' location to develop applications that will deliver personalized information to individuals to attract usage. Hence, the results in this study can educate these developers on the appropriate privacy model to use such that individuals' apprehension for location privacy can be reduced. A reduction in apprehension for location privacy can increase usage intention. Since individuals have more apprehensions over corporate-enterprise level privacy, application developers should work closely with the company to implement measures for privacy protection. An example of such measures could be adopting privacy enhancing technologies, which can be a kind of industrial guidelines for privacy protection. This will increase the individuals' confidence to cooperate with companies to use the LBS that incorporates the corporate-enterprise level privacy.

Individuals should also be conscious of the different types of privacies in LBS to make full use of the benefits provided by LBS. Being conscious would enable individuals to avoid being tempted by untrusted applications. These untrusted applications may be in a form of games, which provides hedonic values, but it may be adopt privacies that are similar to corporate-enterprise level privacy where individuals' location will be monitored implicitly over time.

Regulators can help to reduce individuals' privacy apprehensions by introducing education programs to educate individuals on how to avoid being tempted by untrusted applications. Developers, being the custodian of individuals' location information, should assist the regulators by providing regulations on the measures that each developer should take to protect the location information that is collected.

7   Limitations and Future Work

Like many other studies, this study also has limitations. First, the experiment is done in a laboratory setting, which does not comply, to the actual mobile usage setting where individuals tend to multitask. This experiment can be improved by conducting an ethnographic study where individuals' mobile usage behavior can be observed.

Second, the mobile application we developed for our experiment was in the agriculture context. The participants were asked to play the role of the farmer. The literate participants who have never done farming before might not have a clear idea of the apprehensions that a farmer might have. Future studies may repeat this study by including literate farmers.

Third, the participants who participated in this study were from Asian countries. Asian countries have a very distinct set of cultures, which might not be applicable to other cultures like the western culture. Hence, the results may not be generalizable to other cultures. Future studies may conduct this study with participants that are not from the Asian culture.

8   Conclusion

The growing prominence of mobile application continues to provide increasing value to users, while at the same time creating new channels for user to be exposed to location privacy threats. It is critical for researchers, developers and policymakers to understand how users perceive and weigh the resulting value and risk. Therefore, this study has offered some empirical evidence for this predicament. It has contributed to the existing literatures by spreading knowledge into group level by using the restricted access/limited control theory and the different technological attributes. The findings in our study have proposed that the different type of location apprehension does have impact on the individuals' apprehensions. The semi-literate users have shown similar apprehensions as compared to the literate users. Future researchers could contribute significantly to the foundations laid in this study by extending our theoretical understanding and practical ability to help the literate and semi-literate users to protect their location privacy apprehensions while using mobile applications.

Acknowledgements This research is supported by the National Research Foundation, Prime Minister's Office, Singapore under its International Research Centres in Singapore Funding Initiative and administered by the Interactive Digital Media Programme Office.

References

1. Angst, C., Agarval, R.: Adoption of electronic health records in the presence of privacy concerns: the elaboration likelihood model and individual persuasion. MIS Q. **33**(2), 339–370 (2009)
2. Carolyn, W., Beth, E.: Studying mobile phone use in context: cultural, political, and economic dimensions of mobile phone use. In: International Professional Communication Conference Proceedings, pp. 205–212. IEEE, Limerick, Ireland (2005)
3. Chua, W.Y., Chang, K.T.T., Wan, P.H., Yi, W.: Improving mobile applications usage experience of novice users through user-acclimatized interaction: a case study. In: Twentieth Americas Conference on Information Systems. AIS Electronic Library, Savanna, Georgia (2014)
4. Culnan, M.: How did they get my name?: An exploratory investigation of consumer attitudes toward secondary information use. MIS Q. **17**(3), 341–363 (1993)
5. Culnan, M.: Consumer awareness of name removal procedures: implications for direct marketing. J. Direct Mark. **9**(2), 10–19 (1995)
6. Culnan, M., Armstrong, P.K.: Information privacy concerns, procedural fairness, and impersonal trust: an empirical investigation. Organ. Sci. **10**(1), 104–115 (1999)
7. Dinev, T., Hart, P.: Internet privacy concerns and their antecedents-measurement validity and a regression model. Behav. Inf. Technol. **23**(6), 413–422 (2004)
8. Gefen, D., Karahanna, E., Straub, D.: Trust and TAM in online shopping: an integrated model. MIS Q. 51–90 (2003)
9. Hann, I.-H., Hui, K.-L., Lee, S.-Y.T., Png, P.L.: Overcoming online information privacy concerns: an information-processing theory approach. J. Manag. Inf. Syst. **24**(2), 13–42 (2007)
10. Herman T.H., Moor, J.H.: Privacy protection, control of information, and privacy-enhancing technologies. ACM SIGCAS Comput. Soc. **31**(1), 6–11 (2001)
11. Ling, L.: From data privacy to location privacy: models and algorithms. In: Proceedings of the 33rd international Conference on Very Large Data Bases, pp. 1429–1430. ACM Digital Library, Vienna, Austria (2007)
12. Luhmann, N.: Familiarity, confidence, trust: problems and alternatives. Trust: Making Breaking Coop. Relat. **6**, 94–107 (2000)

13. Masizana-Katongo, A., Morakanyane, R.: Representing information for semi-literate users: digital inclusion using mobile phone technology. Department of Computer Science, University of Botswana, Gaborone (n.d.)
14. Moor, J.: The ethics of privacy protection. Library Trends **39**(1–2), 69–82 (1990)
15. Ning, A.: Mobile internet services personalization customization via Mobile portals. In: Web Information Systems and Mining, pp. 381–385. IEEE, Shanghai, China (2009)
16. Nunnally, J.: Psychometric Theory. McGraw-Hill, New York (1978)
17. Sandys, A.: Key growth opportunities for global smartphone market lie increasingly in developing countries, 31 Oct 2014. Retrieved from Yahoo Finance: https://uk.finance.yahoo.com/news/key-growth-opportunities-global-smartphone-000000662.html
18. Sheehan, K.: Toward a typology of internet users and online privacy concerns. Inf. Soc. **18**(1), 21–32 (2002)
19. Srinivasan, J.: The role of trustworthiness in information service usage: the case of parry information kiosks, Tamil Nadu, India. In: ICTD 2007: Information and Communication Technologies and Development, pp. 1–8. IEEE, Bangalore, India (2007)
20. Tan, Z., Chua, W., Chang, K.: Location based services and information privacy concerns among literate. In: 47th Hawaii International Conference on System Science, pp. 3198–3206. IEEE, Hawaii (2014)
21. Thomas, D., Strauss, J., Maria-Helena, H.: How does mother's education affect child height? J. Human Resour. 183–211 (1991)
22. Venkatesh, V., Morris, M.G., Davis, G.B., Davis, F.D.: User acceptance of information technology: toward a unified view. MIS Q. 425–478 (2003)
23. Westin, A.: Privacy and freedom. Washington Lee Law Rev. **25**(1), 166 (1967)
24. Xu, H.: The effects of self-construal and perceived control on privacy concern. In: 28th Annual International Conference on Information Systems. Montreal, Quebec, AIS Electronic Library, Canada
25. Xu, H., Teo, H., Tan, B.C.Y.: The role of push-pull technology in privacy calculus: the case of location-based services. J. Manag. Inf. Syst. **26**(3), 135–174
26. Xu, H., Teo, H., Tan, B., Agarwal, R.: Research note—effects of individual self-protection, industry self-regulation, and government regulation on privacy concerns: a study of location-based services. Inf. Syst. Res. **23**(4), 1342–1363 (2012)

Towards an Ontology for Enterprise Interactions

Youcef Baghdadi

Abstract Enterprise interactions allow collaborations that add value, in terms of solutions for supporting flexible intra- and cross processes, interfacing the enterprise to its environment, and enabling its objects to act and react within their environment. In addition, they enable emerging knowledge. However, there is a lack of ontologies for interactions. Interaction ontology would share, integrate, and manage knowledge. This paper presents a typology of enterprise interactions towards a lightweight ontology for interactions that facilitate their engineering. First, it distinguishes different types of interactions by their nature, their issues, and their current realizations. Then, it conceptualizes them for the purpose of their modeling, design, realization, evaluation, and analysis. Finally, it proposes a lightweight ontology.

Keywords Enterprise interactions · Conceptualization of the interactions · Lightweight ontology of interactions

1 Introduction

The concept of interactions has been given much importance in many disciplines, including the computing related ones such as artificial intelligence, databases, and distributed systems. An interaction involves two actors that act in re-action to each other action [1]. In information systems, the communities considered the interactions from the perspective of cooperation in different situations such as cooperation between subsystems (e.g., databases), cooperation between people (e.g., groupware), and cooperation at the organization level. Cooperation is considered as solutions, through cooperative information systems, to the distribution that results

Y. Baghdadi (✉)
Department of Computer Science, Sultan Qaboos University, PO Box 36, PC 123, Al-Khod, Muscat, Oman
e-mail: ybaghdadi@squ.edu.om

© Springer International Publishing Switzerland 2016   263
F. Ricciardi and A. Harfouche (eds.), *Information and Communication Technologies in Organizations and Society*, Lecture Notes in Information Systems and Organisation 15, DOI 10.1007/978-3-319-28907-6_17

from the organization of work, but specifically from the widespread information and communication technologies (ICT) [2]. These solutions are primarily integration architectures that abstract syntactic and semantic interoperability to enable cooperation between actors (i.e., subsystems of the information systems.

In addition, we argue that enterprises need to implement interactions for different purposes and in different situation [3]. Indeed interactions do:

- Happen at different levels, as the involved actors may be subsystems of the enterprise information system, employees, customers, partners, suppliers, competitors, and even things of the enterprise and its environment.
- Constitute solutions for the business changing requirements in terms of value resulting from different types of collaborations, as they constitute solutions for supporting flexible intra- and cross business processes (BPs), interfacing the enterprise to its environment, and enabling its objects to act and react within their environment.
- Enable emerging knowledge that does exist anywhere, as the knowledge emerging from the interactions of the involved actors is greater than the sum of their knowledge. This knowledge may be used in day-to-day operation or in the business intelligence.

From a technology perspective, most of the integration for intra- and inter-organizational BPs has been driven by advances in technology [4, 5] and realized, on case-by-case basis, by using adapters, wrappers, object oriented middleware such as CORBA, DCOM, or EJB, which has resulted in the well-known $N * (N - 1)$ integration problem [6]. The distributed architecture SOA based that is based on web services technology has been expected to enable integration, composition, flexibility, and agility [7, 8]. Indeed, web services technology is a de facto internet integration standard. Web services technology allows interfacing, publishing, and binding loosely coupled services on the web. Applications are offered as services both within and across the enterprise with lower development costs [9, 10].

However, still there is a lack of a comprehensive view of the enterprise interactions, within the enterprise architecture, which enables their engineering. In this work, interactions are considered from a conceptual perspective, namely a value added perspective of the work organization and ICT. Indeed, while work organization and ICT have widespread the distribution, they constitute solutions for adding value, specifically in terms of: (i) architectures for integration such as supply chain, extended enterprise, virtual enterprise and integrated enterprise, (ii) interfaces for enterprise social interactions, and (iii) architecture for cooperating objects such as those in the Internet of Things (IoT) paradigm.

Therefore, there is a need for comprehensive conceptualization that leads to a shared, reusable ontology. An ontology is "a formal, explicit specification of a shared conceptualization" [11]. We build on this definition to use conceptualization that refers to a comprehensive, abstract model of the interactions that:

- Constitutes a step towards an ontology for interactions.
- Guides the engineering methods of the interactions, including processes, representation techniques, and tools.

This paper presents a typology of the enterprise interactions, as a first step towards ontology for interactions that facilitate their engineering. First, it separates the interaction activities from the business activities. Then, it distinguishes the different types of interactions by their nature, their issues, and their current realizations with ICT. Finally, it conceptualizes them for the purpose of their modeling, design, realization, evaluation, and analysis.

The remainder of this paper is organized as follows: Sect. 2 introduces the foundation concepts of ontology such as methods, tools and languages to build ontologies. Section 3 details different types of interactions, showing their commonalities and differences. Section 4 details the conceptualization as primordial step towards ontology. Section 5 presents some related work. The conclusion section shows the practical and theoretical impacts and presents further development.

2 Foundation Concepts

This section introduces the foundation concepts of ontology such as methods, tools and languages to build ontologies.

2.1 Definitions

The term ontology comes from philosophy, where philosophers attempted to classify things in the world. It is used to describe the existence of the beings in the real world [12]. Specifically, an ontology is a set of concepts, relationships, instances and axioms, where:

- A concept represents a set of class or a collection of entities, objects, or things of the domain.
- A relationship links concepts. It may be a taxonomy (e.g., 'is-a', 'has') or an association.
- An instance is a specific occurrence of the class/collection.
- An axiom is a kind of constraint on the concept, their relationships and their instances.

The most quoted definition is "an ontology is a formal, explicit specification of a shared conceptualization" by Gruber [11]. The key terms in this definition are: 'conceptualization', 'shared', 'formal' and 'explicit'. Conceptualization means a framework or an abstract model (representation) of some phenomenon in its environment. This abstract model should identify the relevant concepts related to the phenomenon, the relationships between these concepts and the constraints on the concepts and their relationships. In addition, the conceptualization should be shared, which means that the captured knowledge is consensual and accepted by a community. Formal means that the ontology should be machine readable to be exchanged. Explicit means that the concepts, the relationships and the constraints (on the concepts and their relationships) used in the ontology are explicitly defined.

The ontology community distinguishes lightweight ontologies that are taxonomies from heavyweight ontologies that model the domain in a deeper way and provide more restrictions on domain semantics. In other words, heavyweight taxonomy is a taxonomy augmented with axioms and constraints.

2.2 Methods, Tools, and Languages

Methods concern with the process of building an ontology, where the main activities can be summarized as identification of the purpose, development, evaluation, and documentation. The development activities can be further decomposed into specification, conceptualization, formalization, and implementation. There exist many methods such as KACTUS, METHONTOLGY, SENSUS, and On-to-Knowledge.

Automated tools assist all the activities of the process, specifically the development activity. Ontolingua and Protégé 2000 are examples of such tools. Likewise, there exist many languages that aim to formalize ontologies, making them machine-readable. For instance, in Web computing there exist a stack of XML-based markup such as RDF, RDFS, OIL, DAML+OIL, and OWL.

2.3 Ontology for the Interactions

Nowadays, ontologies are widely used by different communities and for different purposes. From a computing perspective, the communities of knowledge engineering and artificial intelligence, databases, software engineering, web computing, or e-commerce are using ontologies for different purposes, namely natural language processing, knowledge management, intelligent information integration, semantic web, or e-commerce (e.g., business to business). For instance, ontologies were first adopted in artificial intelligence to describe what knowledge can be computationally represented in a program. Likewise, databases and software engineering communities build ontologies as domain model by using concepts (e.g., entities, classes), relationships (is-a, has, many-to-many), attributes and properties. In Web computing, several ontologies have been developed by using methodologies, languages, and tools [13], namely XML-based markup languages such as RDF, RDFS, OIL,

DAML+OIL and OWL. In e-commerce standards such as UNSPSC, e-cl@ss and RosettaNet are used as ontologies.

However, there is a lack of ontologies for interactions that would help their engineering; and the cooperative system community should give it the right priority, mainly for the purpose of intelligent information integration and knowledge management. Indeed, the interactions contribute in such types of systems that add value.

The section will introduce taxonomy of the interactions starting by a typology.

3 Typology of Interactions

We characterize four types of the enterprise interactions, by: (1) the nature of the needs: integration of private BPs, sharing of informational and computational resources, integration of inter-organizational BPs, social interfacing of the enterprise, and interfacing the objects of the enterprise with those of their environment; (2) the nature of the issues, and (3) the nature of architectural solutions.

3.1 Interactions Between Subsystems

The interactions between the subsystems (SS_1, SS_2, ...SS_n) of the enterprise support the flexibility of local BPs and the sharing of the enterprise information (e.g., business objects) and computational (e.g., functions or business rules) resources.

Such a type of interactions is mainly meant to make private BPs flexible and to also reduce the IT cost by:

– Reusing the business objects and business function.
– Integrating data and applications.

The main issue facing this type is the interoperability of the subsystems.

3.2 Interactions Between Organizations

The interactions between organizations are mainly used to integrate the enterprise BPs with those of its customers, partners, and suppliers in a supply chain.

This type of interactions is mainly meant to achieve collaborations that adds value such as supply chain, extended enterprise, virtual enterprise, or an integrated enterprise [14] for common business solutions (e.g., serve customers, market opportunities, offer new products/services, focus on professional core activities and skills, or deal with the business changes).

The main issues facing this type of interactions are:

- Autonomy and loose coupling of the actors
- Contract and agreements
- Security.

3.3 Enterprise Social Interactions

The social interactions of the enterprise are used to capitalize on social networks and media of its customers, suppliers, partners, employees, and competitors.

Such a type of interactions enables emerging knowledge that can be used to generate value and competitive advantages. These interactions can transform the company and its relations with its employees, customers, partners, suppliers, and even competitors [15]. Many researchers believe that these networks and social media can facilitate and even lead to the transformation of the company [16, 17]. They see in these interactions a force driving changes such as social commerce (which extends e-commerce) [18]. They are also used to:

- Collaboratively improve and innovate the BPs and their outputs that are products or services
- Create trustful communities around a context
- Help actors involved in making decision
- Trigger new customer's needs
- High visibility and reachability
- Better satisfaction of all involved knowledgeable actors, specifically communities of consumers.

The main issues facing this type of interactions concern with the broader impact of these technologies in various fields. In addition, the complexity of their characteristics, covering various disciplines, poses new challenges for research [16].

3.4 Interactions Between Things

The interactions between things in the real world of the enterprise and its environment (e.g., Internet of Things or IoT) are the next step in increasing the ubiquity of the Internet. It is a new paradigm that quickly gained the ground in the context of wireless telecommunications. The basic idea of this paradigm is the omnipresence of a variety of things or objects such as tags, sensors, actuators, mobile phones, etc. which, through unique addressing, are able to interact with each other and to cooperate with their neighbors to achieve common goals [19].

These four types of interactions have commonalties and differences.

3.5   Commonalities and Differences

The different types of interactions have some commonalities and differences in terms of requirements, issues, and solutions. Indeed, while all of them add substantial value in terms of cost reduction and innovative business solution, they have huge differences in terms of issues and solutions. Actually there exist several challenges and problems related to these types of interactions. These include standardization, naming of objects, mobility, privacy, data integrity, data, etc. [20]. Table 1 summarizes, for each type of interactions, the requirements, the issues, and the potential technology solutions.

Most of the interaction issues traditionally handled by the community mainly focus on the first two types of interactions. They usually focus on networks and communication protocols, interoperability, format and semantics of the exchanged content, integration and coordination mechanisms, standards, middleware, and especially public BPs for supply chains.

We raise the level of abstraction to consider an interaction management perspective through a distributed architecture that must be able to implement interactions, where actors are autonomous and loosely coupled. This architecture (components and connectors) must promote reuse, integration, composition, and

Table 1 Characteristics of each types of interactions

Type	Requirements	Issues	ICT solutions
Subsystems	Informational and computational resources sharing and reuse Internal integration	Interoperability (syntax and semantics) $N * (N - 1)$ integration	Adapter Wrappers EAI SOA
Organizations	Business solution via collaborations such as Supply chain Extended enterprise Virtual enterprise Integrated enterprise	Interoperability (syntax and semantic) $N * (N - 1)$ integration Autonomy Loose coupling Contract Agreement Security	Value added networks Web service SOA Standards such as RosettaNet
Social	Large scale collaboration (internal and external) Enterprise visibility Emerging knowledge	Privacy Legality Social damage Capitalization	Extended social networks and media knowledge management
Things	Value-added services via the interfacing of the objects (things)	Architectures, protocols and algorithms Integration with BPs	RFID Tagging

flexibility of intra- and inter-organizational BPs to make businesses agile, while aligning with them.

The complexity of such architecture, inherent to the different types of interactions, requires not only to solve the above mentioned traditional problems but also to solve the problems related to the management of interactions, in order to create value or use the knowledge that emerges from the interactions.

Managing interactions involves: (i) a cycle: planning-modeling-design-implementation-evaluation, and (ii) an artifact that manages the interaction, in this case the interaction manager (IM). This requires a conceptualization in terms of models of reference or abstract models (theoretical frameworks).

4 Towards an Ontology for Interactions

This section presents first the components of the proposed lightweight ontology, then the concepts of the proposed lightweight ontology of interactions.

4.1 Components of the Lightweight Ontology

The conceptualization provides concepts that are used in the proposed lightweight ontology. To make the conceptualization process easier, we first make a taxonomy, including the four aforementioned types of interactions.

Interactions between subsystems
The interactions between subsystems are summarized in Table 2. These are:

- Interactions between business functions (BF) of the enterprise's functional areas (FA).
- The interactions between the BFs of the same FA.
- The interactions between the BFs and the business objects (BO).

Interactions between organizations
The interactions between organizations involve the enterprise and its partners, suppliers, and customers, as summarized in Table 3 [6]. These are:

Table 2 Types of interactions between subsystems

Type	Relationship	Description
BFs in different functional areas	BF/BF (1)	Support of internal BPs crossing FAs
BFs of the same FA	BF/BF (2)	Support of FA's internal activities
BFs accessing BOs	BF/BO	Support BO's query

Table 3 Types of interactions between organizations

Type	Relationship	Description
B2B1	Enterprise/partners Enterprise/service provider	Focuses on core business activities
B2B2	Enterprise/suppliers	Focuses on agreements
B2B3	Enterprise/customer	Focuses on serving customers
B2C	Enterprise/consumer	Focuses on serving consumers

- The interactions for agreed-upon or virtual enterprises to integrate the private BP to those of the partners or the service providers; we refer to them as B2B1.
- The interactions that integrate the private BPs to those of the suppliers; we refer to them as B2B2.
- The interactions that integrate the private BPs to those of the customers (other enterprises); we refer to them as B2B3.
- The interactions that involve the enterprise and the individual customers; we refer to them as B2C.

Enterprise social interactions
The enterprise social interactions involve the enterprise, its employees, partners, suppliers, customers, regulation authorities, and competitors. The main elements that make enterprise social interactions possible are (i) the participants, (ii) the community, (iii) the participant/community co-created/shared content, and (iv) the relationships between them, as summarized in Table 4.

Interactions between the things
These involve the enterprise and things in its environment. They are expected to provide new intelligent and value-added services available anytime, anywhere. These services, enabled by the interactions among things provided with intelligence, could be integrated with current or new BPs.

Table 4 Types of enterprise social interactions

Type	Relationship
Content-Centered Interactions (CCI)	Interactions between the enterprise and the content
	Interactions between the actors and the content
	Community/content
Participant-Centered Interactions (PCI)	Interactions between the enterprise and the actors
	Interactions between the enterprise and the communities
	Interactions between the actors and the communities
Self-Centered Interactions (SCI)	Interactions between the participant
	Interactions and within the content
	Interactions between the communities

4.2   Lightweight Ontology

The proposed lightweight ontology is made up of a set of concepts and relationships, as summarized in Fig. 1. The main concepts are interaction, actor, collaboration, value, and protocol, whereby we assume the following:

– Content can interact, as it may be intelligent.
– Interactions are required for different types of collaborations.

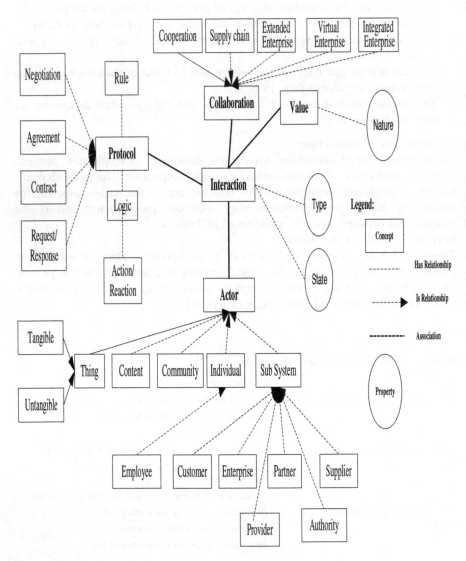

Fig. 1 A lightweight ontology

- Interactions generate value of different natures (e.g., benefit, cost cutting, new customer, etc.).
- Protocols support interactions. They may be specified by a set of rules and logic (action/reaction), depending on their type (negotiation, agreement, contract, a simple exchange).

It is worth noting that this ontology shows:

- The interaction taxonomy, where the actors are categorized into (1) subsystems, i.e., those of the enterprise or other organizations, (2) social such as individuals, communities and shared/generated content, and (3) things (tangible or intangible), as things can interact.
- The interaction intention, represented by the value added by the interactions with respect to the type of collaboration.
- The interactions realization through the protocols, where each protocol has a logic and a set of rules.

5 Related Work

There are only a few works related to conceptualization of the enterprise interactions. For instance, [1] distinguishes: (i) the interactions of units and individuals for whom they are responsible; (ii) the interactions of units with other units within the organization; (iii) the interactions of units with other organizations [1]. In [21], the author characterized interactions and their patterns; he developed a theory, in the social context, that explains the interaction and the outcome of interactions between individuals and groups, and between groups.

In [22], the authors have developed interaction protocols as abstract, modular, publishable specification of interaction in order to develop BPs. The authors argue that when such protocols are instantiated, they yield concrete BPs In [23], the authors argue that protocols for inter-organizational workflow systems can be modeled to be shared, reusable resources, which eases the design of such systems. In [24], the authors extended business process management notation (BPMN) diagram for interaction modeling. In [25], the authors developed enterprise interaction ontology that summaries the entities and relationships representing complex systems.

In a previous work [26, 27], we have developed a framework for the enterprise social interactions, and a Web services-based business interactions manager to support electronic commerce applications.

In this work, we provide a comprehensive framework that captures all the types of interactions to guide their management.

6 Conclusion

The interactions add value to the enterprise and its employees, customers, partners, and suppliers. They are dynamic, as they involve autonomous, loosely coupled participants. They need to be given much attention through their rational engineering and management.

We have provided a comprehensive framework that allows the necessary conceptualization for such an engineering and management. In this framework, we have first categorized the interactions into four types (1) interactions between subsystems of the information systems, (2) interactions between the organizations, (3) enterprise social interactions, and (4) interactions between things.

This kind of taxonomy constitutes a first step towards an interaction ontology to share and integrate emerging knowledge.

This work limits to a description of the different types and how they build on each other.

This work has practical and theoretical impacts. For the integration practitioners, it helps in engineering, namely designing and developing specific artifacts that serve each other. For the research community in cooperative information systems and integration, it opens many issues related to each type of interactions.

This work will be further developed with (1) interaction patterns (architecture, design, and implementation), (2) ontology specification, and (3) ontology building.

Acknowledgment The research leading to these results has received Project Funding from the Research Council of the Sultanate of Oman under Research Agreement No. ORG/SQU/ICT/14/011.

References

1. Ackoff, R.L.: Re-creating the corporation. Oxford University Press, New York (1999)
2. De Michelis, G., Dubois, E., Jarke, M., Matthes, F., Mylopoulos, J., Papazoglou, M., Yu, E.: Cooperative information systems: a manifesto. In: Cooperative Information Systems: Trends and Directions, pp. 315–165 (1997)
3. Baghdadi, Y.: Web-based interactions support for information systems. Informing Sci. **5**(2), 49–66 (2002)
4. Medjahed, B., Benatallah, B., Bouguettaya, A., Ngu, A.H., Elmagarmid, A.K.: Business-to-business interactions: issues and enabling technologies. VLDB J. Int. J. Very Large Data Bases **12**(1), 59–85 (2003)
5. Jung, J.Y., Kim, H., Kang, S.H.: Standards-based approaches to B2B workflow integration. Comput. Ind. Eng. **51**(2), 321–334 (2006)
6. Baghdadi, Y.: Architecture for deploying e-business: business processes, web services-based business interactions manager, and information systems. Int. J. Electr. Bus. **4**(1), 19–38 (2006)
7. Welke, R., Hirschheim, R., Andrew Schwarz, A.: Service-oriented architecture maturity. IEEE Comput. **56**(1), 61–67 (2011)
8. Baghdadi, Y.: A methodology for web services-based SOA realization. Int. J. Bus. Inf. Syst. **10**(3), 264–297 (2012)

9. Fensel, D., Bussler, C.: The web service modeling framework WSMF. J. E-Commer. Res. Appl. **1**(1), 113–137 (2002)
10. Baghdadi, Y.: A comparison framework for service-oriented software engineering approaches: issues and solutions. Int. J. Web Inf. Syst. **9**(4), 279–316 (2013)
11. Gruber, T.R.: Toward principles for the design of ontologies used for knowledge sharing. Int. J. Hum. Comput. Stud. **43**(5), 907–928 (1995)
12. Studer, R., Benjamins, V.R., Fensel, D.: Knowledge engineering: principles and methods. Data Knowl. Eng. **25**(1), 161–197 (1998)
13. Corcho, O., Mariano, F.L., Asunción, G.P.: Methodologies, tools and languages for building ontologies. Where is their meeting point? Data Knowl. Eng. **46**(1), 41–64 (2003)
14. Jagdev, H.S., Thoben, K.D.: Anatomy of enterprise collaborations. Prod. Plann. Control **12**(5), 437–451 (2010)
15. Kim, W., Jeaong, O.R., Lee, S.W.: On social web sites. Inf. Syst. **35**(2), 215–236 (2010)
16. Parameswaran, M., Whinston, A.B.: Social computing: an overview. Commun. Assoc. Inf. Syst. **19**(1), 762–780 (2007)
17. Kaplan, A.M., Haenlein, H.: Users of the world, unite! The challenges and opportunities of social media. Bus. Horiz. **53**(1), 59–68 (2010)
18. Baghdadi, Y.: From e-commerce to social commerce: a framework to guide enabling cloud computing. J. Theoret. Appl. Electr. Commer. Res. **8**(3), 12–38 (2013)
19. Giusto, D., Lera, A., Morabito, G., Atzori, L.: The Internet of Things. Springer, Berlin (2010)
20. Atzori, L., Iera, A., Morabito, G.: The internet of things: a survey. Comput. Netw. **54**, 2787–2805 (2010)
21. Giddens, A.: The Constitution of Society. Polity Press, Cambridge (1984)
22. Desai, N., Malaya, A.U., Chopra, A.K., Sing, M.P.: Interaction protocols as design abstractions for business processes. IEEE Trans. Softw. Eng. **31**(12), 1015–1027 (2005)
23. Andonoff, E., Bouaziz, W., Hanachi, C.: A protocol ontology for inter-organizational workflow coordination. In: Advances in Databases and Information Systems, pp. 28–40. Springer, Berlin (2007)
24. Decker, G., Barros, A.: Interaction modeling using BPMN. In: Business Process Management Workshops, pp. 208–219. Springer, Berlin (2008)
25. Kumar, A., Raghavan, P., Ramanathan, J., Ramnath, R.: Enterprise interaction ontology for change impact analysis of complex systems. In: Asia-Pacific Services Computing Conference, 2008. APSCC'08, pp. 303–309, IEEE (2008)
26. Baghdadi, Y.: Enterprise social interaction patterns for enterprise transformation. J. Enterp. Transform. **3**(4), 307–329 (2013)
27. Baghdadi, Y.: A web services-based business interactions manager to support electronic commerce applications. In: The 7th International Conference on Electronic Commerce, pp. 435–445. ACM (2005)

Employer Branding and Social Media Strategies

Eliane El Zoghbi and Karine Aoun

Abstract Employer branding has nowadays become a strategic tool used by companies to develop the e-relationship with their partners (e-Partner Relationship Management). This article treats the evolution of employer branding on social media platforms, and uses a study to better understand the new facets of employer branding created by social media. Through interviews with a number of hotel managers in Paris, we will present the evolution of this concept as well as summarize the different facets of the e-employer branding within social media.

Keywords E-employer branding · Social media · Facets of employer branding · Strategies of usage of social networks

1 Introduction

Nowadays, companies, in order to build an image of corporate responsibility have gone beyond direct marketing to reach social media (SM). Employer branding has become a strategic tool used to develop the e-relationship with partners (e-Partner Relationship Management). Using social media, employer branding evolves and enables companies to promote their image and reputation in front of their stakeholders: customers, employees, suppliers, partners and governmental entities. Through its e-employer branding, a company looks towards communicating the codes of good conduct it has adopted as well as its engagements in the field of social responsibility. Hence employer branding exceeds its utilitarian vision that

E. El Zoghbi (✉)
Université Paris Ouest Nanterre La Défense, Paris, France
e-mail: elianezoghby@hotmail.com

K. Aoun
Université Saint Joseph, Beirut, Lebanon
e-mail: karine_aoun@yahoo.com

© Springer International Publishing Switzerland 2016
F. Ricciardi and A. Harfouche (eds.), *Information and Communication Technologies in Organizations and Society*, Lecture Notes in Information Systems and Organisation 15, DOI 10.1007/978-3-319-28907-6_18

aimed at making the company attractive to its target employees or potential partners to include more hedonistic and social values [1].

This drives us to ask the following questions: How has the concept of employer branding evolved within social media? What are the different facets of this new construct? What are employer brand strategies adopted by companies to communicate with their different stakeholders using social media?

To answer these questions, we shall start by summarizing the principal theories that tackle employer branding; a concept situated at the crossroad between two fields: Marketing and Human Resources. We will then associate these theories with those related to social media. By doing so, our objective is to update this information through the development of a holistic vision of the notion of employer branding.

Our methodology consists firstly of conducting a qualitative study. This will be followed in the future by the construction of a research model and a quantitative study with a test of hypotheses. Within this paper, we will focus only on our qualitative study. Results are constituted based on the analysis of nine interviews with Parisian hotel managers. The objective of this phase is to restitute a large part of the complexity that accompanies the creation of a holistic employer brand with the help of social media.

2   From Traditional Marketing to Employer Branding

Following the end of the Second World War, the traditional 4P marketing has not ceased to evolve with the aim of pushing products towards consumers. This type of marketing was however accused of being responsible for some of the evils of our modern society [2]. For example, advertising campaigns that encourage consumers to buy fattening food and drinks can lead to obesity and other illnesses. Likewise, companies that pollute are directly and indirectly responsible for climate change.

These misfortunate factors have led to the evolution of the concept of the commercial brand and transformed it into what is known as a holistic brand whose aim is to develop a durable relationship with its partners. As such, the challenge for companies is not only to attract consumers but also to highlight their corporate values and take an active stand in the field of social responsibility (CSR). Hence, companies do not hesitate to communicate with their stakeholders in order to underline the efforts they have exerted to adopt certain moral, social and environmental requirements.

2.1   The Evolution of the Notion of Brand

A few decades ago, the word brand was defined as being «a visible, physical and durable attribute placed on an object to distinguish it from others» [3]. Researchers were however, quick to differentiate between the brand and the product's physical attributes. Hence, Kapferer [4] defined it as «a name and a group of symbols that guarantee the origin of a product or service, which differentiate it from competing products and services and which influence consumer behavior by arousing mental representations and creating an emotional link». The brand has therefore become «a group of associations (...) that allow branded products to achieve sales volumes and margins which are higher than those reached without mentioning the name of the brand» [4].

It represents a value, an expertise, a story, a promise and a guarantee that helps consumers in making a choice [5]. In addition to these definitions, Séguéla [6] recommended a description of brands according to three facets: physical, character and style. The physical concerns products and their performances. The character represents the facets of the personality of the brand. The style concerns the manner in which communication is executed. Darpy and Gomy [7] proposed three central concepts linked to the brand: brand image, positioning and identity. The image is the positive or negative opinion of consumers at any given time [8]. The positioning represents the place a brand occupies in the mind of consumers [9]. The identity as defined by Kapferer [4] is considered to be a prism formed of six facets: physical (material characteristics and product packaging), personality (the set of personality traits that are specific to the brand), relation (the communication between the brand and its customers), culture (the system of values on which the brand is based), reflection (the target chosen by the company and which is often different than the real target), and realization (the ideal a consumer pursues when buying and using a brand).

2.2 The Brand: Beyond the Product

With time, the will to build a brand identity quickly exceeded traditional marketing to reach human resources [10]. The challenge for companies was not only to attract consumers but also to attract qualified employees [11]. Therefore, they did not hesitate to communicate with this new target which was made up of future employees. Their aim was to make their company attractive to targeted employees or potential human resources. This concept thus developed into what has become known as «Employer Branding» [12].

Today, employer branding continues to evolve and aims at targeting all of a company's stakeholders, including the government and public entities, partners, opinion leaders, investors, syndicates... In fact, stakeholders are nowadays more informed and more engaged, and companies tend to look towards positioning themselves as employers that are socially and environmentally responsible. Within this context, employer branding can be defined as «a marketing strategy that promotes the reputation and notoriety of a company as an employer with regards to its stakeholders» [1].

Employer branding has therefore two effects: an internal effect and an external effect. The internal effect concerns employee's loyalty, whereby employees adhere to the values of a company and it becomes their preferred employer. Employer branding, plays on the propensity of employees to show interest in the company, stay, and be motivated to achieve corporate goals. Hence, they add value to the company and are capable of delivering the company's promise [13]. In this case, the company becomes an employer of choice by highlighting the qualities that are dear to employees.

The external effect aims at influencing: potential candidates in order to attract them, consumers within their buying behavior to convince them of the company's social responsibility and sell them products and services, syndicates to show an image of openness, public entities to communicate the company' transparency, and shareholders to show them growth perspectives. The external effect is therefore mainly based on credibility, transparency and business ethics, and growth perspectives.

2.3   The Content of the Employer Brand

In its beginning, the concept of the employer brand consisted solely of utilitarian values such as the benefits associated with an employment and an employer [12, 13]. Therefore, the employer brand was constructed around four dimensions: attractiveness (the capacity to attract and recruit candidates), reputation, employee engagement (employee motivation within the company) and differentiation (the actions that allow a company to distinguish itself from its competitors). However, with time, the definition of the employer brand evolved to include more hedonic and social values [1].

This new facet of hedonic and social values was first defined as the degree to which an individual is attracted to an employer that provides a working environment that is fun, happy, and provides a supportive team atmosphere [14]. But later the target of employer branding has become wider targeting all stakeholders (employees, customers, suppliers, partners, and governmental entities) [15]. Therefore, the hedonistic and social values gained a strategic role in the concept of employer branding. The new concept evolved to promote the company's reputation by communicating the codes of good conduct it has adopted as well as its engagements in the field of social responsibility [16].

Within this context, a company finds itself obliged to communicate accurate and complete information in order to avoid being accused of greenwashing [17]. Hence, social action exceeds the communicational goal to become a 'raison d'être', a managerial philosophy and a long-term vision.

3 Social Engagement and Social Network

Communicating accurate and complete information only works when the organization purposefully employs a "strategic engagement", ensuring that employee actions align with the stated aspiration. Organizations are therefore, investing in social networking because it helps them to identify key employees who are critical to the organization's communication flow it also offers them opportunities for communication on strategic engagement aimed at tuning the network to better promote organizational social engagement [18].

Hence they are using social networks in order to (1) communicate with these key employees; and in order to (2) develop regular sources of feedback from these employees.

Indeed, while firms have long recognized the importance of communicating with customers, they focused mainly on three relationships (firm-to-customer, customer-to-firm, and customer-to-customer) [19]. Employer e-branding using social media not only intensifies these three existing relationships but also creates new options such as firm-to-employee and employee-to-firm relationships. Indeed, social media increases the ability of firms to interact in firm-employee dialog, strengthening firm to-employee and employee-to-firm communications. The fundamental changes in the ease of contact, volume, speed, and nature of these interactions can encourage employees to engage in a social value creation process. Firms can respond to employee ideas quickly and increase their loyalty. For example, rather than the classic suggestion box, firms can use social media to solicit innovations. There is a growing body of work that suggests that employee engagement drives organizational effectiveness [20].

4 Research Methodology

Given the objective of our research, we adopted as a first step an interpretive stance for conducting our study [21]. Data collection took place between September 2013 and December 2013. After a period of intensive e-mail exchange, we were able to schedule nine one-to-one semi-structured interviews with directors of nine luxury hotels in Paris. Each interview session lasted for about 45 min. Prior to the interviews, we developed an exploratory interview guide. In validating our interpretations, we followed the set of principles advanced by Klein and Myers [22].

5 Research Results

The results of our qualitative research show that there are many facets of the employer brand. Indeed, according to the nine interviews conducted with nine managers of Parisian hotels, social networks are used by hospitality companies for new aims, such as underlying the company's engagement in:

- Supporting social progress,
- Co-creating value with all stakeholders,
- Paying back to the society,
- Sharing value: the creation of economic value that also creates value for the society,
- Solving complex social problems,
- Defending human and social values.

The usage of social networks follows the below two strategies:

1. Targeting the natural community of the company by directly targeting the employees and all the company's stakeholders. In this case, the logic is a "Need to know" where the company uses SN to communicate directly with its natural community. The main aim is to install a climate of trust and support.
2. Targeting the network of the company's employees and stakeholders encouraging them to like, to share and participate in the co-creation of content. In this case, the logic is a "Need to share" where the company transforms its community into active followers. This two-step communication aims to broadcast content that is likely to be widely reported beyond the natural community of the company. The aim is to promote social cohesion, innovation and productivity.

6 Conclusion

This study contributes to both theory and practice. By building the foundation of the social facets of employer brands, we provide a theoretical framework to understand the context of online interaction between the company and its employees and stakeholders.

Indeed, with SN, employer brand goes beyond its utilitarian and hedonic facets that aimed at making the company attractive to its target employees or potential partners, to include a third dimension which is mainly social. Our findings help extend the literature on employer brand within the context of social networks. Indeed, our qualitative results show that the social dimension aims clearly to promote the company's image and reputation in front of its stakeholders. The company communicates the codes of good conduct it has adopted as well as its engagements in the field of social responsibility. This is reflected in two strategies: the "Need to know" and the "Need to share" strategies.

Our qualitative research has many limitations. First, it is only based on nine interviews; and what we presented in this paper is only the first level of treatment and analysis. A second reading of the data is necessary. Based on future analysis, these results should be compared to the literature in order to develop an integrative model that will be tested in a quantitative confirmatory phase.

References

1. Maxwell, R., Knox, S.: Motivating employees to "live the brand": a comparative case study of employer brand attractiveness within the firm. J. Mark. Manag. **25**(9), 893–907 (2009)
2. Kotler, P., Keller, K., & Manceau, D. (2012). Marketing Management (éd. 14e édition). Paris: Pearson France
3. Lewi, G.: Sale temps pour les marques. Albin Michel, Paris (1996)
4. Kapferer, J.N.: Maîtriser l'Image de l'Entreprise: le Prisme d'Identité. Revue Française de Gestion, pp. 72–82 (1988)
5. Kapferer, J.N., Thoenig, J.C.: La marque: Moteur de la compétitivité des entreprises et de la croissance de l'économie. McGraw Hill, Paris (1989)
6. Séguéla, J.: Hollywood lave plus blanc. Paris, éd. Flammarion (1982)
7. Darpy, D., Gomy, P.: Le prisme d'identité de marque, outil pour l'analyse historique des publicités - Cahier no. 269 (Mars) Université Paris-Dauphine (1999)
8. Aaker, D.A.: Managing Brand Equity. The Free Press, New York (1991)
9. Dubois, P.L., Nicholson, P.: Le Positionnement, Encyclopédie du Management (1992)
10. Soulez, S., Guillot-Soulez, C.: Marketing de recrutement et segmentation générationnelle: regard critique à partir d'un sous-segment de la génération Y. Recherche et Applications en Marketing **26**(1), 39–57 (2011)
11. Wilden, R., Gudergan, S., Lings, I.: Employer branding: strategic implications for staff recruitment. J. Mark. Manag. **26**(1–2), 56–73 (2010)
12. Ambler, T., Barrow, S.: The employer brand. J. Brand Manag. **4**(3), 185–206 (1996)
13. Uncles, M., Moroko, L.: Employer branding—the case for a multidisciplinary process related empirical investigation. In: Sutar, G., Sweeney, J. (eds.) Broadening the Boundaries. ANZMAC Conference Proceedings, Perth, Australia, pp. 52–57 (2005)
14. Biswas, M., Suar, D.: 'Which employees' values matter most in the creation of employer branding?'. J. Mark. Dev. Competitiveness 93–101 (2013)
15. Das, T.V., Das, H.P.: Employer brand in India: a strategic HR tool for competitive advantage. Adv. Manag. **5**(1), 23–27 (2012)
16. Backhaus, K.B., Stone, B.A., Heiner, K.: Exploring the relationship between corporate social performance and employer attractiveness. Bus. Soc. **41**(3), 292. 27p (2002)
17. Athanasiou, T.: The age of greenwashing. Capital. Nat. Soc. **7**(1), 1–37 (1996)
18. Eisenberg, E.M., Johnson, Z., Pieterson, W.: Leveraging social networks for strategic success. Int. J. Bus. Commun. **52**(1), 143–154 (2015)
19. Gallaugher, J., Ransbotham, S.: Social media and customer dialog management at Starbucks. MIS Q. Executive **9**(4), 197–212 (2010)
20. Mishra, K., Boynton, L., Mishra, A.: Driving employee engagement: the expanded role of internal communications. J. Bus. Commun. **51**(2), 183–202 (2014)
21. Walsham, G.: Interpreting Information Systems in Organizations. Wiley, Chichester (1993)
22. Klein, H.K., Myers, M.: A set of principles for conducting and evaluating interpretive field studies in information systems. MIS Q. Spec. Issue Intensive Res. **23**(1), 67–93 (1999)

The Business with Digital Signage for Advertising

Christine Bauer, Natalia Kryvinska and Christine Strauss

Abstract The market for digital signage has been growing at an accelerated pace for years. The benefits of novel approaches—such as contextualization and inter-action functionalities—were soon recognized for achieving better advertising effects. However, the major types of digital signage currently in use have different requirements on the entire digital signage system. These requirements include components such as the digital signage network, digital signage exchange, scheduling, and pricing. The present paper discusses the differences between these components in depth. The core contribution of this paper is a detailed analysis of the potential of digital signage. Emphasis is placed on challenges in performance measurement and implementation, operating and using a digital signage system, display blindness, and negative externalities. Possible solutions, as well as best practices are presented. At its core, this paper provides an overview of the essentials of doing business with digital signage.

Keywords Digital signage · Contextualization · Interaction · Advertising

1 Introduction

The digital signage market has been growing rapidly for years, and the end of this growth is not yet in sight. According to various recent studies, the growth rates in digital signage market are expected to continuously grow until 2018. Positive

C. Bauer (✉)
Vienna University of Economics and Business, Vienna, Austria
e-mail: chris.bauer@wu.ac.at

N. Kryvinska · C. Strauss
University of Vienna, Vienna, Austria
e-mail: natalia.kryvinska@univie.ac.at

C. Strauss
e-mail: christine.strauss@univie.ac.at

© Springer International Publishing Switzerland 2016
F. Ricciardi and A. Harfouche (eds.), *Information and Communication Technologies in Organizations and Society*, Lecture Notes in Information Systems and Organisation 15, DOI 10.1007/978-3-319-28907-6_19

growth rates will not only appear in digital signage hardware industries, such as digital signage displays, media players, set-top boxes, and PCs, but also in digital signage-related infrastructural markets, such as software and services (cf. e.g., [1, 2]). A major factor in the wide-spread growth of this technology was the fall in the price of LCD screens, which are considered as the crucial hardware component in digital signage. Electronic (i.e., digital) displays used for digital signage offer new opportunities and advantages compared to traditional 'static' signage. For instance, digital technology allows information to be displayed in the form of dynamic multimedia presentations containing audio, video, and animated content (cf. [3]). Additionally, remote access to the digital signs and central scheduling within a digital signage network allows displays to adapt their contents based on both time and location. Adding additional systems and sensors to the digital signage network allows displays to exploit various additional information sources leveraged to better catch the audience's attention.

Digital signage is appropriate for various application areas. The broadest application is the point of sale (POS); the majority of applications in Western Europe take place in (public) transport areas, followed by leisure and gastronomy areas. Compensating for those groups of people that are nowadays quite hard to reach via traditional media such as newspapers and television commercials, digital signage might provide superior opportunities to approach this audience in a target-oriented manner. Several authors (e.g., [4]) claim that, to date, not much attention has been paid to the phenomenon of digital signage in academic literature. The quantity of literature elaborating on this topic might indeed be limited. Nevertheless, several interesting approaches investigate the related dynamics between digital signage and consumer reactions [5], interaction alternatives [4, 6], and strategic issues [7].

This paper will explain the major types of digital signage that are based on currently used technologies (Sect. 2). To provide an insight into the essentials necessary for digital signage business, this paper will outline digital signage system's infrastructure, forms and specific aspects that have to be taken into consideration; digital signage network, digital signage exchange, scheduling, and pricing are discussed in detail (Sect. 3). The core of this paper will analyze the potential and the challenges of digital signage (Sect. 4): challenges in implementation and performance measurement, in display blindness, as well as negative externalities and possible solutions together with best practices will be presented. The paper concludes with a summary and an outlook on further research alternatives.

2 Current Types of Digital Signage

Digital signage is a promising medium that prevails over the information clutter, because digital displays provide new opportunities and advantages over traditional 'static' signage [8]. For instance, digital signage displays dynamic presentations containing audio, video, and animations [3]. In contrast to traditional physical signs, digital signage virtually eliminates the costs of content distribution. In addition, a digital signage system can dynamically change content on its displays within milliseconds. This allows displays to present various advertising messages according to a schedule [9] or that are triggered by particular events.

The term "digital signage" describes networks of displays in public space. While digital signage may be employed for various purposes, e.g., displaying news, tourist information, or flight schedules, this term is most frequently mentioned when a display network is used for advertising [8]. Still, in the context of advertising, the term "digital signage" is quite often misplaced, as it is used to refer to any kind of shop TV or stand-alone screens in stores. For the scope of this paper, in line with [8, 10], we define and use the term "digital signage" for a dynamic, networked, visual or audio-visual information system consisting of several decentralized digital displays, which are interconnected with a central system (consisting of a content management system and a user rights management system) that allows for a remote control of the displays.

There are various types of digital signage solutions used on the market. Based on the location of deployment, we distinguished indoor and outdoor digital signage solutions. Most common examples for indoor solutions are interactive kiosks that are deployed in subway stations, shopping malls, or at airports. In recent days, some fast food chains have also recognized the value of the digital signage and applied those at their point of sale (POS). Most recognized examples of outdoor digital signage solutions are LCD screens deployed in the biggest public areas such as Times Square in New York or Shibuya in Tokyo, stored in a secure and weather proof TV enclosure.

Beyond placement, digital signage may be distinguished based on the application area [11]. Most solutions are deployed at a point of sale (POS). These are typically comprised of in-stores signs that strive for a consumer's attention in order to cause a conversion. At POS, the usual intended conversion is sales uplift. In these cases, the call to action is immediate as the screens are placed directly at the place where the consumer is making buying decisions. Another application area is represented by point of transit (POT). These advertisements are trying to grab attention of passers-by for a short time. The main purpose of these screens lies in the establishment of brand identity. The third application area is point of wait (POW). At such points, consumers have sufficient time to look at the signs and therefore the advertiser may use different tactics to engage the consumer's attention (e.g. more repetitions, longer advertisements with persuasive character). Examples of digital signage at POW are typically found in healthcare, retail banking, and office buildings [8].

2.1 Contextual Digital Signage

Providing relevant content is the key for sustainable advertising effects [12]. For instance, on the Web, contextual keyword advertising is known for its effectiveness:

Advertisements that are related to search keywords appear next to search results (e.g., market leader Google's AdWords [13]). Equipped with respective context-capturing sensors and other technologies, digital signs can adapt instantly to fit the situational context [9, 14]. Regarding advertising, this means that the digital signage system selects and displays advertisements based on contextual triggers such as time, location, weather, characteristics of beholders, etc. [15, 16].

Based on this information, in line with [8], we define contextual digital signage as "displaying an advertisement that is relevant to an individual or to a group of individuals in the present situation based on information about the current situation, which is retrieved, transformed, and/or deduced from any information sources".

In essence, contextual digital signage ensures that the advertisements are better targeted to the consumers as well as the current situations. Hence, the advertisements have a higher probability of being relevant and they gain more attention [12].

2.2 Interactive Digital Signage

Recent research emphasizes that interaction possibilities are able to increase consumer value by raising consumer engagement [17] or emotional perception [18]. In addition, digital signage may be enhanced, allowing consumers to interact with the system.

For instance, consumers may engage actively and intentionally with a digital sign-age system by touching a touch screen. In other implementations, consumers may interact implicitly with the system, with particular movements, for example. Vogel and Balakrishnan [19] presented gesture-controlled displays, interacting with passers-by according to the proximity to the screen. Müller and Krüger [20] developed a solution that can learn from its experience and, based on this information, can influence the advertisement scheduling and selection mechanism.

To conclude, interactive digital signage allows for greater involvement of audience, better user experience, and more accurate targeting.

2.3 Interactive Digital Signage with Mobile Devices

The advancement of information technologies (e.g., Radio-Frequency Identification (RFID), Bluetooth, gesture-sensing technologies) and the increased adoption of personal mobile devices equipped with such technologies (e.g., smartphones) make interaction an increasingly attractive option for furthering consumer engagement.

For instance, when a consumer approaches the coverage of a display, prepared advertisements may be supplied to the connected mobile device of the respective consumer [21]. Thereby, the connection may be accomplished via Bluetooth or Wi-Fi, for instance. A widely known example for this kind of interaction is the sending of vouchers via Bluetooth or SMS to the consumer's mobile device. An additional popular implementation is having consumers scan a Quick Response (QR) code on a display to receiving an advertisement or voucher on their personal mobile devices (cf. [20]).

Other solutions for interaction include using a personal mobile device to control the content on a nearby public display. As the short-range wireless communication technology minimizes delays between user and sign, it may be an effective method of low-latency interaction [1].

3 The Essentials for Digital Signage for Advertising

As outlined in Sect. 2, a digital signage system may be designed and implemented in various ways. Accordingly, there are also different business requirements that have to be considered when deploying a digital signage system. The following subsections provide an overview of a digital signage system's infrastructure, forms and the specific aspects that have to be taken into account in order to achieve a positive business performance.

3.1 Digital Signage Network

A digital signage network (DSN) connecting various displays significantly shortens the conventional CDI (creation, distribution, installation) cycle of a particular advertisement [22]. When an advertising campaign is designed, it can be directly and quickly transferred to some or all displays in the network. Compared to conventional signage, several steps, such as physical sign creation, distribution, and installation have become obsolete in a DSN (Fig. 1). On the one hand, the implementation of digital signage involves relatively high initial investments. On the other hand, the flexibility in content and the promptness of changing the content remotely leads to significant cost savings [8].

If a digital sign is located at the POS, for instance at a supermarket, the retailer's inventory system may be interconnected with the DSN. According to the current availability of a product at the respective retailer, a particular advertisement may be pushed or paused. This scenario is only one of the vast possibilities for *contextual* digital signage. In addition to the information about the inventory status, contextual data is also important when providing dynamically configurable promotion. If further contextual cues should be considered for a contextual digital signage system, the respective hardware and software needs to be interconnected to the DSN. For instance, if an advertisement should be selected based on the current weather situation, a connection to a service providing this information has to be established. For the specific case of weather information, two solutions are viable. Access to a

Fig. 1 Physical sign versus digital signage in the CDI cycle (based on [22, p. 166])

Web service providing weather information for a particular region is one solution, while weather-eliciting hardware (e.g., thermometer, wind gauge, etc.) can also be installed on site to provide the required information. In the event that characteristics of an individual nearby a display should trigger a certain advertisement, additional hardware and software solutions need to be installed on site. First, technology recognizes the presence of an individual has to be implemented; second, personal characteristics of the individual have to be captured (e.g., a camera may take a picture of the individual); and third, the captured information has to be analyzed (e.g., the individual's hair color needs to be analyzed based on the picture) and matched against predefined criteria (e.g., display the suitable hair coloring advertisement for the detected hair color).

For interactive digital signage, respective hardware has to be installed on site with every display on the network that should have the specific functionality. Touch is a typical interaction modality; it certainly requires a display to have touch functionality to enable this interaction type. Using a consumer's posture as the trigger for advertisement selection requires other hardware. Solutions found in literature typically use cameras and/or (Kinect) depth-cameras for being able to capture posture information [23, 24].

For having consumers interact with a digital signage system via their personal mobile devices, hardware has to be available on site (e.g., RFID scanner, Bluetooth). Care must be taken to build on technologies that are supported by widely used mobile devices. For instance, Near-Field Communication (NFC) solutions were implemented in Europe's kiosk systems long before Europe's mobile devices were equipped with such technology. This situation resulted in a wide-scale non-use of those solutions. In addition, consumers developed not-so-positive attitudes towards these systems, as they were not in a position to use them.

3.2   Digital Signage Exchange

To allow for the appropriate distribution of advertising space within a digital signage network, there is a need for digital signage exchange (DSE). Harrison and Andrusiewicz [22] describe DSE as a partially automated, supervised broker that mediates between sellers and buyers. The seller is defined as the entity that owns and controls digital signage solutions. More precisely, the seller may be the platform provider or the space provider. The buyers are usually advertising companies, interested in purchasing time slots for their clients.

Depending on the type of digital signage system employed, there may also be other entities participating in the DSE part, namely an (active) consumer, a space owner, and a context information provider [8]. The interactive feature of digital signage may, for instance, provide consumers with the option to comment on advertisements; these comments may be leveraged to adapt advertisements in future advertising cycles to the specific needs and preferences of the respective consumer or group of consumers.

Overall, DSE is an intermediary between all the involved players on the digital signage market. It is based on schedule management or—if time slots are sold by an auction mechanism—an auction bidding may decide which advertisement is displayed at what time on which display and at which price. This decision process is called transaction management model [22].

3.3 Scheduling

Getting the right message to the right audience and at the right time is the key element for providers of digital signage solutions. Storz et al. [25] state that the scheduling for collaborative displays (i.e., digital signage systems that enable users to share information) is mainly determined by an individual's interaction. Thus, the individual directly decides which content will be shown and there is no need for a complex scheduling system. On the other hand, the informational signs typically employ for scheduling looping playlists where the orders of other players/advertisers may impact the entire selection process.

The main function of DSE is to provide accurate information about available display time to buyer and seller. When a new order is placed, the DSE generates a partial schedule. Based on this schedule, the system calculates how many other orders may be accommodated. If the new or next order is placed, the system compares the partial schedule with the proposal and either accommodates the order as requested or proposes a counter-offer [3].

For contextual and interactive digital signage, Müller et al. [14] propose an autonomous machine learning mechanism using a so-called Naïve Bayes classifier that can apply scheduling strategies obtained from previous observations of the audience. Their concept consists of feedback loops, i.e., the digital signs adapt their content based on audience reactions. Thus, when the system recognizes that a person reacted on a certain sign under certain circumstances, it prioritizes this advertisement next time in a similar situation [14] (Fig. 2). Not only the buyer's order or contextual data, but also other factors may influence scheduling. Each deployment of digital signage is striving for financial sustainability. Therefore, there is a need for appropriate pricing mechanisms, which provide relevant information for an adequate scheduling system.

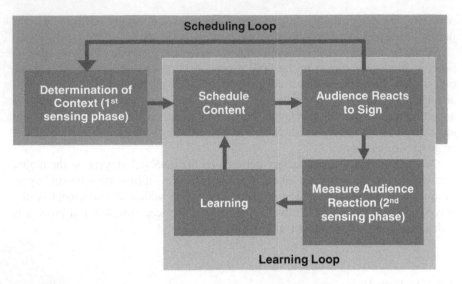

Fig. 2 Machine learning for scheduling in digital signage: information flow and loops (Adapted from [14])

3.4 Pricing System

Assuming that the platform provider (digital signage service provider or seller) aims to fulfill advertisers' needs (i.e., pushing the exposure of an advertisement in the advertising cycle and offering intended conversions), auction mechanisms seem to be a feasible option for pricing. In such cases, auction mechanisms typically lead to much higher conversion rates (up to 64 % as reported by [26]) than classic selection approaches such as the Round-Robin approach or Random approach.

Contextualization and interaction add aspects that have to be considered in a pricing system using auction mechanisms. Based on contextual information such as video captured by an integrated camera, a Bluetooth device connected to the digital sign, location or time, the most suitable advertisement even for lower bidding price may be favored and viable conversion rate achieved [27]. In general, the auctioning selection process consists of an advertising agent that is responsible for purchasing advertising space, and an auctioning agent that saves a history of successful advertising cycles (i.e., history of cycles in which the buyer won the auction, the respective advertisement was shown, and conversion was achieved). Based on these results, the system favors/disfavors an advertiser's bid in the next auctioning cycle [26]. This example is just one of the many used in practice. There are various algorithms for computing bids and consequently displaying advertisements. For example, Google has never completely revealed the bidding algorithm hidden behind its AdWords service. In order to utilize the auctioning process, Google also takes advantage of contextual data and applies it in the AdWords' auctioning mechanism. Buyers with higher Google page rank, more keywords, or better link quality need to bid less than those buyers with a poor rank or fewer keywords. In conclusion, this strategy will favor relevant buyers and produce appropriate results for the audience.

In general, the auctioning mechanism adopted in the field of digital signage in practice currently applies a second price auction [26]. The winning advertiser will never pay more than one bid increment above the bid amount of the advertiser in the second position, meaning that the winning buyer gets the time slot for the price of the bid of the second higher plus an increment, and the second buyer pays just one bid increment above of the bid of an advertiser in the third position; the amount of an increment bid varies between platforms but is generally about USD 0.01 [28].

4 Potential and Challenges of Digital Signage

4.1 Potential of Digital Signage

Digital signage is a promising and very attractive platform that has already gained its fixed place among other advertising tools. Digital signage offers some special features and benefits in comparison to the conventional, static form of campaigns. Based on its direct connection to the provider, a digital signage solution offers quick, effective and flexible controlling and displaying of content. The fast, flexible and on the fly update through the DSB, without the need to interact with the signs physically, eliminates high costs in comparison to creating and distributing print advertisement campaigns. Moreover, the possibility of selling advertising space to their suppliers contributes to the financial advantage of this solution screen providers too. Interactive digital signage is also more engaging, more informative, and offers targeted content that can grab a consumer's attention right at the POS and positively impact sales. Based on the solution deployed, passers-by might be enabled to interact with an advert through several technologies (e.g., Bluetooth, Wi-Fi, motion sensors). As the attention of consumers increases, such solutions also lead to a better Return on Investment (ROI) and lower financial expenses for CDI [8, 22]. However, many retailers still use paper-based promotional material in their retail outlets and are only beginning to upgrade to digital displays ('digital signage') [9].

There are several major arguments supporting the business rationale for deploying digital signage. Current trends demonstrate that the conventional way of attracting consumers is connected with high costs of CDI in terms of labor and material [22] and that using digital signage generates additional business value. Major applications of digital signage and drivers determining the underlying business rationale are selling display time (third party advertising), increasing sales, brand messaging, entertainment, internal communication, and alerting (cf. [29, 30]).

Table 1 The quasi-standards SMIL and POPAI [33, 44]

SMIL	POPAI
XML-based mark-up language for describing playlists, schedules and screen layouts	Similar use like SMIL
	Most commonly supported formats are: MP3,
	.AAC, .PCM, A-law, U-LAW, DiviX, Xvid,
Open standard established by the W3C	x264, .bmp, .jpg, .gif, .png, .avi, .mov, .asf,
Mostly used in USA, Germany, Denmark,	.mp4, TS, PS
France, and India	Pros: no dropped frames for video, no
One hardware vendor may drive about	noticeable distortion of audio and still images
100,000 screens using SMIL-enabled digital	from original
signage devices	

4.2 Challenge of Performance Measurement and Implementation

Deploying any digital signage solution requires, from a managerial point of view, the ability to measure the impact of these signs on the target achievement. Currently, the majority of providers usually give only approximate numbers of passers-by exposed to a screen [31]. However, there are also other approaches such as, for instance, In-Store Marketing Institute and VNU partnership on measuring the impact of digital signs in cooperation with supermarkets. In general, the measurements are accomplished individually, making it impossible to draw a cohesive conclusion on the results [32].

The lack of a *unified* standard represents a major challenge. The existence of such a standard would boost the overall development in this emerging field, but would at the same time interfere with market forces and competition. So far, several approaches have been established as quasi-standards. These standards are POPAI, SMIL, and HTML 5. The W3C consortium is preparing to launch a standard platform, which will potentially result in additional cost reduction of content acquisition and transmission in this field [33]. The initial workshop was held in 2011 where the needs and requirements of big digital signage users were consulted [30]. Table 1 provides an overview on the two most widely used quasi-standards, i.e. SMIL and POPAI.

4.3 Challenges of Operating and Using Digital Signage Systems

Operating the involved technologies poses challenges to advertisers as well as to consumers (cf. Table 2). For instance, many consumers have problems enabling Bluetooth on their mobile devices. Therefore, the camera (which is typically heavily used by most mobile device users) may be the better choice as the main transmitter of information for interactive digital signage. Vogel and Balakrishnan [19] also tested novel interactive public ambient displays that react to gestures and the

Table 2 Challenges of operating digital signage systems for advertisers and consumers (based on [14, 20])

Advertisers	Consumers
• The most important system feature for advertisers was measurability of advertising success followed by optimization of location • Advertisers tend to rely on the proposed scheduling by system, as scheduling effects currently are not sufficiently explored • Advertisers find it difficult to design their own campaigns with respect to contextualization and interactivity • Advertisers expect marketing support for digital signage solutions from advertising agencies due to a lack of knowledge with the technology • Before deployment, advertisers seem interested in controlling their campaigns (which sign, when, how, statistics); thereafter they tend to rely on the efforts by digital signage providers • Location is more important than content	• Consumers tend to prefer taking photos of coupons rather than having to operate Bluetooth or SMS solutions • The location of a display is very important in order to attract a consumer's attention • Younger generation/digital natives may be targeted with highly interactive solutions, while older generations/digital immigrants may have difficulties operating the involved technology • Interaction process may be perceived to be initially difficult for passers-by (understand how to interact with an interactive digital signage system) once they understand how to interact, people state that they enjoy using it • When the purpose of the camera is not explained, people tend to feel being "securely watched"

distance of passers-by to the display. Their research showed that these techniques are essentially easily and fast discoverable and useable. Still, it is very important to bear in mind which target group should be addressed, because it is the younger generation that pays attention to and interacts with interactive digital signage [20], as they are more accommodated to the technologies involved.

Furthermore, as various new technologies may be deployed in digital signage, such as gesture-based recognition (e.g., [6]) or body tracking systems (e.g., [34]), many additional challenges arise. Currently, major efforts are still necessary to bring those systems on a level that allows for easy and user-friendly interfaces for consumers.

Besides consumers, many advertising companies also face challenges in operating digital signage systems. For instance, Müller and Krüger [20] revealed that retailers lack the knowledge and competencies to design and configure their potentially interactive or contextual advertisements. As a result, providers of digital signage systems need to have comprehensive knowledge on complex issues and system properties to offer a full-package product to the potential buyer.

4.4 Challenge of Display Blindness

"Display blindness" is a major challenge for successful digital signage. The term was derived from a similar phrase, namely, from "banner blindness", which is characterized as the phenomenon of website users who are actively ignoring web banners [35]. Studies have confirmed that the "expectations towards what is presented on public displays can correlate with their attention towards these displays" [36]. Such display blindness is connected with an individual's informational overload (cf. [37]). When the advertising space is a scarce resource, digital signage is facing two negative externalities that can influence their deployment. Firstly, the local authorities can regulate the amount of advertising space. For the sake of these regulations, auction systems were recommended [12]. Auction mechanisms seem to be viable in terms of scheduling as well, since, compared to classic selection approaches, the conversion rate is higher [26]. Secondly, studies of [12, 20] revealed that there are still privacy concerns when using and collecting contextual data. Unfortunately, this data is crucial for contextual digital signage. As a result, in some cases the service cannot be tailored to the consumer's needs. There are several legal regulations must be taken into account. Generally, the person has to have the right to opt-out from collection of contextual data [38].

Furthermore, two major factors affecting a person's glance at a display have been identified: bottom-up effects and top-down effects (Table 3). Studies have revealed bottom-up effects that have impact on the display blindness (i.e., generating/increasing or reducing display blindness). Furthermore, studies indicate that displays at a POW receive more attention than displays deployed at a POT [14]. However, the location does not seem to have any effect as long as a person expects interesting information to be displayed. For instance, when the display was deployed in the school area, students expected interesting information, in contrast to

Table 3 Effects influencing display blindness (based on [14, 45])

Top-down effects
Individuals' expectations towards the perceived content can reduce display blindness; e.g., from public institutions people expect more relevant information than from commercial entities, which results in people paying higher attention towards displays placed in public institutions
Location does not have any effect on display blindness if an individual expects some interesting or relevant information
Bottom-up effects
Colourfulness and attractiveness reduces display blindness
Amount of display time; i.e., long distance visibility increases the probability that an individual notices the display
Size of display eliminates display blindness
Placing display in forward direction captures the attraction unintentionally
Displays that show video content tend to capture the eye longer than text
Displays at eye level or positioned considerably above the head draw more attention
Closer distance to other eye-catchers increases display blindness
Small displays may encourage prolonged viewing in public spaces to a greater extent than large displays

the displays placed in the city center, which were considered as "just another ad". As a result, the displays at schools were glanced more often [14]. This underlines the influence of contextualization on consumer perception. Overall, the factors summarized in Table 3 should be taken into consideration when setting up a digital signage system.

Additionally, Dennis et al. [4] examined the mediating factors on perception and emotions in terms of digital signage. People who are in good mood before shopping may have better perception of the products and—as a consequence—tend to buy and spend more [39]. Dennis et al. [4] add that advertisers may enhance this process by using sensory stimuli through the digital signage. They proved that digital signage has significant direct influence on the perception of the mall environment that consequently drives the consumer's willingness to buy and spend more (cf. [4]).

4.5 Negative Externalities and Possible Solutions

Digital signage faces the challenge of increasing effectiveness at locations engraved by information overload [40] as people are exposed to numerous advertisements in public space while the attention of an individual is limited. Paying attention to an advertisement can therefore be regarded as a cost for the consumer ("attention costs"). Only if the advertisement conveys useful information, while at the same time decreasing the attention costs, will the consumer see a 'net benefit'. An overload of signage, which is present at many places that are basically suitable for digital signage, is then simply the result of having more advertisements (causing too much costs) than would be 'optimal' [27]. Advertisers, however, do not directly calculate these costs, as they tend to focus on internal costs, such as costs for space rental or campaign design [9]. Consumers' attention costs are not included in transactions between buyers and sellers of advertising space for digital signage (i.e., transactions between platform/space providers and the advertiser). This situation is described as a negative externality in digital signage advertising [27].

At first thought, one might consider not having any advertisements at all to be a suitable solution in order to deal with negative externalities. Weiser and Brown suggest the opposite: "It seems contradictory to say, in the face of frequent complaints about information overload, that more information could be encalming" [41]. This implies that information overload is not the actual problem. Rather, the fact that consumers become annoyed because they do not receive benefits in return for their attention seems to be the core problem here [42]. Hence, providing sufficient benefits to the consumer is the basis for not consuming attention costs unnecessarily in digital signage advertising, eventually helping to overcome the problem of negative externalities at the same time.

Receiving the consumers' attention is not a matter of bottom-up effects (e.g., screen size, animated advertisements or noise), but rather of providing relevant content [27]. This insight is a crucial starting point when considering solutions to avoid negative externalities. An analogy between the Internet and digital signage confirms this argument: e.g., pop-up advertisements with animations and sounds that appear prominently at the center of the computer screen are far less effective than contextual keyword advertising. Contextual keyword advertising consists of advertisements, which are related to search keywords and which are displayed next to the search results (e.g., Google AdWords [13]). The reason why those advertisements attract more attention is because they are context-driven and, thus, better targeted to the consumers and their current situations and aims, and have a higher probability of being relevant. In contrast, pop-ups appear much more prominently. These pop-ups have many detriments, including a higher risk of unnecessarily consuming attention from the Internet user, causing attention costs [27]. With digital signage, too much advertising can lead to suboptimal consumption of attention, as comparable with pop-ups. The analogy with contextual keyword advertising, in contrast, shows that advertisers could better rethink the relevance of the content, instead of engaging in an arms race of designing their advertisements more attention drawing [27, 43].

Coping with negative externalities by market regulation is an additional possibility. Theoretically, if negative externalities are eliminated, then the average consumer's benefit from giving attention to digital signage at a certain location is maximized. If the consumption of a consumer's attention could be monitored, for example via dual-task performance, one could sell the exact amount of advertisements until this benefit is reached. Müller and Krüger [27] discuss three options to achieve this aim: maximum permissible values, fees, and tradable certificates (cf. Fig. 3). The following paragraphs discuss these three options and their pros and cons in detail.

The first option is regulation by *maximum permissible values*. Regulators may be sure about the amount and style of the advertisements. However, this method seems

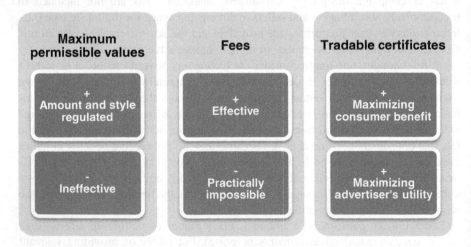

Fig. 3 Options for consumer benefit optimization in digital signage and their pros and cons

to be ineffective, because the costs caused to advertisers cannot be regulated, whereas every advertiser can only attract the same maximum amount of attention. The second option, charging *fees* for each unit of attention would solve the latter problem by letting advertisers pay more in case that an advertisement is worth more to them. This option would be theoretically sound, but practically hard to implement, because it is too difficult to determine how much should be charged for one unit of attention. This value should be equal to the costs induced to society, which is practically impossible to calculate. As a third option, one could work with *tradable certificates* (according to [27] a combination of the both previously stated mechanisms): If one would sell certificates for a certain amount of attention in a certain location, the average consumer benefit will be maximized. An auction can serve as the solution by filtering out which advertiser is valuing the opportunity to advertise at that moment and location most. The drawback of having high transactions costs with this approach might not be too relevant in the case of digital signage, since auctions are applied successfully in this market [26]. Automatic execution of the auction by software agents will then help to decrease these transaction costs to acceptable proportions [27]. This regulation of advertising market will, on the one hand, reduce information overload for consumers, but, on the other hand, it will support advertisers in targeting certain consumers and consumer groups, because just the relevant ones will be able to win the auction.

5 Conclusion

Digital signage plays an increasingly important role in today's advertising industry. This emerging mode of advertising provides new opportunities for consumers and for businesses due to its great array of possibilities. Along with the development of various types of digital signage and their increased application options, the need for diversified business approaches arises. The paper presented and discussed the different requirements and adaptation capabilities for the three major types of digital signage applications that are based on currently used technologies; the three major types are contextual digital signage, interactive digital signage, and the specific form of interactive digital signage with mobile devices. Particularly, this paper discussed the essentials components necessary to create business value for each of the major types of digital signage, i.e., the digital signage network (DSN), digital signage exchange (DSE), scheduling, and pricing. The infrastructure of a digital signage system, its forms and specific aspects, have to be taken into consideration by companies which intend to participate in this promising market. As a result, our work targets both researchers as well as practitioners in the field.

The core contribution of this paper is a detailed analysis of the potential of digital signage; emphasis is laid on challenges of performance measurement and implementation. The lack of a *unified* standard represents one of the major challenges, the existence of which would boost the overall development in all the major types of digital signage. The quasi-standards SMIL and POPAI are already a step into the right direction. Another emphasis of the analysis laid on challenges of operating and using digital signage system; in this context, we discuss display blindness and negative externalities. Possible solution paths were discussed for all challenges and best practices were presented.

As existing studies show diverging results, future research may include empirical studies on immediate as well as indirect effects of digital signage on sales in various sectors. Further issues that could be examined empirically focus on content: Which type of content should be displayed, and should the content be communicated as information or as emotional advertising? Another thread of research will focus on the perception of content that might depend on sequences and/or on schedules of advertisements.

Contextual digital signage is for the time-being in an early phase, thereby facing several drawbacks; from a societal viewpoint the use of contextual signage might well be disapproved due to privacy concerns. Research may focus on technically-oriented and organizational alternatives to offer contextual content that is not only in line with privacy regulations but also meets the consumer's expectations on privacy.

References

1. Want, R., Schillit, B.N.: Interactive digital signage. IEEE Comp. **45**(5), 21–24 (2012)
2. Khatri, S.: Digital signage industry market tracker. https://technology.ihs.com/487712/digital-signage-industry-market-tracker-q2-2014 (2013). Accessed 28 Sept 2015
3. Harrison, J.V., Andrusiewicz, A.: A virtual marketplace for advertising narrowcast over digital signage networks. Electron. Commer. Res. Appl. **3**, 163–175 (2004)
4. Dennis, C., Newman, A., Michon, R., Brakus, J.J., Wright, L.T.: The mediating effects of perception and emotion: digital signage in mall atmospherics. J. Retail. Consum. Serv. **17**, 205–215 (2010)
5. Burke, R.R.: Behavioral effects of digital signage. J. Advertising Res. **49**(2), 180–185 (2009)
6. Chen, Q., Malric, F., Zhang, Y., Abid, M., Cordeiro, A., Petriu, E.M., Georganas, N.D.: Interacting with digital signage using hand gestures. In: International Conference on Image Analysis and Recognition (ICIAR 2009), Montreal, Canada, pp. 347–358. Springer, Berlin, 06–08 July 2009
7. Bauer, C., Dohmen, P., Strauss, C.: Interactive digital signage: an innovative service and its future strategies. First International Workshop on Frontiers in Service Transformations and Innovations (FSTI-2011), in conjunction with EIDWT 2011, pp. 137–142. IEEE (2011)
8. Bauer, C., Dohmen, P., Strauss, C.: A conceptual framework for backend services of contextual digital signage. J. Serv. Sci. Res. **4**(2), 271–297 (2012)
9. Bauer, C., Spiekermann, S.: Conceptualizing context for pervasive advertising. In: Müller, J., Alt, F., Michelis, D. (eds.) Pervasive Advertising, pp. 159–183. Springer, London (2011)
10. Russell, M.G.: Narrowcast pricebook-driven persuasion: engagement at point of influence, purchase and consumption in distributed retail environments. J. Softw. **4**, 365–373 (2009)
11. Kelsen, K.: Unleashing the Power of Digital Signage: Content Strategies for the 5th Screen. Elsevier, Amsterdam (2010)
12. Müller, J., Krüger, A.: How much to bid in digital signage advertising auctions? In: 5th International Conference on Pervasive Computing (Pervasive 2007), Adjunct Workshop, Toronto, Canada, 13–16 May 2007

13. Google.: Google AdWords, 2015. Available http://adwords.google.com/. Accessed 28 Sept 2015
14. Müller, J., Exeler, J., Buzeck, M., Krüger, A.: Reflectivesigns: digital signs that adapt to audience attention. In: 7th International Conference Pervasive Computing (Pervasive 2009), Nara, Japan, pp. 17–24. Springer, 11–14 May 2009
15. Lee, J.S., Lee, J.C.: Context awareness by case-based reasoning in a music recommendation system. In: International Symposium on Ubiquitous Computing Systems (UCS 2007), Akihabara, Tokyo, Japan, pp. 44–58. Springer, 25–28 November 2007
16. Görlitz, G., Schmidt, A.: Digital signage: informal learning in animal parks and zoos. In: World Conference on E-Learning in Corporate, Government, Healthcare, and Higher Education (ELEARN 2008), Las Vegas, NV, pp. 841–846. AACE, 17 Nov 2008
17. Cardoso, J.C.S., Jose, R.A.: Framework for context-aware adaption in public displays. In: Meersman, R., Herrero, P., Dillon, T. (eds.) On the Move to Meaningful Internet Systems: OTM 2009 Workshops, Vilamoura, Portugal, pp. 118–127. Springer, 1–6 Nov 2009
18. Exeler, J., Buzeck, M., Müller, J.: eMir: digital signs that react to audience emotion. In: GI Jahrestagung 2009, Lübeck, Germany, pp. 3904–3910, 28 Sept–2 Oct 2009
19. Vogel, D., Balakrishnan, R.: Interactive public ambient displays: transitioning from implicit to explicit, public to personal, interaction with multiple users. In: 17th Annual ACM Symposium on User Interface Software and Technology (UIST 2004), pp. 137–146, Santa Fe, NM, 24–27 Oct 2004
20. Müller, J., Krüger, A.: MobiDiC: context adaptive digital signage with coupons. In: 3rd European Conference on Ambient Intelligence, Salzburg, pp. 24–33. Springer, Berlin, 18–21 Nov 2009
21. Yoon, C., Lee, H., Jeon, S. H., Lee, H.: Mobile digital signage system based on service delivery platform location based targeted advertisement service. In: 2011 International Conference on ICT Convergence (ICTC), pp. 582–586 (2011)
22. Harrison, J.V., Andrusiewicz, A.: Enhancing digital advertising using dynamically configurable multimedia. In: Multimedia and Expo, ICME'03, 2003 International Conference on, vol. 1, pp. I–717. IEEE (2003)
23. Gollan, B., Wally, B., Ferscha, A.: Automatic human attention estimation in an interactive system based on behavior analysis. In: 15th Portuguese Conference on Artificial Intelligence (EPIA 2011), Lisbon, Portugal, 10–13 Oct 2011
24. Hardy, J., Rukzio, E., Davies, N.: Real world responses to interactive gesture based public displays. In: 10th International Conference on Mobile and Ubiquitous Multimedia (MUM 2011), Beijing, China. ACM, 7–9 Dec 2011
25. Storz, O., Friday, A., Davies, N.: Supporting content scheduling on situated public displays. Comp. Graph **30**(5), 681–691 (2006)
26. Payne, T., David, E., Jennings, N.R., Sharifi, M.: Auction mechanisms for efficient advertisement selection on public displays. In: 17th European Conference on Artificial Intelligence (ECAI 2006), Riva del Garda, Italy, pp. 285–289. IOS Press, 29 Aug–01 Sept 2006
27. Müller, J., Krüger, A.: Competing for your attention: negative externalities in digital signage advertising. In: Workshop at Pervasive 2007, Designing and Evaluating Ambient Information Systems, Toronto, 13 May 2007
28. Amiri, A., Menon, S.: Efficient scheduling of Internet banner advertisements. ACM Trans. Internet Technol. (TOIT) **3**(4), 334–346 (2003)
29. Yackey, B.: A beginner's guide to digital signage: the new banner blindness? Blackbox Network Services, pp. 1–10 (2009). www.blackbox.eu. Accessed 02 Nov 2014
30. ITU-T Stuart Corner: Lack of standards threatens digital signage market, says ITU. http://www.itwire.com/it-industry-news/market/51504-lack-of-standards-threatens-digital-signage-market-says-itu (2011). Accessed on 28 Sept 2015
31. Medias: Outdoor. http://www.medias.sk/outdoor/ba01/ (2013). Accessed 28 Sept 2015
32. Broadcast Engineering: New service to measure digital signage's impact on consumer. http://broadcastengineering.com/news/new-service-measure-digital-signages-impact-consumer (2007). Accessed 28 Sept 2015

33. iAdea: W3C standards now target the digital signage industry. http://www.iadea.com/article/w3c-standards-now-target-digital-signage-industry (2012). Accessed 28 Sept 2015
34. Rymut, B., Kwolek, B.: Real-time multiview human body tracking using GPU-accelerated PSO. In: Parallel Processing and Applied Mathematics, 10th International Conference (PPAM 2013), Warsaw, Poland. Revised Selected Papers, Part I. Springer, 8–11 Sept 2013 (2014)
35. Owens, J.W., Chaparro, B.S., Palmer, E.M.: Text advertising blindness: the new banner blindness? J. Usability Stud. 6(3), 172–197 (2011)
36. Müller, J., Wilmsmann, D., Exeler, J., Buzeck, M., Schmidt, A., Jay, T., Krüger, A.: Display blindness: the effect of expectations on attention towards digital signage. In: 7th International Conference, Pervasive 2009, Nara, Japan, LNCS-5538, pp. 1–8. Springer, 11–14 May 2009
37. Milgram, S.: The experience of living in cities. Sci. New Series 167(3924), 1461–1468 (1970)
38. E-commerce-Gesetz: §§ 1–31 (2015), http://www.jusline.at/E-Commerce-Gesetz_(ECG).html. Accessed 28 Sept 2015
39. Puccinelli, N., Goodstein, R., Grewal, D., Price, R., Raghubir, P., Stewart, D.: Customer experience management in retailing: understanding the buying process. J. Retail. 85(1), 15–30 (2009)
40. Kaupp, M.: Chancen und Risiken von Digital Signage. Master's thesis, Fachhochschule München (2009)
41. Weiser, M., Brown, J.S.: Designing calm technology. Available: http://www.ubiq.com/weiser/calmtech/calmtech.htm (1995). Accessed 28 Sept 2015
42. Müller, J.: Context adaptive digital signage in transitional spaces. Doctoral thesis, Wilhelms University Münster (2008)
43. Burke, M., Hornof, A., Nilsen, E., Gorman, N.: High-cost banner blindness: ads increase perceived workload, hinder visual search, and are forgotten. ACM Trans. Comp. Human Interact. (TOCHI) 12(4), 423–445 (2005)
44. POPAI: Screen media formats. http://popai.com/docs/DS/ScreenFormat%20Standards%20Dras%20rev097.pdf (2009). Accessed 28 Sept 2015
45. Huang, E.M., Koster, A., Borchers J.: Overcoming assumptions and uncovering practices: when does the public really look at public displays? In: 6th International Conference, Pervasive 2008, Sydney, Australia, LNCS-5013, pp. 228–243. Springer, 19–22 May 2008

Trust, but Verify: The Role of ICTs in the Sharing Economy

Sami Dakhlia, Andrés Davila and Barry Cumbie

Abstract Successful peer-to-peer sharing platforms open the door to new markets by relying on feedback-driven reputation mechanisms to reduce transactions costs. In particular, the reputation-based mechanisms go a long way towards reducing informational asymmetries and opportunistic behavior. Nevertheless, they are not 100 % impervious to abuse. The challenge for ICTs is to further boost trust by reducing risk while keeping transaction costs small. This can be achieved with the help of two complementary approaches: (1) develop ID verification solutions that link and aggregate a user's reputation profiles from various communities and (2) use connected monitoring devices. Both approaches raise privacy concerns that must be taken into account. This pedagogical note offers a short primer on some of the underlying economic concepts.

Keywords Collaborative consumption · Collaborative production · Global village · Sharing economy · Reputation · Information technology · Internet · Privacy

1 Introduction

"As a greater number of economic activities become mediated by computers, sophisticated monitoring of transactions will become feasible, allowing for more efficient contractual arrangements in rental markets" [1].

S. Dakhlia (✉) · A. Davila
ESCE International Business School, Paris, France
e-mail: sami.dakhlia@esce.fr

A. Davila
e-mail: andres.davila@esce.fr

B. Cumbie
University of North Alabama, Florence, AL, USA
e-mail: bcumbie@una.edu

© Springer International Publishing Switzerland 2016
F. Ricciardi and A. Harfouche (eds.), *Information and Communication Technologies in Organizations and Society*, Lecture Notes in Information Systems and Organisation 15, DOI 10.1007/978-3-319-28907-6_20

In [2], DeLong and Froomkin cautioned that the new economy would create more of the types of goods and services, such as mp3-encoded music files, that lack the essential features of private goods, namely excludability and rivalry; moreover, they argued, commerce would be hampered by a loss of transparency—what you see online is not what you may get—so that the very foundations of Adam Smith's world and its efficient allocation of resources would be eroded.

With the benefit of hindsight, we can now plausibly argue that the new economy brought about net benefits: the corporate music industry has shrunk significantly, but thanks to innovative business models, from iTunes to Spotify, it is still alive and kicking; more importantly, musicians aren't starving, despite their growing ranks. Electronic commerce, whether via eBay or Amazon, is thriving, and their online feedback reputation mechanisms appear to be working well enough.

Our focus here is on the so-called peer-to-peer (P2P) sharing economy, in which individuals monetize idle or underutilized resources, for instance by renting their car, a power tool, or a room to a stranger.[1] Such trades were inconceivable less than ten years ago: friends were invited to stay for free and strangers were not let into the house under any circumstances. In a nutshell, sharing platforms have brought us closer to, not farther away from, an economy with low transactions costs and more complete markets.

The term "sharing economy" has been used to designate many new services or marketplaces. While the term may be an apt descriptor for some of these IT-driven transactions, it can be misleading for many others. Techno-utopian theories promising a new golden era of zero-marginal cost societies only lead to further confusion. It therefore seems important to address, upfront, various misperceptions about the sharing economy.

First of all, despite the utopian connotations of the words "sharing" and "community", the transactions are fully compatible with and generally motivated by dollars and cents: what's mine is indeed yours, but for a fee. Sharing platforms facilitate a more complete market economy as reduced friction improves the efficiency of free trade of goods and services. Bardhi and Eckhardt [4], for instance, argue that the term "access economy" far better captures the fact that these are market transactions, not reciprocal, informal exchanges within small social groups.

Second, collaborative consumption is predominantly not about providing access to digital information goods, but to physical ones. The distinction is important: thanks to Intenet, digital information goods could be duplicated and distributed at a very low marginal cost so that these files became neither excludable (the original producer can, in the worst case, only charge a price for the first copy), nor rival in consumption (my copy of your copy does not affect your copy's consumption value).

---

[1]Botsman [3] proposes a definition that also includes ethical criteria, such as "transparency, humanness, and authenticity".

2 The Sharing Economy Is About Club Goods

Rivalry (in consumption) and excludability are two basic criteria used to classify goods (and services) and help determine whether they can be efficiently provided by the private sector or whether they should potentially be provided, or at least regulated, by governments. A good is said to be rival if your use of that good reduces my own enjoyment of it. For example, if you take my car, I cannot use it. Conversely, a good is said to be non-rival if multiple people can use it simultaneously: an FM radio signal is such an example, since your signal reception does not impede mine. A good is said to be excludable if the provider has the means of withholding the good from specific users; he might choose to exercise that power if the user fails to pay for the good, for instance. A gym, for instance, is excludable, since only members in good standing will be granted access. Conversely, a good is considered non-excludable if the provider cannot limit access, as would be the case for a fireworks show, since anybody within a few miles would be able to enjoy it.

These two criteria define four types of goods: private goods, which are rival and excludable; pure public goods, which are neither rival, nor excludable; commons, which are rival, but not excludable, and club goods, which are excludable, but not rival. The four types are shown in Fig. 1, in which we recognize that the concepts of excludability and rivalry are not strictly binary (yes or no), but that there can be degrees of rivalry (e.g., I can still use a road even if it is congested), and that access control can be more or less costly.

The distinction is useful, since it helps us categorize the various services in the new economy. Wikipedia, for example, provides a public good: millions of people can access the service simultaneously (non-rival) and it is freely accessible (non-excludable, or, at least, non-excluding).[2] Uber, in contrast, arguably provides access to private goods (or, rather, services), since transportation service is created on demand, the client chooses the destination, and is the sole user of that particular ride. A ride-sharing platform such as Blablacar, on the other hand, provides access to a club good, since the driver is not only the producer but also the consumer of the trip; in particular, she chooses both the trip's destination and timing, while passengers can merely claim empty seats. Furthermore, the platform helps the driver offset part of her variable cost (gas and tolls), but she cannot generate a profit, that is, revenue over and above her explicit and implicit opportunity costs.

Peer-to-peer sharing platforms, then, provide access to club goods, goods that are excludable and rival in consumption—to a degree. The degree of rivalry largely defines a club's optimal size (see Buchanan [5]). For instance, a sedan can comfortably seat at most four adults. Clubs are nothing new, of course: the treadmill in a home gym, for example, may only see 30 min of use a day; the much higher utilization of the same treadmill at a neighborhood fitness center may lead to a

---

[2]One might argue that Wikipedia could opt to restrict access to paying subscribers (or to those willing to watch ads); this would, however, most likely upset its business model and negatively affect the goodwill of its countless contributors.

Fig. 1 The four types of goods

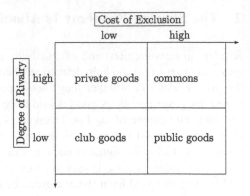

substantial reduction in cost per minute. These savings, however, can only be realized if the number of club members is sufficiently small so that they can coordinate sequential use and if access to the gym is sufficiently convenient; in short, if the transactions costs are sufficiently low.

3 Reputation Is Key, but not Always Sufficient

The interesting twist is that many of the club goods and services accessible via sharing platforms have heretofore been considered private goods: sequential use had been impractical and the associated transaction cost prohibitive. Entrusting a personal, valuable resource to a stranger was fraught with peril: how could one guarantee that the good would not be damaged? What type of enforceable contract would have to be drafted to resolve any potential claim or conflict?

For the sake of comparison and to understand the power of reputation, consider the case of so-called micro-credits in developing countries: access to micro-loans was limited because the transaction cost associated with verifying the borrower's identity, securing a collateral, and filling out the paperwork far exceeded the loan amount. Yet, in the absence of such verifications, a bank would face a high probability of default. Loan sharks could fill the void, but at usury rates. The Grameen bank (see Yunus and Weber [6]) solved this dilemma by leveraging peer-pressure and merely requiring that four of the borrower's peers co-sign the loan; as such the borrower's reputation among his peers was on the line. While reputational collateral is of no intrinsic value to the bank, it nevertheless solves the problem of trust, because the bank knows that it is valuable to the borrower.

In much the same way, peers in the sharing economy prize their reputation, and with it the ability to engage in future transactions. A history of positive feedback earned in prior transactions is a bond of trust and opens the door to more potential transactions. The ability to trust people not to engage in opportunistic behavior is key to the continued success of platforms such as Airbnb or Zilok. Unfortunately, a few bad apples may spoil the barrel for the rest of us.

Moral hazard is one of two fundamental problems with entrusting equipment, say, a car, to a stranger: she may not treat it as carefully as the owner would. She may drive it harder or park it in a risky neighborhood. When the car is returned, the owner may generally not be able to tell how the car was treated; in the case of mechanical failure, the owner can usually not assess if the failure is an Act of God or the user's fault. As a consequence, a mechanism based solely on reputation cannot provide perfect and complete protection from negligent behavior.

Neither can it fully protect owners from adverse selection, the second fundamental problem, where sharing platforms attract a disproportionate number of inherently risky users, not merely young drivers who are unable to rent from traditional rental agencies, but rather, malicious users who prey on a trusting community: a scammer could potentially game the system and boost his reputational score by creating multiple fake digital identities that exchange positive feedback among themselves. Furthermore, as discussed in Friedman and Reznick [7], online pseudonyms are disposable and replaceable so that bad reputations can easily be shed.

The success of online sharing platforms, the ability to unlock new markets, hinges on the platforms' ability to limit opportunistic behavior by reducing the informational asymmetries that underlie moral hazard and adverse selection. Unfortunately, as pointed out by Reznick et al. [8], eliciting useful feedback is not easy since users do not always have a strong incentive to rate their experience and to rate it truthfully. Providing feedback is a tax on time; and providing negative feedback can be an emotional burden and may potentially lead to further conflict.

Taking the case of an Airbnb transaction, because both parties benefit from feedback (provided it's positive), it suffices to merely withhold access to received feedback until one takes the time to evaluate the other. On the other hand, in the wake of a dispute, both parties could agree to leave neutral comments (or no comments at all) rather than mutually damage each other's reputation. In theory, Airbnb's policy of concealing feedback until both have responded does nothing to encourage or dissuade this type of collusive behavior; in game-theoretic parlance, there are many Nash equilibria. In practice, however, parties nevertheless often collude. Designing robust truth-revealing mechanisms is no easy task. Jøsang et al. [9] offer an excellent survey of online reputation systems.

Because of these issues, Airbnb or peer-to-peer car sharing platforms such as Getaround and Relayrides have evolved from offering mere matchmaking services to providing not only screening (identity and driving record verification) but also, most importantly, insurance. Of course, these extra expenses increase the transaction cost.

One method to counter increasing transaction costs and complexities of identity enforcement in a sharing economy platform is to link and aggregate reputation data that peers accumulate in various online communities. The proposed model of cross-community reputations (CCR) (see Grinshpoun et al. [10], for example) also promises to effectively reduce the burden of burgeoning start-ups to fully construct their own verification and enforcement mechanism in a sharing platform.

Furthermore, individual platforms would also sidestep the need to attain a critical mass of users, transactions, reviews, and ratings that are needed to establish the reputation of the actors involved. An individual would not have to use a single sharing platform many times over to establish their reputation but could leverage their reputation from their goodwill accrued elsewhere. My favorable eBay seller rating would inform and bolster my Airbnb reputation and also connect with my Uber experiences and so forth.

Last, but not least, Facebook and Google Plus have significantly increased the cost of pseudonym replacement. Not only does Facebook require (with varying success) people to provide their real life name, but erasing an old and opening a fresh account brings with it the tedious process of rebuilding one's network.

4 The Evolving Role of ICTs

The problems of verifying identity and associated reputations that are faced by sharing economy platforms are not without analogy to previous and ongoing developments in other ICT-facilitated economic platforms. There is still a trade-off between simplicity and robustness of protocols for authentication of digital identity. Biometric techniques such as face, retina, or voice scan may help overcome the trade-off, although they raise not only privacy concerns, but also issues of development cost for platform providers. Nevertheless, the more valuable the shared equipment and the higher the stakes, such as housing and vehicles, the more it may make sense for a platform to impose robust authentication of a person's identity and for vehicle or apartment owners to invest in monitoring devices.

Trust in e-commerce transactions in both digital or physical goods from buyer to seller are moderated by several controls including the technological protocols to secure and encrypt transmitted data during the ICT-facilitated transaction. In this regard, payment methods are more trusted and secure than ever before. Emerging players in this market are further able to incorporate industry standards of accepting and processing payment, not by building their own from the ground up, but by sidestepping this onerous process and using preexisting and well-known third-party services such as PayPal.

In the same manner, many smaller online and information services can outsource the complex, risky, and fundamental feature of user login and authentication to technology giants. The tasks of developing, maintaining, and securing user data and profile become unwieldy and detracting and—with more user data collected— expose an organization to greater risk. The solution to this are protocols such as oAuth or OpenID that allow third-party websites, services, or applications to use preexisting user login credentials (those from Facebook or Google, for example) to create and access an account. Users can login to many sites using the same credentials, at greater convenience, but the sites themselves do not have to store, protect, or maintain user passwords.

These two cases of incorporating third-party payment or authentication services form the backdrop of a cross-community reputation service. The crux of the problem is ensuring persistent reputation versus transient digital profiles. Digital profiles—the user names and associated information provided—are shaped by what the user provides, what the platform allows, or the interaction among the user, platform, and the network of users (Kane et al. [11]). Digital profiles provided by users that are not linked to a network of users (e.g., Facebook) are susceptible to being discarded and recreated and are thus not persistent in the true identity of the user. This is not necessarily problematic for product-based transactions; a seller may tolerate a user terminating and recreating accounts so long as the user continues to make purchases. This behavior does however become a serious issue when trust and reputation are important factors in a transaction, as is the case for the unique situation of the sharing economy, in which the parties are in closer contact, if not meeting in-person, then connecting via a shared resource that is used and then returned to the lender.

These issues do seem to point to the need for a cross-community reputation aggregator. Online payment and user authentication are two areas that are not without ongoing security risks but have also gained in user trust by adopting third-party services or standards to achieve higher levels of service and security. Reputations in a sharing economy platform also may benefit from the presence of third-party agencies that maintain persistent reputations across many platforms, especially when digital profiles can be discarded and recreated.

Ultimately the clearest analogue for a CCR service is that of a credit agency, which assigns an index score (i.e., credit score) to individuals based on relevant debt, income, and other factors. A reputation score that stays with you across all platforms and user names would alleviate concerns in ICT-facilitated transactions. The solution may lie in additional layers of systems and complexity that represent an Identity or Reputation Economy of third-party agencies that verify users across platforms and link digital profiles with a persistent reputation score.

However, until a CCR system is widely adopted, sharing platforms must continue to engage in painstaking weeding of fake accounts, if only to keep insurance premiums and user complaints to a minimum. They may also encourage the adoption of monitoring devices.

Housing is far less fragile than a vehicle and while it is far more valuable, the potential damage is typically lower and is more easily revealed upon post-rental inspection. The cost-benefit ratio of monitoring devices, such as cameras, may thus be less favorable, especially considering the very serious privacy considerations.

In the case of car sharing, on the other hand, owners may opt to retrofit their cars with vehicle telematics, i.e., various sensors and monitoring devices. These may include geolocalization to record road types, speed, and neighborhoods where parked. An accelerometer can provide information on driving style and detect small shocks. Access to the engine's CPU can provide data on fuel consumption. These technologies have already found their way into usage-based insurance, such as Metromile's pay how you drive (PHYD), whose premium is, in part, based on driver behavior.

Both CCR services, which collect and store data, and monitoring devices raise serious ethical and privacy issues. Dambrine et al. [12] contend that reputational systems are capable of protecting user privacy and concealing identity until a transaction takes place, while preserving transparency and channels of feedback and response for users. As for monitoring, which would necessarily occur with the informed consent of the user, privacy concerns could be significantly alleviated by ensuring that the flow of usage data is restricted to a neutral third party. This third party would preserve the data for only a limited time period and only release it to the platform's arbitrators if "foul play" is suspected. Langheinrich [13] and Cavoukian and Jonas [14] develop further measures, principles, and best practices for what is known as Privacy by Design (PbD).

5   Conclusion

Reputation and trust-based mechanisms have opened the door to new markets and to a higher rate of resource utilization. Unfortunately, the mechanisms are not bulletproof and cannot fully resolve the problem of informational asymmetry. The continuing success and development of the so-called sharing (or access) economy thus hinges on its ability not only to develop more robust game-theoretic truth-revelation mechanisms, but also to link and aggregate persistent reputation profiles across platforms and to develop protocols that permit monitoring while still protecting users from unwarranted privacy intrusion.

Acknowledgments The authors wish to thank Nabil Georges Badr, Antoine Harfouche, Kirsten Ralf, Alexandre Sokic, ICTO 2015 participants, and an anonymous referee for valuable comments.

References

1. Varian, H.R.: Buying, sharing and renting information goods. J. Indus. Econ. **48**(4), 473–488 (2000)
2. DeLong, J., Froomkin, A.: Speculative microeconomics for tomorrow's economy. In: Kahin, B., Varian, H.R. (eds.) Internet publishing and beyond: the economics of digital information and intellectual property, pp. 6–44. A Publication of the Harvard Information Infrastructure Project (2000)
3. Botsman, R.: The currency of the new economy is trust, TEDGlobal 2012, http://www.ted.com/talks/rachel_botsman_the_currency_of_the_new_economy_is_trust (2012)
4. Bardhi, F., Eckhardt, G.M.: Access-based consumption: the case of car sharing. J. Consum. Res. **39**(4), 881–898 (2012)
5. Buchanan, J.M.: An economic theory of clubs. Economica **32**(125), 1–14 (1965)
6. Yunus, M., Weber, K.: Creating a world without poverty: social business and the future of capitalism. PublicAffairs, New York (2007)
7. Friedman, E., Resnick, P.: The social cost of cheap pseudonyms. J. Econ. Manage. Strategy **10**(2), 173–199 (2001)

8. Resnick, P., Zeckhauser, R., Friedman, E., Kuwabara, K.: Reputation systems. Commun. ACM **43**(12), 45–48 (2000)
9. Jøsang, A., Ismail, R., Boyd, C.A.: A survey of trust and reputation systems for online service provision. Decis. Support Syst. **43**(2), 618–644 (2007)
10. Grinshpoun, T., Gal-Oz, N., Meisels, A., Gudes, E.: CCR: A model for sharing reputation knowledge across virtual communities. In: Proceedings of the 2009 IEEE/WIC/ACM international joint conference on web intelligence and intelligent agent technology, Vol. 01 (WI-IAT '09), Vol. 1. IEEE computer society, pp. 34–41, Washington, DC, USA (2009)
11. Kane, G.C., Alavi, M., Labianca, G.J., Borgatti, S.P.: What's different about social media networks? A framework and research agenda. MIS Q. **38**(1), 304–375 (2014)
12. Dambrine, B., Jerome, J., Ambrose, B.: User reputation: building trust and addressing privacy issues in the sharing economy. Future of Privacy Forum (2015) http://www.futureofprivacy. org/wp-content/uploads/FPF_SharingEconomySurvey_06_08_15.pdf (2015)
13. Langheinrich, M.: Privacy by design—principles of privacy-aware ubiquitous systems. In: Ubicomp 2001: ubiquitous computing, pp. 273–291. Springer Berlin (2001)
14. Cavoukian, A., Jonas, J.: Privacy by design in the age of big data. Information and Privacy Commissioner of Ontario, Canada (2012)

Internet Service Providers: The Italian Scenario

Francesco Bellini, Fabrizio D'Ascenzo and Valeria Traversi

Abstract This paper shows the characteristics of the Italian Internet Providers' market. The study is divided into three parts where different factors are analysed providing an observation of the targeted sector from different perspectives. After having identified the research objectives and the characteristics of the internet providers' sector, the Italian Internet market is described through fundamental parameters such as the analysis of demand, global turnover and the analysis of different methods of access to the network. In the second part, we analyse the technical, economic and financial characteristics of the sector, through the study of fundamental elements such as technological readiness of ISPs and the structure of supply, taking into account operating areas and services provided by companies; the survey provides then a study of the companies' size in order to have a clear market segmentation. The last part provides an analysis of the economic and financial structure exploring companies' efficiency through performance indicators. The final result is a critical analysis of findings from which emerges that medium sized ISPs are more performing in terms of business indicators while policies still seem to be in favour of big operators.

Keywords Internet service provider · Services · Technologies · Geographical distribution · Companies' performance · Dimension · KPIs

F. Bellini (✉) · F. D'Ascenzo · V. Traversi
Department of Management, Sapienza University of Rome, Rome, Italy
e-mail: francesco.bellini@uniroma1.it

F. D'Ascenzo
e-mail: fabrizio.dascenzo@uniroma1.it

V. Traversi
e-mail: valeria.traversi@uniroma1.it

© Springer International Publishing Switzerland 2016
F. Ricciardi and A. Harfouche (eds.), *Information and Communication Technologies in Organizations and Society*, Lecture Notes in Information Systems and Organisation 15, DOI 10.1007/978-3-319-28907-6_21

1   Introduction

The present research[1] provides an analysis of the Italian market structure for Internet access services in order to define size classes of operators (ISP—Internet Service Providers) and study the main characteristics of these companies and their offered services in the current operational context. Our analysis starts from the hypothesis that the different sizes of operators enable different levels of techno-logical, economic and financial efficiency [1] and we wanted to identify which is the optimal dimension for ISP that want to face the Italian market where industrial policies still appear to be favourable to big operators [2].

Our methodological approach is grounded upon the set-up of a database (DB) which will be further improved and used for future analysis. The DB contains the information of relevant elements characterizing the single companies—from operational/technical details to economic/financial figures—that will be used for the elaboration of indicators needed for the study and comparison between companies within the ISP sector.

After having observed the elements of the market situation, an economic-financial analysis was carried out with the aim of identifying the main sector features, weaknesses and strengths, emphasizing the attractiveness in order to improve operational solutions.

The composition of ISP operators' sector can be represented in various ways given all the characteristics of the target market. The Fig. 1 shows "accesses to the fixed network" provided by Telecom Italia and Other Licensed Operators (OLO) [3].

The diagram shows the increasing OLO role in the domestic market. The per-formance is clearly shown when taking into account the class "others" representing small and medium service providers that are consolidating over the time their position on the market. The next Fig. 2 makes it even clearer showing the market breakdown among OLO: here all operators' market shares are shown without considering the position of Telecom Italia (which is the former monopolist and the bigger incumbent on Italian market).

This figure clearly represents the increasing role of the operators categorized as "others" with a market share that rises from 4.7 % in 2012 to 6.3 % in 2013.

As regards broadband accesses, Fig. 3 shows a similar situation to the fixed network accesses.

The data comparison clearly shows an increasing development of small and medium ISPs' market share, which is improved by almost one point percentage in one year.

In short, we can say that small and medium internet service providers are or have been considerably growing by absorbing even more large market shares despite the delay Italy has experienced in digitalization, computerization and opening the market to an actual concurrency.

---

[1]This research was carried out thanks to the support of AIIP (Associazione Italliana Internet Providers) and NAMEX (Nautilus Mediterranean eXchange point).

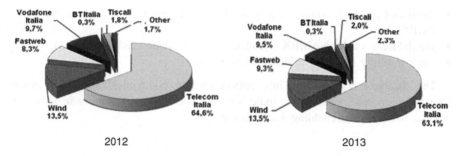

Fig. 1 Accesses to the fixed network a comparison between 2012 and 2013. *Source* AGCOM

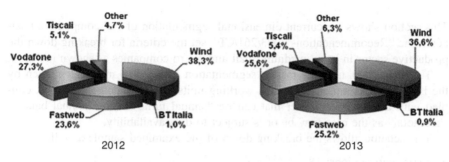

Fig. 2 Accesses to the fixed network OLO between 2012 and 2013. *Source* AGICOM

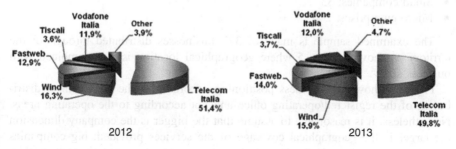

Fig. 3 Broadband market shares between 2012 and 2013. *Source* AGICOM

2 Internet Service Providers in Italy: A Methodological Approach for the Analysis

In order to perform our analysis, we built our database of Italian ISPs by merging together the information coming from:

- "Registro degli Operatori di Comunicazione" (ROC) maintained by the Italian Agency for Communication Market Control AGCOM;

- the list of members maintained by the Italian Association of Internet Providers (AIIP);
- the database of the NAMEX (Nautilus Mediterranean eXchange point);
- other publicly available information sources.

The database contains the information on the companies' size, their main financial-economic performance indicators and the operators' supply in terms of Access, Services and enabling Technologies.

2.1 ISP Size and Segmentation on Indicators Basis

This section shows the current dimensional segmentation of ISP competitive business. The "Recommendations 2003/261/CE" set the criteria for breaking down the productive sector in large, medium small and micro companies as shown in Fig. 4.

The parameters used for market segmentation follow two main rules given by the European Commission: "annual working units" must be considered first, coupled with a second parameter that can be "annual turnover" or "annual balance sheet total" as the case may be or is subject to data availability.

This scheme allows the breaking down of the examined sample as follows:

- Large corporations: 18
- Medium sized companies: 30
- Small companies: 83
- Micro enterprises: 246

The examined sample is made of 377 businesses distributed throughout the territory as shown in Fig. 5 where geographical location is also combined with business size.

Figure 5 shows the business positioning according to the geographical distribution of the registered/operating office and not according to the operating areas. Nevertheless, it is reasonable to assume that the bigger is the company dimension the larger is the geographical coverage of the services provided: big companies cover the whole domestic territory and medium enterprises may cover more than one region while small and micro companies are local operators.

2.2 Overall Supply Analysis: Areas of Operation and Offered Services

For the selected companies Table 1 shows the type of offered services in a scheme relating two main elements: that of size and type of service.

The table describes the composition of access, services and technologies by using the size class segmentation. The availability of IPv6 technology represents a

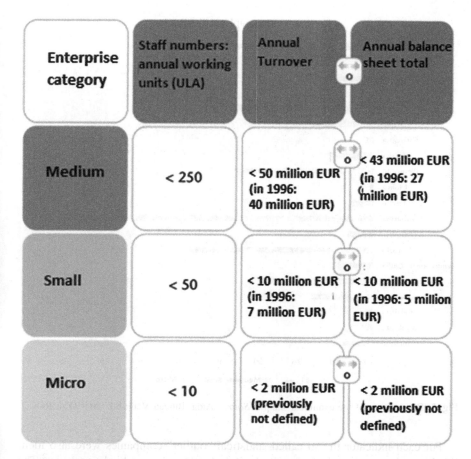

Fig. 4 EU definition of medium, small and micro companies

meaningful information that can be interpreted as the readiness of providers to manage internet products accordingly to the developing trends and technologies such as "Internet of Things" that need wider structural configuration and more advanced qualitative characteristics.

3 Analysis of the Financial Structure in Relation to the Performance Indicators

In this section, the analysis is developed in order to measure the ISPs' performance. The available financial statements' data made possible to obtain an in-depth representation of the companies' economic-financial conditions.

Geographical distribution

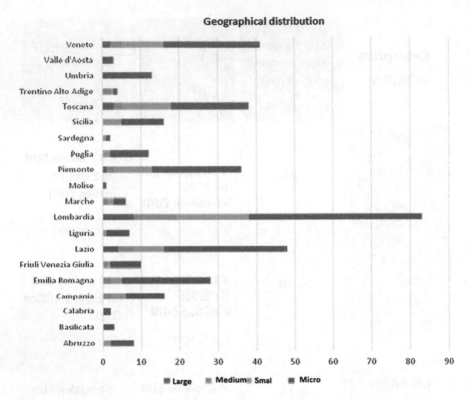

Fig. 5 Break down of the examined sample. *Source* Aida, Bureau Van Dijk, AGCOM, ROC

For each indicator the so called statistical "outlier" companies were also identified in order to avoid distortions and get a clearer and more likely analysis.[2] The red columns in the following charts show the results obtained without the outliers (NO) while the blue columns represent the full sample.

3.1 Trading Profitability (EBITDA/Sales)

The analysis starts from the ratio EBITDA[3]/Sales. This is used to constantly monitor the developments of the business activity. The purpose of this indicator is to highlight the developments of the business activity and their trends over the time in order to better "know" the company. EBITDA is then used to compare the

---

[2]For calculating the outliers we used the Inter Quartile Range (IQR) algorithm.
[3]Earnings Before Interest, Taxes, Depreciation and Amortization.

Table 1 Access, services and technologies

Dimension	Access (%)			Services (%)				Technologies (%)		
	WIMax/Wi-Fi	ADSL/HDSL	Fibre optics	VoIP	Cloud services	Domain	Data center	IPv4	IPv6	ASN
Large	57	67	50	56	72	67	72	83	72	61
Medium	43	53	30	33	37	27	27	57	50	47
Small	51	57	20	47	29	37	35	60	42	47
Micro	48	48	16	45	15	28	24	49	34	34

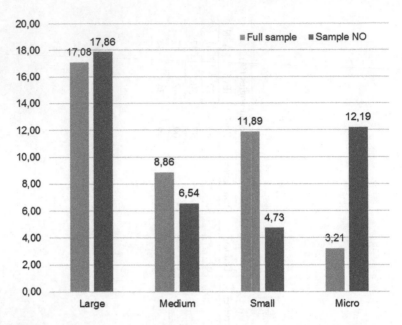

Fig. 6 Trading profitability (EBITDA/Sales—%)

company's profitability over several financial years, comparing it with sales as profitability is heavily influenced by the business sector.

Figure 6 shows that large corporations are more performing when considering the overall turnover while Fig. 7 shows that SME have a better profitability when selling cost are considered and consequently SME appear to be more efficient.

3.2 Asset Profitability (Net Profit/Total Assets)

In this paragraph, we consider the ratio between net income and total assets (or invested capital); the Return On Assets (ROA) index enables to check how much a company's total assets are profitable (Fig. 8).

This indicator also shows that SMEs have a more efficient asset profitability than large corporations.

3.3 Return on Equity (Net Profit/Capital)

This indicator enables us to investigate the profitability of shareholders' capital (Fig. 9).

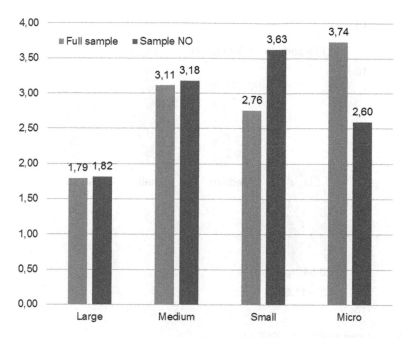

Fig. 7 Profitability on sales (EBITDA/net revenues—%)

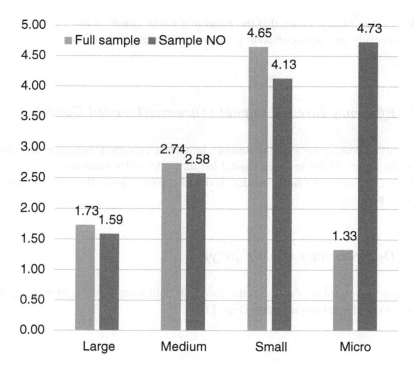

Fig. 8 Total asset profitability (ROA—%)

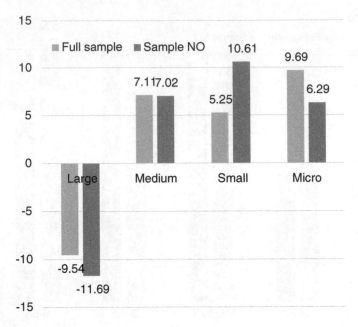

Fig. 9 Total asset profitability (ROE—%)

Return On Equity shows that the economic performance of risk capital is positive especially for small companies. Conversely, large corporations show a negative result.

3.4 Efficiency Invested Capital (Turnover/Invested Capital)

With this indicator, we measure another important efficiency indicator that illustrates the ability of the invested capital to "turn into" sales revenues.

Figure 10 confirms that the SMEs' invested capital is more than that the one of large corporations.

3.5 Debt Structure (Debt/Equity)

This indicator enables to measure the company debt sustainability, identifying the debt ratio or the debt/equity ratio (Fig. 11).

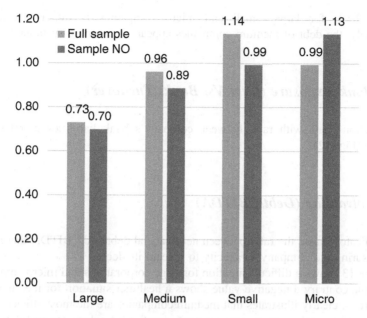

Fig. 10 Invested capital turnover

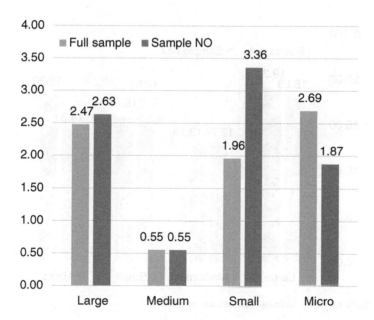

Fig. 11 Debt/equity ratio

Debt level for large, small and micro companies is rather widespread. Conversely, the debt of medium companies appears to be more sustainable.

3.6 Bank Exposure (Debt Vs. Banks/Turnover)

This section deals with ratio between company's bank liabilities in relation to turnover (Fig. 12).

3.7 Solvability (Debt/EBITDA)

This indicator shows the ratio between net financial debt and EBITDA that is used for measuring the company's capacity to redeem its debt.

Figure 13 shows a difficult situation for large corporations and micro companies and on the contrary a negative value shows a healthier situation for medium ones.

Figure 14 clearly illustrates that medium companies are the most efficient as the calculated value takes on a very positive significance when compared to other categories.

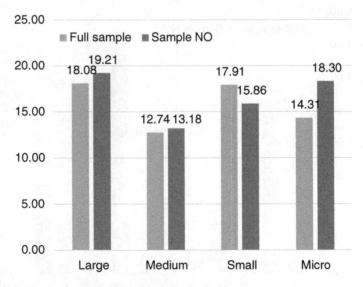

Fig. 12 Bank exposure (debt vs. banks/turnover—%)

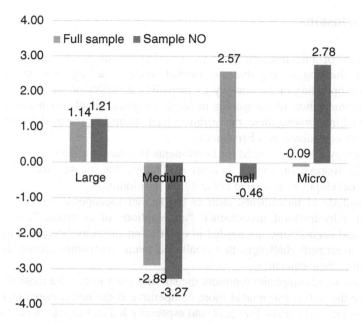

Fig. 13 Debt/EBITDA ratio

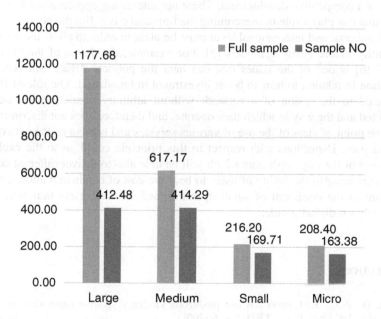

Fig. 14 Turnover per employee

4 Conclusions

The results of this research provide an overview of Italian Internet Service Providers showing a very dynamic market made of a large number of active companies operating in the territory by providing a variety of services.

The segmentation of companies in large, medium, small and micro provides interesting hints: among these, the medium sized enterprises is a model of efficiency that can be considered as a benchmark.

The survey reveals the need for investments in order to seize market challenges as ultra high-speed Internet or Internet of Things, that are key technologies for business development and solid competitive positioning.

The attitude of incumbents, such as the former monopolist, suggests a lower trend for infrastructural investments; "aggregations of companies", as well as mergers and acquisitions, are needed in order to enable consolidation policies and to meet investment challenges that small and micro companies cannot singularly bear despite their efficiency.

Medium sized companies represent the starting point to achieve these objectives and make the Italian ISP market more competitive at the international level.

Moreover, world crisis, European and especially Italian low rate of development are obstacles to the boost of this sector. The objectives of Italian Digital Agenda [4] are very clear and require great efforts to overcome present difficulties and identify areas for a competitive development. There are interesting opportunities in the ISP sector that can play a role in overcoming the financial crisis. But the policy strategy, both at national and international level must be clear in order to allow the operators to identify viable business models [5]. For example, the theme of the "net neutrality" [6] is one of the issues that can heat the political debate and economic regulation in relation to how to boost investment in broadband. The role of ISPs is connected to the vision of a network without arbitrary restrictions on devices connected and the way in which they operate, and therefore does not discriminating from the point of view of the use of various services and content of the network by the end user. Distortions with respect to this principle could go to the exclusive advantage of the large operators which will be able also to deliver different content based according to the ability of users to bear the cost of bandwidth allocation and therefore to the detriment of small operators and low-end users thus will affect negatively on digital divide.

References

1. Lien, D., Peng, Y.: Competition and production efficiency: Telecommunications in OECD countries. Inf. Econ. Policy 13(1), 51–76 (2001)
2. Manenti, F.M., Nicolò, A., Tedeschi, P., Valbonesi, P.: Caso AIIP vs telecom Italia: nuovi mercati, antiche condotte. Economia e Politica Industriale, 191–206 (2001)

3. Autorità Garante per le Telecomunicazioni.: Osservatorio trimestrale sulle Telecomunicazioni agg. 31 dicembre 2013 (2013)
4. Agenzia per l'Italia Digitale.: Strategia Italiana per l'Agenda Digitale (2014)
5. Keskin, T., Kennedy, D.: Strategies in smart service systems enabled multi-sided markets: business models for the internet of things. In: System sciences (HICSS), 2015 48th Hawaii international conference on (pp. 1443–1452). IEEE (2015, January)
6. Bourreau, M., Kourandi, F., Valletti, T.: Net neutrality with competing internet platforms. J. Indus. Econ. **63**(1), 30–73 (2015)

ICT and Retail: State of the Art and Prospects

Daniele Pederzoli

Abstract In this paper, we analyze the diffusion of technologies in the retail sector. Technologies are disrupting the traditional way of selling products and services and the relations between companies and consumers. In our paper we categorize four different fields for technologies impacting retail activities and we analyze some examples for each category that can illustrate these trends.

Keywords Consumer enhancement · Store atmosphere · Ubiquitous consumption · Store management · Technology and retail

1 Introduction

Retail has been a "low technology" sector for many years because its main purpose was to distribute products manufactured and branded by industrial companies and the competition was mainly between traditional small mom and pop stores and modern large formats.

This situation started to change in the 1970s, and the rate of change accelerated in the following decades, especially when ICT disrupted many sectors, introducing profound changes in relations with consumers and the other players in the distribution channel.

One of the main reasons for investment in innovation and technology in the retail sector is increased competition in each main subsector and in every developed country. The retail sector in the most developed countries is characterized by strong concentration in all the main sectors from FMCG to clothing, from DIY to digital products; this concentration leads to strong competition between huge multinational companies who develop the same formats and need to differentiate their brand to avoid merely price-based competition.

D. Pederzoli (✉)
NEOMA Business School, Rouen Campus, Rouen, France
e-mail: daniele.pederzoli@neoma-bs.fr

© Springer International Publishing Switzerland 2016   329
F. Ricciardi and A. Harfouche (eds.), *Information and Communication*
Technologies in Organizations and Society, Lecture Notes in Information
Systems and Organisation 15, DOI 10.1007/978-3-319-28907-6_22

Technology is a key component of retail companies' strategies for building differentiation and gaining competitive advantage both nationally and internationally. The real divide in the retail sector is no longer between modern and traditional retailers, but between "high tech" retailers, able to use technology to create competitive advantage, and "low tech" retailers, without the necessary resources to invest in technology, or unable to fully exploit this technology.

Research has explained innovation and technology adoption by retail companies in terms of push factors (consumer demand for technology adoption) and by pull factors (company needs and strategic orientations) [1].

However, innovation is also a way to alter the focus from products sold to services provided, thus enhancing the store and shopping experience [2].

Introducing new digital technologies into its stores can also improve the image of a retail company, building more modern and up-to-date customers perceptions [3–5].

In this paper, we classify the technologies adopted by retailers in different categories according to consumer needs or to company expectations. Some of these technologies are already well established in the market and have been adopted by the vast majority of retailers, whilst others are at a more experimental stage. It is currently very difficult to forecast whether the latter will become mainstream in the future.

2 Ubiquitous Consumption (Maximize the Number of Contact Points with Customers)

The first trend we analyze is the attempt by all major companies to increase the number of contact points with end customers. The aim of this trend is to respond to a certain number of strategic issues:

- The companies' strategy of increasing consumer awareness of their brands;
- Changing consumer behavior concerning consumption time and location; according to the concept of "multiple selves" [6], consumers tend to use different channels and formats in various situations and for different needs;
- Consumer expectations of increased convenience throughout the purchasing process, from information collection to after-sales service;
- In some sectors, notably seasonal and fashion goods, stock management has become more complex and clearance activities have become important ways relevant to guarantee company profitability.

To respond to these issues, all retailers are now engaged in multi-channel or omni-channel strategies, including e-commerce, m-commerce and "buy" buttons on social networks pages. However, it is very interesting to notice major innovations by "pure players" and other omni-channel companies.

This strategy offers retailers not only opportunities to target consumers more precisely, but also to respond better to each shopper's varying states of need [7].

Pure players are experimenting with new customer contacts points, including lockers for product delivery and popup stores, before developing "brick and mortar" outlets.

Zalando, the German footwear and clothing retailer, opened two stores in 2014 to sell their end of season stock and products returned by customers. For fashion retailers using a free of charge return policy, inventory management is a vital point, especially if they update their range frequently, as it is the case in the "fast fashion" sector. The risk of receiving products returned by customers that cannot be sold in their physical stores is one of the main reasons why companies like Zara and H&M take a very cautious approach to e-commerce.

Omni-channel retailers try to increase shopper convenience, creating delivery points at very busy locations with high commuter flow at least twice a day; Tesco in the UK is experimenting with delivery lockers in train and subway stations. Meanwhile, CDiscount in France is developing delivery points in the convenience stores of its parent company, Casino, located in city centers or subway stations.

Some retailers are using shopping windows to extend the opening hours of their stores and as a way to attract consumers into the store during opening hours through an interactive, entertaining shopping experience; Adidas Neo is an example of this use of technology. Its shopping window allows customers to "play" with a virtual model, browse the brand offer and place articles in a shopping bag before paying with their smartphone. The shopping window is a powerful tool for customer attraction during the day, but it also represents a virtual shop in the evening and at weekends.

Other examples of virtual shopping windows are the Kate Spade store in New York and the Eye Candy vending machine tested by the Italian brand Luxottica, also in New York City [8].

It is interesting to underline also that the paper catalogue, one of the oldest forms of "non-store retailing", has not been killed by the on-line catalogue, but it is now returning as a way to promote omni-channel experiences; even an established department store chain, JC Penney, announced at the end of 2014 that they would resume publication of a paper catalogue for home decoration and home improvement products, some year after they abandoned the concept. As indicated by McGoldrick and Collins [7] we are perhaps moving away from the concept of "clicks and bricks", and towards retail companies that are "bricks, flicks and clicks."

3 Pro-sumerism and Product Co-creation

Another very interesting trend is the use of technology to involve consumers in the product creation process.

This trend responds to two main issues:

- The consumer search for "customized" products, matching a very specific need or desire and enabling them to escape from "mass market" standardization;
- Corporate use of "crowd creativity" to go beyond their own innovation capacity and to reduce the risk of failure for new product launches.

Some interesting examples in this field are the pure player Made.com, in the area of furniture, and the C'vous.com site, created by the French Group Casino to collect and share customer ideas about new products and services.

The international brand Nike is well known for allowing customers to customize products through the Nike ID site; what it is less known, perhaps, is that it is now possible to customize shoes, t-shirts and other products in some flagship Niketown stores around the world.

In France, Auchan, one of the market leaders in the FMCG retail sector, has reached an agreement with the crowdsourcing platform Qwirky to sell products created using customer ideas in a specific area near the entrance of some Auchan hypermarkets.

This kind of technology can also improve consumer engagement towards the brand. Some customers can become "brand ambassadors," a very important function in an era when consumers increasingly seek out peer recommendation before buying. In general, this kind of promotion is also better perceived and evaluated than direct communication by the brand.

4   Store Experience Improvement

Following the development of non-store retailing [9], it is becoming vital for companies to reinvent the functions of physical outlets; virtual channels have now totally outstripped one of the main sources of competitive advantage for large superstores, the possibility of offering a very wide range. Virtual channels can offer an almost unlimited range, as described in the celebrated "long tail" theory, first presented by Wired magazine in 2004 [10].

If outlets are not able to offer customers something genuinely different from on-line channels, the risk of store "commoditization" could become a reality. Stores might become simply irrelevant for customers that can buy products or services at the same price as in store, but in the comfort of their home or office, or as they travel to work.

To avoid this catastrophic scenario, retailers are investing heavily to create shopping experiences that encourage customers to visit their stores and purchase through the physical channel.

The value of customer experience, as originally described by Holbrook and Hirshmann [11], is now becoming a fundamental part of retail strategy in the omni-channel, 21st century world. In a study of "e-atmospherics", Poncin and Ben Mimoun [12] demonstrate that technology is an important tool that can construct an appealing store atmosphere, even for brick and mortar stores.

One of the main attempts to link stores and online channels is the introduction of virtual catalogues into stores, allowing customers to browse the entire product range, order online a product unavailable in the store and choose between home or in-store delivery. The introduction of a virtual catalogue into the store allows retailers to develop a multi-format strategy in different locations; retailers from different sectors are modifying their location strategy, formerly based on large, out-of-town superstores, and are tending to locate new outlets close to where customers live and work, very often in city centers and at commuter hotspots. However, these smaller formats can offer customers the entire brand range using virtual catalogues, or the possibility of picking up products purchased online.

Virtual reality is another way to create an in-store experience and to facilitate the purchasing process: virtual fitting rooms, magic mirrors and other technologies allow customer to test products, combine different items and share the images with friends and family via social networks.

Beacon technology is another possible way to improve customer experience, but also to get closer to one of the marketer's dreams, a completely customized offer, or one-to-one marketing.

Some technologies are used to facilitate the consumer purchasing process or to make more information available for consumers. One of the main examples of this is NFC technology, used by some FMCG retailers in France like Casino and Leclerc to give information to customer on the nutritional components of products. However, the real development of this technology is expected to occur in the payment activities, one of the longest and more boring parts of the purchasing process for many customers. With the arrival of Apple Pay in 2015, many experts predict the real take-off of mobile payments and the competition among different payment systems like the existing Paypal, Google Wallet, Apple Pay, but also the announced Current C, will become harsher in the next four to five years.

Another way of improving customer experience is to help them to find the required product easy and quickly inside the store. Store maps and store navigators are now available for many different brands and some applications developed by retailers allow the consumer to link the shopping list to the navigator to create an optimal route inside very large food or non-food superstores.

It is not always easy to conduct a shopping activity and to look at the smartphone screen at the same time, so some companies started developing technologies "hand free"; the best example was perhaps the Google glasses, even if the recent announcement of Google stopping the production of this item raises many questions. In the same area, the French company Intermarché has tested connected glasses in association with the French technology firm Digitas; this model of connected glasses guides customers around the store to find the items on their shopping list, but also enables them to scan products using a simple head movement. They also receive customized suggestions for additional products or special offers directly on the glasses, and can make their payment by nodding their head.

The expected mass development of other wearable technologies in 2015, such as smartwatches, will very probably increase the number of hands-free solutions inside stores.

5   Store Management Technologies

Technology can also be used to help sales assistants and store or department managers. The principal inspiration behind these technologies is certainly the development of customer relationship and satisfaction, but in some case also the improvement of store employee productivity.

In France, Sephora, the leading perfumes and cosmetics chain, introduced tablets in 2013 to assist the sale process; sales assistants use these tablets to scan customer loyalty cards, to analyze their purchase and visit history and to recommend purchases during the shopping trip. The system is far from perfect; some sales assistants complain that the recommendations are not always very targeted and specific to the individual customer. However, the use of tablets allows shopping assistants to retrieve the entire purchase history of each customer with the Sephora brand, both on and off line, seamlessly integrating all the channels for the final consumer.

Another interesting example is Lowe's, a world leader in the field of home improvement and decoration. The American company has developed a specific application to enable department and store managers to check stock levels for each item sold in all stores; with this application, a manager can inform customers about the availability of a specific item, delivery time if the product is out of stock, and the availability of the product in a nearby store.

Another application, also based on iPhone, enables Lowe's store managers to perform administrative tasks directly on a mobile device.

In Japan, Toshiba is testing electronic scales than can recognize fruits and vegetables visually, enabling sales assistants to scan these rapidly, and removing the need for customers to weigh and label them.

In some apparel stores, companies are testing a "smart model" that counts store entries and helps the store manager to plan the exact number of cashiers required depending on average shopping time and to prevent queues forming at checkouts.

One interesting avenue for future research would certainly be technology acceptance by retail staff; many studies have concentrated on the process of technology acceptance by consumers, but very little is known about staff reaction to technological innovations adopted in stores [8].

6   Conclusions and Discussion

In this paper, we have analyzed some of the most important technologies in the field of retail, grouping them in categories according to retailer strategy and consumer needs and expectations. We have also linked some major trends described in recent literature concerning consumer behavior and company strategies in the field of technology to corporate investment and experiments in technology use.

We have not analyzed the technologies used by retailers in the back-office or in supply chain management. These are of course key tools in modern markets and can create significant competitive advantage, but they were beyond the scope of this paper, which concentrates on retailer-consumer relations.

The use of technology in the retail sector has developed drastically over a very short period. Some trends and some technologies have already become mainstream, such as self-service checkouts in large superstores, whilst others are still in their infancy or at an experimental stage, such as contact-free payments using mobile phones. It is very difficult to forecast which of the current experimental technologies will become dominant in the future, and will give some retailers strong competitive advantage, but it is certain that in this fast-changing environment, strategies are altered very quickly. Company size, which had been one of the main components of competitive advantage in the retail sector for at least a century, is losing its importance, and companies need to become more nimble to adapt to change and respond to customer evolution. Technology is changing the retailing environment in a very disruptive way and some large, well-established firms may lose their position in the market very quickly if they do not adapt, as an analysis of world retail rankings over the last 15 years clearly demonstrates [13].

At the same time, retailers need to reassure customers concerning security and the use of personal information disclosed by consumers or collected by retailers during shopping interactions. Consumers may agree to share personal information with retailers in exchange for hedonic or utilitarian values, but major data breaches such as those that befell Ebay, Target and other retailers during 2014 can seriously hinder long-term consumer technology acceptance.

References

1. Pantano, E., Viassone, M.: Demand pull and technology push perspective in technology-based innovations for the point of sale: The retailers evaluation. J. Retail. Consum. Serv. **21**, 43–47 (2013)
2. Zott, C., Amit, R.: Creating value through business model innovation. MIT Sloan Manage. Rev. **53**(3), 41–49 (2012)
3. Bodhani, A.: Shops offer the e-tail experience. Eng. Technol. **7**(5), p46–49 (2012)
4. Pantano, E., Viassone, M.: Demand pull and technology push perspective in technology-based innovations for the point of sale: the retailers evaluation. J. Retail. Consum. Serv. **21**, 43–47 (2014)
5. Pantano, E., Iazzolino, G., Migliano, G.: Obsolescence risk in advanced technologies for retailing: a management perspective. J. Retail. Consum. Serv. **20**, 225–233 (2013)
6. Solomon, M., Bamossy, G., Askegaard, S., Hogg, M.K.: Consumer behaviour: a European perspective, Prentice-Hall (2006)
7. McGoldrick, P.J., Collins, N.: Multichannel retailing: profiling the multichannel shopper. Int. Rev. Retail. Distrib. Consum. Res. **17**(2), 139–158 (2007)
8. Pantano, E.: Innovations drivers in retail industry. Int. J. Inf. Manage. **34**(3), 344–350 (2014)
9. Berman, B.R., Evans, J.R.: Retail management: a strategic approach, International edn. Pearson, London (2013)
10. Anderson, C.: The long tail, Wired, Issue 12.10, (October 2004)

11. Holbrook, M.B., Hirschman, E.C.: The experiential aspect of consumption: consumer fantasies, feelings and fun. J. Consum. Res. **9**(2), 132–140 (1982)
12. Poncin, I., Ben Mimoun, M.S.: The impact of "e-atmospherics" on physical stores. J. Retail. Consum. Serv. **21**, 851–859 (2014)
13. Deloitte.: Global powers of retailing (different years from 2005 to 2015)

Printed in the United States
By Bookmasters